MASS VIOLENCE IN AMERICA

MASS VIOLENCE IN AMERICA

REPORTS ON CRIME INVESTIGATIONS

ARNO PRESS & THE NEW YORK TIMES

New York • 1969

Editorial Note

NATIONS, LIKE MEN, ARE SOMETIMES INTERESTED IN BURYING THE PAST.

In early 1968, after more than five years marked by political assassinations, racial uprisings, campus disorders, mass demonstrations and the violent suppression of protest, *The New York Times Magazine* asked a group of distinguished scholars to reply to the question, "Is America by nature a violent society?" In answer, University of Chicago anthropologist Clifford Geertz wrote:

> "We do not know very well what kind of society we live in, what kind of history we have had, what kind of people we are. We are just now beginning to find out, the hard way . . ."

The proposition was astonishing but correct: what was least understood about domestic political violence was its role in American history. It was common knowledge that the United States had had a Revolution, a Civil War, some trouble with the Indians and a period of labor-management conflict. But one could search the shelves of the nation's great libraries without discovering more than a handful of works on the subject of violence in American history, and these hopelessly out of date.

Historians had generally ignored or soft-pedaled the history of farmer uprisings, native vigilantism, labor-management struggles, ethnic conflicts and race riots; comparative work in the history of social conflict was particularly weak. Sociologists and political scientists in the grip of "consensus" theory tended to treat episodes of mass violence in America as insignificant or aberrational—temporary exceptions to the norm of peaceful progress. Psychologists and behavioral scientists discussed "mob violence" in terms which suggested that riots, revolts, insurrections and official violence were the products of individual or group pathology. All such interpretations had the effect not only of minimizing group violence in America, but of depriving it of political content—hence, of relevance to the present.

As a result, as late as 1968, the rich, multifarious and often terrifying history of domestic political violence was still largely *terra incognita*. So long as most Americans wished to keep certain skeletons locked away in their closets, few scholars would attempt to open doors. Conversely, once the American people, frightened yet emboldened by the sudden reappearance of intense social conflict, began to ask new questions about the past, so did the scholars.

Our purpose in helping Arno Press and *The New York Times* select and publish significant documents in the history of political violence has not been to compound past errors by overemphasizing the role of conflict in American history. On the contrary, our aim has been to provide materials which will aid in the search for an accurate perspective on the present. MASS VIOLENCE IN AMERICA includes eyewitness reports, government documents and other descriptive and analytic material relating to mass political violence in the United States. These documents not only provide information—they give the "feel" or "flavor" of past eras of civil disorder by evoking the emotional and political context in which revolts took place. Most of them have long been out of print and are obtainable, if at all, only in the nation's largest libraries.

The scope of this series is wide, ranging from accounts of Indian warfare to descriptions of labor-management violence, from narratives of colonial insurrections to reports on modern racial uprisings. It is not, however, limitless, nor were the constituent volumes carelessly selected. The principle of coherence which guided the selections is implicit in the phrase "mass political violence." "Mass" denotes activity engaged in by large groups rather than individuals acting alone; "political" suggests a relationship between such activity and competition among domestic groups for power, property and prestige; and "violence" is narrowly construed as resulting in physical damage to persons or property. In short, the materials reproduced herein are intended to illuminate the resort to violence by American groups seeking to change or to preserve the status quo. Although historical, they are of interest to any who wishes to understand the causes, nature and direction of domestic political violence, whether they be social scientists, historians or just interested Americans.

Of course, we are particularly hopeful that these volumes will prove useful to those now engaged in curriculum-revision and the teaching of high school and college courses in the area of American studies. What Christopher Jencks and David Reisman term "the Academic Revolution" has made difficult demands on all educators, not the least of which is the demand for courses which are both relevant to the condition of modern America and of the highest academic quality. These volumes are meant to provide raw material for such courses— primary source matter which will help both instructors and students to deepen and enrich their views of the American experience.

Most important, the editors and publisher recognize that these volumes appear during a national crisis which is also a crisis of the spirit, a time in which the public response to various manifestations of civil disorder is increasingly governed by anger, fear and hysteria. In such an atmosphere it is important to recognize that one is not alone in time—that such events have taken place before in America and, unless fundamental changes in our social and political life take place, will probably recur in the future. Our fondest hope is that this work, and others like it, will help to keep alive, in a time of growing unreason, the spirit of reasoned inquiry.

RICHARD E. RUBENSTEIN
The Adlai Stevenson Institute
Chicago, Illinois

ROBERT M. FOGELSON
Harvard-MIT Joint Center
for Urban Studies
Cambridge, Massachusetts

REPORTS ON CRIME INVESTIGATIONS

REPORTS ON CRIMINAL REVELATIONS

82D CONGRESS : : : : 1ST SESSION

JANUARY 3–OCTOBER 20, 1951

SENATE REPORTS

VOL. 6

REPORTS ON CRIME INVESTIGATIONS

UNITED STATES
GOVERNMENT PRINTING OFFICE
WASHINGTON : 1951

CONTENTS

NOTE.—The 1st report on crime investigation pursuant to S. Res. 202, 81st Congress, was issued as Senate report 2370, 81st Congress, 2d session, and was bound in volume 5 of Senate reports of that session, serial number 11371.

82D CONGRESS ⎫
  1st Session ⎰   SENATE   ⎰ REPORT
          ⎱ No. 141

SECOND INTERIM REPORT

OF THE

SPECIAL COMMITTEE TO INVESTIGATE ORGANIZED CRIME IN INTERSTATE COMMERCE

PURSUANT TO

S. Res. 202

(81st Congress)

FEBRUARY 28 (legislative day, JANUARY 29), 1951.—Ordered to be printed

UNITED STATES
GOVERNMENT PRINTING OFFICE
WASHINGTON : 1951

SPECIAL COMMITTEE TO INVESTIGATE ORGANIZED CRIME IN INTERSTATE COMMERCE

(PURSUANT TO S. RES. 202, 81ST CONG.)

ESTES KEFAUVER, Tennessee, *Chairman*

HERBERT R. O'CONOR, Maryland   CHARLES W. TOBEY, New Hampshire
LESTER C. HUNT, Wyoming   ALEXANDER WILEY, Wisconsin

RUDOLPH HALLEY, *Chief Counsel*
JOHN L. BURLING, *Associate Counsel*
ALFRED M. KLEIN, *Associate Counsel*
DOWNEY RICE, *Associate Counsel*
GEORGE S. ROBINSON, *Associate Counsel*
HAROLD G. ROBINSON, *Chief Investigator*

The committee wishes to express its appreciation to Judge Morris Ploscowe, of New York City, and the Commission on Organized Crime of the American Bar Association for assistance in the preparation of this report.

CONTENTS

SECOND INTERIM REPORT OF THE SPECIAL SENATE COMMITTEE TO INVESTIGATE. ORGANIZED CRIME IN INTERSTATE COMMERCE

FEBRUARY 28 (legislative day, JANUARY 29), 1951.—Ordered to be printed

---

Mr. O'CONOR (for Mr. KEFAUVER), from the Special Committee To Investigate Organized Crime in Interstate Commerce, submitted the following

SECOND INTERIM REPORT

[Pursuant to S. Res. 202]

INTRODUCTION

I

The Special Committee of the United States Senate To Investigate Organized Crime in Interstate Commerce had its genesis in Senate Resolution 202 of the Eighty-first Congress, second session, filed January 5, 1950, adopted on May 3, 1950.

Its primary purpose was precisely what is implied by its title. Before and beyond the date of the adoption of this resolution by the Senate, a considerable segment of the thinking population of the country had come to the inescapable conclusion that organized crime had developed into a serious national problem.

In the daily press and in countless periodicals appeared numberless indications that organized criminals had achieved such power as to be able to infiltrate into our very Government and to corrupt law enforcement in many local communities. Into the ears of millions of the population via radio went warnings that well organized mobs engaged in crime were operating from one border of the Nation to the other without regard for State lines and thus were avoiding responsibility for their criminal actions in local jurisdictions.

In many places it was open and notorious that these things were transpiring. Efforts to curb them had proved of such little effectiveness that in many places they had been abandoned and, through public apathy, they became accepted as part of the normal way of life.

In February 1950, under the auspices of the Attorney General of the United States, the American Municipal Association and the American Conference of Mayors, a conference of the mayors of most of

1

the large cities of the United States was held in Washington. Some of them like Mayor de Lesseps Morrison of New Orleans, La., and Fletcher Bowron of Los Angeles, Calif., took the lead in stating the situation for the record and admitting frankly that organized crime had become such a serious problem that disparate localities were unable any longer to suppress it.

On the other hand, there was a body of opinion which expressed doubt that there was any serious organized crime problem in the Nation. Among those who held this view respected by many, were men charged with the responsibility for suppression of crime. It found expression by some who were present at the United States Attorney's Conference in Washington, at about the same time as the mayors' conference.

The conflict of opinion thus was shared not only with the public but manifested itself as well in the Halls of the Congress and for some time it was debated at length whether or not the Congress was warranted in adopting legislation to deal with a condition that might not in reality exist.

This debate and the attendant public reaction released a flood of opinion and from the accompanying tide of information that poured into the congressional offices more facts began to come to light. These facts have been amplified by this committee over 10 months of the most intensive investigation of its kind ever attempted.

ORGANIZED CRIME DOES EXIST

It cannot now be denied, as will appear more fully later in the report, that the doubt which originally existed in the minds of many intelligent and careful persons as to whether crime is organized in the United States was in great measure deliberately planted there. It was created by criminals who have vast resources and incalculable power. They have amassed and hoarded tremendous wealth out of the proceeds of their criminal activities and with it they have sought to purchase respectability so that the true nature of their operations would not become known. They have insidiously cultivated the association of persons whose integrity and character are unquestionable. They have sought membership in social clubs and other organizations where they might acquire the status of respectability in their respective communities. They have been lavish in their gifts to charity and they have publicly promoted philanthropies, all in an effort to hide their crimes behind the shielding cloak of respectability.

And to carry out this fiction, in many cases they have invested in legitimate businesses so that they could always point to these false fronts and claim that they were no longer engaged in crime in the event that a question might ever be raised as to their former criminal associations.

Nor was this situation confined to any one particular community or State. It was an open secret in the State of Florida, one of the Nation's best-known playgrounds, where at certain seasons of the year affluent Americans from all parts of the country would gather for their vacations, presumably well provided with money and seeking excitement, that criminals from Chicago had moved in during the early part of 1949 and were attempting to take control of the largest and most lucrative bookmaking operation in the entire State.

It was no secret in the State of Florida at the same time that a criminal gang basing its operations in New York and northern New Jersey had taken control of the largest gambling casinos in Florida and New Jersey and were mulcting millions of dollars out of these gambling games from anyone who would play.

CONNIVANCE OF LOCAL AUTHORITIES NECESSARY

It was no secret that these operations could not continue without the protection of police and with the connivance of local authorities. Yet when this committee, as one of its first official acts, wrote a letter of inquiry to municipal heads and law-enforcement officers in the States of Florida and Missouri, among others, asking for information on the subject, the reply was virtually unanimous that there was no serious crime problem whatsoever, not even in the Miami-Miami Beach area where gambling was so open and notorious as to be a stench in the public nostrils.

It was no secret in the State of Missouri, and particularly in Kansas City, that the State government and its administration had narrowly escaped falling under the control of gangsters with criminal affiliations in the election of 1948. These gangsters had for their objective making the State of Missouri, and particularly Kansas City "wide open," and they were willing to spend money on an election campaign for the governorship in order that they might not have to pay for protection thereafter. The racket contamination in Missouri, festering for a long time, finally erupted in the double murder of Charles Binaggio and Charles Gargotta followed by a full-dress investigation by an aggressive Federal grand jury conducted by Max H. Goldschein, an able prosecutor, who is special assistant to the Attorney General of the United States.

It was no secret in New York and in the counties of New Jersey directly across the Hudson from America's biggest city that the most notorious hoodlums in Manhattan were operating a chain of gambling houses that showed, conservatively, profits of from five to ten million dollars a year. There was no secret about this. For New Yorkers with money in their pockets, transportation in private limousines to the casinos of north Jersey was available. The customers were told they need not eat their dinners before departure for lavish food was available without cost on the casino premises to those who played. The district attorney of New York County succeeded in 1949 in convicting the one minor figure in this tremendous gambling ring over whom he had jurisdiction. This gangster's contribution to the crime set-up consisted of cashing checks for the ring in a New York bank.

The facts brought to light by this individual's trial goaded the New Jersey authorities into action and as a result of their efforts a minor participant was imprisoned, this time on a plea of guilty. But no attempt was made to obtain the books or records of the gambling houses so that those who were principally in control and who shared principally in the profits might also be prosecuted. Although the name of one of the other participants in this operation appeared as endorsee on every one of the checks used to convict the check-casher in New York, no prosecution by the local prosecutor was brought against him. The "fall guy" pleaded guilty and that was that.

It was no secret in Chicago that the head of a Nation-wide wire service which furnished news of horse racing over leased wires from one corner of the country to the other was ambushed and shot after a lengthy dispute with a gang of criminals who were trying to take over control of this lucrative service.

It was no secret that this man had been threatened with death if he did not cut the organized mob in. He died because he fought the gang; after his death the mob took over and again, that was that.

It was no secret to the newspapers of the United States during the year 1949 that from time to time meetings of notorious characters with police records would be held in various places, preferably resorts like Miami Beach, Hot Springs, Ark., Phoenix, Ariz., and others. Articles to this effect were printed. The comings and goings of crime operators like Frank Costello, Joe Adonis, Meyer Lansky, Willie Moretti and many others were considered as newsworthy as the activities of heads of foreign states and received comparatively as much space in news columns.

What brought about this public state of mind that approached almost respect for these underworld characters? Why were they permitted to proceed with the organization and integration of their criminal activities throughout the country?

POWER AND INFLUENCE OF THE GANGS

Prior to the investigation by this committee, which is only now approaching its conclusion, the only reason that could be surmised was that these criminal gangs possess such power and had access to such sources of protection that they constituted a government within a government in this country and that that second government was the government by the underworld.

This committee at the outset of its investigation found it difficult to accept such a hypothesis. But the mass of detailed testimony that covers thousands of printed pages taken from hundreds of witnesses, a good number of them at the very top of America's criminal hierarchy, has forced this committee to the ineluctable conclusion that there is such an underworld government.

This phantom government nevertheless enforces its own law, carries out its own executions, and not only ignores but abhors the democratic processes of justice which are held to be the safeguards of the American citizen.

This secret government of crimesters is a serious menace which could, if not curbed, become the basis for a subversive movement which could wreck the very foundations of this country. There is no doubt that the confidence of millions of citizens in the protection which their Government should give them has already been undermined by these gangs and to that extent has left many otherwise law-abiding citizens ripe for an approach to do the bidding of anyone willing to pay a price.

GAMBLING NOW BIG BUSINESS

A preliminary consideration of this menacing situation brought new views on gangs and gangsters. It was apparent that since the entire approach of the criminal mobs had been revised many of the classic aspects of crime would probably have been abandoned. The striving for respectability, if only as a false facade, would undoubtedly bring with it many new side ventures and devious paths. The lush traffic in alcohol beverages during the violent years of 1920 to 1933 had laid the base of organization for a number of criminal gangs. The termination of the ban on liquor deprived these gangs of their most lucrative source of money and they were obliged to turn in to some other avenue of activity. Simultaneously with the advent of repeal came the turning point of the depression. Money began to become more plentiful and as the years went on became more and more so. What could be more desirable for these criminal gangs than a business whose sole commodities consisted of money and information? The answer was the promotion of gambling in the forms that are now so prevalent.

Strangely enough, for the last three decades there appears to be a continuity of identity not only in the operating gangs but in the individuals who comprise them. Reports were current, that for reasons best known to the insiders, some had been eliminated—liquidated— by the secret enforcers of this underworld government, but many of the same names that achieved such notoriety during the frenetic days of prohibition were still foremost in the news when the activities of these mobs were reported.

One conclusion was inescapable: That somewhere along the line there was a force operating which permitted these lawbreakers not only to shift from one illegal operation to another but to continue in those operations without effective harassment or cessation.

Because there can be only one paramount government at any time in any one place, it was necessary to determine to what extent law and order were in jeopardy of being completely destroyed by these organized outlaws. It became manifest that it was also necessary to arouse the public to the threat that was implied by permitting these dangerous and unscrupulous individuals, possessed of neither morals nor conscience, to prey upon the weakness and indifference of the average citizen. Finally, if any action were to be taken to curb or suppress these activities, it was also apparent because of the complex interstate ramifications that the impetus would have to come from the Federal Government and toward that end information to the fullest extent of the over-all picture was imperatively necessary.

ORGANIZATION OF CRIME INVESTIGATING COMMITTEE

Out of a distillation of all these considerations came Senate Resolution 202 of the Eighty-first Congress, second session. The enabling resolution directed the committee to determine whether organized crime operates in and through interstate commerce; to identify the persons or firms so operating; to determine whether organized crime utilizes interstate facilities to develop corrupting influences, and to decide what changes and amendments in Federal laws are necessary so that the various States might more adequately meet the threat of organized crime within their borders.

To arrive at a thorough, accurate, and over-all picture of the problem of organized crime in interstate commerce, the committee, consisting of Senator Estes Kefauver as chairman; two other Democratic members, Senators Herbert R. O'Conor and Lester C. Hunt; and two Republican members, Senators Charles W. Tobey and Alexander Wiley, has visited and held hearings in many parts of the country. As of the date of this report they have held executive sessions and public hearings in Miami, Kansas City, Washington, Chicago, Philadelphia, New York, St. Louis, Las Vegas, San Francisco, Los Angeles, Tampa, New Orleans, Cleveland, and Detroit. Approximately 500 witnesses have been heard. The minutes of these hearings constitute the basis of this report.

Under the pressure of a national emergency, with the Congress in session during most of the life of the committee, and with a strict limitation of time within which to survey the interstate crime situation throughout the Nation, the committee has had to place a great measure of reliance on its staff.

While due acknowledgment of the splendid manner in which the committee's staff performed this herculean task will be made at length in the final report, the committee believes it would be remiss if it did not, at the outset, express to its able and indefatigable chief counsel, Rudolph Halley, its gratitude and appreciation of his work.

At the sacrifice of his own lucrative law practice, he has, for the better part of a year devoted himself continuously to this inquiry, assiduously and without regard to his own comfort and convenience. To Mr. Halley and his loyal, hard-working staff, the committee here records its sincere thanks.

Augmenting the investigative efforts of its own staff, the committee has had the valuable assistance of numerous national, State and local organizations, notably the crime commissions of several States and cities.

Of particular help have been the activities of the commission on organized crime of the American Bar Association, headed by former Secretary of War Robert P. Patterson. Indeed, to Hon. Morris Ploscowe, of New York City, the executive director of that commission, the committee is especially indebted for assistance in the preparation of this report.

During the course of this inquiry a good many material witnesses deliberately dodged service of subpenas issued by the committee. Some of these elusive witnesses fled beyond the borders of the country in a willful attempt to sabotage the committee and its purposes.

Within the past 2 weeks, the Senate has directed that warrants of arrest issue for these missing witnesses. This step has been followed by the voluntary surrender of a number of these individuals. Their testimony will be taken before the committee ends its activity.

As long as this committee retains the authority to do so, it will continue to search for those who have flaunted its process; after the expiration of its authority, the members of the committee hope that the Senate will follow its established procedure for bringing these recreant witnesses to book for their contumacy.

It should likewise be noted again that the purpose of the committee has been solely to obtain information to be used as a basis for legislation should the need for new law be established.

It has no prosecutive power; prosecution is a province reserved exclusively for the judicial branch of government.

Toward the end of acquiring information, the committee has issued many subpenas; some of the witnesses summoned have not, however, been called upon to testify.

As the committee has taken great pains to make clear at every hearing it has held, no inference of guilt of any offense, or criminal association, should be drawn from the fact that an individual was summoned, whether he testified or not.

II

HOW CRIMINAL GANGS OPERATE

In every large city that it has visited the committee has found similar patterns of organized crime.

These patterns may be summarized as follows:

(1) Groups of individuals work together to operate for profit one or many forms of criminal activity.

(2) These individuals and groups do not hesitate to use murder, bombing, or any other form of violence to eliminate competition, silence informers, persuade potential victims, or to enforce gang edicts. They frequently import associates from other areas of the country to perform these tasks in order to make detection more difficult.

(3) They use bribery or some other form of corruption to secure the noninterference by law-enforcement agencies with gang activities.

(4) They maintain profitable arrangements and relationships with like-minded criminal groups and individuals in other cities and in other areas of the country.

(5) They employ the gains and profits from these illegal activities to infiltrate into legitimate enterprises, to which they bring the operational methods of their criminal business, i. e., monopoly, enforced by intimidation and strong-armed violence.

Evidence of widespread organized criminal activity has been found by the committee particularly in connection with various forms of gambling such as bookmaking, slot machines, the numbers or policy game, punchboards, gambling casinos, and in connection with the sale and distribution of narcotics. The committee has also heard testimony in many communities concerning organized criminal activity in connection with the violation of the liquor and prostitution laws, business and labor rackets, and extortion and blackhand shake-downs.

Conditions similar to those spread upon the record by the committee have from time to time been uncovered by legislative investigations, grand jury inquiries, or exposés by daily newspapers and crime surveys on a local, isolated, sporadic basis. Many of the individuals who appeared before the committee have been the targets of these investigations, inquiries, exposés, and surveys. However, previous revelations of organized crime have normally been limited to occurrences in a single community or State. What is startling about the present evidence is that it demonstrates quite clearly that organized crime today is not limited to any single community or to any single State, but occurs all over the country. Conditions in Tampa or Miami may be duplicated in Philadelphia, or in Bergen County, N. J. Conditions in Kansas City have their counterpart in Los Angeles and New York. The leading figures active in one section are either active themselves or have been shown to have working arrangements with the leading figures in another. Whether out of ignorance or indolence is not clear, but some local authorities insisted, orally and in writing, that there was no organized crime in their jurisdictions, although the subsequent testimony proved them pathetically in error.

III

ADVANTAGES OF GANG MEMBERSHIP

Organized criminal activities are run in our big cities by professional criminals with long arrest records and with well-documented criminal reputations but who remain immune from prosecution and punishment.

Many large metropolitan centers can match Chicago's Tony Accardo, Jake Guzik, Charles Fischetti, and Murray Humphreys; persons known to be engaged in illegal activities, the top racketeers of the community, whom the law rarely touches. There are basic similarities in the past history of these big-time racketeers. They have usually had a long apprenticeship in the cruder forms of criminal activity—ranging from petty larceny to armed robbery and murder. In this period of their lives, they are arrested frequently and are occasionally imprisoned in State and Federal prisons and local jails. However, their arrests, convictions, and prison sentences scarcely interrupt their criminal careers.

Membership in a gang brings advantages. The gang has means of protecting its members. A bondsman is ever ready to "spring" them from jail. Expensive and able counsel is provided. One of the peculiar coincidences that occurred time after time was the revelation that the identical lawyer appeared for many of the bookmakers working for the same major outfit. In Miami, Ben Cohen, brother of one of the members of the S. & G. Syndicate, turned up as counsel for many of the bookmakers who were arrested there. In St. Louis, Morris Shenker appeared to have a substantial portion of the legal trade involving bookmakers who had fallen into the clutches of the law. It is noteworthy that Shenker appeared before the committee as counsel for William Molasky, one of the owners of Pioneer News Service, the racing wire news distributor in that city. He also appeared as counsel for Joe Uvanni, race-track "comeback money" agent for John Mooney, of St. Louis. According to testimony before the committee, Molasky contributed $2,000 to the gubernatorial campaign fund of Forrest Smith on condition that Smith would name Shenker to the police board (of control) of St. Louis if elected.

Witnesses are intimidated or bribed on occasion. The case is dragged out as long as possible with a view to obtaining eventual dismissal. Even where a conviction is ultimately obtained, an effort is made to keep the sentence as light as possible or to obtain an early release on parole.

One example of many in the minutes of this committee is the prosecution of Charles Gargotta for the murder of a deputy sheriff in Kansas City. There were 29 continuances before the case finally came to trial. It is alleged that the gun with which the deputy sheriff was killed was switched by Kansas City police officers, so that ballistics tests were made on the wrong gun. Gargotta was acquitted of the homicide charge although he had been practically caught in the act. However, he was convicted of the illegal possession of a gun, sentenced to a minimum term, and released promptly. Eventually, over the protest of the police department, he was pardoned by the Governor.

About 20 years ago a noted authority on criminology, after a survey of organized crime in Chicago, concluded:

> The leading criminal profiteers in bootlegging, gambling, vice, and labor and merchant racketeering run little risk of prosecutions and conviction in conducting these illegal operations. Underlings occasionally receive punishment, almost without exception, of a minor kind.

The data of the Senate Crime Investigating Committee on the careers of top criminals and racketeers indicates that this conclusion is still true today, not alone for Chicago, but for every metropolitan center in which we have held hearings. In Miami, for example, the sheriff of Dade County, James A. Sullivan, presented considerable information on the careers of the big-time racketeers and gamblers who infest the Miami area. Florida has a statute requiring persons with a felony record to register. But Sheriff Sullivan, though he admitted familiarity with the criminal records of police characters like Joe Adonis, said he did not know whether the latter and others like him had complied with that statute. Sheriff Sullivan boasted of the gambling arrests by his office, but he admitted that the men taken in were the bookies, the "leg men," never the operators and owners of the local gambling syndicate.

IV

INTERSTATE RELATIONSHIP OF LEADING GANGS

The evidence before the committee indicates that the top racketeers do not restrict their criminal operations to one section of the country. They are frequently found operating in entirely different geographic areas. Moreover, individual gangsters and gangs from different parts of the country frequently enter into profitable working relationships with each other.

The grand jury of Dade County, Fla., complained that—

> our community is fast becoming the national capital wherein the so-called leaders of the criminal element of numerous communities throughout the land are congregating.

Recreation was not the only interest of the mobsters in the Miami area. Such gambling operations as the Colonial Inn, Greenacres, and the Club Boheme were run by such leading mobsters as the two Lanskys, Joe Adonis, Frank Erickson, William Bischoff, Joe Massei, and others. This is apparent from the chart introduced as an exhibit from the Florida report which was substantiated in the testimony.

Harry Anslinger, United States Commissioner of Narcotics, who has had considerable experience in dealing with organized crime, supported the notion that the leading figures in organized crime know each other, do business with each other, get together in places like Miami and Hot Springs, and on occasion do each other's dirty work when a competitor must be eliminated, an informer silenced, or a victim persuaded. He summarized the situation as follows:

> I would say that all of the members of this combine are very well acquainted with everybody else throughout the country. The fellows in New York, Florida, California all know each other. Seizing their telephone lists, they are all on there, you find. It is interlaced and intertwined.

He did not think that the activities in one part of the country occur as a result of instructions given in other parts of the country, as a general rule. In some sections, he said, "it is pretty well organized in that particular way, but I wouldn't say that one section of the country controls another section." What happens, Mr. Anslinger testified, is that "they confer together, or talk to each other, deal with each other." He agreed with the characterization of Rudolph Halley, chief counsel to the committee, that "they confine their dealings pretty well to the family." "That," he said, "has been our experience. They have offshoots. They have associates in other rackets. They make connections for persons outside of their own combine."

V

CONTACT AND LIAISON BETWEEN GANGS

There is no doubt in the minds of the members of the committee that there do exist at least two major crime syndicates. There is one with an axis between Miami and the Capone Syndicate now headed by Tony Accardo, the Fischetti brothers, and Jake Guzik. There is another with an axis between New York and Miami headed by Frank Costello and Joe Adonis. These axes have branch lines that extend into many cities and areas and there is apparently a gentleman's agreement, if the operators of these mobs can truthfully be called gentlemen, not to infringe on the activities of each other. Between them there are contact and liaison carried on by individuals known to and trusted by both, and if there can be said to be one head who sits as an arbiter of any disputes between the two, it is Charles "Lucky" Luciano, who is now in Italy, but who maintains associations with both groups through his former racketeer affiliates.

About 20 years ago, a study of the situation in Chicago by the Illinois Crime Survey concluded:

> There exists in Chicago today an underworld system of control which enforces its decrees by bombs and murder. Its history, traced for 25 years in this study, discloses its various interlocking manifestations in commercialized vice, gambling, bootlegging, and gang crimes.

Today, the major criminal organization in Chicago still is the Capone syndicate which is active in various forms of gambling, in prostitution, in the distribution of narcotics, and in various legitimate and quasi-legitimate activities such as the sale and distribution of beer and liquor, the operation of dog tracks, the control of various union activities, and the control of the wire services which transmit gambling information.

The evidence shows that the Chicago crime syndicate has extended its operations to other cities beyond the borders of the Chicago metropolitan area.

RACING WIRE SERVICE CONTROLS BOOKMAKING

In Miami, Harry Russell, a representative of the Chicago mob, muscled his way into a one-sixth partnership in the S. & G. Syndicate, a $26,000,000-a-year bookmaking operation, for a nominal consideration of $20,000, which was probably never actually paid in the real sense of the word. Accardo's and Guzik's partnership income tax returns showed that they, and not Russell, took the deduction for 1949 for losses sustained in the S. & G. operation.

The principal evidence of nation-wide operation by members of the Chicago crime syndicate is tied up with the apparent control by by the Capone mob of the wire services to bookmakers. As we shall see presently, the control of the wire services provides a stranglehold over large bookmaking operations. To the extent that the Capone crime syndicate controls the wire service, it is in that proportionate measure a partner of every bookmaker of any consequence in the country. These matters will be developed subsequently in greater detail since the committee's inquiry into all these matters is still proceeding.

THE MAFIA—WHAT IS IT?

One of the persistent matters that has received intensive attention from the committee has been the repeated statement that there exists in the United States a crime syndicate known as the Mafia, operating Nation-wide under centralized direction and control.

Many of the witnesses who were heard by the committee were individuals suspected of membership in this shadowy organization. They were virtually unanimous in their complete ignorance of the existence of such a group, or, if they admitted they had heard of it, knew nothing about it beyond hearsay of its existence. Yet their very denials had a hollow ring.

There is a great deal of testimony in the committee records that would indicate beyond peradventure that such an organization exists; that its members have inter-related ties in various unlawful activities and that these are so coordinated that the Mafia is the adhesive between the major crime syndicates. All this is too coincidental to be merely accidental.

The investigation into the existence and organization of the Mafia is still under way, and the results of this investigation and the conclusion of the committee with respect to the Mafia will be reported to the Senate by this committee in its final summation.

VI

HOW BIG IS THE GAMBLING RACKET?

Gambling is the principal source of income for organized criminal gangs in this country.

The "take" from such forms of gambling as bookmaking, policy or numbers, slot machines, punchboards, and gambling casinos is fantastic in amount. Gambling has supplanted prostitution and bootlegging as the chief source of revenue for organized crime. Before the First World War, the major profits of organized criminal gangs were obtained from prostitution. The passage of the Mann White Slave Act, the changing sexual mores, and public opinion, combined to make commercialized prostitution a less profitable and more hazardous enterprise. After World War I, prohibition and the illicit-liquor traffic provided golden opportunities for organized crime. Since prohibition has been repealed, organized criminal gangs have found a new bonanza in the conduct of various forms of gambling.

Testimony before the committee indicates that in every community, a tremendous amount of the effort and attention of organized gangsters goes into gambling operations. No form of gambling is overlooked. The slot machine, the punchboard,' the gambling casino, the policy or numbers game in all its variations, and above all, bookmaking on horse races and other sporting events are all exploited to the limit by organized mobsters.

The moneys derived from these sources are positively staggering. For example, Theodore Roe had a one-fifth interest in two policy operations on the South Side of Chicago, called the Maine-Idaho, and the Ohio policy wheels. According to him there are eight operations of similar size in Chicago, and some seven or eight smaller ones. His policy wheel had a drawing which averaged $25,000 a day. He had a one-fifth interest in the wheel. This netted him approximately $200,000 a year. The committee estimates that $150,000,000 has been played on numbers in 5 years in Chicago on the basis of figures obtained from the files of the operators of a number of wheels in that city.

The committee has considerable data on the take from slot machines. From this data the committee estimates that the average take from a slot machine is $50 per week per machine. For the fiscal year June 30, 1949, the $100 coin-operated Federal tax was paid by approximately 70,000 premises. Since only one tax receipt is issued to each location regardless of the number of machines, the number of machines in operation is far greater than this. It is estimated that each location has an average of three machines. This would make an average of $50 per week from 210,000 machines at premises that paid the Federal tax, or a take of approximately $540,000,000 in a year. It is impossible to estimate the number of machines to be found in premises which have not paid the Federal tax. Profits from the machine are usually split on a 50-50 basis between location owner and the operator. A mobster who places 200 slot machines, which is a comparatively small operation, can reasonably assure himself approximately $5,000 a week.

LOSERS CASH MILLIONS IN CHECKS

The returns from the gambling casinos are equally fantastic. One Max Stark was the check cashier for the mob operating the gambling casinos in north Jersey. He would bring into the Merchants Bank of New York City, a small private bank in which he was a shareholder, 60 to 70 checks daily, resulting from this gambling operation. These were checks cashed at the gambling casino and most of the money was undoubtedly used for gambling. Over a space of about 6 months, these checks totaled $5,000,000. Admitted gambling house operators testified that a player seldom cashed a check in a gambling house unless he had lost and was trying for a "come-back."

Some confirmation of the large sums wagered and won or lost in these establishments is had from the testimony of one witness who said he lost about $14,000 on four occasions. He stated that from 200 to 300 people were present on these occasions and there might be as much as $2,000 on the crap table at any one time.

The amounts reported to the income tax authorities for these gambling casinos are, of course, considerably less than what might be expected from these figures. Nevertheless, they are still substantial.

For example, the G. & R. Trading Corp. ran a gambling operation in northern New Jersey in the year 1945–46. Gross receipts were shown on the tax return of this corporation of $488,698 and a net of $255,271 which was divided between the following underworld characters as follows:

James Rutkin	$51, 054
Anthony Guarini	38, 290
Joe Adonis	76, 581
Jerry Catena	51, 054
Salvatore Moretti	38, 290

Similar sums are reported from the operation of other gambling casinos. For example, the Club Boheme in Broward County, Fla., in 1947 paid $205,470 to its owners, among whom was Meyer Lansky, according to the tax returns. The Greenacres Club paid $133,233 to W. H. Bischoff in 1948 for a 40-percent interest. Some idea of what the returns from a gambling casino may be when it is operated in a legalized setting is had from testimony of Clifford Jones, Lieutenant Governor of Nevada, who testified that his 1-percent interest in the Golden Nugget at Las Vegas netted him $12,000 a year.

The returns from bookmaking are astronomical. The report of the McFarland Committee on the Transmission of Gambling Information points out that estimates made by law-enforcement authorities have put the total amount bet off-track at figures ranging from $3,000,000,-000 to $10,000,000,000 annually. Best informed guesses are that the total is somewhere between $3,000,000,000 and $5,000,000,000 annually, based primarily on the $2,000,000,000 that is bet legally at the tracks every year. On the basis of a $3,000,000,000, off-track operation, and estimating the net profit to the bookmaker to be 20 percent of the amount bet, the net profit to the bookmakers would be approximately $600,000,000 in a year.

TWENTY BILLIONS CHANGES HANDS YEARLY

The figures obtained on specific illegal bookmaking operations by this committee, indicate that the McFarland estimates have a close relation to reality. The S. & G. Syndicate, which dominated bookmaking operations in Miami grossed upward of $26,000,000 a year. The Guarantee Finance Co. bookmaking operation in Los Angeles County admitted grossing upward of $7,000,000 a year. Tony Gizzo, a Kansas City mobster who was a member of Binaggio's gang, admitted that his bookmaking operation at the newsstand of the Coates House, netted him upward of $100,000 in a year. Charles Gioe, a Capone syndicate mobster was a partner in a bookmaking operation which took in bets approximating $20,000 a week.

The Carroll-Mooney bookmaking operation which had been going in wide-open fashion for years in East St. Louis, Ill., took bets of approximately $16,000 a day, according to one of its employees. The prosecuting attorney of St. Louis County, Mo., testified before the committee that the E. J. Rich Co., which used over 100 Western Union agents to solicit bets on a 25 percent commission basis took in between $150,000 and $300,000 a month in this operation.

It is apparent from these figures how rich a prize the control of bookmaking operations represents.

In all, the committee figures conservatively that $20,000,000,000 changes hands every year in the United States as a result of organized illegal gambling, a net inconsiderable portion of which stays with the promoters and operators of this illicit activity. Millions of dollars, it is safe to say, are paid out of this "take" as "ice," or protection money, in various forms.

VII

BOOKMAKING IS AN ORGANIZED INDUSTRY

Of all the forms of gambling, the one showing the greatest degree of organization and syndication, the one which depends most on interstate commerce and interstate communications, is bookmaking.

From the Senate investigation of wire services in 1909 to the current committee hearings, there have been many explorations of the operations of bookmakers in the United States. The McFarland committee report of last year gives a detailed explanation of its operations and ramifications.

While race-track betting is legal within the enclosures of race tracks in 27 States, off-track betting is illegal everywhere except in Nevada. But the McFarland report estimates that the number of bookmakers today far exceeds the estimate of 15,000 individual bookmakers made 10 years ago by the Internal Revenue Department in connection with the inquiry into the M. L. Annenberg tax returns. The California Crime Commission asserted that bookmaking reached into every community in the State, and the present testimony—such as that in Miami for example, where one syndicate controlled some 150 to 200 bookmakers—indicates that these estimates and assertions have basis in fact, and that bookmaking is as widely prevalent as is commonly believed.

It is apparent from the record that there are various levels of bookmaking. There is first the individual independent bookmaker who operates out of his pocket, on a capital of about $1,000, taking bets ranging from $2 to $10. When he contacts his clients, they have usually already made their selections from newspaper or scratch sheet information. The following day, he checks the papers for results and the odds paid, makes his rounds, and settles his accounts. He rarely lays off bets with a larger operator and he has little use for the wire service.

The second type of bookmaker, who probably handles the largest volume of bets, accepting wagers up to $100 a horse, maintains an office either in his own home or behind some innocent-looking front such as a newsstand or cigar store. He has from 2 to 15 telephones to receive incoming bets from clients. He has agents who work industrial plants, office buildings, and the like, possibly as adjuncts of their own employment, and turn the bets over to him on a commission basis. He gets up-to-the-minute race-track information from a still larger operator who is a direct subscriber to a wire service. He must have this information because he accepts bets from his agents and individual clients over the phone up to the very last minute before the race begins and must maintain a balanced book by constant check on all bets made and by laying off any excess bets on one horse.

On the third level are the large operators. They subscribe directly to the news service coming in usually over the ticker. Where law enforcement is especially lax, this type of bookmaker might have quarters roughly resembling those of a prosperous stockbroker where race information and changing odds are posted and can be watched by large crowds who place their bets just as clients of stockbrokers watch changing stock prices on the board and place their orders. These bookmakers may own an interest in smaller bookie establishments which place part of the bets with them and all their lay-off bets. To service the smaller bookies they have a battery of telephones kept open for the relay of the race-wire news service. The Mooney-Carroll bookmaking operation in East St. Louis, the Guaranty Finance Co. operation in Los Angeles, and the S. & G. Syndicate operation in Miami, all described in detail in the committee minutes are of this general character.

VIII

WIRE SERVICE ESSENTIAL FOR MONOPOLY

Big-time bookmaking operations largely monopolized by the big mobsters with their rich returns cannot be carried on without the rapid transmission of racing information and information about other sporting events.

We find—

stated the California Commission on Organized Crime—

that to conduct successful bookmaking, the operators must have information in excess of that which can be obtained through regular news and radio channels. Accordingly, there has grown up a specialized wire service which has for its principal purpose the dissemination of detailed racing information within a matter of minutes after the occurrence of actual events. This information includes details of track conditions, betting odds, jockey changes, and other facts occurring immediately prior to the running of the race and the results thereof. These wire services sell this information to bookmakers who in turn use it in conducting their business.

The bookmaker who has the wire service has a considerable advantage over one who does not have the service. He can book his bets with a far greater degree of certainty and in far greater volume if the necessary information about horse races and sporting events comes to him promptly. No bookmaker who does not have the wire service can hope to compete with one who does, any more than a stockbroker who hasn't got a ticker service could hope to compete with one who has it. This was confirmed by several professional bookmakers in their testimony before us.

The bookmakers themselves recognize the great value of the wire services in the prices they pay to distributors and subdistributors of the news service. It is apparent from the testimony before this committee that the price normally is what the traffic will bear. There is pressure to obtain as large a proportion of the bookmaker's profits as possible. One distributor testified that the bookmakers in his area paid anywhere from $40 to $350 a week for the news service and that there was no difference between the type of service offered to customers who paid $40 a week and the type offered to customers who paid $350 a week. Since the entire business is done in cash without records, it is impossible to verify these statements. The amounts paid by the bookmakers may be compared with the $20 a week which the New York Daily News pays to the Continental Press Service for the same news. Actually, there is little doubt that, in many localities, the distributor makes arrangements with the bookmaker to supply service not for a fixed price, but for a fixed percentage of the bookmaking profits. This makes the distributor a partner in the bookmaking operation.

IX

CONTINENTAL PRESS SERVICE A MONOPOLY

The wire service today, insofar as purveying information to book-makers is concerned, is a monopoly throughout the country.

On the surface, the Continental Press Service, the central distributor of racing news, is a sports news distributing company which is wholly owned by Edward McBride, Jr., a young law student at Miami University, who takes no part at all in its management. It is run by Tom Kelly, McBride's uncle, who is the general manager. Technically the Continental Press Service has nothing to do with book-makers. It does not sell directly to them. It sells news to from 20 to 24 supposedly independent regional distributors who in turn deal either with subdistributors or with bookmakers. One finds, however, the most extraordinary business arrangements between the Continental Press Service and its distributors, which indicate quite clearly that the latter are nearly all dummies, set up to insulate the Continental Press Service against the charge that it deals directly with persons engaged in illegal occupations. For example, the Illinois Sports News is one of the top distributors of Continental Press Service. Its ownership consists of Tom Kelly's brother and his son. It has no written contract with Continental Press Service, but news is provided to the Illinois Sports News on an oral agreement to pay as much of the profits as possible. "I told my brother," testified Tom Kelly before this committee, "to pay Continental Press as much as he possibly could and don't short them. I told him to send Continental whatever he could afford and to make sure it was a good substantial amount of what his profits was." This varied from $2,000 to $10,000 a week.

Another distributor paying what he thinks he should is Ed Mc-Goldrick, who, according to his testimony, was permitted to buy a business that averaged $2,800 to $3,000 a week, for a total purchase price of $3,000, which he conveniently borrowed from Henry M. Hilton, the attorney for Continental Press Service. According to his testimony, he pays Continental a fluctuating rate which varies from $500 to $2,000 a week. A third illustration of how Continental Press Service operates through dummies is the Howard Sports News, a Baltimore distributor. This is a corporation consisting of three individuals who pay all the operating expenses and pay themselves salaries and then remit all the profits to the Continental Press Service. It is obvious that these three individuals are merely acting as employees of the Continental.

It is apparent from the testimony before the committee that Continental controls its distributors, and that it can determine who in the last analysis will get betting news. The monopolistic character of Continental News Service was previously recognized by the McFarland committee report when it stated:

The facts support the thesis that Continental today has a near monopoly in the transmission of racing news which ultimately reaches the bookmakers in the country. Continental does choose its distributors, assigns them exclusive territory, and charges them for service on the basis of size and amount of business done in such territory.

X

CAPONE GANG CONTROLS BOOKMAKING

From the preponderance of evidence before the committee a conclusion is warranted that the Continental Press Service is controlled not by Edward McBride or Thomas Kelly but by the gangsters who constitute the Capone syndicate.

The Senate Crime Investigating Committee has elicited considerable testimony which supports this conclusion as to the ownership of the wire service. As a corollary it must follow that since the Capone syndicate controls the wire service it likewise controls the resultant power over bookmaking operations of any size in the United States.

The racing wire news service is such a phenomenon and of such great importance in the scheme of interstate criminal operations that a discussion of its development is appropriate at this point. It first assumed importance under the ownership of M. L. Annenberg some 30 years ago. Annenberg had been circulation manager for several large metropolitan newspapers and had likewise interested himself in the distribution of racing news publications known as scratch sheets. These scratch sheets contained information with respect to various aspects of horse racing which was intended to guide prospective bettors.

He conceived the idea of establishing a telegraphic news service which would carry over the wires fast and accurate information on racing for bookmakers and, with the big daily news distribution loops as his model, set up his own method of racing news coverage.

In the days when Annenberg, now deceased, was building newspaper circulations, competition between daily papers in metropolitan areas was intense. It was the era when newspapers were numerous. Since then many have become defunct and many others have been merged. The fight for circulation was a rough and tumble affair. Often violence was resorted to in order to cut down the circulation of a rival journal. Obviously many of those who participated in the circulation wars were strong-arm individuals to whom street brawls for control of newsstands and distribution outlets were everyday affairs.

To obtain the news from race tracks was the first problem of the new wire service. Some track owners were willing to sell the privilege of reporting from their enclosures to the news service which Annenberg named Nationwide News Service. However, some tracks were unwilling to cooperate and here it was necessary for the news to be purloined. For this purpose it was only natural for Annenberg to employ some of the individuals who had been associated with him in the newspaper circulation wars. Crews were formed to telegraph racing information from some point near the track, if not inside it, to a central location in Chicago, whence it was relayed to other distribution points in the various States. From these latter subcenters of distribution local distributors furnished it to bookmakers.

Annenberg and his principal associates, including James A. Ragen, Sr., not only controlled Nationwide in Chicago; they also apparently owned considerable interests in the suboutlets which in turn purveyed the racing information to the bookmakers. The profits accruing to the owners of this system were enormous.

In view of its limited time and facilities, this committee was unable to study exhaustively the various subcenters that constituted the provincial capitals of the old Annenberg empire but to complete its study it was considered necessary to make a detailed investigation of one typical point and for this purpose the committee selected the Pioneer News Co. of St. Louis, a relict of the old Annenberg distributorship.

The testimony shows that Annenberg, Ragen, and one Al Kruse of Chicago owned 50 percent of the stock of Pioneer News Co. when the latter was an affiliate of Nationwide.

Their participation in the business was not active but another Nationwide associate, William Molasky, who then lived and still lives in St. Louis, was their representative on the spot. There came a time in 1939 when Annenberg divested himself of all his interest in the racing wire news service, at about the time when the Internal Revenue Bureau opened an investigation into his income tax returns. Molasky purchased the entire Annenberg interest in Pioneer News Co. for $1; its actual value had no relation to the nominal purchase price.

Annenberg's disassociation with the racing wire news service was complete. He did not attempt to sell it to anyone or to realize any salvage from it; he simply walked out.

At that same time Ragen was also under indictment for violation of income-tax regulations. Ragen turned to an old friend, an associate of the newspaper war days, Arthur V. McBride of Cleveland. McBride was, like Ragen, a veteran of the vicious street battles for newspaper circulation. Moreover, Ragen's man Friday, Thomas Kelly, had been married to McBride's deceased sister.

It is one of the amazing aspects of this whole story that without any break in the service, without any dislocation of the facilities used in the entire process of obtaining, legitimately or illegitimately, from the race tracks and without any disruption in its distribution, one man stepped out of this complicated business and another man took it over without any formal transfer or without the passing of a single dollar.

It is hardly believable that no one else made any attempt to acquire the race news wire service either by purchase or by force. It happened just that way. The old management closed the door and a new management walked in and sat down and started operating.

ARTHUR M'BRIDE TAKES OVER

McBride, in his testimony before the committee, said he believed that without him the organization would have fallen apart. But his testimony is also on record to the effect that when he went into the wire service he knew nothing about it, had no time to devote to it and that if, at Kelly's asserted plea, he did go into the business, it would have to be run by Kelly and Ragen.

From McBride's testimony, the committee finds it hard to discern just how his person was indispensable to the conduct of the racing wire service. McBride said that it was necessary for him to provide the original working capital of $20,000 but this does not appear to be convincing because $20,000 in the operation of the new racing wire service which was given the appellation Continental Press Service appears to have been small money. As a matter of fact, McBride got his $20,000 back out of net profits before 2 weeks had elapsed. It was also apparent that Ragen could have put that amount up out of his own pocket or could have borrowed it without any difficulty whatsoever.

McBride testified that the only reason he went into the business was to help his brother-in-law, Kelly, and another old friend, Ragen. It was suggested by counsel for the committee that he could have loaned Kelly $20,000 and allowed Kelly to become the owner of the business but McBride said that he did not feel Kelly was sufficiently seasoned in business to be trusted with a loan of that size—this despite the fact that McBride had loaned similar amounts to known gangsters on at least two occasions and also despite the fact that when he did take the business over he had to trust Kelly to run it.

McBride stayed in Continental until 1941. Then he sold out to Ragen.

The story continues with Ragen and Kelly operating Nationwide until 1943 when McBride says Ragen came to him and said that he simply had to have McBride or a member of McBride's family in the organization. Nobody has given a clear reason for this because McBride, in his testimony before the committee, said that he had not learned anything further about the business up to that time and he had neither the energy nor available time to give to it.

McBride had a son, Edward, who at that time was overseas with the Armed Forces. Obviously Edward could not give any attention to the business. But for him McBride purchased a one-third interest for $50,000. Why McBride had to be brought into a business which was operating successfully and did not need capital is obscure unless it was to make available to the business such advantages as might result from McBride's powerful connections with John Angersola (King) and the important leaders of the Mafia in Cleveland.

Continental Press Service continued to operate without serious trouble until about 1946. During this period Ragen and McBride operated it as partners and there is no indication on the record that during this period it was dominated by any out-and-out gangster element although, beyond any doubt, Continental Press enjoyed amicable relations with the gangsters who were building up large-scale bookmaking operations in the bigger cities of the country.

CAPONE GANG STARTS MUSCLING IN

It was in 1946 that trouble began.

The first eruption came in California where Mickey Cohen and Joe Sica, undoubtedly acting on behalf of Jack I. Dragna, a leader of the Mafia in California, entered the premises of Russell Brophy, who was in charge of the local distribution agency for Continental. Brophy, incidentally, is Ragen's son-in-law. Sica is a reputed member of the Mafia under indictment on a narcotics charge; his trial has been delayed because the chief witness against him was recently mysteriously murdered. Brophy took a beating from the two hoodlums. At about the same time, back in Chicago, Ragen himself was having serious trouble with the R & H Publishing Co., a subdistributor of the racing news service controlled by the local Capone syndicate. R & H serviced several hundred bookmakers from Chicago. R & H, which was operated by Hymie Levin, Phil Katz, and Ray Jones was actually controlled by Tony Accardo and the Chicago syndicate.

Ragen threatened to tell what he knew about the Chicago mob to the Federal Bureau of Investigation and also threatened to report R & H to the Federal Communications Commission so that the sub-distributor would be forced out of business. He made a number of attempts to get R & H out of the business, saying that the wire service could not tolerate the gangster element or it would itself be put out of business.

Ragen offered to buy out R & H but he would not pay the enormous price that the gang set as the consideration for their elimination. The syndicate in turn appears to have been anxious to ease Ragen out and to take over the entire wire service.

Then, from nowhere, suddenly appeared a new racing information distribution service known as Trans-American Publishing & News Service, Inc.

One of Trans-American's first customers was R & H which withdrew from the Continental Press set-up. Heading Trans-American were three nonentities, not one of whom had any address or stature in gangdom. Two of them were former employees of Continental who had been lured away by Trans-American for the new set-up. One of the three was Ralph O'Hara, a minor gangster of Chicago. O'Hara was a witness before the committee in Chicago. The books and records of Trans-American were supposed [to be in his custody, but many of them proved to be missing. But from those that were available it would appear that in its first year's operation Trans-American lost about $200,000, most of which was put up by R & H Publishing Co.

In addition to the huge "loans" from R & H, Trans-American received a "loan" of $12,000 from Benjamin (Bugsy) Siegel, who at that time had a monopoly of the bookmaking and wire-news service in Las Vegas. Carlos Marcello, the reputed Mafia leader of Louisiana, also provided funds for Trans-American's operation, and still additional money was provided by William (Butsy) O'Brien, who had formerly controlled the racing-news service for Continental in the State of Florida and who continued throughout Trans-American's operations to give support to Continental, thus playing both ends against the middle.

TRANS-AMERICAN EXPANDS ITS ACTIVITIES

Trans-American made no attempt to operate directly in St. Louis; it utilized one of the partners in Pioneer News Service to work from the Illinois side of the Mississippi in East St. Louis, thus competing directly with Pioneer. In Kansas City, Trans-American was directed and operated by four of Binaggio's henchmen who included two notorious Mafia members with outstanding records for violence. They operated independently for a few days and then moved into the office of Continental which they took over lock, stock, barrel, and personnel. The Kansas City group spread its wire-service tentacles out into a number of neighboring States, including Iowa, Nebraska, and Colorado, taking with it Continental wire outlets and utilizing them for Trans-American set-up.

Police officials in the cities involved confidently anticipated that there would be considerable violence but the outburst did not reach the height which they expected. It is possible that the reason for this is that before local violence became too acute Ragen, the head of Continental Press Service, was assassinated in Chicago in a fashion typical of gangland.

A few weeks prior to his slaying, he had gone to the district attorney of Cook County, Ill., and had made a very lengthy statement saying that his life had been threatened and he fully expected the threats to be carried out. If he were killed, he said the probable killers would be Accardo, Guzik, and Murray ("The Camel") Humphreys, the top echelon of the Capone syndicate. Ragen said that the Capone syndicate wanted to be cut in on Continental and that he was resisting with all his might even though his life was thereby endangered. Ragen's statement to the district attorney of Cook County is a part of the record of this committee. It is corroborated, at least in part, by the testimony of Dan Serritella, Jake Guzik's partner in the Capone syndicate's scratch sheet.

After Ragen's death, active management of Continental was taken over by Tom Kelly; Kelly and McBride arranged to buy the two-thirds interest in Continental which belonged to the estate of Ragen and the latter's son. Title was taken in the name of Edward McBride, Arthur McBride's son, but Edward had no part in the negotiations and was not present except when the papers were executed. Edward McBride thus became the sole owner of Continental. He remained in Florida where he was attending law school and had absolutely nothing to do with the management of the company. When questioned at a committee hearing he could not even recite elementary facts about the important personnel of his news transmission system but had to refer to his uncle or to his counsel for the replies. It is obvious that, although he now owns Continental Press of record, he knows nothing whatever about its operation or management.

The acquisition of Continental by McBride's son had a mysterious paralyzing effect on the hostilities between Continental and Trans-American. Like the Arabs in the poem, Trans-American quietly folded its tents and silently withdrew from the scene—just at the point, according to the testimony of Kelly of Continental Press, where the latter seemed doomed to be forced out of business.

TRANS-AMERICAN MOBSTERS DODGE SUBPENAS

Although the most diligent efforts were made, the committee was unable to serve subpenas on any of the persons connected with R & H Publishing Co. It did obtain the presence of Ralph O'Hara, the head of Trans-American, but he refused to answer any questions whatsoever about the business on the ground that his answers would tend to incriminate him. He did not change his attitude when it was pointed out to him that the McBrides and their counsel insisted that the Continental operation, parallel in all respects to that of Trans-American, was wholly legitimate and in no way in violation of any law. Kelly and McBride insisted in their testimony that Trans-American discontinued doing business on its own initiative and not as a result of any deal.

After Trans-American folded, Continental took back into its employ one Pat Burns and his sister, both of whom had walked out on Continental to take jobs with Trans-American. Why Continental gave reemployment to these persons and others who had left to go into the employ of its competitor has not been satisfactorily answered. Nor has any convincing explanation been given as to why Continental then gave racing wire service in Kansas City to the same group who in effect had stolen the local outlets of Continental for Trans-American. In fact, the Mafia operators who took over the Reliable News Service in Kansas City received much better terms than the old wire service in that city had received from Continental before the fight and certainly got better terms than other distributors in various cities who had not fought Continental but who are not connected with the Mafia or the Capone gang. R & H in Chicago continued to receive service from Continental on terms far more profitable than those given to another racing service distributor in Chicago who had no connection with either Mafia or the Caponites. R & H paid $750 a week for its service, whereas its competitor, for precisely the same service, paid between $4,000 and $5,000 a week. In New Orleans, Continental made Marcello its distributor; on the west coast, Dragna was rewarded for his part in the fight with Continental by being given a contract at $25,000 a year to steal news from the race tracks and send it into Continental's headquarters for interstate distribution.

In Florida, "Butsy" O'Brien held on to his distributorship for Continental. The testimony taken by the committee in Florida shows particularly that it was not until after Trans-American took itself out of the picture that the Capone henchmen infiltrated the racing-news service in that State.

One of the most significant aspects of the racing wire story in Florida was the manner in which service from Chicago was cut off from the S. & G. bookmaking syndicate and its operatives in order to force that syndicate to take into partnership the Capone gang whose front man was Harry Russell, a Chicago gambler and former partner of Tony Accardo. A representative of the Western Union Telegraph Co., over whose wires the racing news to Miami Beach was carried, testified that the cut-off was ordered by William (Butsy) O'Brien.

Continental Press claimed that if all these things occurred, they were done by independent news-distributing companies to whom Continental sells the news, but over whom it has no control. Continental, it is claimed, stands simon-pure as a central news-distributing agency, which does not steal news or deal with bookmakers or characters of the underworld.

The facade of legality which Continental Press has erected for itself on the advice of eminent and learned counsel is a sham. In a court of law, as a corporate structure, it might stand up. But this is all the more reason why the true facts must be called to the attention of the Senate.

Continental Press is said to be owned by Edward McBride, a young man in his early twenties studying law in Miami, Fla. He knows nothing of its operations. Continental Press is operated by young McBride's uncle, Tom Kelly, who says he simply sells a news service to Illinois Sports News, Inc., and he does not know, he says, what Illinois Sports News does with it thereafter. It is significant that Illinois Sports News hired Pat Burns and the other dissident Continental employees back after Trans-American went out of business. It was Illinois Sports News that resumed business with R & H after

Ragen was shot. Strangely enough, Illinois Sports News is operated by two other Kellys, the brother and son of Tom Kelly of Continental.

On the business side, Illinois Sports News does not keep the considerable profits that it earns but it remits to Continental all of its net profit beyond a certain amount which has been agreed upon as a fair payment to Kelly's relatives for their services for running the outfit.

CONTINENTAL PULLS THE STRINGS

Illinois Sports News is a dummy. It is a typical dummy, but it is not the only one of its kind. Everywhere this committee looked among the subdistributors of Continental it found other dummies which are captained and manned by former long-time affiliates of the wire service chiefs and the Capone mob. They go through the fiction of stockholders' meetings, of meetings of board of directors, of voting themselves salaries which, in terms of the huge returns that roll in from the wire service, are picayune—they pay themselves $90 or $100 a week sometimes—and each year, by a solemn vote of the board of directors, arrange to pay into either Illinois Sports News or Continental Press everything that has come in over and above their actual operating expenses and these peanut salaries so that the subdistributors make no profit and pay no dividends. There is nothing left, after Continental Press gets its share, from which to pay any dividends.

Continental's operators and counsel contended in the face of all this that these subdistributing companies are independent operators and that their actions are their own. On its face, this contention is almost insulting and can be rejected out of hand. In every case investigated by the committee the purpose of attempting to insulate Continental Press was clearly obvious. As an example, in the case of Howard Sports News, which operates out of Baltimore and is one of the most flagrant of Continental's dummies, Continental wants to be isolated because Howard Sports News has for one of its functions the procurement of news from most of the race tracks. By the admission of its manager, Kelly, and the assertion of its lawyers, Continental has been very careful to divorce itself by every legal maneuver from any possible connection with activities as sordid as the stealing of news or selling the same to bookmaers who it cannot deny are engaged in an illegitimate business.

In fact, the testimony is uncontroverted that Continental deliberately set out to erect a business structure of such a kind that if its activities were ever questioned it would be able to defend itself with the half-truth that its news is sold only for a legitimate purpose. This fictional attempt at legality was attempted to be supported by distributors at the second level of the Continental set-up who had the temerity in their testimony before the committee to assert that they did not know they were selling their service to bookmakers.

The efforts of the subdistributors to keep up the legal fiction sought to be established by Continental collapsed under persistent questioning before the committee. The various distributors finally admitted that they sell racing news service to bookmakers and that they are fully aware that they are doing so.

These second-level outfits also groped for a pretense at legality by offering highly favorable rates to any legitimate publication which would buy their services. For example, a New York newspaper with one of the largest circulations in the country pays no more than $30 a week for Continental's news service, although other customers are billed as much as $5,000 a week for the same identical service.

One of the fundamental faults in the racing wire system is the discrimination between customers as to price and the allocation of the news service. This discrimination became so serious a threat to law and order in the State of Nevada where bookmaking is legal that a law has been passed requiring racing-news service to be made available on equal terms to all who apply for it. The testimony shows that this was necessary to prevent a serious outbreak of gang warfare. The Nevada law is in sharp contrast to the practice of Continental Press in other cities and States where Continental's service is supplied only to those selected by the distributor at rates fixed by him either at his own discretion or, as it was testified, after a conference with representatives of Continental Press in Chicago.

Here is another typical example test'ied to by William P. Brown, manager, operator and owner of the controlling interest in the Pioneer News Service of St. Louis:

Brown stated in his testimony that some customers pay about $100 a week for service and other customers of Pioneer pay as much as $350 a week for service. He was then asked, "What is the difference between the service given a $100 a week customer and the service given a $350 a week customer?", to which Brown replied, "Really none."

Question: "Really no difference whatsoever? Can you justify that difference?" Answer by Brown: "No; I can't."

FACADE OF LEGALITY A SHAM

The committee believes that the facade of legality which was set up by Continental's counsel with such great particularity must be rejected. It must also reject the insulation erected between McBride and the ultimate customers of Continental's service, the bookmakers, and, having rejected both of these factors, the inference becomes inescapable that Arthur V. McBride created a machine in which Edward McBride, through his agents, operates a racing wire service which is an integral part of a Nation-wide system employing discrimination in service and price against various persons seeking to purchase a commodity.

The conclusion is also inescapable that through agents and subagents McBride's organization steals news from race tracks and supplies this news through direct and indirect channels to bookmakers operating in violation of the law throughout the country. Whether this constitutes violation of local laws on the part of McBride is a matter for the determination of the courts in the respective States. The sole function of this committee in respect to the circumstances is to ascertain the facts and to determine whether or not any Federal legislation or regulation is required.

It also becomes inescapable, once the fiction of the divorce of Continental Press and McBride from the various distributors of Continental's news service, particularly in Chicago, has been rubbed out, that Arthur McBride is deliberately making a gift to the Mafia-affiliated Capone mob in Chicago of about $4,000 a week, which represents the difference in price paid by the Capone-controlled R & H service and the price paid by their competitors in the same city. In Kansas City, the Mafia group operating the wire service receives largesse of several hundred dollars a week on the same comparative basis. It is also clear that in many other cities the Capone affiliates and the Mafia are now in control of the distribution of racing wire news with a resultant source of enormous profits and power over bookmaking.

The committee has given careful thought to a proposal which might remedy this situation. It is essential that legislation or regulation be devised which will cure the evils that have been set forth so extensively above and at the same time will not impinge upon any constitutional rights guaranteed to those whose legality of operation is not a sham. These considerations are highly involved and for the purpose of this interim report the committee merely wishes now to state that a thorough study of the situation with respect to corrective legislation is proceeding and recommendations will be forthcoming in the committee's final report.

XI

BOOKMAKERS' PROFITS SHARED BY GANG

There is evidence that the wire service is being used to siphon off the profits of local bookmakers all over the country.

The use of control over the wire service in Miami in order to obtain a substantial share of the profits of bookmaking operations is not an isolated occurrence. From the testimony elicited by this committee in Miami, it is evident that the Capone syndicate had sufficient control over the wire service to cut off all service to the S. & G. bookmaking syndicate. This came at a time when this organization was also being pressured by raids conducted by W. O. Crosby, the investigator from the Governor's office. Under the combined pressure of the lack of wire service and the raids on its operations, the S. & G. Syndicate capitulated. The wire service was then restored and with Russell as their front man, Accardo and Guzik were cut in for a partnership, interest.

In Las Vegas, Benjamin (Bugsy) Siegel (since assassinated in gangland style) used his power as the local distributor of the wire service to make himself a partner of every bookmaker that took his service. He would refuse service to any bookmaker that would not give him the share of the profits that he demanded. The bitterness and threatened violence resulting from these practices resulted in the passage of a Nevada statute requiring racing-wire service to be furnished to bookmakers on a nondiscriminatory basis.

This technique of making the person who controls the wire service a partner of everyone who uses the service is an old one. In the early 1900's, Monte Tennes had the exclusive right to wire service in Chicago. He demanded and received a large cut of the profits of every subscriber to his service and kept a daily check on each subscriber's business. It is interesting to note that Continental Press is still doing business at 431 Dearborn Street, the address where Monte Tennes made his headquarters 30 years ago.

The policy of providing service to bookmakers on the basis of a share of the profits of the bookmaker was continued under Annenberg and

Ragen. Roselli, a tough mobster from California, who went to prison in the Bioff-Browne extortion case, was a partner in the gambling news distribution service for the southern California area. He testified that his job was to persuade bookmakers to buy the wire service and not "steal" it. He also asserted that Ragen was always clamoring for more revenue. He would always call every week or send out his field men to see if somebody was stealing money or failing to give Nationwide News Service (the predecessor to Continental) "the right count."

XII

RECORD OF OFFICIAL CORRUPTION

The most shocking revelation of the testimony before us is the extent of official corruption and connivance in facilitating and promoting organized crime.

The committee has found evidence of corruption and connivance at all levels of government—Federal, State, and local. Such evidence of the corruption of Federal Government officials as we received is primarily in connection with the enforcement of the income-tax laws. The evidence of corruption and connivance with organized crime in State and local government is present in five different forms:

(1) Direct bribe or protection payments made to law-enforcement officials, so that they will not interfere with specific criminal activities.

(2) Political influence and pressure of important officials or political leaders used to protect criminal activities or further the interests of criminal gangs.

(3) Law-enforcement officials found in the possession of unusual and unexplained wealth.

(4) Law-enforcement officials participating directly in the business of organized crime.

(5) Contributions to the campaign funds of candidates for political office at various levels frequently made by organized criminals without reference to political affiliation. Not infrequently, contributions are made to both major political parties; gangsters operate on both sides of the street.

Referred to elsewhere in this report are contributions made to the campaign of Fuller Warren for the governorship of Florida and to the campaign of Forrest Smith for the governorship of Missouri. There is no doubt from the testimony that both these candidates were assisted in their campaigns by contributions from known gamblers. The only purpose that this committee can conceive in the making of such contributions by persons engaged in gambling on the scale at which they operated was in the expectation that the contribution might prove an ultimate quid pro quo.

Striking evidence concerning direct payments of protection money to high State officials is the shocking story revealed by the California Commission on Organized Crime and repeated by Warren Olney, its former counsel, before this committee. Representatives of the attorney general's office, with the apparent blessing of Fred Howser, then attorney general, attempted to organize a State-wide system of protection for slot-machine operations and for the distribution of punchboards. This unsavory episode is described as follows:

The years 1947–50 have witnessed a persistent attempt to organize a system of State-wide protection for the operation of criminal rackets in California with primary emphasis on the gambling racket. This is something unique in the history of the State. In the 100 years of the State's existence, there have been from time to time in the cities and in the counties of California attempts to organize systems of local protection for gambling, prostitution, the narcotics traffic, and other activities prohibited by law. Occasionally and for brief periods such attempts have been successful, or partially successful, but more often than not they have ended in disaster for their originators. But never before has an attempt been made to organize a State-wide system of protection for any racket.

It was many months, and only after the receipt of a very large amount of evidence coming from many widely separated places, that the commission became convinced that an actual attempt was being made to organize a State-wide system of protection for rackets.

After summarizing reports from the various counties of the State concerning the incidents, the commission states:

> The conclusion became inescapable that these incidents were not separate one from the other, but on the contrary were diverse evidences of a single plan to organize in the name of the attorney general's office a system of protection for criminal rackets covering as much of the State as possible.

GANGS SEEK INFLUENCE IN HIGH PLACES

There is no direct evidence of the payment of protection money to any high State official in the Florida story of the Senate Crime Investigating Committee. The committee, however, points to the apparent connection between the $100,000 contributed to the gubernatorial campaign of Fuller Warren, by William Johnston, an associate of Capone mobsters and the designation by the Governor of W. O. Crosby as an investigator to conduct gambling raids, which, by a peculiar coincidence, only involved S. & G. Syndicate bookies. The raids ceased as soon as Russell, an associate of Johnston in the Capone mob, was taken in as a member of the S. & G. Syndicate.

In Missouri, one can perceive a more than passing connection between Governor Smith's appointment of two members to the Kansas City Police Board who favored a "wide-open town" and Binaggio's support during the election. Binaggio, who had important gambling interests to further, went so far before his slaying as to offer former Attorney General McKittrick a bribe to withdraw from the gubernatorial race. Binaggio's statement, as reported by McKittrick was: "I have to have a governor." He also tried to get Governor Smith to discharge Colonel Holzhausen, who was president of the St. Louis Police Board, because of the latter's lack of cooperation with the gambling interests.

CORRUPTION AT LOWER LEVELS RAMPANT

At the local level, this committee received evidence of corruption of law-enforcement officers and connivance with criminal gangs in practically every city in which it held hearings, with only one or two rare exceptions. The testimony at the Tampa hearings, for example, indicated that Sheriff Hugh Culbreath, of Hillsborough County, was the center of the criminal conspiracy to violate the gambling laws. Not only was evidence received of direct and regular payments of protection by gamblers, but there was also evidence of Culbreath's business association with "Red" Italiano, the "boss man" of the racketeers in Tampa. Unexplained, moreover, is a peculiar real-estate transaction of Culbreath with John Torrio, the predecessor of Al Capone in Chicago.

The sordid story of direct payments to law-enforcement officials in return for the protection of ciminals, is repeated in Philadelphia, where the "bag" man for Police Captain Vincent Elwell, would reportedly come into the station house with his pockets bulging with money. From $3,000 to $4,000 a month was alleged to have been paid in each of 38 police districts in that city or approximately $152,000 a month, not counting payments to the higher-ups. In Dade County, Fla., during a 5-year tenure in office, Sheriff James A. Sullivan's assets increased from a reported $2,500 in 1944 to well over $75,000 by 1949, and one of his deputies made enough money in 4 years to retire to a farm he bought for $26,000. Both the sheriff and his deputy John Burke did not deposit their money in banks, but used old fishing-tackle boxes and blankets as hiding places. In the adjoining Broward County, Sheriff James Clark acquired a fortune in real estate and business holdings over a period when not only did he fail to enforce the laws he had sworn to uphold, but he personally participated in their violation. In Jackson County, Mo., some deputy sheriffs were on the payrolls of machine distributors and taverns that violated the liquor laws. In Los Angeles, Calif., at least half a dozen police officers "borrowed" money from the Guarantee Finance Co., a big bookmaking operation. One suspended policeman worked as a collector from bookmakers for the Guarantee Finance Co., during the period of his suspension.

Law enforcement or rather the neglect thereof has been an easy road to affluence for many law-enforcement officials. The case of "Tubbo" Gilbert, "the richest police officer in the world," who was chief investigator in the States' Attorney's office in Chicago, is well known. There are many other illustrations in the testimony before the committee. Typical of this is the fortunate economic position of John English, the city commissioner in charge of the police department of East St. Louis, Ill., who was able to acquire a $100,000 summer home, various interests in real estate in East St. Louis, ownership participation in a restaurant and a gas station, all on a salary of $4,500 to $6,000. The fact that the city was wide open for years and only two or three gambling arrests were made in 1950 may have had some relation to the commissioner's wealth.

LAW ENFORCEMENT PARALYZED BY GANGSTERS

The attempt to paralyze law enforcement by political means is encountered again and again in the testimony. The committee developed at great length the extraordinary attempt by Binaggio, a powerful political leader to acquire control of the Police Board of Kansas City so that he could install as police chief a man named Braun, who had been disciplined because he had run a crap game in his station house. Binaggio finally offered a substantial bribe to one of the commissioners who had refused to go along with his program. Gene Burnett, police chief of Granite City, Ill., was apparently willing to close down the gambling places and the handbooks in his town, but the orders from the mayor of his town were to let them operate because that was how the city council wanted it.

In Miami, the committee heard a dictaphone recording of a conversation between the Chief of Police Luke Short and City Councilman Melvin Richard in which Short averred that he had been told "to lay off" gambling.   Short admitted that "the city could be closed up in a matter of hours."   It is noteworthy in this connection that one of the city councilmen of Miami to whom the chief of police was responsible had had a number of extremely profitable business deals with Harold Salvey, a member of the S. & G. Syndicate.

There is considerable evidence in the minutes of the testimony concerning contributions to political campaigns by gamblers and gangsters.   For example, William Molasky contributed $2,500 to the gubernatorial campaign in Missouri in the hope that he would begiven the right to name a member of the St. Louis Police Board.   When he was unable to do so he claimed to have been double-crossed.   Pat Noonan, an associate of the mobsters in the Binaggio gang, did considerable political work in the campaign to elect Governor Smith. Some of his expenses were paid by Binaggio and other persons involved in violations of the gambling laws.   The fact that Emilio Georgetti "the Gambling King of San Mateo County" in California, worked like a beaver for the election of Sheriff McGrath and "accumulated a little money for the campaign," did not hurt him in his gambling operations.

Evidence has also been presented to the committee that certain law-enforcement officials not only received protection money from gangsters but that they actually ran gambling operations themselves. The bookmaking operation which was run right in Sheriff Culbreath's office by his brother and an employee of the sheriff, may or may not have been as insignificant as the sheriff tried to show.   But the same thing cannot be said for the partnership which Sheriff Clark of Broward County had in the Broward Novelty Co.   This company operated bolita games (policy) and slot machines and provided the sheriff with his principal source of income.

It is obvious that a law-enforcement official who is himself engaged in gambling operations can have no special desire to enforce gambling statutes.

XIII

OLD METHODS OF ENFORCEMENT INEFFECTIVE

Traditional patterns of law enforcement are ineffective in dealing with organized crime in many localities, it would appear.

Throughout the country, law-enforcement agencies are organized on a strictly local basis.   Each county has a prosecuting attorney, a sheriff, and as many independent local police departments as there are incorporated cities, towns, and villages.   Testimony before this committee indicates that this law-enforcement organization tends to break down when confronted with the problem of organized crime, and particularly with the enforcement of gambling laws.

In the first place, jurisdiction between the local police, the sheriff and the district attorney is poorly and vaguely defined in the statutes of many States.   The result is very frequent conflict between these agencies, particularly where they have different policies with respect to the suppression of particular crimes.   This is illustrated by States Attorney Boyle's testimony concerning conditions in Cook County, Ill.   His office was conducting slot machine raids throughout the county.   However, he felt that the repression of handbooks was the job of the sheriff.   He has sent "thousands of letters" to the sheriff of

Cook County reporting handbooks.   There is no apparent reason why slot machines are within his jurisdiction and handbooks are the sheriff's job.   Boyle also testified that he has continuously called the sheriff's attention to gambling within the county in the towns outside of Chicago, but nothing was done about these conditions.   According to Boyle the sheriff has taken the attitude that what happens in incorporated cities is not his business, even though he is the principal law-enforcement officer of the county.   A key to the conflict between the State's attorney and the sheriff of Cook County is found in the statement that a sheriff's assistant named Gleason "raised the devil" with the State's attorney's men for coming out there (outside of Chicago) and "bothering the gambling places and slot machines." Boyle cited one instance where the sheriff's men were actually directing persons into the gambling places.

This Cook County testimony is similar to the situation in Los Angeles, where the city police department officials wanted to do something about the bookmaking operations of the Guarantee Finance Co., which was located outside city limits, and not only failed to receive any cooperation from the sheriff, but were told to stay on their own side of the line.

JURISDICTIONAL OVERLAPPINGS CONFUSING

When a Governor like Adlai Stevenson in Illinois feels that the State has a responsibility when local law enforcement breaks down and uses the State police in the attempt to enforce the laws, he is likely to be plagued by the same problem of inadequate definition and implementation of the powers and jurisdiction of law enforcement agencies.   This same "out" makes it possible for a judge in Madison County, Illinois, to construe narrowly the powers of the State police and hold that they have no power to interfere in local law enforcement and that their jurisdiction extends only to the State highways. As a result a gambling raid on the notorious Hyde Park Club was declared an illegal exercise of power and the money and the gambling equipment seized in the raid were ordered returned.

Conflicts of this character give point to the observations of Judge Stanley Milledge of Dade County, Fla., to the committee.   Indictment, he said—

doesn't represent anything beyond the technical power of the local people to deal with.   There our difficulty is our unwillingness to do so   *   *   *   We seem always to have the misfortune of having in office at any given time, some people who want to enforce these gambling laws and other criminal laws dealing with organized crime, but we always have some who wouldn't   *   *   *   You never can get the team organized at any one time to do something.   It isn't the fault   *   *   *   of any one officer   *   *   *   The judiciary are not entirely blameless.   Elective officers are always apparently concerned about re-election   *   *   *   and the power of the money that is behind the rackets and the fear of antagonizing this business, the fear that so much money will be put behind them at the next election that they will be defeated.

It is apparent from the testimony before our committee that many of our law-enforcement agencies are not properly equipped to deal with organized crime even if they had the will to do so.   Many of the gang killings in Tampa, for example, are done by imported gunmen. But the Tampa Police Department, according to Chief Beasley, has no way of carrying on criminal investigations outside of Tampa.

The entire travel fund of the police department is $200. Many law-enforcement agencies, like the Cook County sheriff's office, are run on a patronage basis. When a new head comes in there may be a complete personnel turn-over. As a result inexperienced men may be charged with complex law-enforcement operations and inefficiency is inevitable. But while law-enforcement officers may change, organized criminal operations continue to be manned by the same racketeers over the years who learn new tricks of deception, and devise more effective methods of thwarting law enforcement agencies.

XIV

GOVERNMENT CHEATED OF VAST SUMS

The Federal Government is being defrauded of many millions of dollars, perhaps running into hundreds of millions, of tax revenues by the mobsters engaged in organized criminal activities.

Assistant Commissioner of Internal Revenue, Daniel A. Bolich, made a statement before the committee that—

unlike the gangsters of the thirties, many of our modern big-time racketeers take deliberate and carefully contrived steps to defend themselves against the possibility of successful tax prosecutions. They obtain professional tax advice, and in numerous cases, they report substantial net income on their returns. They frequently attempt to insulate themselves from direct attack by operating through a maze of corporations, dummy stockholders, and "fronts." Under these conditions, investigation on the part of the Bureau aimed at determining whether the returns or supporting records of these individuals are false or fraudulent so as to sustain a charge of criminal tax evasion, is frequently a long, difficult, and time-consuming process.

There is no doubt that the top racketeers are using able tax accountants and lawyers to prepare their tax returns. These accountants and lawyers tend to specialize in gangster accounts. For example, Eugene Bernstein in Chicago, represents Tony Accardo and many other members of the Capone mob. George Goldstein in Newark represented all the well-known mobsters of North Jersey. Harry Sackman prepared tax returns for Mickey Cohen, the Guarantee Finance Co., and other gangster and racketeer customers in southern California. Louis Roth, a New York accountant, who has represented Joseph Profaci for 18 years, turned up as accountant for Frank Livorsi, Max Eder, convicted narcotics dealers, and for William Giglio, a black market sugar partner of Livorsi's.

How strong is the dependence of organized mobsters on their accountants and lawyers is revealed by the fact that without taking any receipts for their money, a number of unidentified persons handed sums totaling $190,000 to Bernstein to pay delinquent income taxes for Louis Campagna and Paul DeLucia, members of the Capone mob, so that they could be paroled from a Federal prison.

However, there is doubt as to whether the Bureau of Internal Revenue has been making a real effort to check on the income-tax returns of known gamblers and racketeers. It is apparent from the testimony before the committee that returns are being submitted by gangsters and racketeers which the Bureau would not accept from ordinary citizens. In these returns, a general statement is made as to the amount of income during the year, and a general statement of expenses. There is no itemization or detail concerning the sources of the income, nor any itemization or detail concerning expenses. No books or records are shown to the accountant or lawyer who prepares the return and only gross figures are submitted to him. These figures are accepted by the person preparing the return. "We took our client's word for it," says Bernstein, "based on information they gave us." According to him, he knows nothing of his client's business or the sources of their income.

Goldstein, who prepared the returns for the north Jersey gambling operations, was well aware of the fact that the whole operation was in cash and that "honest men did not do business that way" and that there was no way of checking the returns. Nevertheless, he had no hesitancy in submitting them.

MANY TAX RETURNS FRAUDULENT

It is apparent that many, if not all, of the returns submitted for the gamblers and gangsters are fraudulent, and that the Government is losing huge sums in tax revenue from the illegal ventures run by them. For example, John O'Rourke was a bookmaker who was in partnership with Frank Erickson at the Boca Raton Hotel in Miami. He also owned a large crap game at West Palm Beach. There was no attempt to keep these individual operations separate. All transactions were in cash. His accountant, Ralph Hart, testified that the net profit of O'Rourke from all operations in 1948 was $1,700 although the gross return from the Boca Raton operation alone was over $750,000.

William Brantman, a tax consultant in Chicago, prepared tax returns for Ralph Capone. The latter did not maintain books and records although he owned a cigarette vending company, a tavern, a mineral water company and apparently had gambling interests. Brantman accepted lump-sum figures from Capone as a basis for the preparation of the return. The income reported by Capone was less than $5,000 from all these varied sources.

Mickey Cohen's return showed a gross income for 1949 of $14,845. In 1947, according to his tax lawyer, Sackman, he built a lavish and costly home. The greater part of this money was "borrowed" without security. He has also "borrowed" in similar fashion over $50,000 a year since 1947. These so-called borrowings are not reported as income. At least one "lender" denied under oath making any "loans" to Cohen. O'Rourke in Florida must have contributed to these "borrowings" for there is testimony in the Florida hearings that Cohen laid off bets with O'Rourke and that Cohen won on 14 consecutive occasions. In any event all the checks on balance were going out to Los Angeles, none came from Los Angeles to Florida. In the preparation of Mickey Cohen's return, Sackman stated:

> I always ask him each year to give me the detail and he says "here is the figure and this is the only thing I can present to you. If the Government accepts the figure, that is their responsibility."

When it is remembered that Cohen was the reputed head of a bookmakers' association with almost 500 members, and is engaged in other profitable rackets, it is manifestly apparent that he has ridiculously understated his income for 1949.

DIFFICULT TO DETERMINE GAMBLING INCOMES

There can be little question that gamblers and racketeers conduct their businesses in such a way that it is extraordinarily difficult to determine their gross or net incomes. Wherever possible business is done exclusively in cash. No records of any kind are kept. Where individual enterprises are conducted their returns are confused with other enterprises of an entirely diverse character. If a bank is used by a racketeer or a gambler there is never any certainty that all the moneys handled by him pass through the bank account. Where bank accounts exist, claims are made that the deposits frequently represent the accommodation of cashing of checks and not income. Employees of gambling rooms even went so far as to state under questioning that they entered upon this employment having no idea how much they were going to be paid, and were simply handed an envelope containing money at the end of a week.

Not only is there no way of establishing through records such as ordinary businessmen keep what the gambler's gross receipts and net income are; there is also no way of establishing through usual business bookkeeping methods the expenses which they claim. There can be no question from the testimony we have taken that the gangsters, mobsters, and gamblers are literally "getting away with murder" in their tax returns.

The scandal in the Bureau of Internal Revenue in the California area may partially explain why even ordinary care was not used in scrutinizing the tax returns of gamblers and gangsters. Certain top officials of the Internal Revenue Bureau in that area conceived the brilliant scheme of selling stock which they owned in a company that they controlled to persons who were likely to have trouble with their income taxes. The stock was worthless, but its purchase tended to assure immunity from a too careful scrutiny of income-tax returns. One wonders also whether there was any relationship between the kind of returns that Harry Sackman filed for his gangster clients and the fact that he took a member of the Intelligence Unit of the Bureau of Internal Revenue into full partnership with him.

XV

GANGS INFILTRATING LEGITIMATE BUSINESS

The vast profits from organized crime are being used to buy up legitimate businesses.

One of the most perplexing problems in the field of organized crime is presented by the fact that criminals and racketeers are using the profits of organized crime to buy up and operate legitimate business enterprises. There is considerable evidence of this in the testimony which will be more fully developed in the committee's final report. "Nig" Rosen, a tough Philadelphia mobster, is in the dress business, as are other well-known gangsters. Louis Crusco, a "numbers" operator in Philadelphia, bought for cash ($34,000) a substantial interest in a steel company. Frank Livorsi, a New York gangster, went into the jelly business at a time when there was a shortage of sugar. The two Di Giovannis, Kansas City gangsters with long criminal records, are in the liquor distributing business. Both have exclusive distributing agencies for most important liquor lines. Tony Gizzo, member of the Binaggio mob, has an interest in a soda water company which sells "Canadian Ace," a Capone brewery beer. Jerry Catena, a New Jersey mobster, has a 50-percent interest in an express business. Joe Adonis is the principal stockholder of the Automotive Conveying Co. which hauls assembled Ford automobiles. Frank Costello has been active in many legitimate enterprises although he is the outstanding underworld leader in the New York City area. He has had a very profitable interest in a liquor company, in a moderately sized manufacturing concern; he has recently disposed of large real-estate holdings and he still retains some productive oil and gas leases. In Miami, the S. & G. Syndicate members obtained control of some of the choicest real estate in the city. In various parts of the country large office buildings, hotels, and night clubs are owned in whole or in part by outstanding gang leaders and gamblers.

A gangster in a legitimate business does not suddenly become respectable. The methods which he uses to achieve success in racketeering and gambling enterprises are not sloughed off. Thus there is evidence in the testimony concerning the use of homicide, intimidation, and strong-arm violence to eliminate competition or to compel customers to take merchandise sold by the mobsters. Monopoly and unfair competitive methods are the keys to the big money in criminal activities. It is also sought by the mobsters when they enter legitimate business. In addition to attempting to secure monopolies, there is considerable evidence of their black-market practices, tax evasion and unjust enrichment from legitimate businesses. These practices add further to the tremendous economic and political power which is wielded by the forces of organized crime.

XVI

STATUS OF CONCLUSIONS AND RECOMMENDATIONS

Although the authority of the committee expires 1 month hence by virtue of the limitations of Senate Resolution 202, the inquiry is proceeding apace, with open hearings scheduled to be held during March, 1951, in San Francisco, New York City, and Washington.

Certain tentative conclusions are under consideration; they are still to be formulated in the final report to the Senate which will be completed for presentation by March 31, 1951.

Accompanying these conclusions will be a series of proposed suggestions for corrective and repressive legislation. At this time the committee desires only to indicate the tentatively drawn lines that some of these recommendations will follow:

1. Legislation to be directed at the prohibition or control of transmission of gambling information in interstate and foreign commerce.

2. Legislation to be directed at the prohibition of interstate transmission of bets, wagers, and/or moneys used for betting or wagering in any form.

3. Recommendation that special procedures and rules be adopted by the Bureau of Internal Revenue for dealing with the income-tax returns of known criminals.

4. Legislation to provide for the establishment of a committee or commission to be created by the Congress having for its purpose the

continuing study of organized crime and its utilization of the avenues and vehicles of interstate commerce in all of its ramifications and aspects and the better coordination of the investigative activities of the law-enforcement agencies of the Federal Government.

5. Legislation recommending that consideration be given to augmenting the law-enforcement and criminal investigative agencies of the United States Government and that additional funds be made available for their operation.

The committee desires to stress that these references to proposed recommendations are not all-inclusive. Others are intended for submission; they are presently being studied and will be included in the committee's final, definitive report.

ESTES KEFAUVER, *Chairman*,
HERBERT R. O'CONOR,
LESTER C. HUNT,
CHARLES W. TOBEY,
ALEXANDER WILEY.

O

THIRD INTERIM REPORT

OF THE

SPECIAL COMMITTEE TO INVESTIGATE ORGANIZED CRIME IN INTERSTATE COMMERCE

PURSUANT TO

S. Res. 202

(81st Congress)

A RESOLUTION TO INVESTIGATE GAMBLING AND RACKETEERING ACTIVITIES

MAY 1 (legislative day, APRIL 17), 1951.—Ordered to be printed

UNITED STATES
GOVERNMENT PRINTING OFFICE
WASHINGTON : 1951

83229

SPECIAL COMMITTEE TO INVESTIGATE ORGANIZED CRIME IN INTERSTATE COMMERCE

(PURSUANT TO S. RES. 202, 81ST CONG.)

ESTES KEFAUVER, Tennessee, *Chairman*

HERBERT R. O'CONOR, Maryland   CHARLES W. TOBEY, New Hampshire
LESTER C. HUNT, Wyoming   ALEXANDER WILEY, Wisconsin

RUDOLPH HALLEY, *Chief Counsel*
ALFRED M. KLEIN, *Associate Counsel*
DOWNEY RICE, *Associate Counsel*
GEORGE S. ROBINSON, *Associate Counsel*
JOHN L. BURLING, *Associate Counsel*
JOSEPH L. NELLIS, *Associate Counsel*
HAROLD G. ROBINSON, *Chief Investigator*

The committee wishes to express its appreciation to Judge Morris Ploscowe of New York City and the Commission on Organized Crime of the American Bar Association of which Hon. Robert P. Patterson is chairman, for their valuable assistance in the preparation of this report.

II

TABLE OF CONTENTS

REPORT OF THE SPECIAL SENATE COMMITTEE TO INVESTIGATE ORGANIZED CRIME IN INTERSTATE COMMERCE

MAY 1 (legislative day, APRIL 17), 1951.—Ordered to be printed

Mr. KEFAUVER, from the Special Committee To Investigate Organized Crime in Interstate Commerce, submitted the following

REPORT

[Pursuant to S. Res. 202, 81st Cong.]

GENERAL CONCLUSIONS

1. Organized criminal gangs operating in interstate commerce are firmly entrenched in our large cities in the operation of many different gambling enterprises such as bookmaking, policy, slot machines, as well as in other rackets such as the sale and distribution of narcotics and commercialized prostitution. They are the survivors of the murderous underworld wars of the prohibition era. After the repeal of the prohibition laws, these groups and syndicates shifted their major criminal activities to gambling. However, many of the crime syndicates continued to take an interest in other rackets such as narcotics, prostitution, labor and business racketeering, black marketing, etc.

2. Criminal syndicates in this country make tremendous profits and are due primarily to the ability of such gangs and syndicates to secure monopolies in the illegal operations in which they are engaged. These monopolies are secured by persuasion, intimidation, violence, and murder. The committee found in some cities that law-enforcement officials aided and protected gangsters and racketeers to maintain their monopolistic position in particular rackets. Mobsters who attempted to compete with these entrenched criminal groups found that they and their followers were being subjected to arrest and prosecution while protected gang operations were left untouched.

3. Crime is on a syndicated basis to a substantial extent in many cities. The two major crime syndicates in this country are the Accardo-Guzik-Fischetti syndicate, whose headquarters are Chicago; and the Costello-Adonis-Lansky syndicate based on New York. Evidence of the operations of the Accardo-Guzik-Fischetti syndicate was

1

found by the committee in such places as Chicago, Kansas City, Dallas, Miami, Las Vegas, Nev., and the west coast. Evidence of the Costello-Adonis-Lansky operations was found in New York City, Saratoga, Bergen County, N. J., New Orleans, Miami, Las Vegas, the west coast, and Havana, Cuba. These syndicates, as well as other criminal gangs throughout the country, enter profitable relationships with each other. There is also a close personal, financial, and social relationship between top-level mobsters in different areas of the country.

4. There is a sinister criminal organization known as the Mafia operating throughout the country with ties in other nations, in the opinion of the committee. The Mafia is the direct descendant of a criminal organization of the same name originating in the island of Sicily. In this country, the Mafia has also been known as the Black Hand and the Unione Siciliano. The membership of the Mafia today is not confined to persons of Sicilian origin. The Mafia is a loose-knit organization specializing in the sale and distribution of narcotics, the conduct of various gambling enterprises, prostitution, and other rackets based on extortion and violence. The Mafia is the binder which ties together the two major criminal syndicates as well as numerous other criminal groups throughout the country. The power of the Mafia is based on a ruthless enforcement of its edicts and its own law of vengeance, to which have been creditably attributed literally hundreds of murders throughout the country.

5. Despite known arrest records and well-documented criminal reputations, the leading hoodlums in the country remain, for the most part, immune from prosecution and punishment, although underlings of their gangs may, on occasion, be prosecuted and punished. This quasi-immunity of top-level mobsters can be ascribed to what is popularly known as the "fix." The fix is not always the direct payment of money to law-enforcement officials, although the committee has run across considerable evidence of such bribery. The fix may also come about through the acquisition of political power by contributions to political organizations or otherwise, by creating economic ties with apparently respectable and reputable businessmen and lawyers, and by buying public good will through charitable contributions and press relations.

GAMBLING SUPPORTS BIG-TIME RACKETS

6. Gambling profits are the principal support of big-time racketeering and gangsterism. These profits provide the financial resources whereby ordinary criminals are converted into big-time racketeers, political bosses, pseudo businessmen, and alleged philanthropists. Thus, the $2 horse bettor and the 5-cent numbers player are not only suckers because they are gambling against hopeless odds, but they also provide the moneys which enable underworld characters to undermine our institutions.

The legalization of gambling would not terminate the widespread predatory activities of criminal gangs and syndicates. The history of legalized gambling in Nevada and in other parts of the country gives no assurance that mobsters and racketeers can be converted into responsible businessmen through the simple process of obtaining State and local licenses for their gambling enterprises. Gambling, moreover, historically has been associated with cheating and corruption.

The committee has not seen any workable proposal for controlled gambling which would eliminate the gangsters or the corruption.

7. Rapid transmission of racing information and gambling information about other sporting events is indispensable to big-time bookmaking operations. This information is presently being provided by a monopoly operated by the Continental Press Service. The Continental Press Service, at critical times and in crucial places where monopoly of bookmaking is at stake, yields to the domination and control of the Accardo-Guzik-Fischetti crime syndicate, to which it is beholden for its own monopoly in the wire-service field. The wire service is so vital to large bookmakers that they are compelled to pay what the traffic will bear to the Continental Press Service. This makes it possible for the Accardo-Guzik-Fischetti crime syndicate to participate in the profits of bookmaking operations throughout the country.

8. The backbone of the wire service which provides gambling information to bookmakers is the leased wires of the Western Union Telegraph Co. This company, in many parts of the country has not been fully cooperative with law-enforcement officials who have been trying to suppress organized criminal rackets which make use of telegraph facilities. By permitting its facilities to be used by bookmakers, Western Union has given aid and comfort to those engaged in violation of gambling laws. In some cases, Western Union officials and employees actually participated in bookmaking conspiracies by accepting bets and transmitting them to bookmakers. It should be noted that during the latter months of the committee's investigation, Western Union has taken steps to prevent this practice and has been more cooperative with the committee.

In many areas, of which New York is a notable example, the telephone companies have cooperated fully with law-enforcement officials. However, in still other areas, telephone companies have been much less cooperative. Local legislation is apparently necessary in many States to require telephone company officials to refuse facilities and remove existing facilities of suspected bookmakers and to call to the attention of local law-enforcement officials the use of telephone facilities by bookmakers.

9. Crime is largely a local problem. It must be attacked primarily at the local level, with supplementary aid, where appropriate, from State and Federal authorities. The conduct of various forms of gambling enterprises, houses of prostitution, the distribution of narcotics, the use of intimidation, violence, and murder to achieve gang objectives are all violations of State laws. The public must insist upon local and State law-enforcement agencies meeting this challenge, and must not be deceived by the aura of romanticism and respectability, deliberately cultivated by the communities' top mobsters.

10. The Federal Government has the basic responsibility of helping the States and local governments in eliminating the interstate activities and interstate aspects of organized crime, and in facilitating exchange of information with appropriate safeguards between the Federal Government and local and State law-enforcement agencies as well as between law-enforcement agencies in the various States.

The task of dealing with organized crime is so great that the public must insist upon the fullest measure of cooperation between law-enforcement agencies at all levels of Government without buck-passing. The committee feels that it has fully demonstrated the need for such cooperation.   The time for action has arrived.

11. Wide-open gambling operations and racketeering conditions are supported by out-and-out corruption in many places.   The wide-open conditions which were found in these localities can easily be cleaned up by vigorous law enforcement.   This has been demonstrated in the past in many different communities and has received added demonstration during the life of our committee.   The outstanding example is Saratoga, N. Y., which ran wide-open through the racing season of 1949 but was closed down tight in 1950.

12. Venal public officials have had the effrontery to testify before the committee that they were elected on "liberal" platforms calling for wide-open towns.   The committee believes that these officials were put in office by gamblers and with gamblers' money, and that in the few cases where the public was convinced that gambling is good for business, this myth was deliberately propagated by the paid publicists of the gambling interests.   In many wide-open communities, so-called political leaders and law-enforcement officials have sabotaged efforts of civic-minded citizens to combat such wide-open conditions and the crime and corruption that they entailed.

13. The Treasury of the United States has been defrauded of huge sums of money in tax revenues by racketeers and gangsters engaged in organized criminal activities.   Huge sums in cash handled by racketeers and gangsters are not reflected in their income tax returns. Income tax returns filed with the Federal Government have been inadequate since, as a rule, they contained no listing of the sources of income nor any itemization of the expenses.   Gangsters and racketeers, moreover, do not keep books and records from which it might be possible to check tax returns.

14. Mobsters and racketeers have been assisted by some tax accountants and tax lawyers in defrauding the Government.   These accountants and lawyers have prepared and defended income tax returns which they knew to be inadequate.   At the very least, those who are guilty of such practices could be convicted of a misdemeanor and sent to jail for a year for every year in which they have failed to comply with the law.

The Bureau of Internal Revenue states that it has, to the best of its ability, considering its limited manpower, been investigating these returns.   It states further that when it pursues the case of one of these individuals, it prefers to set up against him a case of criminal tax evasion which is a felony, rather than the lesser offense of failing to keep proper books and records, which is a misdemeanor.

Despite this, the committee believes that the Bureau of Internal Revenue could, and should, make more frequent use of the sanctions provided for failure to keep proper books and records than it has heretofore.   In any event, the Bureau of Internal Revenue should insist on adequate returns and proper books.

While the great majority of agents of the Bureau of Internal Revenue are honest and efficient, there have been relatively few instances in different parts of the country of lack of vigorous and effective action to collect income taxes from gangsters and racketeers.

15. A major question of legal ethics has arisen in that there are a number of lawyers in different parts of the country whose relations to organized criminal gangs and individual mobsters pass the line of reasonable representation. Such lawyers become true "mouthpieces" for the mob. In individual cases, they have become integral parts of the criminal conspiracy of their clients.

16. Evidence of the infiltration by organized criminals into legitimate business has been found, particularly in connection with the sale and distribution of liquor, real-estate operations, night clubs, hotels, automobile agencies, restaurants, taverns, cigarette-vending companies, juke-box concerns, laundries, the manufacture of clothing, and the transmission of racing and sport news. In some areas of legitimate activity, the committee has found evidence of the use by gangsters of the same methods of intimidation and violence as are used to secure monopolies in criminal enterprise. Gangster infiltration into business also aggravates the possibility of black markets during a period of national emergency such as we are now experiencing. Racketeers also have used labor unions as fronts to enable them to exploit legitimate businessmen.

17. In some instances legitimate businessmen have aided the interests of the underworld by awarding lucrative contracts to gangsters and mobsters in return for help in handling employees, defeating attempts at organization, and in breaking strikes. And the committee has had testimony showing that unions are used in the aid of racketeers and gangsters, particularly on the New York water front.

RECOMMENDATIONS

INTRODUCTION

The committee has received many recommendations for controlling organized crime and improving the enforcement of the criminal law and the administration of criminal justice. Those recommendations have been received from a variety of sources: from public officials, experts on law enforcement, lawyers, accountants, and interested laymen. They all have been given careful attention.

The committee is convinced that there is no single panacea for the widespread social, economic, and political evils that have been uncovered in the many cities in which it has made investigations and held hearings. The committee feels, nevertheless, that while organized crime cannot be completely eliminated from our society, this is no reason for defeatism, for vigorous law enforcement can control organized crime to the point where it is no longer a menace to our institutions.

Any program for controlling organized crime must take into account the fundamental nature of our governmental system. The enforcement of the criminal law is primarily a State and local responsibility. While channels of interstate communication and interstate commerce may be used by organized criminal gangs and syndicates, their activities are in large measure violations of local criminal statutes. When criminal gangs and syndicates engage in bookmaking operations, operate gambling casinos or slot machines, engage in policy operations, peddle narcotics, operate houses of prostitution, use intimidation or violence to secure monopoly in any area of commercial activity, commit assaults and murder to eliminate competition, they are guilty of violating State laws and it is upon State and local prosecuting agencies, police and courts, that the major responsibility for the detection, apprehension, prosecution, and punishment of offenders rests.

The crisis of law enforcement which has been uncovered by the committee is basically a State and a local crisis. The Federal Government does not have responsibility for the widespread gambling and vice conditions it has found in such places as the Miami area; the parishes outside of New Orleans; the Covington-Newport areas of Kentucky; Bergen County, N. J.; several counties in California, Illinois, and Saratoga, N. Y. The responsibility is basically one that must be shared by local and State agencies of law enforcement, as well as by the citizens of the various communities who tolerated such conditions. Nor can a remedy for these conditions be found merely by shrugging off local and State responsibility and declaring that only the Federal Government can do the job of cleaning up wide-open conditions. As J. Edgar Hoover pointed out in his statement to this committee, "The Federal Government can never be a satisfactory substitute for local self-government in the enforcement field."

The Federal Government, moreover, can do relatively little to assist local citizens and officials in the removal of local law-enforcement officials who have accepted money from gangsters and racketeers or who have actually participated in criminal operations. The Federal Government can do little about the influence which gangsters and racketeering elements exert upon local political organizations. The Federal Government can do even less about the inefficiency and ineffectiveness of local law-enforcement agencies. Nor can the Federal Government correct the diffusion of responsibility and the "buck passing" which take place between independent law-enforcement agencies operating in the same county or in the same metropolitan area. Finally, the Federal Government can do nothing to correct the misguided leniency of State and local judges who impose small fines or short jail sentences in racketeering situations.

While the Federal police and prosecuting agencies cannot be substituted for State and local law enforcement in dealing with organized crime, the Federal Government still has a major and vital responsibility in this field. The Federal Government must provide leadership and guidance in the struggle against organized crime, for the criminal gangs and syndicates have Nation-wide ramifications. It should establish additional techniques to provide maximum coordination in law-enforcement agencies to insure complete efficiency. It must help work out techniques for securing better interstate cooperation in dealing with crime. In addition, the Federal Government is under certain positive obligations to use powers presently available to it against organized criminal gangs. It is the responsibility of the Federal Government to see that the channels of interstate commerce, transportation, communication, and the United States mails are not used to facilitate the operations of organized criminal gangs and syndicates. It is up to the Federal Government to see that gangsters and racketeers are stripped of as much of their ill-gotten gains as possible through vigorous enforcement of the income-tax laws. Only the Federal Government can take affirmative action to rid our shores of alien criminals who have become members of predatory criminal groups. Finally, the Federal Government has the responsibility for revision of existing statutes where legal technicalities are permitting the guilty to escape just punishment.

It is with the aforementioned goals in mind that the following recommendations are formulated:

I. The Congress through a continuation of this committee should for a further limited period continue to check on organized crime in interstate commerce. The basic function of the committee should be to scrutinize the efforts made by the Federal agencies to suppress interstate criminal operations, and particularly the racket squads described in later recommendations. It will also follow up the legislative recommendations made in this report

The committee should receive periodic reports from the racket squads recommended to be established in the Justice and Treasury Departments. It should continuously scrutinize the effectiveness of these squads. It should also take steps to facilitate greater cooperation between Federal and State law enforcement agencies. The committee should use its subpena power to hold hearings from time to time concerning crime situations in which there is a great public interest, or which should be called to the attention of the public.

However, it should be clearly understood at the outset that the continued committee should have as its prime function the task of pursuing its legislative inquiries and program and of stimulating law enforcement officials to direct action against criminals rather than the exposition of situations which can only give cumulative support to the now overwhelming evidence that there is a serious organized crime problem which must be met.

II. A racket squad should be organized in the Justice Department

The function of this racket squad, which might appropriately be placed in the Criminal Division of the Department, must be to clean the country of racketeers, gangsters, and organized criminal gangs by utilizing any lawful means available, including

(*a*) Prosecution for Federal crimes;

(*b*) On-the-spot racket grand jury investigations and inquiries; these, as suggested by the Attorney General, should be held in each judicial district at least once each year;

(*c*) Gathering and correlating information about gangsters and criminals from all sources, both Federal, State and local;

(*d*) Stimulating local prosecutions by turning information concerning local criminal situations over to State and local authorities for action. Of course, in such cases proper caution must be exercised to avoid turning information over to corrupt officials or to officials who would use it for political advantages;

(*e*) Turning information on criminals and gang activities over to specific Federal agencies such as Immigration and Naturalization, Customs and the tax-collecting authorities, for action thereon;

(*f*) Reporting to this Senate committee and its successor as well as other appropriate committees.

In this connection, it should be observed that the Department of Justice has had such a squad functioning on a limited scale since 1947, under the able direction of Special Assistant Attorney General Max H. Goldschein. The committee urgently recommends that the size of this squad be increased.

III. Appropriate legislation should be enacted to set up an independent Federal Crime Commission in the executive branch of the Government

This Commission should be appointed by the President with the advice and consent of the Senate. It should be composed of three members, all of whom are prominent citizens and not otherwise members or employees of the Federal Government. It should be organized promptly and be ready to function on September 1, 1951, the date set for the expiration of authority of this committee.

The Commission should hear witnesses and hold hearings from time to time, but should not have the power of subpena. In such cases as the Commission may find it necessary to subpena witnesses, or to hear them under oath, it should apply either to the Senate Committee on Interstate and Foreign Commerce, which by virtue of Senate Resolution 129 succeeds to the functions of this committee, or in the alternative, it may apply to any other appropriate committee of the Congress which has jurisdiction over the subject matter when it deems it desirable to have hearings. The hearings, in such instances, will be held by the appropriate committees.

The functions of the Federal Crime Commission should be—

1. The continuing study and surveillance of operations of interstate criminal organizations throughout the country.

2. Reports on such criminal activities at periodic intervals to the Interstate and Foreign Commerce Committee of the United States Senate.

3. To make recommendations for hearings to the Interstate and Foreign Commerce Committee of the United States Senate or any other appropriate committee in cases in which the Interstate and Foreign Commerce Committee may not be the most appropriate, for more intensive investigation requiring the testimony of witnesses under oath.

4. The maintenance of liaison between Federal investigative and law-enforcement agencies and crime commissions at the State and local levels with the dissemination to the latter of information respecting criminal operations as may be required in the public interest.

5. Suggestion and encouragement of legislation designed to expedite, facilitate, and encourage better and more intensive law enforcement at all levels of government.

6. The initiation and development of appropriate social study relating to crime, its punishment, and law enforcement.

7. The maintenance of files and records as a national clearing house of information respecting criminal activities in interstate commerce to be made available, to properly authorized individuals and groups, subject to suitable security measures, but not to conflict with the interests of any presently established Federal, State, or local law enforcement agency.

Recommendation III is concurred in by all members of the committee except Senator Alexander Wiley who, while appreciating some of the advantages which might be achieved under a Federal Crime Commission, believes that the possible abuses of such a new agency require his opposition to the proposal.

It is Senator Wiley's contention that the Commission could conceivably result in (a) the basis for a national-type police force which is contrary to America's tradition and which has been vigorously opposed by all outstanding Federal law enforcement agencies; (*b*) unnecessary harassment and interference with Federal investigative agencies; (*c*) an unnecessary and costly superstructure imposed upon the present operating agencies; (*d*) dissipation of the function on the part of the legislative branch.

Senator Wiley believes that voluntary cooperation among Federal investigation agencies can achieve most of the objectives which the committee majority believes can only be obtained by a Federal Crime Commission.

This is the only point on which Senator Wiley dissents from his agreement with this unanimous report. The committee notes at this point that there has been no previous dissent by any member on any major point of policy.

IV. The establishment of the Special Fraud Squad by the Bureau of Internal Revenue of the Treasury Department is one of the most effective and useful steps taken to collect taxes from the criminal element. The committee applauds the Department for this act and recommends that it be supported with necessary appropriation and that it work in close cooperation with the special racket squad if set up by the Department of Justice as is recommended by the committee. The Bureau of Internal Revenue should maintain on a current and continuing basis a list of known gangsters, racketeers, gamblers, and criminals whose income-tax returns should receive special attention by a squad of trained experts. Procedures leading to prosecution should be streamlined and speeded up

In our second interim report, we noted that "The Federal Government is being defrauded of many millions of dollars—perhaps running into hundreds of millions—of tax revenues by the mobsters engaged in organized criminal activities" (p. 31); and also that "It is apparent that many, if not all, of the returns submitted for the gamblers and gangsters are fraudulent and that the Government is losing huge sums in tax revenues from the illegal ventures run by them" (p. 32).

Under these circumstances, it becomes absolutely vital for the Federal Government to enact new legislation and to modify and strengthen existing administrative procedures and regulations so that gangsters, racketeers, gamblers, and other persons engaged in illegitimate enterprises shall be compelled to turn over as much of their illgotten gains as possible to the Government in the form of income taxes. Money is the key to power in the underworld. It buys protection for illegitimate enterprises and enables underworld characters to buy up legitimate business and to claim respectability by contributions to worthy causes. The large financial resources at the disposal of criminal gangs and syndicates make such gangs and syndicates a serious menace to our institutions. The Federal Government must make every effort to reach these resources and curb the power of organized crime. Accordingly, we recommend that the Bureau of Internal Revenue should set up and maintain a list of known gamblers, gangsters, racketeers, and other criminals whose income-tax returns must be given special attention. A similar list is already in existence and was submitted to this committee by the Department of Justice. This list should be supplemented by names furnished by all Federal law-enforcement agencies, by the racket squads of the Justice and

Treasury Departments, and by names solicited from the leading State and local law enforcement agencies throughout the country. The committee notes with strong approval the notice of the Treasury Department of April 30, that the tax returns of 2,500 leading gangsters are being given special attention by the Bureau of Internal Revenue.

The mere existence of a known criminal list in the Bureau of Internal Revenue is not enough. Special attention must be given to the tax returns submitted by the persons on this list. Thus, their returns cannot be left for examination by routine procedures. The Bureau of Internal Revenue has organized a special racket squad of picked men known as the Special Frauds section whose function would be to subject the tax returns of known criminals to close scrutiny and investigation. These men will be familiar with the accounting methods, techniques, and procedures of the Bureau, and they should also have familiarity with the modus operandi of gangsters, racketeers, gamblers, and other offenders. Since income-tax men are not expected to know the habits and methods of criminals, training for the Bureau of Internal Revenue squad might be arranged with such Federal agencies as the FBI, the Narcotics Bureau, and other law-enforcement agencies of the Government.

It is obvious to anyone familiar with income-tax prosecutions that the procedures presently employed by the Department of Justice and the Bureau of Internal Revenue are entirely too laborious and time consuming. Many complex steps are necessary before an income-tax prosecution is finally decided upon. The committee urges the Bureau of Internal Revenue to make a study with a view to simplifying its procedures in connection with the processing of prosecutions for income-tax frauds. Swift prosecution and punishment are deterrents to crime in the tax field as much as anywhere else.

V. The Bureau of Internal Revenue should enforce the regulations which require taxpayers to keep adequate books and records of income and expenses, against the gamblers, gangsters, and racketeers who are continually flouting them. Violation should be made a felony

The committee has been continually hampered in the course of its inquiry into the activities of known criminals and their political and official allies, by the failure of these individuals to keep and maintain books and records of their income and expenses. Though they may handle moneys running into hundreds of thousands of dollars, they have not felt it necessary to keep books and records which explain the nature, source, and amount of the moneys they receive, nor the nature and extent of their disbursements. Income-tax returns in most instances merely give gross figures of income and expenses without explanation of the nature of these items. A typical attitude of gamblers toward the maintenance of records is found in the testimony of one successful gambler who calmly informed the committee that although he kept no records of his gambling activities during the year, he was able to keep a running balance in his head. At the end of the year, he entered the final balance in his return. It is true that the present regulations of the Bureau of Internal Revenue require tax-payers (except wage earners and farmers) to keep such permanent books of account or records as are sufficient to establish the amount of the gross income and the deductions (Regulation 111, sec. 2954-1).

While honest businessmen comply with this regulation, hoodlums, venal officials, some politicians with underworld affiliations, do not. Nevertheless, the Bureau of Internal Revenue has not utilized this regulation to its full potentialities. The committee feels that the obligation to keep adequate books and records of account should bind not only honest businessmen but also those who profit from crime. Willful failure to comply with this obligation should subject the offender to prosecution and punishment. At present such failure is a misdemeanor. The law should be amended to make it a felony. The regulations should also require that these books and records be kept for a sufficiently long period (e. g., 7 years) and not be destroyed as soon as income-tax returns are submitted.

VI. Gambling casinos should be required to maintain daily records of money won and lost to be filed with the Bureau of Internal Revenue. They also should be required to maintain such additional records as shall be prescribed by the Bureau. Officials of the Bureau of Internal Revenue should have access to the premises of gambling casinos and to their books and records at all times. Where the casino is operating illegally, in addition to the aforementioned obligations, the operators of the casino should be required to keep records of all bets and wagers

The cash returns from gambling casinos are fantastic in amount. There is also, at the present time, no way in which the tax returns filed with the Bureau of Internal Revenue by the proprietors of these casinos can be adequately checked. The committee feels that one way of placing gambling casinos under control is to require them to keep daily returns to be filed with the Bureau of Internal Revenue and maintain prescribed books and records. These returns and the books and records should be checked frequently by visits from responsible revenue officials. Only through some such means can the Government obtain its proper share of the moneys which pass through the hands of proprietors of gambling casinos.

In order to maintain even a closer check upon the operations of the illegal gambling casinos, the committee recommends that such casinos be compelled to keep a record of all wagering and betting transactions which take place within its walls. They should also be subject to the obligation to maintain daily records for the Bureau of Internal Revenue and the obligation to permit inspection of premises and inspection of books and records at all times.

The committee is well aware that these provisions may well put illegal gambling casinos out of business.

VII. The law and the regulations of the Bureau of Internal Revenue should be amended so that no wagering losses, expenses, or disbursements of any kind, including salaries, rent, protection money, etc., incurred in or as a result of illegal gambling shall be deductible for income-tax purposes

Under present income-tax law and regulations, criminals and racketeers in computing their incomes for tax purposes are permitted to deduct from their gross incomes the operating expenses and wagering losses of their illegitimate gambling enterprises.

In the opinion of the committee, this is not only incongruous but highly undesirable.

If organized professional gambling is to be stopped by any Federal enactment, this recommendation is best calculated to do so.

Even under present tax law (title 26, sec. 23h) there is some recognition of this principle. Gambling profits are taxable but gambling losses are not deductible when they exceed the winnings. The present law primarily hits the amateur gambler and the little man. The suggested revision would hit the big professional gambler.

VIII. The transmission of gambling information across State lines by telegraph, telephone, radio, television, or other means of communication or communication facility should be regulated so as to outlaw any service devoted to a substantial extent to providing information used in illegal gambling

Information is vital to large-scale bookmaking operations. The elimination of wire service to bookmakers is therefore of such importance that a practical law must be devised to effect this end. The need is all the more essential because such wire service to bookmakers is now in the hands of Continental Press Service which enjoys an almost complete monopoly of this activity insofar as it exists on a Nation-wide scale. The committee points out elsewhere in this report that the control over the wire service exercised by the Chicago crime syndicate has made it possible for this crime syndicate and others to organize bookmaking operations throughout the country and to participate in their profits.

The need for such suppressive legislation was pointed out by the Senate Committee on Interstate and Foreign Commerce in its excellent and well-considered report on the bill to prohibit the transmission of gambling information (S. 3358, 81st Cong.). This conclusion was also reached by the mayors, State attorneys general, and other State and local law-enforcement officials who attended the Attorney General's conference on organized crime in Washington on February 15, 1950, and who adopted the following resolution:

Be it resolved, That this conference go on record as favoring Federal legislation making interstate use of telephone, telegraph, or radio facilities for dissemination of horse-race results for illegal gambling purposes a Federal crime. Such a law would not be designed to prohibit dissemination of sports information through he generally accepted press associations and newspapers.

The committee is now working on a specific bill for the purpose of accomplishing these ends, and at the same time, minimizing disadvantages which may incidentally accrue to those who are engaged in the wholly lawful dissemination of news. To the extent that they may unavoidably cause incidental inconveniences to such persons engaged in wholly lawful operations, the committee desires to suggest and urge that these disadvantages be accepted as inevitable and necessary in order to accomplish a very important public purpose. It is believed that the specific legislation will hold any such disadvantages to an absolute minimum.

In general, the committee has in mind a proposal which would require all persons engaged in the dissemination of any information concerning horse-racing or dog-racing events or betting information on any other sporting event by means of interstate or foreign communication to receive a license solely for these purposes from the Federal Communications Commission.

It is proposed that such licenses shall be freely granted to any applicant unless the Commission establishes that the granting of such application would not be in the public interest, that the applicant is not of good moral character, or that the information will intentionally be disseminated directly or indirectly to any substantial number of persons who would utilize it primarily to facilitate gambling activities or other activities in violation of the laws of the various States.

No one seeking a license shall be able to evade responsibility for the ultimate use of the information provided by him merely because the ultimate user or any number of intermediate subscribers are independent legal entities. If an applicant seeking a license has failed to obtain available information concerning the use to which the information is put, the burden shall be on him to show proper intent. Licenses may be revoked for the same reasons for which they are denied.

Every common carrier or other supplier of information concerning racing and sporting events should be required to maintain a list of its terminal points and drops, both for receiving and sending. The address of such terminal point shall be noted, together with the name of the person or persons operating such terminal facility. Such lists should be open to inspection by appropriate local, State, and Federal law-enforcement agencies.

The committee has given consideration to the added burden which this proposal would place on the Federal Communications Commission. But it feels that this Commission is well equipped to handle the problem, particularly if it is enabled to employ the necessary but small number of additional personnel, and if it receives full cooperation from this committee, from the successor to this committee, from the various executive departments and from the proposed Federal Crime Commission.

The committee has given consideration to proposals that all dissemination of betting information in interstate commerce be declared illegal, but has rejected this proposal at least for the present in the hope that the elimination of racing-wire service primarily for gambling will effect the desired result, with the minimum disruption of legitimate news dissemination activities. The committee has also considered various proposals relating to delay in furnishing information concerning horse and dog races and other sporting events and believes the proposals set forth here will accomplish the result without the inconveniences and difficulties attendant upon such alternative proposals.

The committee intends to propose in the legislation to be submitted that the operation of such a wire service without the requisite license suggested shall be made a felony.

IX. *The internal revenue laws and regulations should be amended so as to require any person who has been engaged in an illegitimate business netting in excess of $2,500 a year for any of 5 years previously, to file a net-worth statement of all his assets, along with his income-tax returns*

The necessity for a net-worth statement in connection with checking upon the income-tax returns of persons engaged in criminal activities was clearly stated by Assistant Attorney General Caudle in his statement to the committee:

Cases involving racketeers are difficult to prove. Gamblers and gangsters do not keep books to show their receipt of income. Therefore, it is usually necessary for the Government to rely on their year-by-year increases in net worth and their known expenditures. To make this type proof stick in court we must establish a beginning point from which to figure annual increases in wealth. And because these characters must hide their activities it is always difficult and sometimes impossible to establish a starting net worth which excludes the possibility of other hidden wealth.

In order to facilitate a check upon the income-tax returns of known criminals and racketeers, the committee recommends that they be required to file net-worth statements so that this essential beginning point for investigation will be available to the Government.

X. The transmission of bets or wagers, or the transmission of moneys in payment of bets or wagers, across State lines by telegraph, telephone, or any other facilities of interstate communication, or the United States mails, should be prohibited

Large bookmaking operations cannot be carried on without using facilities of interstate commerce and interstate communication. The Ericksons, Carroll-Mooneys, Rosenbaums, Gizzos, S. & G. Syndicates, and the Mickey Cohens all do a considerable lay-off business with each other as well as with other bookmakers throughout the country. All this business is carried on by telephone and telegraph. In addition, bets in large volume are also laid off by telephone or telegraph at the tracks, thus depressing pari-mutuel odds and robbing legitimate bettors of their fair shares of the winnings. We have also seen that in the S. J. Rich Co. situation in St. Louis, the facilities of a telegraph, company were actually used to receive bets and money from bettors, as well as to pay off bettors.

The Federal Government should not permit interstate communication facilities or the mails to carry on bookmaking and gambling operations. It may be argued that the prohibition of all use of interstate communication facilities or the mails to place bets or send money for wagers will throw an unreasonable burden on Federal law-enforcement agencies. Thousands of small bets are made over the telephone to bookmakers. However, the Federal Government should leave the elimination of these transactions to State and local officials. It should concern itself only with the larger bookmaking operations, where the link to organized crime is more clearly apparent.

XI. The prohibition against the transportation of slot machines in interstate commerce should be extended to include other gambling devices which are susceptible of gangster or racketeer control, such as punchboards, roulette wheels, etc.

The passage of the bill to prohibit the interstate transportation of slot machines was a blow to racketeering interests. The underworld has drawn great profits from slot machines for years. In the past, the manufacture of such machines was concentrated in the Chicago area, and the machines were distributed throughout the country. The recent statute makes a crime the transportation of a slot machine into a State where the operation of such machines is illegal. However, slot machines are not the only gambling devices from which gangsters and racketeers draw substantial profits. The lowly punchboard has attained the proportions of a major racketeering enterprise in many sections of the country. The committee has had before it evidence that the sale and distribution of punchboards are pushed by methods similar to those used in connection with slot machines. Since this is so, then, just as slot machines are barred from interstate commerce, so punchboards should likewise be barred. Other gambling devices, such as roulette wheels, might similarly be barred from interstate commerce because they too are used by racketeering interests in illegitimate gambling operations.

XII. The penalties against the illegal sale, distribution, and smuggling of narcotic drugs should be substantially increased

We have seen that there has been a serious increase in the narcotics traffic, particularly among teen-agers. One of the ways to curb that traffic is through the imposition of severe penalties. Mr. Harry Anslinger, Commissioner of Narcotics, testified before this committee that—

The average prison sentence meted out in the Federal courts is 18 months. Short sentences do not deter. In districts where we get good sentences the traffic does not flourish. * * * Both the League of Nations and the United Nations have recommended more severe sentences as one of the best methods to suppress the traffic.

In many countries that has been very effective.

* * * * * * *

There should be a minimum sentence for the second offense. The commercialized transaction, the peddler, the smuggler, those who traffic in narcotics, on the second offense if there were a minimum sentence of 5 years without probation or parole, I think it would just about dry up the traffic.

In the light of this testimony, Congress should pass legislation to provide for increased penalties for drug peddlers and others engaged in the commercialized aspects of the drug traffic. Mandatory penalties of imprisonment of at least 5 years should be provided for second offenders. Such legislation is now pending in the House of Representatives where it is receiving the careful consideration of the Committee on Ways and Means.

XIII. The immigration laws should be amended to facilitate deportation of criminal and other undesirable aliens. To this end, the committee recommends the adoption of the legislative proposal heretofore recommended by the Commissioner of Immigration and contained in section 241 of S. 716 (82d Cong.), now pending before the Senate Judiciary Committee

Some of the criminals who occupy key positions in criminal gangs and syndicates are alien-born. Some came into this country illegally. Some have never been naturalized. Others obtained naturalization certificates by concealing their criminal activities.

XIV. The Immigration Act of February 5, 1917, should be amended to provide punishment for smuggling, concealing, or harboring aliens not entitled by law to enter or reside in the United States

Legislation to this effect has been proposed by the Department of Justice and is endorsed by the committee. This legislation (H. R. 2793) is intended to overcome the decision of the United States Supreme Court in the case of *U. S.* v. *Evans* (333 U. S. 483) which is authority for the statement that there is no provision of law under which a person may be punished for committing any of the acts mentioned.

XV. The Attorney General should be authorized to revoke suspensions of deportation and to make such revocation ground for the cancellation of certificates of naturalization granted aliens who have succeeded in getting their immigration status recognized but who are later found to be ineligible for such relief

A bill to make this proposal effective is also pending with the House Committee on the Judiciary (H. R. 2258) and is endorsed by the committee and recommended for passage.

XVI. The personnel of Federal law-enforcement agencies should be materially increased. Consideration should be given to eliminating inequities in the salaries of law-enforcement officers, many of whom are woefully underpaid for the duties they perform and the risks they undertake.

In its interim report, the committee drew attention to the fact that Federal law-enforcement agencies were seriously undermanned, and recommended that increased appropriations be granted to such agencies. This action becomes particularly necessary because of the new duties which are thrust upon these agencies in connection with the struggle against organized crime.

One of our most important law-enforcement agencies, the Bureau of Narcotics, operates today with an appropriation which is the same as or even less than appropriations granted it 20 years ago. The Bureau has only about 180 agents to cover the entire country at a time when narcotics violations are on the increase. The Bureau of Internal Revenue, as of May 31, 1950, had a total of 3,416 suspected tax-fraud cases either under or scheduled for investigation, with a total backlog of 9,110 cases under consideration. Many of these cases involve gangsters and racketeers. The size of the staff seriously limits the Bureau in following up and prosecuting these cases. The United States Secret Service, which investigates counterfeiting and forgery cases, is way behind in its case load, with but 18 agents in its New York office to handle a backlog of over 3,000 cases.

Similar circumstances confront the Federal Bureau of Investigation, which is now called upon to perform much of the investigative work associated with the Nation's internal security.

This phase of its work, all-important as it is, should not be permitted to impair the crime-investigative aspects of the Bureau's functions through lack of manpower.

Under these circumstances the committee therefore recommends that investigative and enforcement staffs of the Government's law-enforcement agencies should be materially increased. This is particularly vital in connection with the Bureau of Narcotics. Consideration should also be given by the appropriate committees of Congress to increasing the pay of Federal law-enforcement agents to a point which will be commensurate with their responsibilities.

It should be borne in mind that higher salaries for persons engaged in law enforcement will not necessarily result in a drain on the Treasury. Better law enforcement will bring increased revenues to the Government through collection of taxes which are undoubtedly now being avoided by the underworld.

Spending of more money to compensate enforcement employees adequately will mean that reduced tribute will be paid to racketeers and gangsters by persons who unknowingly depend on gangster-infiltrated businesses for the purchase of commodities or services in their own communities. It is indeed a fact, well established by testimony before this committee, that where crime has enabled the gangster to infiltrate into legitimate business the average consumer has to pay increased costs, as witness the water-front rackets, through which millions of dollars in tribute are exacted by the racketeer—all of which ultimately comes out of the pocket of the consumer.

XVII. The existing Federal law with respect to perjury should be tightened; the committee endorses H. R. 2260 (82d Cong.) and recommends its passage

Under existing Federal law, a person may not be convicted of perjury for making contradictory statements under oath unless the indictment charges and the prosecution proves which of the statements is false. Under the rules of proof in perjury cases, for a conviction to be had, the falsity of the statement made under oath must be established by the testimony of two independent witnesses or by one witness and corroborating circumstances.

The committee favors a revision of the law to provide that perjury shall consist of giving under oath or affirmation, within a period of 3 years, willful contradictory statements on a material matter, either in proceedings before a grand jury or during the trial of a case; and such perjury could be established by proof of the willful giving or making of such contradictory statements without proving which one is false. The Attorney General has vigorously recommended this bill.

XVIII. The Attorney General of the United States should be given authority to grant immunity from prosecution to witnesses whose testimony may be essential to an inquiry conducted by a grand jury, or in the course of a trial or of a congressional investigation

The fifth amendment to the Constitution provides that no person "shall be compelled in any criminal case to be a witness against himself." The courts have construed this to mean that a person may remain silent if it appears that a criminal charge, however remote, may be made against him on account of any matters concerning which he is questioned.

In the light of the history of the constitutional provision, it is clear that the granting of immunity from prosecution would present a means of obtaining needed testimony from one who might otherwise hide behind the constitutional protection against self-incrimination. If any witness, benefited by immunity, refused to testify, he could then be punished for contempt; or if he committed perjury in his testimony he could be convicted and punished. This power should, of course, be exercised only with the greatest caution, and only upon the written permission of the Attorney General after he has cleared the granting of immunity with other Federal agencies which might have an interest in the matter.

XIX. The committee favors the passage of legislation providing for constructive service by publication or otherwise upon a witness whose testimony is desired who evades personal service upon him

Because of its experience with recalcitrant witnesses who evaded service of subpenas willfully and with obvious intent to hinder and delay the committee's investigation, the committee believes that legislation is necessary to compel the presence of evasive witnesses; hence the foregoing recommendation.

This would give congressional committees the same right to perfect service of subpenas upon witnesses as is now provided for in the Federal code for the appearance of witnesses required to appear before Federal courts.

Once construction service has been obtained, the witness would be subjected to punishment for contempt as contrasted with the present situation where the witness may be arrested and held for appearance but not punished for contempt.

XX. The committee favors passage of the legislation recommended by the Alcohol Tax Unit of the Treasury Department to prevent racketeering elements from entering the liquor industry and to eliminate any now in it. The committee also favors passage of legislation which will extend the same Federal protection to local option States as is now extended to the wholly dry States against the illicit transportation of liquor into the dry areas

With respect to the question of racketeering elements in the distribution of liquor there are now pending in the Congress bills S. 22 and H. R. 137, which were introduced by Senator McCarran and Congressman King and which heretofore have in previous sessions been sponsored by them and other Members of Congress. The bills as they now stand require the annual renewal of basic permits to the liquor industry. The committee is of the opinion that annual renewal may impose too much of a burden upon the industry and the Alcohol Tax Unit, and the committee recommends that the proposed requirement be relaxed to the extent of requiring renewal biennially. The Committee is also well aware of objections to the bill by the wholesale end of the liquor industry, which has made the point that such a bill would seriously impair the industry's ability to obtain credit. However, the committee believes that the problem of racketeering elements in the liquor industry is sufficiently serious to justify the passage of the basic permit sections of this legislation with the change noted above, and the committee is also of the opinion that the industry is overfearful of the effect it will have upon its ability to obtain credit.

In recommending to the committee the passage of this bill, the Alcohol Tax Unit, through its representatives, has pointed out that many of the racketeering elements now in the industry are blanketed under the original post-repeal legislation with the result that the only effective means of eliminating them would be such new legislation.

The committee does believe that the licenses of some individuals might be revoked on a positive determination that they are not persons of good moral character who would hold licenses against the public's interest. However, the committee is aware of the practical problem involved and therefore feels that the Alcohol Tax Unit must receive the support of the Congress if it is to perform its functions effectively. The committee takes no position on features of this legislation other than the ones specified above.

The bootlegging of liquor into dry and local option States has become a very serious problem because of the great volume of such illicit traffic. Many racketeers with connections in other illegal activities are engaged in this traffic. It has proven extremely lucrative, and is a substantial source of income to organized criminals. Moreover, it is a very vicious influence in the States affected. To cope with this evil the committee is recommending that the Bureau of Internal Revenue take steps to require better identification of applicants for special tax stamps required of retail and wholesale liquor dealers.

While this will aid local law enforcement officers in identifying the traffickers in illicit liquor, it does not provide a complete solution to the problem. Accordingly, the committee recommends the adoption of the bill introduced by Congressman Camp, House bill 1278, which would extend the same Federal protection to local option States as is now extended under Federal law to the wholly dry States.

Under this amendment, the local option States would still be able to control the local traffic within their borders and to determine whether or not they want Federal assistance in preventing illicit shipments of liquor into dry areas. Even the Camp bill would not bring a complete solution to the problem. However, with additional enforcement personnel, plus a vigorous effort to identify all applicants for special tax stamps, it is believed that much can be accomplished. It is true that the cost of investigation of applicants for special tax stamps cannot be paid out of the $27.50 fee, but the public policy question involved is so great that this should not be too serious a consideration.

XXI. The committee recommends that the present Federal regulation and application forms which require a listing of individual owners, partners, and holders of Alcohol Tax Unit permits, be amended, so that, in addition to the present requirements, the names of all beneficial owners will be stated: also that the application forms require the disclosure of all previous arrests and convictions. A report should be filed with the Alcohol Tax Unit of every change in such interests or in management as such occurs

On November 8, 1950, the committee called an advisory meeting of the liquor and beverage industry, representatives of the Alcohol Tax Unit, and others interested to meet with the committee. An advisory committee was formed of which Carroll E. Mealey, Deputy Commissioner, Alcohol Tax Unit, was named as chairman. This committee made an extended study of the problems of the industry with particular reference to weeding out racketeers and other undesirable elements. The representatives of the industry and the Commissioner did not come to an agreement on all pertinent matters under discussion. However, the industry and the Alcohol Tax Unit agreed that the foregoing recommendation would be one beneficial in preventing infiltration by racketeers into the industry, particularly at the wholesale level. They joined in this recommendation and it is highly recommended by the committee.

XXII. The committee recommends that the Interstate Commerce Commission be required by law to consider the moral fitness of applications for certificates of necessity and convenience as one of the standards in acting upon applications for such certificates or transfers of certificates

The transportation industry, including interstate transit systems, is especially vital to the economy and security of the Nation. The committee does not by this recommendation imply that there has been a substantial infiltration by racketeers into the industry. There have, however, been some incursions, and in view of the fact that the economy of the country depends upon a competitive and completely gangster-free management of this vital segment of business, the committee feels that every means should be used to weed out the criminals and prevent them from obtaining a further foothold.

In the section of this report dealing with racketeer infiltration of legitimate business, the committee has noted the intrusion of persons into the industry who could not be expected to have the public interest in mind. Situations in New Jersey and Michigan which have been investigated by the committee show the necessity for this recommendation. There are indications that possible competitors are fearful of filing applications for competitive permits where the territory is being served by a gangster-permeated company.

The statute and regulations should require a listing under oath of officers, directors, and principal stockholders of companies and corporations making application for permits. The committee is aware of the difficulties in enforcement, but believes that the public interest necessitates such action.

The committee is giving further consideration to and expects in a later report to deal with the problem of revocation of existing permits where it has been shown to the Interstate Commerce Commission that the holders of such permits do not have the requisite moral fitness.

Where the foregoing recommendations call for new legislation, it will be drafted and submitted to the Senate by members of the committee at the earliest possible time.

INTRODUCTION

The Special Senate Committee To Investigate Organized Crime in Interstate Commerce had its genesis in Senate Resolution 202, which was submitted on January 5, 1950, by Senator Estes Kefauver, Democrat, Tennessee, who subsequently became chairman of the committee. The resolution was referred to the Committee on the Judiciary, and upon being reported by the chairman of that committee on February 27, 1950, was referred to the Committee on Rules and Administration.

It was reported out of the Rules Committee on March 23, 1950, and on May 3, 1950, was considered and agreed to by the Senate.

A week later, the President of the Senate appointed a committee consisting of the author of the resolution, Senator Kefauver, Senator Herbert R. O'Conor, Democrat, Maryland; Senator Lester C. Hunt, Democrat, Wyoming; Senator Alexander Wiley, Republican, Wisconsin, and Senator Charles W. Tobey, Republican, New Hampshire.

The function of the committee was to make a full and complete study and investigation to determine whether organized crime utilizes the facilities of interstate commerce or whether it operates otherwise through the avenues of interstate commerce to promote any transactions which violate Federal law or the law of the State in which such transactions might occur.

The committee was also charged with an investigation of the manner and extent of such criminal operations if it found them actually to be taking place and with the identification of the persons, firms, or corporations involved.

A third responsibility which was charged to the committee was the determination as to whether such interstate criminal operations were developing corrupting influences in violation of the Federal law or the laws of any State. For purposes of the resolution there was included in the area to be covered the District of Columbia, the respective Territories, and all possessions of the United States.

The committee was originally intended by resolution to submit a report to the Senate not later than February 28, 1951, as to its findings with such recommendations as might be deemed advisable. The authority conferred by the resolution was to have terminated on March 31, 1951, but both dates were extended, the date for the report to May 1, 1951, and the date for the committee's expiration to September 1, 1951.

The committee held hearings in pursuance of its charge in 14 cities. They included Washington, D. C.; Tampa, Fla.; Miami, Fla.; New York City; Cleveland, Ohio; St. Louis, Mo.; Kansas City, Mo.; New Orleans, La.; Chicago, Ill.; Detroit, Mich.; Philadelphia, Pa.; Las Vegas, Nev.; Los Angeles, Calif., and San Francisco, Calif.

In all, it heard testimony from more than 600 witnesses. Many of these were high officials of the Federal, State, and city governments in various areas visited by the committee. The record of testimony covers thousands of pages of printed matter and constitutes one of the most valuable documents of its kind ever assembled. This record has for the most part been put into print and has been made available to law enforcement officials and public authorities all over the country for their guidance and information. The balance of the record is being printed for publication, and with the extension of the life of the committee, will also be sent to parties in interest upon completion.

ACKNOWLEDGMENT OF APPRECIATION

At the outset of its report, the committee desires to acknowledge with its deepest appreciation the immense cooperation it has received from countless sources in the execution of its commission.

The vast record it has compiled from testimony taken in 14 cities, which presented facts relative to conditions in most of the States of the Union, amply bespeaks the immensity and complexity of the task. The task has been performed within a short space of time, with a limited personnel which, although small in number, was able and zealous. The committee operated under a modest budget, considering the enormity of the assignment.

Not only was this cooperation most helpful but it was stimulating and encouraging because it indicated unquestionably to the committee and its staff that the people of the Nation, and particularly in those cities visited by the committee, were awakening to the menace of organized crime and were looking to this committee for guidance in an effort to cope with the problem.

From the very first day of its organization the committee received communications from individuals and organizations throughout the Nation offering information for investigation and, where this was not available, tendering moral support for the committee's undertaking.

This tide of communications, which started as a modest flow, swelled into a veritable flood as the committee's activities approached a crescendo in its New York hearings. The thousands of letters and telegrams directed to the committee were augmented by similar thousands addressed to individual Senators and Representatives.

Again, the tenor of these communications was most heartening to the committee and its staff and although an attempt has been made by the committee to acknowledge receipt of these letters and telegrams, a word of thanks to the senders is herewith expressed.

To catalog the individuals, organizations; local, State, and Federal agencies to which the committee is indebted for valuable assistance is virtually impossible.

Many public-spirited citizens gave liberally of their time and knowledge of local and national criminal operations to provide information to the committee and in numerous cases to appear as witnesses before it. It is significant of the high civic-mindedness that prompted the appearance of many individuals before this committee that a great many waived their rights to witness fees and reimbursement for travel expense. The committee also commends the numerous witnesses who, at personal risk of gangland retribution, testified in open or executive sessions.

One of the greatest aids in ferreting out the activities of the underworld was provided to the committee by the President of the United States, in his Executive order making available not only pertinent income-tax returns of individuals under investigation as interstate criminals or having associations with such individuals, but calling on the respective Government departments and bureaus to make available to this committee their files and knowledge. It must be apparent that the President's order was most effective and was probably the greatest single weapon at the committee's disposal. Particularly, because of the trust in the committee implied by the President in his order, the committee has attempted to use its power impartially and judicially and has tried scrupulously at all times to protect and guard the rights of all persons involved.

The vast files and limitless experience of the various Federal enforcement and investigative agencies proved fertile sources for many phases of this committee's inquiry. Among the agencies in this group whose cooperation was of great help should be named the Department of Justice, including the Federal Bureau of Investigation, the Immigration and Naturalization Service; the Attorney General, his assistants and United States attorneys; the Treasury Department, including the Bureau of Internal Revenue, the Customs Bureau, the Alcohol Tax Unit, the Secret Service, and particularly the Bureau of Narcotics; the Post Office Department and such other agencies which the committee called on for assistance.

In naming the various Government agencies mention should also be made of the contribution to the committee's investigation by Hon. James V. Bennett, Director of United States Prisons.

Most encouraging and helpful to the work of the committee in its travels around the country was the volunteered cooperation of countless numbers of individuals who offered to make themselves available for any service the committee desired.

To these public-spirited citizens, the committee acknowledges their assistance with deep appreciation.

Outstanding in the ranks of those whose volunteer efforts added inestimably to the committee's successful operation was Mr. Julius N. Cahn, executive assistant to Senator Alexander Wiley of Wisconsin, a member of the committee. Mr. Cahn's innumerable helpful suggestions were always welcome. Through the kind cooperation of Senator Wiley, his assistant attended many sessions of the committee both in Washington and in the field and thus became very familiar with the background and detailed activities of the group. Mr. Cahn was, therefore, in an excellent position to help with sound advice in formulating decisions in the public interest as situations arose. The committee therefore takes this occasion to voice its thanks to him.

Also of great assistance in many varied ways during this inquiry were Mr. A. J. Bourbon, administrative assistant to Senator Herbert R. O'Conor, of Maryland, and Mr. Charles Neese, administrative assistant to Senator Kefauver, the Chairman. To both these gentlemen go the committee's thanks.

The staffs of other members of the committee were also called upon in many instances and always responded eagerly. George Green, of the Senate Judiciary Committee, and Mrs. Vivian Lynn, formerly of the Senate District of Columbia Committee, have materially aided the committee.

An expression of appreciation should be recorded for the cooperation and assistarce of the Commission on Organized Crime of the American Bar Association, of which former Secretary of War Robert P. Patterson is chairman.

All members of the Commission actively participated in the program. Through them, the American Bar has rendered a tremendous service to the committee. The Commission members included: Walter P. Armstrong, Jr., Memphis, Tenn.; Howard L. Barkdull, Cleveland, Ohio; Arthur J. Freund, St. Louis, Mo.; Phillip S. Habermann, Madison, Wis.; Laurance M. Hyde, Jefferson City, Mo.; and Chief Judge Bolitha J. Laws, Washington, D. C.

On several occasions it has made available the talent and wide experience of Judge Morris Ploscowe, of New York City, executive director of the Commission, who has been of outstanding service in the preparation of the committee's reports, as noted elsewhere herein.

Throughout the country where hearings were held by the committee facilities were made available for holding these sessions by the judges of the United States district courts, to whom gratitude is freely acknowledged, as well as to the various Federal district attorneys and members of their staffs who also facilitated the holding of hearings by providing office space and in many cases stenographic assistance.

Service of subpenas was expedited by United States marshals and their assistants, to whom thanks are due. Building custodians and their staffs frequently had to work overtime by reason of the protracted sessions of the committee that sometimes continued into the night. These are only a few of the many in Federal service who helped in facilitating these hearings.

State and local officials, from governors of States and mayors of cities, down to policemen on their beats went out of their ordinary paths to be of assistance to the committee. Crime commissions composed of citizens, like those in Greater Miami, Chicago, St. Louis, and the State of California, provided dossiers on local crime conditions which advanced the starting point of committee investigators. Special thanks are expressed to Daniel Sullivan of the Greater Miami Crime Commission and Virgil Peterson of the Chicago Crime Commission and their officers and staffs. The work of these two crime committees through their courageous officers and most able directors is outstanding and serves as a splendid example for other voluntary crime commissions.

Another source from which the committee received splendid cooperation in its investigative activities was the American Telephone

& Telegraph Co., and its affiliates whose help is herewith gratefully acknowledged.

One of the most effective means of establishing whether a hoodlum in one State had affiliations or associations with a fellow-gangster in another State was by tracing telephone calls. This called for the expenditure of much manpower and time by the American Telephone & Telegraph Co., and it should here be recorded that all this tremendous research was conducted at the sole expense of the telephone companies.

The committee regards as invaluably helpful the splendid direct and indirect aid and support given by the mass media of public information of the United States in the committee's work.

It is doubtful indeed if the activities of any similar governmental group has received such widespread coverage as was given to the hearings and reports of this committee.

Newspapers were particularly helpful because in their own particular locales they have, over the years, amassed archives of information about crime, all of which were freely made available to the committee. The crime reporters of many great newspapers have been of invaluable assistance to the committee. The willingness and courage of the press in printing full information on the activities of gangsters, criminals, and their political protectors have achieved many notable results in improved law enforcement. At times, the committee was helped by the constructive criticism of some of the local press. It is noteworthy that many of the country's foremost journalistic specialists in crime news were assigned by their respective publications to travel the length and breadth of the Nation with the committee to cover its hearings. The committee regrets that some inconvenience has been caused the press because of the difficult circumstances under which the committee has had to operate.

Magazines, too, should be credited with independently researching the subject of interstate crime operations and with furnishing committee investigators many fruitful leads that helped to round out the picture of organized crime in the United States.

The committee subscribes most heartily to the statement of J. Edgar Hoover, Director of the Federal Bureau of Investigation, that if there were in every town in the United States a crusading newspaper which, without fear or favor, would turn the spotlight of pitiless publicity on corruption, gambling, and vice in its area, major progress would have been made toward cleaning up that particular community.

Testimony before this committee was carried into millions of American homes by wireless, first by radio and toward the closing stages via the newest electronic communications device—television.

The committee recognizes that a major part of the credit for the vital impact of this committee's most recent hearings on the public was due to the televising of the sessions. Never, prior to that time, had a congressional hearing received such a public airing or viewing, nor before such a huge audience. It has been estimated that the hearings in New York were watched by upward of 30,000,000 persons.

These telecasts, in the opinion of the committee, have had a most salutary effect in awakening the public to the menace of organized racketeering that now confronts our national life. For the first time the public was able to see and hear the notorious hoodlums to whom it was, in one form or another, paying tribute, to determine for itself whether or not these men are wholesome influences in public affairs, and whether they should be permitted to wax even more powerful than they are now.

Television can undoubtedly be a tremendous power for good; as a means of public education it is superb. But its employment involves serious consideration of many new factors.

One of these is the possible invasion of the rights of privacy—a claim which was raised by several witnesses who refused to have their faces screened although they did not object to the broadcast of their voices over wireless radio. This broad legal question has already been the subject of considerable learned debate; there will undoubtedly be more before a final adjudication is made by the courts.

It should be noted that two of the committee's witnesses, Morris Kleinman and Louis Rothkopf, raised this issue of privacy and the alleged onerousness of the conditions under which they were asked to testify—conditions which included the presence of microphones, news-reel cameras, television cameras and still photographers—to all of which they objected. These individuals were cited for contempt for refusing to reply to pertinent questions at a properly constituted hearing of the committee. It was strongly felt by the committee that their stated ground for refusal to testify was actually a subterfuge for a more cogent reason.

In addition to the legal implications, our committee sees in television a medium which raises whole new or intensified issues of public policy insofar as the screening of congressional activities is concerned. It is for that reason that the committee feels that a code of congressional procedure should be worked out so as, among other things, to insure the continuing dignity and maximum effectiveness of legislative proceedings which might be televised as well as to preserve the constitutional rights of citizens. Nevertheless, our committee commends the television industry which devoted so much time at considerable cost to our committee's proceedings.

The dignified and restrained handling of the television broadcasts of the hearings by the respective stations and networks involved, and their personnel, speaks most highly for the public spirit of this relatively new medium and for its judicious approach to a new problem.

Through the motion-picture newsreels, millions of American theatergoers were able to follow the committee's activities in all parts of the country. The newsreels were particularly cooperative in New York City where limited space in the hearing room necessitated a pooling arrangement under which two or three cameramen made the pictures which were then made available to all film companies on an equal basis.

One innovation that marked the newsreel coverage of this committee's hearings was the release of a film nearly an hour long that graphically depicted the highlights of the entire series of hearings and was seen by an audience estimated in the millions.

Finally, the committee, speaking for the Senate and the American people whose servant and representative it is, acknowledges with deep gratitude and respect the contribution of every member of the committee staff to this most notable result.

Seldom, if ever before, has a congressional committee been favored with such a splendid group, working as a team with but one objective in mind. Dispassionately and intelligently this group attacked one of the most complex and widespread fronts and drove wedges of information into it that enabled the committee to throw light on it not only from the front but from the rear, and even from underground whence more than a few witnesses came to testify to the evil prevalence of Nation-wide crime.

The sparking genius behind this excellent staff deserves the commendation not only of the Senate but the entire Nation—the committee's chief counsel, Rudolph Halley, of New York.

From the very inception of our committee, Mr. Halley displayed the keenest of insight into the nature of the problem, and an indefatigable energy that overcame the limitation of time imposed on the committee prior to its extension of authority. In a spirit of sacrifice of his own personal comfort and aggrandizement, Mr. Halley relentlessly and tirelessly pursued his course against the most feared underworld gangs in America.

How well he earned the plaudits of the Senate and the public is now, through television, a familiar story. This record would be incomplete, however, without a final accolade bestowed on him, and this expression of merit: "Well done!"

SUGGESTIONS FOR ACTION BY STATE AND LOCAL GOVERNMENTS

The enactment of the afore-mentioned recommendations will do a great deal to break up criminal gangs and syndicates and make considerably more difficult the use by organized crime of the facilities of interstate commerce and interstate communication. The committee, however, has stressed above that if organized crime is to be brought under control, State and local law-enforcement agencies must do their part.

The violations of criminal statutes committed by.the members of criminal gangs and syndicates are, for the most part, violations of State laws. In order that State and local law-enforcement machinery and procedures be strengthened and become more effective in dealing with organized crime, the committee makes the following suggestions of a broad nature, believing they may be helpful and in the public interest and in conformity with the letter and spirit of Senate Resolution 202.

I. A committee might well be appointed in each State to make a thoroughgoing investigation of the problem of organized crime

The fact that so many of the conditions which breed organized crime are beyond the reach of Federal authority makes it absolutely vital that the various States institute sweeping inquiries into organized criminal conditions within their borders. The able reports and recommendations of the special crime study commissions appointed by Governor Warren in California indicate how effective such inquiries can be in formulating State and local policies in dealing with organized crime. Noteworthy State action has been taken in Ohio and Illinois by Governors Lausche and Stevenson. It should be noted that the disclosures resulting from our hearings in New York prompted the appointment by Governor Dewey of a five-man crime commission to investigate and act against racketeers and "the links between organized crime and units of State government in New York State." The action of these and of other Governors should be emulated in other States.

II. Grand jury investigations could well be instituted in every community in which wide-open gambling and racketeering conditions exist, so that local responsibility for such conditions can be fixed and determined

The grand jury is the traditional organ of law enforcement charged with the responsibility of uncovering corruption in Government and misfeasance and nonfeasance in office of public officials. Under adequate leadership grand juries can do a great deal to help local communities clean house. Steps should be taken in each State so that grand jury attention can be focused upon local conditions that contribute to organized crime. In order for grand jury inquiries to be effective, they must be freed from such hampering restrictions as are found in the Illinois laws which limit the terms of grand juries to 30 days.

III. It might be advantageous for each State to institute a survey of its law-enforcement agencies with a view toward bringing about greater cooperation between agencies, greater centralization of responsibility for lax enforcement of the criminal law, and greater efficiency

The committee has been impressed by the failure of independent local units of law enforcement to work together harmoniously to eliminate gambling and racketeering conditions from their communities. In metropolitan areas, there usually are large numbers of independent city, town, and village police forces which work together or refuse to cooperate, as they please. The sheriff of the county operates independently of other law-enforcement agencies and frequently pursues law-enforcement policies which are diametrically opposed to theirs. The district attorney, or the State's attorney, sometimes works with and sometimes against both the police and the sheriff. Exactly who is responsible for what in the law-enforcement field is frequently a matter of conjecture and dispute. The very organization of law-enforcement agencies in local communities makes it difficult to fix responsibility for widespread violations of the criminal law. This necessarily leads to "buck passing" and evasion of responsibility.

The committee cannot find the answers to the problems which local organization of law enforcement presents with the data presently available. The patterns of local law enforcement are deeply embedded in the constitutions and laws of the several States. They were evolved at a time when conditions of life were much simpler and when crime conditions were not as complex as they are today. They require thorough overhauling, and a thorough re-examination in the light of what is required to combat present-day syndicated and organized crime. The several States cannot hope to control jet-plane criminality by the horse-and-buggy methods evolved in the early nineteenth century.

Any survey of State and local law-enforcement agencies must consider such problems as:

1. The combination of small independent local police forces into larger regional units which will be adequately staffed and equipped to make criminal investigations and to deal with organized crime.

2. The elimination of the law-enforcement responsibilities of the sheriff's office.

3. The more adequate policing of rural areas by State police units.

4. The closer integration of local police forces and local police activities with the work and efforts of State police units.

5. The provision of better methods of recruiting and training local and state police officials.

6. The provision of higher standards of pay for persons engaged in local law-enforcement work.

7. The elimination of the traditional coroner's office and substitution of adequately staffed and equipped medical examiner's offices.

8. A clearer definition of the function and the responsibilities of the local prosecutor in connection with the investigation of criminal cases.

9. The steps necessary to secure greater stability of tenure and greater professionalization in the local prosecutor's office.

10. The provision of a greater degree of centralized control of the work of local prosecutors, either through the Attorney General or the Governor's office.

11. The tightening of legal provisions concerning the removal of lax and faithless law-enforcement officials, who fail to carry out their sworn duties.

12. More law enforcement officials should be brought under civil service regulations; in some places these regulations should be revised in order to facilitate the separation from the service of corrupt and/or inefficient enforcement officials.

Surveys of State law-enforcement agencies which come up with answers to such problems will make vital contributions to the improvement of methods of dealing with organized crime.

IV. Organization of rackets and special purpose squads in each State with sufficient manpower and authority to make investigations and arrests in connection with organized criminal activities would be helpful. Such squads are particularly desirable on both the State and local levels, in connection with the suppression of narcotics traffic

State surveys which would provide data for fundamental changes in law-enforcement organizations, will take a long time. In the meantime, the State governments must take the initiative in dealing with the immediate problems presented by organized crime.

The need for State law-enforcement activity is particularly acute in the suppression of the illicit sale and distribution of narcotics. In narcotics there has been, as we have seen, a tremendous upsurge in activity. A great deal of narcotics drugs are presently being sold to our "teen-age" youth, resulting in their consequent demoralization. Energetic methods are necessary to combat the drug traffic. A well-trained squad of men operating throughout the State who are thoroughly familiar with the methods of narcotics peddlers and who will cooperate closely with the Federal Narcotics Bureau, could do a great deal to stem this vicious traffic which lives from the slow murder of its customers. Similar squads might also be organized in the larger cities to cooperate with State officials and with the Federal Government.

Racket squads would also be very valuable in other fields of criminal activity in which organized criminal gangs are presently engaged. Where local enforcement breaks down in connection with gambling operations, for example, conditions can be materially improved by State police squads acting under the direct authority of a vigorous governor.

V. Each State would do well to analyze the provisions of its criminal law and its sentencing practices so as to make certain that deterrent sentences are imposed upon offenders engaged in criminal activities connected with organized crime

Organized criminal activities cannot be controlled by the imposition of small fines. Yet this is the normal technique for dealing with such racketeering activities as bookmaking and the numbers, or policy game. Persons convicted of taking bets and engaging in bookmaking operations and persons who collect policy numbers are usually punished only by small fines. This has absolutely no deterrent effect upon key individuals who control the rackets or upon the small fry who are normally brought before our courts. The fine is looked upon merely as an expense of doing business and is usually paid by the banker of the policy game or the backer of the bookmaker. A fine may be called for in connection with a conviction for the first time of a violation of the gambling laws. But certainly second and subsequent convictions should be more severely dealt with. Such severity is vital if mobsters who run the bookmaking and policy rackets are to be controlled. When subordinates in the racket understand that they are exposing themselves to prison sentences and that their employers cannot absorb penalties imposed upon them, they will be less likely to engage in illegal activities. Similarly, more drastic penalties appear to be indicated in connection with the violation of State narcotics laws. It is the considered opinion of the Federal Bureau of Narcotics that drug peddlers can only be controlled by drastic penalties. Surely the harm that these individuals do to others clearly warrants such action.

Here again, the committee can make only the general recommendation that each State review its criminal penalties and the sentencing procedures used by its judges. If these follow the pattern which has been indicated above, then a revision so as to provide more deterrent penalties would appear to be indicated.

VI. Each State should consider legislation making it possible to deprive any establishment of its license which permits gambling games or gambling operations on its premises

Local and State licenses are required from many different types of establishments, hotels, night clubs, taverns, restaurants, candy stores, etc. Racketeers frequently use such establishments as locations for slot machines, punchboards, and other gambling games or conduct other types of gambling operations, such as bookmaking or the collection of policy numbers on these premises. In Minnesota, Wisconsin, and Iowa, statutes have been enacted which make it possible to strip such establishments of their license to do business if they are permitting gambling operations to be conducted on their premises. The committee commends such statutes to the attention of other States. If a businessman knows that he may lose his license if he permits a violation of the gambling laws to take place in an establishment that he operates, he is less likely to listen to the racketeer who is seeking to use his establishment as a base for enterprises that violate the law.

*VII. A citizen crime commission charged with the duty of observing the
activities of local law-enforcement agencies and with the duty of
observing and reporting on local crime conditions would be helpful
in each large community*

Public apathy has in large measure been responsible for many of
the conditions disclosed by the committee. This apathy is due in
large part to a lack of knowledge of crime conditions on the part of
the citizens living in the cities visited by the committee. Even
where some knowledge was present, the leadership to do something
about malodorous crime conditions was frequently lacking. The
function of a local crime commission is to provide both knowledge and
guidance. Its task is to expose pitilessly the racketeers who grow
fat on crime and their allies in law enforcement and in political
organizations. Local crime commissions have contributed considerably to more effective methods dealing with crime in such cities
as Chicago and Miami and have pointed the way to the kind of public
service that such organizations can render. The committee notes
with approval the organization of the Greater New York Crime
Committee in New York City. Similar organizations should be set
up in every metropolitan area.

THE CITY STORIES

MIAMI

The principal activity of organized criminal groups in the Miami
area at the time of the committee hearings was gambling. Card games,
dice games, numbers games, roulette and other gambling wheels
operated in establishments varying from the well-appointed air-con-
ditioned casinos set up for the purpose, to night clubs and restaurants
and private rooms in various hotels. Bookmaking operated out of
newsstands, cigar stands or elaborate horse rooms, in most hotels,
and even from specially fitted cabanas on the beach.

Bookmaking was largely in the hands of local residents with long
experience in the field. The gambling casinos and games, on the other
hand, were almost wholly owned and operated by the racketeers and
criminals from all over the country who had made the area their
gathering place, and several Miami hotels, their headquarters.

At one time 52 more or less elaborate gambling casinos operated
in Broward County alone. At the time of the hearings, the principal
casinos operated by the out-of-town gangsters and racketeers were the
Greenacres, the Club Boheme, the Island Club, and the Club Collins.
The Greenacres and the Club Boheme were operated by a group
including Frank Erickson of New York, Joe Adonis and the Lansky
brothers of New York, and Mert Wertheimer of Detroit. In Greenacres, William Bischoff (Lefty Clark) and Joseph Massei operated a
crap game.

Erickson, his agents and associates, made the Wofford Hotel
their headquarters. The hotel was operated by a former New York
lawyer, Abe Allenberg, brought to Florida to represent Erickson
in his race-track interests, and set up in the hotel business with money
provided by Erickson. Allenberg's partners in this venture included
the notorious gangsters Anthony Carfano from New York and John
Angersola from Cleveland.

Allenberg testified that crap and card games for high stakes were conducted in upstairs rooms by racketeering associates of his partners. Erickson's agents lived in the hotel, while they conducted his large-scale illegal lay-off and come-back betting operations and used the banking facilities of the hotel for cashing checks tendered in payment of lost wagers on horse races.

Two other nearby hotels, the Grand and the Sands Hotel, served as headquarters for the Detroit, Philadelphia, and Cleveland mobs.

The operations of the gambling casinos showed tremendous profits. The net reported income from the Greenacres-Club Boheme combination, totaled $348,821.48 in 1948, and $599,073.44 in 1949. In addition, the cash operation of the single crap table yielded $222,056.47 in reported income for the 1949 season.

S. AND G. SYNDICATE REPORTS $26,500,000 GROSS

Testimony disclosed that the largest organized bookmaking operation in the Miami area was conducted by the S. and G. Syndicate, a group of five local bookmakers who, until 1944 had operated independently. In 1944, they agreed to eliminate competition among themselves and make the financing of other bookmakers their business. By 1948, this business, according to its own books, controlled concessions at 200 hotels and grossed over $26,500,000 in bets. The Federal Government, investigating the individual returns of the partners, has contended that even on the basis of the reported gross, the net reported income of $466,504 is substantially below the true income.

On the basis of the reported gross bets, and the mathematically established minimum net return used at the pari-mutuel tracks, the committee calculated that the net profit for the members of the syndicate must have been over $2,000,000. Other observers of the Florida bookmaking scene put the S. and G. gross income at between $30,000,000 and $40,000,000 and its net income at between $4,000,000 and $8,000,000 a year.

The S. and G. Syndicate maintained an executive office, with Edward Rosenbaum as the active manager, where the daily collections from bookmakers were received, their records kept and the periodic accountings made. At an elaborate penthouse office atop a midtown hotel, telephone connections to all parts of the country from California to New Jersey and from New Orleans to New York, made it possible to keep a constant check on bets at the Nation's important race tracks. Here, the up-to-the-minute racing news coming in over the wire service was received. At branch offices throughout Miami Beach, S. and G. received information from their bookies and the bookies in turn could receive information from the wire service.

200 BOOKIES DEALT WITH S. AND G.

Just under 200 bookies dealt with the S. and G. Every bookie made his own arrangements with a hotel for permission to take bets on its premises, and paid for the concession and necessary employees out of his own pocket. As bets were placed, the bookie would telephone them in to an S. and G. branch office, and at the end of each day he either deposited his winnings with the S. and G. office, or had them picked up by a collector. On the rare occasions when his losses exceeded his winnings, he picked up cash from the S. and G. to make his payoffs. At the end of the month or the season, depending on individual arrangements, the bookie and the S. and G. made a 50–50 division of the profits from the operation. However, certain expenses of operation—an agreed-upon portion of the rent for the concession, which might range from $3,000 to $50,000 a year, salaries of employees hired by the bookie, and fines levied on the bookie—were deducted from the profit before the division of profit was made. But after the division, from his own half of the profits, the bookie paid the syndicate upward of $75 a week for the racing news service, and another $50 to $75 a week for operating expenses. The partners denied the contention of one bookie, that the money for operating expenses was "ice" or protection money, that independent bookies understood that they would be raided, while bookies belonging to the S. and G. were not. But the committee established that the S. and G. suffered little from police interference. The attorney for the syndicate admitted that from 1944 to 1950 the syndicate bookies had suffered no greater indignity than fines; that they never received a jail sentence, and that as soon as their fines were paid, they went back into business. Two members of the syndicate, Levitt and Salvey, admitted to a record of arrests years back. The former, despite several convictions, had never been to jail. The latter had never even gone to trial. Both admitted to the offenses of bookmaking, with which they had been charged.

It was also apparent that the S. and G. syndicate members enjoyed cordial relationships with members of the city government and law-enforcement agencies. Their attorney admitted he had been influential in getting a former law associate selected as a judge. In their numerous and extremely profitable real estate transactions, members of the S. and G. were represented by the city attorney, who was later expected to oppose for the city a change in the rezoning law which would have more than tripled the profits of the S. and G. members on their holdings in one of the most valuable sections of the beach. One partner, Salvey, inactive in the actual syndicate operation almost from the time of its formation in 1944, admitted to business relationships with William Burbridge, an influential city councilman, which had been extremely profitable to Burbridge.[1] A former police chief and a sheriff gave testimony indicating that the syndicate attorney was friendly enough with someone in the department so that he could be present at any raid of a syndicate book or a horse room or casino in which its members had an interest, or could appear on the scene almost immediately thereafter. There was evidence, too, that the syndicate made an effort to present a fair face to the community; records of donations to religious charities, to Boy Scout and Red Cross chapters, to hospitals, to firemen's and policemen's associations were shown.

Until 1949, the syndicate members with their local contacts had been able relatively well to protect themselves from outside incursions. Erickson, and a local independent gambler named John O'Rourke, had managed to get the gambling concession at the Boca Raton, and at the

---

[1] Salvey, a member of the syndicate, had taken a 99-year lease with Burbridge for $6,000 a year, for a piece of land on which Salvey was to pay the taxes. The other half of the property Salvey had bought outright for $25,000. Salvey had taken loans of $40,000 from Burbridge for short periods and paid interest at the rate of 20 percent. A cashier's check for $1,000 sent by Salvey to Burbridge from California could not be explained by either man; they simply did not know what it was for

Roney Plaza, at the seasonal rentals of $22,000 and $45,000, respectively. Both had previously been operated by S. and G. concessionnaires. But Erickson was soon forced to give up his concession. Meyer Schine, owner of the hotel, testified that Pat Perdue, the Miami Beach one-man vice squad, urged him to give the concession to the S. and G. When he refused, the Roney Plaza was raided by Perdue with great attendant publicity, and forced to discontinue gambling, in contrast to the usual discreet raids which ended in a fine and the resumption of gambling.

The following season, the Roney Plaza gambling concession was operated by an S. and G. member bookie.

THE STORY OF THE RUSSELL "MUSCLE"

In 1949, the S. and G. suddenly acquired a sixth partner, a Chicago resident, Harry Russell, whose connections with the Capone group are clearly established. The original members of the syndicate, questioned about Russell, stuck to a consistent story: they had heard he was attempting to take over concessions in Miami hotels owned by Chicago men, and further, they understood that he knew a great deal about baseball pools, into which they intended to expand. But they had made no similar approaches to any other competitors, nor could they show any baseball operations in their records after Russell became a partner. They claimed that they knew nothing of Russell's Chicago connections. One of the members insisted that he had first approached Russell about the partnership.

Just prior to Russell's entry into the partnership, the S. and G. had been subject to pressure from two sides. In January of 1949, shortly after the election of Gov. Fuller Warren, a special investigator named W. O. Crosby appointed by the Governor presented himself to the sheriff of Dade County and asked for help in raiding gambling establishments. In their testimony, neither Sheriff Sullivan nor Crosby could recall raids on any but S. and G. bookies. Crosby admitted that he knew Russell and had seen and become friendly with him in Miami during the period of the raids. Crosby had also seen and talked to William H. Johnston, a Chicago and Florida race track owner, a long-time associate of the Capone gang, and a friend of Russell. There is more than a casual connection between the fact that Johnston contributed $100,000 to Governor Warren's campaign fund and the fact that Crosby raided only S. and G. locations with the knowledge of Russell.

At about the same time, the Continental Press Service, which is controlled by the Capone gang, cut S. and G. off from the wire service, without which no large-scale bookmaking enterprise can dare to do business. When S. and G. attempted to get the news service from other bookmakers in Florida, service was cut off throughout the State. For some unexplained reason, though the syndicate found it could get the news from its bookie contacts in New Orleans, it did not do so. The lack of wire service compelled the syndicate to shut down operations for about 2 weeks. Service was resumed and the raids from Crosby miraculously ceased when Russell was taken in as a full partner of the S. and G. syndicate. He was said to have paid $20,000 for his share in the $26,000,000-a-year business. But a few months later, the S. and G. partners bought a boat owned by Tony

Accardo, an associate of Russell and the alleged leader of the Capone gang, for just exactly $20,000. Further evidence that the Capone mob merely muscled into the lucrative S. and G. syndicate using Russell as a pawn is had from the fact that the 1949 tax returns for the partnership of Accardo and Guzik show a loss of $7,240 attributed to the operations of S. and G.

No business on the scale of the S. and G. Syndicate and the various gambling casinos, operated by notorious gamblers, could be run under cover. In fact, the business was run openly in violation of Florida laws, with the full knowledge of the community. Grand juries in 1944 and 1947 had no trouble in finding evidence of operations. A 1949 jury reported:

> We could not see any purpose in repeating the work of our predecessor juries to discover officially and at great length that crime and corruption do exist here (p. 736). Conditions have apparently not changed since the writing of the 1944 grand jury report (p. 737). There is present in our community a large number of individuals of unsavory reputation. These persons are criminals of national stature (p. 736). All forms of gambling are flourishing, the 1949 jury found, and there appeared to be little effort to curb them, although they were being carried on right under the eyes of the police (p. 737).

SHERIFF WAS TOLD ABOUT GAMBLING

Daniel P. Sullivan, director of the Greater Miami Crime Commission, set before the committee a detailed statement as to the gambling and bookmaking operations, the criminal records and backgrounds, the infiltration of these criminals into legitimate businesses in Florida, and their out-of-State connections. The crime commission and the Law Enforcement League of Dade County, had both called the attention of the sheriff of the county to the open and notorious gambling operations. These activities went on, not only with public knowledge, but with a considerable amount of public acquiescence. In the words of the director of the crime commission:

> There is quite a large group of people that think that gambling is an asset in that it is an inducement to the tourists. They feel that it is just a question of placing a dollar bet, and the average person does not realize the ramifications of what happens when it becomes highly organized and operated by syndicates.

Attorney General Ervin also called attention to the segment of public opinion which believes it is impossible to stop gambling, and that in any event it is good for business. Certain public officials with a demonstrated antipathy to law enforcement supported this viewpoint; the sheriff of Broward County flatly stated that he had been elected because he was known to have a liberal point of view, that he favored a wide-open town; the sheriff of Dade County observed that $20,-000,000 legal gambling at the tracks creates an atmosphere so favorable to gambling that the illegal off-track gambling is hard to stop.

The laxity of public officials in the face of this situation was described by the officials themselves. Sheriff Walter Clark of Broward County admitted that he knew the gambling places operating in his area. He had eaten in some of them at charity affairs, though he had never seen gambling there except when he went on raids. Raids were conducted only on complaint. He never checked up to see whether operations were resumed. Former Police Chief Short admitted that he had said he would have nothing to do with gambling. He left the job entirely to one detective, Pat Perdue. Sheriff Sullivan admitted that although Florida has a statute compelling visitors with a felony record to register upon entering the State, he had no idea whether the notorious criminals in his area, of whose background and presence he was completely aware, had complied with the law. Nor had he ever made any attempt to prosecute them for conspiracy to violate the laws of Florida.

TECHNICALITIES USED TO BLOCK ENFORCEMENT

The attempts of public-spirited citizens to remedy conditions were blocked by obstructive tactics of law-enforcement officials who took advantage of every technicality to avoid action within the State. When the Greater Miami Crime Commission offered the full facilities of its organization to Sheriff Sullivan in closing down the gambling casinos, Sullivan countered with a long brief to show that sheriffs had no responsibility for the repression of gambling, and with another describing the rigid restrictions of the law of search and seizure which would hamper him in obtaining evidence of gambling operations.

Honest law-enforcement officials ran into the same obstructive tactics. Since it was felt that the elected officials would not undertake to get evidence of gambling that would stand up in court, Judge Stanley Milledge acted under the statutory provision and appointed an "elisor" to get such evidence. The efforts of the elisors so appointed were hampered by the local police who appeared on the premises while a raid was in progress, and interfered with the work of the elisors. After arrests were made, an action was brought with the approval of the sheriff, contending that the elisor warrant was illegal.

Where law-enforcement agencies took any action, it was apt to be for the protection of racketeers or the elimination of their rivals. The efforts of Pat Perdue to drive competitors of the S. and G. Syndicate out of business, and of Crosby to use the local sheriff's office for raids on the S. and G. but on no other bookies or gambling joints, have already been mentioned. The prompt appearance of the mouthpiece of the S. and G. Syndicate during the Crosby raids leads to the suspicion that someone from the sheriff's office was tipping him off. Sheriff Clark admitted deputizing the guards who ran the armored trucks in which Broward County gamblers kept their bank rolls overnight. Three former deputy sheriffs in Sullivan's office stated that they were instructed to refrain from making arrests for bookmaking. One of them was discharged after making inquiries about a bookmaking establishment which happened to be run by a relative of the deputy.

In the opinion of many witnesses, criminals from all over the Nation were able to act freely in the Miami area because the concentration of economic power they brought in from outside, enabled them to control local government and corrupt substantial portions of the community. "The profit motive in this thing is tremendous," said Attorney General Ervin, "and they naturally have to protect their investment; and, if they can bribe or buy anybody, they naturally will do it." Bookmaking and gambling, he stated, were dominated by syndicates including men so big that they can bribe and influence public officials.

ROCKETLIKE RISE IN SHERIFF'S ASSETS

Considerable evidence of direct bribes to law-enforcement officials was presented to the committee. Where no direct bribes could be traced, there was the unmistakable evidence of wealth of public officials acquired during their terms of office. Sheriff Sullivan's assets increased during his 5-year term from $2,500, which, was his net worth as given in a bank loan, to well over $70,000. This apparently does not include $26,000 which Sullivan and his wife sent to members of Mrs. Sullivan's family in Maryland. His deputy, whose purchase of a new Cadillac in 1949 caused Sullivan a certain amount of uneasiness, retired after 4 years to a farm for which he paid $26,000, although his salary was never more than $4,200 a year. Both Sullivan and his deputy distrusted banks, and testified to keeping large amounts of cash in their homes in a tin box, an old fishing box, or in a blanket. Melvin Richard, a young councilman who had kept up an effective opposition to the machinations of the S. and G. Syndicate, and who was largely responsible for revealing their members' close connections with the city government, testified that immediately after his election he was offered a share in the profits of the punchboard games in the area, if he would refrain from interfering with their operations.

Sheriff Clark, of Broward County, made a very large fortune by participating in the profits of gambling ventures, and as a partner in the Broward Novelty Co., which operated an illegal bolita and slot-machine business. The gross income of this company from 1945 to 1947 was more than $1,000,000.

In Florida, illegal gains from gambling and bookmaking, including funds rightfully due the Federal Government in taxes, were largely invested in homes, hotels, and other real estate. Like the local members of the S. and G., the visiting gamblers and bookmakers from Detroit and Chicago, and Cleveland and New York owned large expanses of property in Miami Beach and nearby sections of Florida. For years, Capone maintained a vast estate, and his successors and associates from other areas followed his example in buying elaborate homes for themselves and their families in the area. It has already been pointed out that the hotels which operated as headquarters for these gangsters and as locations for their gambling games, were owned and operated by the gangsters or their associates. There was also testimony that the racket element had an interest in a wired-music organizations whose chief stockholder was the operator of the Club Collins, one of the gambling casinos.

But the director of the Greater Miami Crime Commission, under questioning by Senator Hunt, estimated that a large proportion of the money made in gambling and bookmaking in Broward County and elsewhere was not invested or spent in Miami, but siphoned out of Florida by the visiting racketeers. It therefore represented not a boon to business, but a net loss to the Florida community.

REINSTATEMENT OF SHERIFF JAMES SULLIVAN

The committee cannot understand and strongly condemns the reinstatement by Gov. Fuller Warren, of Florida, of Sheriff James Sullivan without a full and public investigation of all the facts brought out by this committee and by the Dade County grand jury.

KANSAS CITY

The committee held hearings in Washington and in Kansas City, Mo., to study the extent and interstate implications of organized crime in Kansas City. In the conduct of its hearings, the committee was greatly aided by the Federal law enforcement agents in Kansas City, and by the Kansas City Crime Commission. In addition, the committee had the benefit of the findings of the Federal grand jury which held extensive hearings in Kansas City in 1949 and 1950. In the course of its executive and public hearings, the committee heard a total of 48 witnesses, including Gov. Forrest Smith, and representatives of the law enforcement agencies of Kansas City as well as a number of the city's known gamblers and racketeers.

The committee's investigations indicated that while bootlegging and narcotics peddling still exist on a small scale in Kansas City, the vigilance of the Federal alcohol tax investigators and the investigators for the Federal Bureau of Narcotics has greatly reduced such violations from previously bad conditions. The committee found that there were a number of gambling houses operating in and around Kansas City and that, with the end of prohibition and the dissolution a decade later of the organized narcotics racket in Kansas City, the majority of the city's racketeers had concentrated their energies on gambling or activities relating to gambling.

As in other cities, a number of Kansas City racketeers have entered into legitimate business, sometimes as a front for gambling activities, but in other cases, purely for the revenue that can be secured from combining otherwise legitimate enterprises with hoodlum methods to make sales and maintain monopolies. The committee found evidence of criminal infiltration and hoodlum tactics in the wholesale and retail liquor business, in the distribution of juke boxes and pinball machines, in the operation of a Kansas City bakery, and the operation of the horse race wire service. The problem of infiltration of legitimate business by criminals and racketeers is discussed at length elsewhere in the committee's report.

GAMBLERS GROSS $34,000,000 A YEAR IN KANSAS CITY

The Federal grand jury investigating crime in Kansas City, Mo., found that the gambling business had, in years past, grossed more than $34,000,000 a year.

Until his violent death in April 1950, Charles Binaggio was generally conceded to be one of the central figures in Kansas City gambling circles. Binaggio occupied a dual position in Kansas City. In addition to his extensive gambling activities, he was the leader of the First Ward Democratic Club, and it was generally conceded that he could control an important segment of the Democratic vote in the city. Binaggio and Charles Gargotta (who was murdered with Binaggio), Anthony Gizzo, and Thomas Lococo were among the racketeers who dominated Kansas City gambling. The testimony before the committee indicated that these men and their close associates, most of whom had criminal records, had an interest in most of the gambling carried on in the city. Binaggio held a one-fourth interest in Coates House, a bookmaking establishment which in the year 1948 made a net profit of $100,000. He was associated with

Gizzo and several others in this enterprise, and also had an interest at various times in other gambling operations, including the Last Chance Tavern, where he ran a dice game in partnership with Gargotta and Lococo and Morris "Snag" Klein and Phillip E. Osadchey (alias Eddie Spitz) who generally worked with or for Binaggio. From the point of view of the committee, one of the most interesting aspects of the gambling operations in and around Kansas City was the existence of a sort of interlocking directorate of all gambling operations, Binaggio, Gizzo, Lococo, Gargotta, Osadchey, Klein, or one or more of their known associates, were almost invariably named among those participating in any given gambling operation.

Testimony before the committee indicated that several bombings and a killing had preceded the taking over of the Last Chance Tavern and that a number of bombings and a robbery took place before Osadchey and Klein, without putting up any money, became partners in the Stork Club, a gambling casino in Council Bluffs, Iowa. In a number of cases, members of the group had moved into existing gambling operations after bombings or other evidences of violence had persuaded the previous operators to share profitable operations.

MAFIA PLAYS LARGE PART IN NARCOTICS

The extent to which Kansas City operations are integrated with rackets in other cities is difficult to determine from the testimony before the committee. In past years, Kansas City was known as a center for the activities of the Mafia, or Unione Siciliano, which is said to be a secret organization operating throughout the country and internationally. The narcotics ring which was broken up in Kansas City in 1942 was made up entirely of men believed to be members of the Mafia, operating through alleged Mafia members in other cities. Lococo and Gizzo are believed to be members of the Mafia, as were Binaggio and Gargotta. Gizzo, who testified before the committee, admitted to familiarity with a large number of men believed to be members of the Mafia in Chicago and in other parts of the country.

The two men believed to be the leaders of the Kansas City Mafia at the present time, James Balestrere and Joseph Di Giovanni, are not on record as being presently engaged in gambling, although Balestrere, who is an older man, was active in the 1930's. Di Giovanni and his family are engaged in lucrative liquor operations described elsewhere in this report. Information about the operations of the Mafia is difficult to secure, and is generally hearsay, due largely to the record of violence toward persons testifying against alleged Mafia members. Carl Carramusa, who testified for the Government in the Kansas City narcotics trial, was shot to death 3 years later in Chicago where he had gone to escape retribution by the Mafia. Thomas Buffa, who testified for the Government in a collateral matter affecting the narcotics trial, fled to California after an attempt had been made on his life, but was shot to death in California in 1946. Kansas City now has a record of 16 unsolved murders believed to have been committed by or at the direction of Mafia members. Among these is the shooting of Wolf Riman, who was shot shortly after he secured a liquor distributing franchise in competition with one of the Di Giovannis.

Witnesses before the committee, believed to be Mafia members, claimed to be completely ignorant of the organization, and its operations. Joseph Di Giovanni refused even to admit to having heard of the Mafia, which is patently incredible since almost all persons of Sicilian extraction are at least familiar with the existence of the Mafia but when confronted with his criminal record he admitted that he had been involved in a black hand (Mafia) charge.

KANSAS CITY BOOKIES USE CONTINENTAL PRESS SERVICE

As in other cities investigated by the committee, the race horse wire service played a vital part in the gambling operations of Kansas City. In 1946, Kansas City was a distribution center for the race wire service furnished by the Continental Press Service, then operated from Chicago by James Ragen, Sr. The up-to-the-minute racing information distributed by Continental was received in Kansas City by the Harmony Publishing Co. and from there, was redistributed by leased wires and/or by telephone to various bookmakers in Missouri, Kansas, Nebraska, Iowa, and Oklahoma, where it was used as the basis for their illegal bookmaking operations. It may be noted in passing that the Coates House was one of the subscribers to the Harmony Co. service. From 1939, the Harmony Co. was run by one Simon Partnoy who was responsible for distributing information, securing customers, collecting fees, and remitting the collections to Continental.

In 1946, a rival wire service was set up in Chicago, known as Trans-American News Service. The nominal head of the Trans-American Service in Chicago was Pat Burns, but the forces behind Burns were the members of the old Capone gang. When Trans-American was set up, Burns visited Kansas City and made a deal with Osadchey to serve as Kansas City distributor for the news service. Osadchey agreed to pay Burns $1,000 a week and put up a $5,000 deposit. He then went into partnership with Klein, Gargotta, and Lococo but these four never set up a distributing office of their own. Instead, Osadchey approached Partnoy and he and his partners took over the facilities of the Harmony Publishing Co. which thereafter subscribed to the Trans-American Service. Osadchey and his partners paid Partnoy $7,500 for his equipment and contacts, plus a 15-percent interest in the business. The $7,500 was paid out of the operations of the business and not out of the pockets of Osadchey and company. It is interesting to review the criminal records of the four new owners of the Kansas City distributorship: Osadchey and Klein have been convicted of violations of Federal statutes; Klein is now in a Federal penitentiary serving a sentence for vote fraud violation. Gargotta was in a Federal penitentiary for stealing arms from an armory, and was convicted of assault with intent to kill. Lococo has been arrested on numerous occasions and is now confined to Federal prison for income tax evasions in connection with his gambling enterprises in Missouri.

Partnoy continued the actual operations for a percentage of the company's take, and Osadchey appears to have traveled through the neighboring States to "induce" customers to subscribe to the new Trans-American Service. Among his customers were two bookmakers who took both the Continental and Trans-American Service. Klein, Gargotta, and Lococo had no duties in connection with their partnership in the service.

Shortly after Trans-American went into business, Ragen was killed, and early in 1947, about 6 months after it came into being Trans-American ceased operations. The Kansas City distributor of Trans-American, which was now known as the Standard News Service, switched back to the Continental wire service without difficulty and continued to operate with Gargotta, Klein, Lococo, and Osadchey as partners in the enterprise which netted an average of $45,000 a year. After the death of Binaggio and Gargotta, the Kansas City wire service closed down and the bookmakers who continued to operate had to get their information by telephone from St. Joseph or St. Louis.

CRIME AND POLITICS

The committee heard considerable testimony relating to attempts by Binaggio to exert political influence to open up for gambling and other illegal operations, the State of Missouri, and particularly St. Louis and Kansas City. Prior to 1948, Binaggio's political influence was rather limited, but it seems clear that at the time of the Democratic primary for Governor in 1948, Binaggio had gained considerable influence at the expense of the Pendergast element which opposed Smith in the primary. Estimates of the number of votes that Binaggio could control in Kansas City ranged up to 35,000, but these estimates seem to be highly inflated in the light of the fact that Forrest Smith, whose candidacy for governorship was supported by Binaggio and by a number of other factions more or less independent of Binaggio, realized only 27,000 votes in Kansas City. However, it seems undisputed that Binaggio was the dominant member of the pro-Smith coalition and that after the election, he was considered by many to be the leading pro-Smith politician in the city.

During and after the gubernatorial elections, rumors were prevalent that Binaggio had contributed sums as large as $150,000 to the Smith for Governor campaign, but the most diligent efforts of the committee's investigators failed to disclose any large-scale contributions by Binaggio or his associates. Certain irregularities in bookkeeping on the part of B. E. Ragland, assistant treasurer of the Missouri State Democratic Committee, were disclosed but these irregularities had no real relevance to Binaggio's attempt to exert political influence to open up Kansas City.

It is abundantly clear that Binaggio did support Forrest Smith, and that his organization was active in the Governor's campaign. Osadchey testified that he and Binaggio had campaigned for Smith, and some of Binaggio's supporters contributed sums to finance the activities of John K. Noonan who was campaigning on behalf of the Governor. But whatever Binaggio's expectations may have been as a result of his efforts in the campaign for Governor Smith, there is no substantial evidence that Governor Smith made any kind of commitment to Binaggio, or that Binaggio was successful in opening up the town.

On the other hand, it is inconceivable that Governor Smith, being an experienced politician, could have failed to know of Binaggio's background, or that Binaggio expected a quid pro quo for his support. Smith's assertions under oath that he did not discuss politics with Binaggio, or discuss Binaggio's expectations, are simply not credible.

Smith did appoint two police commissioners who were at least acceptable to Binaggio and who appeared willing to go along with him. The two hold-over appointees showed a determination to remain on the board. Smith did not take aggressive action to remove them, or to influence them. He did call one of them to the State capitol, after Binaggio had predicted that this would occur. But in the ensuing conference, he neither put any pressure on the commissioner, nor did he act on the commission's statements to him that Binaggio was trying to influence and even to buy the board. Much of the conjecture about Binaggio's death lays it to his inability to satisfy the organized gambling element which had expected him to open Kansas City up for gambling. It was, of course, extremely desirable for the gambling element to be able to control the police department. As pointed out by Osadchey before the committee, gambling is a lucrative business if you can operate. Without police cooperation, operations must necessarily be conducted on a sneak basis and suspended whenever pressure is exerted by the police.

Under Missouri law, police commissioners are appointed by the Governor and the police department is under the jurisdiction of the State government. One commissioner, Mr. Robert Cohn, was a Republican; another, Mr. Hampton Chambers, was a Pendergast man and had not supported Governor Smith in the primary campaign. Mr. J. M. Milligan, a Governor Smith appointee, testified that he tried to give Binaggio some patronage but it seems clear that he did not go along with Binaggio's sponsorship of an ex-police captain called Joseph Braun for the position of police chief. Braun had previously been dismissed from the police force because he had permitted gambling to go on in his own station house. Sheridan Farrell, the remaining commissioner appointed by Governor Smith, testified that he believed that a little gambling was a good thing. In the final analysis Police Chief Johnston, whom Binaggio was most anxious to replace, remained in office.

Mr. Chambers and Mr. Cohn both testified that Binaggio had attempted to persuade and then to bribe them to go along with his plans for transferring police officials who would not cooperate with him and his associates in refusing to enforce the gambling laws. Mr. Cohn testified that at his last meeting with Binaggio in June 1949, Binaggio appeared to be most disturbed by his inability to open up the town and stated that "The boys were behind in their schedule and making it hot for him."

On April 6, 1950, Binaggio and Gargotta were murdered. On April 21, the Kansas City Chamber of Commerce directed a letter to Governor Smith indicating its lack of confidence in the police board, particularly in Milligan and Farrell, because of their associations with Binaggio. Farrell resigned shortly thereafter and after repeated requests by the chamber of commerce, Milligan also resigned. Chambers and Cohn later resigned at the request of the Governor. The present board is made up of four men of undoubted integrity.

ATTEMPT TO CONTROL ST. LOUIS POLICE BOARD

An analogous situation seems to have arisen in St. Louis during the same period that the board of police commissioners in Kansas

City was causing so much difficulty. In St. Louis, William Molasky, a large stockholder in the Pioneer News Service, a local racing wire distribution agency, made a $2,000 campaign contribution to Forrest Smith. He attempted to obtain appointment of his nominee to the board of police commissioners in St. Louis. There was testimony that he was interested in getting Morris Shenker named to the commission. Mr. Shenker was attorney for him and for many St. Louis witnesses who appeared before our committee. Although the contribution was accepted and handled as an anonymous contribution under the fixed name of J. J. Price, no such commitment was made. The appointment to the board of police commissioners was Col. William L. Holzhausen. Apparently the gamblers erroneously thought he would permit them to operate. When Holzhausen set out to enforce the law, vigorous efforts were made by Binaggio to have him removed. The story of the conversations in negotiations surrounding these efforts is complicated and the fact is that Holzhausen was not removed and has done an excellent job as chairman of the St. Louis Board of Police Commissioners.

Another interesting facet of the link between crime and politics is to be found in the testimony of Roy McKittrick, former attorney general of the State of Missouri, who had sought the nomination for Governor in 1948, on which McKittrick contends that Binaggio swung his support from McKittrick to Smith, and that after this occurred, Binaggio offered McKittrick a large sum of money to refrain from running against Smith. McKittrick also charged that Smith asked McKittrick to obtain for him the support of Gully Owen, one of the partners in the Pioneer News Service in St. Louis.

Governor Smith has categorically denied all these charges. Whether they are true or not, it stands out at least that the former attorney general of the State of Missouri and the prominent aspirant for the post of Governor, admitted to having intimate dealings with Binaggio and the operators of the Pioneer News Service in connection with political matters.

While the committee did not find any evidence that the board of police commissioners responded to Binaggio's efforts, this is not to say that individual police officers were not guilty of cooperating with known gamblers in the city. Handbooks and gambling casinos were operating in the city both before and after the gubernatorial elections. Although police officers were forbidden by law from becoming members of political clubs, a number of the members of the police force were known to frequent Binaggio's clubhouse.

While the committee feels justified in saying that on the whole, the racketeering elements did not succeed in their efforts to control the Kansas City police force, a different situation prevailed in that portion of Jackson County which lies outside of Kansas City.

CONDITIONS IN JACKSON COUNTY

The committee's investigation showed that Sheriff Purdome, who was responsible for law enforcement in the county, was notably lax in his enforcement of the liquor and gambling laws. He also permitted his deputy sheriffs to use their badge of office to promote their personal business interests. Until his murder in 1949, Wolf Riman was the owner of the Western Specialty Co., which placed juke boxes and pinball machines in taverns and other establishments in Jackson County and Kansas City, Kans. Riman, who was himself a deputy sheriff, used the services of a number of Sheriff Purdome's deputies in placing his machines. Harry Hundley, Riman's assistant and successor, testified that although it was illegal for county taverns to sell liquor except by the bottle, it was the general practice for the county taverns to sell drinks over the counter. Hundley testified that although the Western Specialty had a number of active competitors in the placing of machines, Riman's machines were used in 75 percent of the county taverns. Hundley testified that on one occasion Riman himself used his badge to threaten a tavern owner who was reluctant to take his machines. Although Sheriff Purdome admitted that he was aware of Riman's activities, Riman continued to be a deputy sheriff until his death.

Mike Manzello, a county tavernkeeper, testified that he had been arrested for selling drinks over the counter after he had refused to join a tavernkeeper's association. He had no further trouble with arrests after he began paying a weekly stipend to two of Purdome's deputies.

There was also testimony that Purdome overlooked gambling activities by Walter Rainey, a gambler who could control a large number of votes in the county, and that Rainey moved his gambling activities, so as to remain under Purdome's jurisdiction when the Kansas City police force interfered with his operations at his original location. In general, as a result of poorer law enforcement, gambling and liquor law violations are more widespread in the county than in Kansas City proper.

KANSAS CITY ENFORCEMENT NOW IMPROVED

Since the death of Binaggio, there has been a diminution of gambling activities in Kansas City. The formation of the Kansas City Crime Commission and the appointment of a new board of police commissioners has led to improved morale in the police department and increased efficiency in law enforcement. The closing down of the race wire service has hampered bookmaking operations, although the information is still available to bookies through phone connections to nearby wire services. The work of the Federal and State grand juries, the indictments issued by those grand juries and the publicity attendant on this committee's investigations have contributed to the closing up of many of Kansas City's gambling houses and the general decrease in criminal activity. However, these recent improvements in law enforcement can be sustained and extended only through the continued support of the local citizenry and continued cooperation between local and Federal law-enforcement agents.

ST. LOUIS

Col. William L. Holzhausen, chairman of the St. Louis Board of Police Commissioners, stated that the principal law-enforcement problem in St. Louis is organized gambling, which was facilitated by the dissemination of interstate racing information. Colonel Holzhausen testified that the national wire services give impetus to the creation of gambling joints and sneak books and that no police department, no matter how efficient, could fully cope with the situation unless Federal legislation outlaws the dissemination of "hot" racing information by interstate wires.

Attorney General J. E. Taylor, of Missouri, told the committee in detail of his legal efforts to put an end to the dissemination of gambling news within the State. In 1938 the St. Louis Police Board endeavored to cut off the race wire telephone service furnished by Pioneer News, which for approximately 25 years has had a monopoly of the dissemination of racing news to bookmakers in St. Louis. This attempt was defeated by legal action. A long and complicated legal struggle then followed to compel the Southwestern Bell Telephone Co and the Western Union Telegraph Co. to discontinue furnishing service to Pioneer News Co. The effort by the attorney general to cut off Pioneer's telephone and telegraph facilities was only partially successful. Even when orders were obtained compelling the telephone company to cut off Pioneer's phones, Pioneer continued to supply racing information to bookies by illegal stratagems. When the attorney general testified, telephone service had legally been cut off from Pioneer. Nevertheless, the committee discovered that the Pioneer was still furnishing service to bookmakers, for its customers were paying for service as late as February 1951.

Although Attorney General Taylor was much opposed to Federal intervention in State affairs, he felt that it was proper for the Federal Government to stop interstate transactions carried on for the sole purpose of fostering violations of State law.

Continental Press Service (of which Pioneer is a subsidiary)—

stated the attorney general—

is a giant monopoly whose slimy tentacles reach into every metropolitan area in the country. It serves no useful purpose; its sole business is supplying information to bookmakers which enables them to carry on their illegal enterprises It has brought about and financed gangsterism; it has caused bloodshed and led to the corruption of public officials. That it not only knows the kind of business its customers are engaged in, but also the volume of business they do is evident from the fact that they charge some customers a few hundred dollars a week and others as much as $6,000 a week for the same service.

He further stated:

If the transmission of this racing information by Continental or any other similar agency in interstate commerce could be stopped it would, in my opinion, eliminate racing news distributing agencies, take the profit out of bookmaking and prevent a great deal of gangsterism which results from fights over the control of such illegal enterprises.

THE CARROLL-MOONEY ENTERPRISE

The largest bookmaking operation in the St. Louis area was the Carroll-Mooney enterprise operated from 318 Missouri Avenue, East St. Louis, Ill. Its annual volume of bets might reasonably be approximated at $20,000,000. To enable the enterprise to carry on its business, wire service was obtained from Continental Press, through Pioneer News. Most of the business done by the partnership was in the nature of lay-off betting, i. e., betting by professional bookies to insure themselves against excessive loss. The partnership employed men to represent it at various race tracks whose function was to bet what is known as comeback money at the pari-mutuel machines. This type of betting had two basic purposes: (a) to provide a second round of reinsurance for Carroll and Mooney, and (b) to distort the track odds by the sudden placing of heavy bets about a minute before post time. Since track odds determine pay-offs to successful bettors, it is obvious how important the come-back operation is in holding down the losses of bookmakers. The committee received detailed testimony about this operation from men employed by Carroll-Mooney, as well as from men employed by Rosenbaum, a bookmaker in the Cincinnati area.

Carroll has long described himself and been accepted by the public under the glorified term "Betting Commissioner." This term was intended to signify some sort of respectability. The committee found him to be an ordinary bookie operating clandestinely behind locked doors which had to be broken down, in order to gain entry to the premises in broad daylight, when many employees cringed behind the locked barrier.

C. J. RICH & CO.

C. J. Rich & Co., which has also operated under the name of Rich & Wyman, was one of the most unusual bookmaking operations studied by the committee. This enterprise did a gross business of between 4 and 5 million dollars a year and used Western Union telegrams, money orders, and Western Union agents to carry on operations. Most of the business of C. J. Rich Co. came from more than a hundred miles away from St. Louis through Western Union. Telegrams placing bets would be sent to C. J. Rich & Co. at an address in East St. Louis, Ill. Bets were covered by Western Union money orders. During every operating day the Western Union Telegraph Co. would accumulate the incoming money orders and would issue a single check for all the moneys bet. The fact that bets could be placed through Western Union with C. J. Rich & Co. was made abundantly clear in the advertising literature, which this company distributed. Western Union agents were used as runners and solicitors for bets and were paid a percentage of winnings for their services or commissions. Cash or presents were also given by the C. J. Rich Co. to various Western Union representatives. The Western Union Co. itself profited from the bookmaking business, for C. J. Rich Co. would receive between 500 to 1,000 telegrams a day. In the month of May 1950, the telegraph bill of C. J. Rich Co. was $26,700.

It is quite clear that in the C. J. Rich Co. operation, the Western Union aided and abetted the violation of the gambling laws of the State, because it was profitable to do so. Only when the C. J. Rich Co. was raided on June 26, 1950, did the Western Union do anything to stop its participation in the bookmaking conspiracy. All charge accounts with Western Union of this company were canceled after the raid. One wonders whether the Western Union's obliviousness to its public responsibility not to permit its facilities to be used in violation of State law, was in part due to the fact William Molasky, of St. Louis, a well-known gambler, is one of its outstanding stockholders.

PIONEER NEWS SERVICE

Pioneer News Service is a local racing wire outlet. One of its chief stockholders, William Molasky, is also a very substantial stockholder in Western Union Telegraph Co., and although he claims that there is no particular reason for this coincidence, the fact remains that he does not own any other large stockholdings and that he has made his substantial interest in Western Union known to the local Western Union management.

Molasky and the Pioneer News Service, together with Annenberg, Ragen, and Kruse, were all associates of the Chicago Annenberg news service. Their local partners were Gully Owen and Bev Brown. Annenberg and Ragen gave up their interest at the time of their income-tax indictments, and Annenberg sold his to Molasky for $1. When the Capone Syndicate organized the Trans-American Service, hoodlums from East St. Louis attempted to gain control of the Pioneer News Service. When this failed, Bev Brown, without relinquishing his interest in Pioneer, moved across the river and opened the Reliable News Service in East St. Louis. It is significant that during this period, Brown's son worked for Buster Wortman, the local East St. Louis hoodlum, in a coin machine operation.

When peace was made, Reliable News went out of business, and Bev Brown and his son, William, moved back into Pioneer. After about that time, William Brown bought out the interest of Kruse and of Gully Owen. He accomplished this by declaring a dividend in Pioneer, but not advising the Chicago trustees of Kruse's estate that his dividend had been declared. After he purchased Kruse's interest, he was able to reimburse himself in effect out of the dividends which had been declared. After this time, Brown and his mother each recived $25,000 a year from the news service, his mother being considered honorary. The relation between Pioneer News Service, William Brown, and Buster Wortman's gang of racketeers, is very close and indicates to the committee's satisfaction that the Pioneer News Service today like the Harmony Publishing Co. in Kansas City is now under the domination and control of the Capone Syndicate.

PHILADELPHIA

The Philadelphia story differs only slightly from the pattern of organized crime that the committee has found to exist in a number of other cities. The principal organized crime is the numbers game. To be sure, there is a volume of horse betting but there does not appear to be any open activity along these lines nor is the existence of any big gambling houses apparent.

The numbers game in Philadelphia has achieved the size of a big industry and, like big industry, it appears to be organized on a highly efficient scale. It operates through tight control, manipulated by a politico-gambler-police tie-up that makes it impossible for any intruder to edge his way in from the outside. The city is organized into a number of geographical territories, each with its own bank, in turn affiliated apparently with sufficient political connections to be able to operate without too much fear of molestation.

This geographical allocation of territory with lines of area definitely fixed, beyond which the operators in one area do not overstep, was confirmed by the director of public safety of Philadelphia, Samuel H. Rosenberg, but in the absence of definite knowledge, he did not believe that this territorial allocation was reached through any alliance or agreement. He would not say that there were no police in the pay of the numbers racketeers, he limited his commitment to the statement that he had never been able to prove such payments.

LACKED CONFIDENCE IN POLICE OFFICIALS

Nevertheless, he admitted that he lacked confidence in four of the highest police officials under his direction, not because he had any proof of their violation of trust but because he believed that under the circumstances as they existed, they had failed to pursue the circumstances with what he considered adequate aggressiveness. That these men in whom he lacked confidence were still able to hold high positions in the Philadelphia Police Department, he ascribed to the shackles imposed on him as director by civil-service regulations.

It is notable that one of the four officials named in the "no confidence" category by Director Rosenberg has since been suspended by the director from his duties and has made the action the subject of a court review, not yet heard.

Another aspect of the situation in Philadelphia was the attitude taken until comparatively recently by the judges before whom violators of the gambling laws had been brought. This chapter of the Philadelphia story is a repetition of the same situation that was turned up in other cities canvassed by the committee. It was described as a "casual and cavalier outlook" by one of the very judges before whom these miscreants were brought for trial and sentence. Judge Joseph Sloane, who was a witness before the committee, said that many of his colleagues on the bench were content to impose only fines upon guilty offenders, that only the little people came before them and that no serious attempt was made by the judges to get beyond the lower echelons in the sizable gambling industry in Philadelphia. He pointed out that although defendants came before judges with records of numerous previous arrests and discharges without trial, and although the maximum fine possible was $500 with an accompanying year in jail, the usual first offense brought a fine of only $25 or $50 and no jail sentence. In many years on the bench, he said he had seldom seen a fine imposed in excess of $250.

5,000 OFFENDERS IN 5 YEARS; 2 JAILED

Judge Sloane testified that in many cases pressure was brought by politicians for reduction in sentence, reduction in fines, and reconsideration of punishment previously imposed. It is to be noted that in 5 years prior to 1950, out of thousands of arrests that were made for gambling in connection with the numbers game and horse booking in Philadelphia, only two defendants had gone to jail.

There has been a change in this attitude on the part of the judges since the committee held its hearings in Philadelphia. More and more jail sentences are beginning to be imposed and it is a fact, reported by municipal authorities, that the numbers game is no longer as easy to carry on in Philadelphia as it was prior to the committee's advent.

The principal police witness was the assistant superintendent of police, George F. Richardson, one of the four officials in whom Director Rosenberg said that he reposed less than full confidence. Richardson testified with some vehemence with respect to Harry Stromberg, alias Nig Rosen, and his henchman, William Weisberg, who, he had previously informed the committee, he believed to be the kingpin of the numbers game in Philadelphia. His oral testimony seemed to be in

variance with the information he had previously given the committee
in a letter, as well as information he had given the Crime Commission
of Greater Miami in a previous communication. He stated that
Rosen was persona non grata in Philadelphia as long as he had anything to do with the police department, even to the point of physical
violence if he should meet him on the street.

Subsequently, Rosen, who was a witness before the committee,
testified that he had been engaged in the numbers game in Philadelphia but was no longer active in it. However, during the period
when he was active, Rosen testified, he had made numerous gifts to
Richardson and, on occasion, had entertained him at various public
functions and in public places in the city of New York. The committee considered the testimony of these two witnesses as being so
diametrically at variance the entire record was referred to the United
States attorney for the District of Columbia for his review and any
further action that might seem to be justified by the testimony.

Indicative of the tie-up of gamblers, politicians, and police heretofore referred to, was a case of Michael McDonald, a Philadelphia
policeman, who, while on duty, arrested a numbers writer named Jack
Rogers. While Rogers was being booked in the station house,
McDonald said, there came into the station one Mike Caserta who
had been named by Rogers as his backer. McDonald said that
Caserta had offered him a bribe if he would change the charge from
gambling to disorderly conduct. Upon McDonald's refusal, he said,
Caserta threatened to frame him and he thereupon arrested Caserta
for disorderly conduct. At that point, a police captain, Vincent
Elwell, entered the picture and when he learned that McDonald had
arrested both Rogers and Caserta, he reprimanded the policeman.
Rogers was then brought in and accused McDonald of reporting less
than the money found on Rogers' person which, under police regulation, had to be turned in. On the basis of Rogers' statement, which
McDonald said he believed had been written out and signed under
Elwell's direction, Elwell suspended McDonald.

It is interesting to note that after McDonald's story had been
brought out, he was given a retrial on these charges by the civil
service board and was reinstated to his position on the police force.
He thereupon resigned and entered the United States Army in which
he had served during World War II with distinction.

"CONVENIENCE ARRESTS" PATTERN DESCRIBED

McDonald gave a picture of the operations of the politico-gambler-
police triumvirate. He named a policeman who he said was known
as the collector for Captain Elwell. He named a political leader who
was the boss of one of the wards in Philadelphia and who, he said,
he had often seen in the stationhouse and conferring with the captain
in the latter's office. He calculated that the payment of protection
money to police in Philadelphia in the lower echelon totaled more
than $150,000 a month, and he said that his own captain, Elwell,
was reported to be getting $1,000 a month. McDonald said that the
police were discouraged from making arrests of the numbers writers
and if they persisted in doing so, they would be moved to beats where
there were none. The general picture in this respect, given by McDon-

ald, indicated that there is a tie-up between the three elements in Philadelphia which permits these operations to continue with the token "convenience arrests" that are characteristic of the same kind of operations in other cities.

Captain Elwell was given a chance to tell his side of the story and did. He denied, of course, that any of McDonald's charges were true. He said that he had heard that there was a regular system of payoffs to police but that he had no personal knowledge of it and that he had not taken any money from racketeers.

One of the most significant statements given to the committee in Philadelphia was that of William A. Gray, for 53 years a member of the bar of that city, one of Philadelphia's most distinguished lawyers and the undisputed leader of its criminal bar. Gray told the committee that several years ago Weisberg had come to him and had told him that Assistant Superintendent Richardson had warned him to keep out of the central part of Philadelphia on pain of personal treatment by Richardson if he found him there. Incensed by this, Gray had gone to see Richardson, whom he knew personally, had protested this treatment of Weisberg and suggested that if Richardson knew of any offense committed by Weisberg he should have him arrested on a warrant. Richardson truculently said that he would not have a warrant issued, but that the next time he saw Weisberg in Philadelphia he would wreak such personal injury upon him that Weisberg would have to go to a hospital.

Gray then went over Richardson's head, but instead of going to Richardson's superior, he went to see a judge, the late Harry S. McDevitt, who, he said, had some measure of control over Richardson to exercise his control. If this were not done, Gray said, he told McDevitt, "I am going to take some steps in this matter which won't be very pleasant for a lot of people in the city of Philadelphia."

After this conversation with the judge, Gray related, Richardson withheld further harassment of Weisberg for a while; later it was resumed.

NUMBERS GAME PROTECTED IN PHILADELPHIA

The committee has no doubt that the numbers game in Philadelphia is a big operation. It is, however, operated in the main by local characters, obviously under protection. It lacks the interstate connections of similar operations in other cities; it is reasonable to infer that outsiders find it too difficult to come into the picture from out of State. As it happened, shortly before the committee hearings were held in Philadelphia on October 13 and 14, 1950, a Federal grand jury was convened to delve into the operations of organized crime in the eastern district of Pennsylvania and it was decided by the committee that further committee investigations and hearings would be postponed pending the outcome of the grand jury investigation so that there would be no conflict or hindrance in the activities of the latter body. This grand jury is still in session. Its investigation has been augmented by a local grand jury inquiry which has just gotten under way and to which this committee has offered, as it has to the Federal grand jury, such information as has been disclosed by this committee's inquiries in the Philadelphia area.

CHICAGO

Chicago, by virtue of its size and its location as a center of communications, transportation, and distribution of goods, has been and remains a focal point for the activities of organized criminals in the United States. This does not mean that the law-enforcement officials of the city have been uniformly lax in the performance of their duties, although the committee has found evidence of deplorable laxity on the part of individual officials. It does mean that because of the history of the city, its physical location and its great size, the job of law enforcement in Chicago remains a tremendous responsibility and challenge to the law-enforcement agencies and to the citizens of Chicago and its surrounding areas.

GANG ORIGINS IN 1920's

The roots of the criminal group operating in Chicago today go back to the operations of the Torrio-Capone gang which terrorized Chicago in the 1920's. Records seized by the police during that period indicated that John Torrio, Al Capone, Jacob Guzik, Tony Accardo, Joseph Fusco, Frank Nitti, John Patton, Murray Humphries, Paul (Ricca) DeLucia, Alexander Greenberg, and others had built up an illegal empire netting millions of dollars a year. In the late 1920's, Torrio abdicated his leadership and Al Capone took over. The activities of the Capone gang at this time consisted largely of illegal liquor rackets, prostitution, gambling, and the control of horse-racing and dog-racing tracks. During this period the gang was particularly powerful in Burnham, Ill., a suburb of Chicago, whose mayor, John Patton, was closely associated with Torrio and Capone.

In 1924, the Torrio-Capone gang manned the polls during the mayoralty election in Cicero, another Chicago suburb, as part of a plan to take over the local government in Cicero. Following the 1924 election, Cicero became the headquarters for gang operations, and gang influence is still strong there today. In 1931, Al Capone was brought to trial and sentenced for Federal income-tax evasion after all attempts to establish his bootlegging operations had failed to put him in prison. Capone's place as leader of the gang was then taken by Frank Nitti, who, like Capone, was believed to have an interest in the Manhattan Brewery Co., and was an old-time member of the Torrio-Capone gang. At the time of Capone's conviction, the men who were believed to be important members of his underworld empire were, among others, Nitti, Louis Campagna, Paul Ricca, Jacob Guzik, Tony Accardo, Charles Fischetti, Edward Vogel, Hymie Levin, and Ralph Capone. Nitti committed suicide in 1943, while under indictment with a number of other Capone henchmen who were tried and convicted for a conspiracy to extort millions of dollars from the movie industry through their domination of the Motion Picture Operators Union. In 1943, Campagna, Ricca, Charles Gioe, Phil d'Andrea, Nick Circella, and John Rosselli, all of whom had been close to Capone, went to prison in connection with the movie extortion case. They have since been released from the Federal penitentiary.

CAPONE GANG REACTIVATED

Until the repeal of the eighteenth amendment in 1933, the manufacture and distribution of bootleg liquor constituted an important source of revenue for the Capone syndicate. After repeal, the Chicago underworld, like racketeers all over the country, concentrated its attention on the revenue possibilities of illegal gambling, extortion rackets, and infiltration of legitimate enterprises.

In Chicago, in many of the service industries, in the liquor industry, and in the unions, there has been a long history of activity by former Capone mobsters. Violence and bombings still occur. There is little doubt that members of the Capone syndicate use proceeds from their illegitimate activities to buy their way into hotels, restaurants, laundry services, dry-cleaning establishments, breweries, and wholesale and retail liquor businesses. In all such businesses their "contacts" give them a substantial advantage.

The extortion cases in the moving-picture industry, successfully prosecuted in New York, marked a milestone in governmental ability to cope with union infiltration by gangsters and the use of the powers of unions by gangsters in order to shake down business enterprises. The astonishing aftermath of the prosecution deserves detailed discussion. Paul Ricca, also known as Paul the Waiter and Paul DeLucia, undoubtedly one of the two or three leading figures in the Capone mob; Louis "Little New York" Campagna and Charlie "Cherry Nose" Gioe, who had been in partnership with Tony Accardo, were prominent in the mulcting of the movie industry. After their conviction and sentence, these three mobsters were visited in prison by Tony Accardo and Eugene Bernstein, the mouthpiece and tax lawyer for the mob. Bernstein and Accardo were indicted as a result of these visits because Accardo used the assumed name of another lawyer, Joseph Bulger. The trips to the prison from Kansas City to Fort Leavenworth were made in the automobile of Tony Gizzo, a prominent Kansas City mobster who has a history of close connections with the Capone syndicate.

The three mobsters were released on parole after serving a minimum period of imprisonment although they were known to be vicious gangsters. A prominent member of the Missouri bar presented their parole applications to the parole board, which granted the parole against the recommendations of the prosecuting attorney and of the judge who had presided at their trial. In the opinion of this committee, this early release from imprisonment of three dangerous mobsters is a shocking abuse of parole powers.

"YOU DON'T ASK QUESTIONS"—BERNSTEIN

Another example of the efficiency of the underworld in releasing its leaders from the toils of the law is the story of the raising of funds for a tax settlement effected by the three above-mentioned mobsters, which they had to complete before they would be eligible for parole. Eugene Bernstein testified that he arranged this settlement. The Government's original claim against Campagna and DeLucia was about $470,000, including penalties. This liability was settled for $120,000 plus penalties of $70,000. Bernstein testified that $190,000 was delivered to his office in cash at various periods over a month by

persons unknown to him. He had the almost inconceivable effrontery,
as a member of the bar, to assert to the committee under oath that
although he saw some of the persons who delivered the money he
never asked them their names and that his office had no record whatsoever to indicate their identities. "You don't ask those fellows
any questions," said Mr. Bernstein. He testified that he told Campagna and DeLucia that the money would have to be raised and that
he also told this to Accardo. He testified that he visited Mrs. Campagna's home but did not remember what he told her. Neither
DeLucia, Campagna, nor Mrs. Campagna had any idea of who might
have been interested in providing funds or in how the funds were
raised. Each had several hundred thousand dollars in cash hidden
away in safety boxes in their homes. "It was a friend of mine," said
DeLucia, "I would put up $190,000 for a friend of mine who needed
it." The combined testimony of these witnesses represents a graphic
demonstration of the willful, sullen, vicious contempt for the law still
dominant in their hearts and minds. The connivance in this plot of a
lawyer who obviously could provide the essential clues, if not the actual
answers, brands the entire matter as even more shocking.

The most recent evidence of the intricacy of gangland's financial
operations was provided in 1948 and 1949 when Ricca received loans
totaling $80,000 from one Hugo Bennett, a salaried underling in the
Sportsmen's Park Race Track and Florida dog tracks, formerly controlled by Edward O'Hare, John Patton, and the Capone syndicate.
Bennett and his present boss, William H. Johnston, who figures
prominently in our discussion of the Miami area, both worked at
Sportsmen's Park under O'Hare. Patton, through his son, still has
an important interest in the dog tracks. Several prominent Capone
mobsters worked at the dog tracks when this committee began its
investigation.

THE MYSTERIOUS $80,000 LOAN

Ricca did not need the $80,000. By his own testimony, he had
$300,000 in cash "stashed away." He owned a very valuable and
pretentious farm of 700 acres and an elaborate home in a Chicago
suburb. Bennett, on the other hand, had very meager assets and in
order to make the loan to Ricca, borrowed $20,000 from Johnston and
$15,000 from Max Silverberg, Johnston's restaurant concessionaire at
the race tracks. Most of the remainder of the $80,000 was made avail-
able to Bennett by a highly questionable real-estate deal through which
Johnston and a group of his own friends sold some land to the Miami
Beach Kennel Club and made a huge profit. Bennett was cut in on
this deal and the proceeds to him enabled him to complete the loan
to Ricca.

Although Bennett went through the motions of obtaining mortgages, it was apparent to the lawyer who drew up these instruments
that Bennett was determined to make the loans whether or not they
could be properly secured. The evidence of the attorney and of
Bennett, conflicting as it is on many points, clearly demonstrates that
the mortgages were simply for the record. There is also ample reason
to suspect that the $80,000 may have been a payoff for Ricca's ap-
proval of the wire service deal in which Accardo, Guzik, and Russell
obtained an interest in the lucrative Miami Beach S. and G. gambling
syndicate.

Several unions which were racketeer-infested and whose treasuries were raided by racketeers, had their headquarters in the same building where Tony Accardo operated his gambling enterprises and where he was in partnership with both Charlie Gioe and Harry Russell, whose Silver Bar tavern was also located there. The entire gang of union extortionists appear to be living in luxury in Florida, California, or Chicago and many of them have already acquired a thick veneer of respectability.

BOOKMAKING AND THE RACE WIRE

As the committee pointed out in its second interim report, the form of gambling which depends most on interstate commerce and interstate communications is off-track betting on horse racing and dog racing. The backbone of illegal bookmaking operations throughout the country is the up-to-the-minute information furnished by the Continental Press Service through its Nation-wide network of telephone and telegraph wires, and the intricate organization of distributors and subdistributors that gather and disseminate the news for Continental.

The heart of the racing news service centers in Chicago, where Continental has its main operating office, and from which most of its wires fan out to the rest of the country. While in Chicago, this committee focused its attention to a considerable degree on the operations of the Continental Press, its relations with the distributors through whom racing news flows, and the increasing domination of the wire service by the same racketeering elements who control the large-scale and lucrative handbook operations.

The headquarters of the race wire service have been established in Chicago since before John Torrio became the underworld king of the city in 1920. Interestingly enough, the building which was occupied by Monte Tennes and his General News Bureau racing service now houses the offices of the Continental Press Service, some 30 years later. But the story of the race wire service, while inextricably linked with Chicago's past and present, is not only a story of Chicago but of every city and town in the country into which the tentacles of the wire service reach. For this reason, the committee discusses the history and operations of the wire service in a separate section of this report.

The committee has described the workings of the Continental Press Service and exposed its facade of respectability and attempted insulation from the handbook operators who depend on it for information and on whom it depends for revenue. Just as the race wire service is essential to the success of large-scale betting operations, the substantial income which channels into Chicago from the wire service depends on the continuous operation of a flourishing handbook business. United Press and Associated Press pay a nominal fee of from $70 to $80 a month for the information that Continental distributes; the Illinois News Service, a single distributor, pays about $250,000 annually for the same service. The difference in these rates is the profit of the handbook operators which is passed on, in part, to the subdistributor and distributor for Continental, and ultimately to Continental.

SUBDISTRIBUTORS SERVICE BOOKMAKERS

Since the last reorganization of the wire service in the Chicago area, the city of Chicago has been serviced by the R. and H. wire service, owned by the Capone mobsters, Ray Jones, Phil Katz, and Hymie Levin, and by Midwest News, now owned by John Scanlon, who participated in the Guzik-Accardo-Russell maneuver to take over the S. and G. wire service in Florida. The list of wire service drops compiled by the Senate Committee on Interstate and Foreign Commerce indicates that R. and H. services over 100 individual drops in Chicago. The Midwest Service sends racing news to over 200 drops in Chicago, as well as to about 50 drops in the surrounding area in Illinois. The list does not designate the occupation of the subscribers or drops, but in the case of R. and H. and Midwest, both of which are themselves subdistributors, it is safe to assume that the listed drops are, almost without exception, handbook or lay-off establishments. Some idea of the magnitude of the operations involved can be obtained from a review of the income of a number of the members of the Capone syndicate who have been actively engaged in gambling. Louis Campagna told the committee that his bookmaking operations in Cicero netted about $80,000 to $90,000 a year before his conviction in the movie extortion case. Harry Russell, who operated as a lay-off man for bookies in Kansas City, Omaha, and locations in Indiana and Michigan, was a partner with Accardo in the Owl Club, a bookie operation in Calumet City. In 1946, Russell reported an income of $26,000 from the club, and Accardo's share in the take has been as high as $45,000 in 1 year. In 1948, Joseph Corngold and Willie Heeney, members of the Cicero contingent of the Capone mob, grossed $51,000 on the handbook operation of the El Patio Club in Cicero.

The committee also heard testimony as to the extent of large bookie operations outside the immediate environs of Chicago. The income tax return of Charles Fischetti, who with his brother Rocco ran the lavish Vernon Country Club, showed a total net income of over $22,000 believed to be attributable to the gambling operations of the club. The Big House, a gambling place operated in nearby Indiana by William Gardner, Sonny Sheets, and Harry Hyams, who have close connections with the Chicago syndicate, took in $9,000,000 in 1948. William Spellisy, who operates on the Midwest wire service in Morris, Ill., testified that his handbook operations grossed $200,000 per annum, and Thomas Cawley, who operates on the Midwest wire service in La Salle County, showed a net profit of $68,000 from a half-interest in handbook and other large-scale gambling operations in La Salle and Streator.

Jack Doyle, gambling king of Gary, Ind., another subscriber to the wire service, conducts a large-scale handbook operation in that city along with other forms of gambling. Because of his political connections he is unmolested by law-enforcement officials. The profits from his illegal operations are enormous. Doyle told the committee nothing, but his detailed records on horse-race betting, poker roulette, craps, and slot-machine operations told much. From a mere $8,000 in 1943, his profits jumped to $120,000 in 1948.

SLOT MACHINES MADE IN CHICAGO

Most of the coin machines in use throughout the country are manufactured in and around Chicago, and a large number of the machines have been purchased and operated inside the State of Illinois. The manufacture and distribution of slot machines has been a lucrative field of operation for a number of Capone mobsters. The Taylor Manufacturing Co. in Cicero, one of the largest manufacturers of gaming equipment in the country, is partially owned by Claude Maddox, a Capone mobster with a long criminal record, and Joseph Aiuppa, a close friend of Accardo and one of the leading members of the Capone syndicate. Over the past 3 years, the gross income of this operation has averaged between $200,000 and $300,000 a year.

Listed in its record of customers are some of the largest gambling establishments in the country. Total sales of gambling equipment by this company to one plush gambling establishment alone, the Hyde Park Club, were $75,000 for a period of 3 years.

The merchandising of coin machines and particularly slot machines is a business peculiarly adapted to the sales technique of the underworld, and a number of Chicago mobsters have been active in this field. Ed Vogel, old-time Capone henchman who evaded service of subpena by the committee, is believed to control the distribution of slot machines in the North Side of Chicago and in the northwest suburbs. Vogel has a partnership interest in lucrative cigarette vending and juke box distributing business. Through arrangement with the owner of a privately operated golf club, Vogel has been collecting for years from the operation of the slot machines at the club on the basis of 60 percent for the club and 40 percent for Vogel. It is conservatively estimated that from this one source alone the revenue received by Vogel is $50,000 annually. Each week Vogel's representative and an employee of the club lock themselves in a room at the club and divide the take. The club was reimbursed by Vogel for the expense of new machines purchased by it. In the past year, the State police, on direction of Governor Stevenson and the State's attorney of Cook County, have made a concentrated effort to break up slot-machine operations in the State. State's Attorney Boyle testified that since November 1, 1949, his office had confiscated and destroyed 564 slot machines. Boyle testified that it was clear to him that a syndicate was behind the operations of the slot machines found in small taverns and gambling joints throughout the country because of the regularity with which slot machines reappeared in clubs that had been raided. During the period when the raids on slot machines were most intense, a number of hold-ups took place in private clubs that owned their own slot machines and the machines were removed from the premises. It seems apparent that the seizure of these slots was an effort by the syndicate to recoup their losses of machines seized by the law-enforcement agents.

SLOT-MACHINE PROFITS TEMPT RACKETEERS

The take on some of the slot machines operating in large gambling establishments, while not comparable to the sums taken in by some of the larger bookies, are tempting bait to the organized vultures operating in this field. Jack Doyle of Gary, Ind., reported ownership of 129 slot machines which brought in $60,000. Indicative of the size of Doyle's slot machine operation is the fact that in one year his expense for machines and parts totaled $24,000. The El Patio Club in Cicero grossed $23,000 on its slot-machine operations, and the Seven Gables, referred to before in connection with handbook operations, took in about $15,000 annually in the operation of its six slot machines. The 40-percent cut which Vogel, Francis Curry, and other members of the Capone syndicate are believed to take on the machines that they control constitutes a large-scale gambling racket, operating in the southern part of Illinois and across State lines into neighboring territories.

POLICY—BIG BUSINESS—BIG MUSCLE

The large sums of money which annually pass into the hands of the Chicago bookmakers are the accumulations of large and small bets placed by occasional bettors and professional gamblers alike. The committee's investigations revealed that the city of Chicago harbors another huge gambling operation whose income in the millions is built upon a foundation of nickels, dimes, and quarters. It is estimated that the play on the policy wheels in Chicago's south side totaled for the past 5 years $150,000,000.

The densely populated South Side area of Chicago has for years been a fertile territory for the operation of policy wheels. Theodore Roe, a long-time policy operator estimated before the committee that 60 to 70 percent of the population of this area bet on the numbers to be drawn in the so-called policy wheel. There are approximately 15 to 20 wheels in operation in Chicago, 7 or 8 of which have a total play approximating 3 to 5 million dollars annually. The payoff on the wheels rarely goes above $50 to a bettor. In some instances when combinations are hit, the payoff may be 100 to 1. The placing of bets is handled by hundreds of low-paid employees and so-called commission writers who take and report the thousands of small wagers made each day. Bets are either made with a writer who goes from door to door with a book on which numbers can be played, or a would-be bettor can go to an established betting station and place a bet on the number to be drawn. In 1942 a number of the important policy racketeers, including Peter Tremont and Pat Manno (alias Manning), long-time associates of the Capone syndicate, were indicted by a Cook County grand jury for a conspiracy to operate a lottery. The subsequent trial resulted in a verdict of not guilty because of failure of the principal grand jury witness to testify. With the exception of this unsuccessful grand-jury action no major efforts have been made to break up Chicago's huge policy operation.

Theodore Roe could recall only one of his employees who had ever received a jail sentence in connection with his policy operations. Fines average from $25 up, and are absorbed by the wheel operator. Judging from sums taken out of the policy operations by the men who control them, these fines amount to no more than a reasonable expense of doing business.

Although for the most part the policy racket has operated in predominantly Negro sections of the city, the Capone syndicate has found the territory a fertile source of revenue. Peter Tremont and Pat Manno control the operations of the Rome-Silver Wheel and the Standard Golden Gate. From their gaudily named operations

Tremont and Manno have averaged an annual take of from $80,000 to $100,000. The lesser partners in these two wheels, Fred, Tom, Jeff, and Sam Manno, brothers of Pat, have netted $50,000. The play on the wheels runs over $5,000,000 annually. In 1946, Pat Manno was linked with others in an effort by Chicago racketeers to take over a $14,000,000 annual gambling policy and other racket activities in Dallas County, Tex. The committee heard testimony to the effect that a hoodlum known as Paul Jones came to Dallas in 1946 in an attempt to make arrangements with the Dallas police and sheriff-elect of Dallas County on behalf of the Chicago syndicate for undisturbed racket operations in Dallas. Lt. George Butler, one of the police officials approached, testified that Pat Manno had appeared in Dallas to convince the Dallas officials and local racketeers of the authenticity of Jones' scheme. A recording was made of Manno's conversation during this visit. On the record, Manno stated that he had been in the policy business for 17 years in the city of Chicago.

Jones and others involved in the scheme to take over Dallas County were indicted and convicted of attempted bribery, but the Texas police never took any action against Manno in this connection.

The frankness of the recorded statement in the files of the committee is an interesting contrast to Manno's testimony, or lack thereof before this committee. He refused to answer most of the committee's questions on the grounds that he might incriminate himself, questions relating to his visit to Dallas, his acquaintance with Jones, his business associations with Peter Tremont or any aspects of his policy operations.

GANGSTER'S OWN DESCRIPTION OF OPERATIONS

The records of Paul Jones' and Pat Manno's negotiations with the Dallas officials amply corroborates the existence and method of operation of organized criminals. Typical are the following recorded statements of Manno, whom his associate called the No. 5 man in the Chicago syndicate:

Sure. Once you get organized, you don't have to worry about money. Everything will roll in in a nice quiet manner, in a business-like way. You don't, he don't have to worry about it personally. Everybody will be happy I'm sure. * * *

We're not going to come from Chicago down here * * * all local fellows. We're leaving that to him. He's representing us * * * and keep the, like calls, the muscle men, these petty * * *. These people can be called in too, you know * * *

One thing I'm against, always was against. I don't like, like I was telling you last night, five or six joints in the radius of six blocks, a joint every block. That's one thing I've always talked against. I like one big spot and that's all. Out in the country, out of the city entirely. * * *

I don't run any of those places up there, gambling or anything like that. I got my own territory. I got certain business that I take care of for the last 16 or 17 years. I do very well, living comfortably, worry about nothing. As far as the set-up, these places like dice rooms or horse rooms and things like that, that's like another department I would call it. If I had a fellow sitting here with me that runs a certain game, he could give it to you in a minute. He could tell you what to expect and all that sort of stuff you see. But I have my own little concession, and that's the end. * * * Well, that's my business, policy. Policy is my business. That I could run. * * * I've been at it for 17 years.

The oldest, and probably the largest wheel now operating in Chicago is the Maine-Idaho-Ohio wheel, originally known as the Jones brothers wheel. Theodore Roe and the Jones brothers are partners in this wheel. The play on this wheel amounts to about $6,000,000 per-year; the net income for 1949 was close to $700,000 and for 1948 it came to over $997,000. It is interesting to note that the gross for 1949 was about $1,000,000, and the gross for 1948 was about $1,300,000. In 1946, Edward Jones, one of the partners in the Jones brothers wheel, was kidnaped and held for ransom. The ransom demanded was $250,000. George Jones, a brother of the kidnaped Edward, negotiated with the unknown persons who were holding Edward. One hundred thousand dollars in ransom was paid, and Edward Jones was released. He left Chicago about a week later and has since resided in Mexico, although he continues to draw sums approximating $200,000 a year from the operations of the wheel. In his testimony before the committee, Jones stated that he had no idea who his kidnapers were, and that they had made no mention of the proceeds of the policy wheel. It may be noted, however, that Jacob Guzik recorded, simply as "from various sources," without explanation a single item of income in the amount of $100,000 for the year 1946.

The only large policy wheel operated by white persons other than the Rome-Silver and Standard-Golden Gate, which are owned by the Capone mobsters, Peter Tremont and Patrick Manno, is the Erie-Buffalo. This wheel, the gross play of which runs to $5,000,000 annually, was for years operated by the Benvenuti brothers. Because of favors done for Al Capone by the elder brother Julius, the mob laid off this wheel.

After the death of Capone and Julius, conditions changed rapidly. In 1947, Caesar and Leo owned the Erie-Buffalo wheel which netted them approximately $105,000 each from its operation. As a lucrative side line, the Benvenutis operated a paper company which supplied policy slips to wheels within and outside of the State of Illinois. This same year, Sam Pardy received as income $1,500 from the Benvenutis. His total income had never exceeded $5,000. In the same year, the homes of both Caesar and Leo were bombed. The muscle started.

In the year 1948, drastic changes took place in the internal organization of the Erie-Buffalo wheel. Suddenly Sam Pardy and Tom Manno, a brother of Pat and a junior partner in the Rome-Silver and Standard-Golden Gate wheels, appear as partners in Erie-Buffalo, each netting for 1948 from the operation of Erie-Buffalo $305,000 each. Tom Manno's income from the two Capone wheels in past years had been a mere $40,000. His vacancy was filled by his brother Sam Manno. Caesar and Leo Benvenuti contented themselves with receiving payments of $50,000 each from the wheel they previously owned.

In 1949, the new partners, Pardy and Manno, received $135,000 each from the Erie-Buffalo. Their "associates" Leo and Caesar Benvenuti were paid the same $50,000 each.

In the Erie-Buffalo records, a single significant item appeared in 1949 under the heading of "Special services." The amount covered under this item was $278,000, which was paid to the partnership of Anthony Accardo and Jacob Guzik. What the special services were bore no explanation. The result is self-evident. Three of the largest policy wheels in operation were under the dominance and control of the mob. In the middle of 1950, the Benvenutis left for an extended visit to Europe.

LEGISLATORS OPPOSE ANTICRIME LAWS

Substantial testimony was adduced before the committee that certain members of the State legislature, particularly those living in districts most heavily infested by racketeers, vote against legislation designed to curb gangster activities and urged for passage by the vigorous Chicago Crime Commission and associate freely with their gangster constituents. Roland Libonati, Democratic State senator from the West Side, and a close associate of Capone's, spearheaded the opposition to the reform legislation proposed by the Chicago Crime Commission and Governor Stevenson and backed by the bar. Representative James J. Adducci, Republican member of the bipartisan coalition against reform, has represented Chicago's West Side for 17 years. Adducci has been arrested a number of times in company with Capone mobsters and admitted to accepting campaign contributions from Lawrence Mangano, a well-known figure in the Capone hierarchy, explaining that in his district it was necessary to "accept finances from any kind of a business." Adducci has recently been indicted on the basis of his testimony before the committee that he received commissions amounting to $6,000 a year for securing orders from the State for printing and supplies.

It was perfectly obvious, as must be the case wherever large-scale law violations exist, that many of the law enforcement officials have been corrupted, although in the time available to the committee, only a few cases could be found where direct payments to police could be established. On the other hand, the committee heard and saw shocking evidence of inefficient or nonexistent law enforcement; of unexplained wealth enjoyed by low-salaried police officials; of brazen neglect of duty on the part of local officials, and in some localities, of apathy amounting to approval on the part of the public.

Evidence of individual police payoffs is difficult to uncover, and it was neither possible nor desirable for this committee to engage in a prolonged search for specific instances of corruption. As John Rosselli, onetime Capone henchman, frankly stated before the committee, the wire service, the handbooks, the slot machines, and the other rackets which have thrived in the city of Chicago cannot operate without local corruption; if the handbooks are open, the conclusion is inescapable that the police are being paid off.

PUNCHBOARDS

There are 30 to 40 punchboard manufacturers in the United States. The boards are shipped in interstate commerce. Their use in most of the States is contrary to local law. The Sax interests in Chicago are probably the largest makers of punchboards. There are about six or seven other leading producers. Total sales by all manufacturers is about $10,000,000 annually.

Of the total number of boards produced, 95 percent are so-called straight money or gambling boards. The remaining 5 percent are used for the merchandising of candy, cigars, cigarettes, etc. But even this type of board is often used for gambling.

Punchboards vary in price from $2 up, depending on the type and elaborateness of the board. A common type of board which sells for $2 will pay out $80 in prize money on a $120 total play, a

$38 profit on a $2 investment. If, as sometimes happens, the board is destroyed before the large money prizes are punched, the profit may be greater.

Some distributors and jobbers place the boards in locations on a commission basis, splitting the profits with the proprietor on a 50–50 basis.

Testimony was given to the committee that some concerns, for an additional cost over and above that of the board, will furnish a key to the board. In such circumstances, the probable profits to the proprietor and the chance of winning by the gullible gambler are obvious. The victimizing of the proprietor by a confederate of the jobber who has the key to the winning numbers is another method of operation.

The use of punchboards for gambling is on the increase. They provide a great incentive to gambling. A variation of the punchboard is the penny pushcards which have great attraction for children. Cease and desist orders of the Federal Trade Commission against the use of these boards have been upheld by the courts.

It is, of course, not possible to estimate with any great degree of exactitude the annual sum played on punchboards. In view of the number of boards manufactured, the committee believes that to estimate this figure to be $100,000,000 would be conservative.

CRIME CONDITIONS IN ILLINOIS

Cook County.—Law enforcement in the city of Chicago is primarily the responsibility of the mayor and the commissioner of police. Outside the city, but within the boundaries of Cook County, lie a number of incorporated villages each with its own mayor and its own chief of police. These areas are also under the jurisdiction of the State's attorney and the county sheriff, but the testimony before the committee revealed a pattern of continuing attempts to shift responsibility from one law enforcement agency to another.

As in other cities, the committee found that gambling operations were even more extensive and wide open just outside the city limits. The committee found evidence of lush gambling operations in Cicero, Burnham, Melrose Park, and other of the incorporated villages just outside Chicago.

Law enforcement in the areas outside the city has been particularly lax because of the ineffectiveness of the sheriff's office under former Sheriff Elmer M. Walsh, who did not stand for re-election, and his predecessors, and the indifference or outright dishonesty of the local chiefs of police. Sheriff Walsh's excuse for this laxity was lack of adequate personnel and lack of jurisdiction. The ward sponsorship system, which results in a complete turn-over of personnel in the sheriff's office with the election of each new sheriff, cannot possibly yield an effective enforcement agency.

In 1949, gambling conditions in the area outside Chicago had reached proportions which made it necessary for the State's attorney for the county to undertake gambling raids. Anthony A. Gherscovich, administrative assistant to the State's attorney, told the committee that prior to that time, the State's attorney's office had notified the sheriff and the chiefs of police of gambling operations within their jurisdiction but that nothing had been done to stop them. As a result of the raids conducted by the State's attorney, a number of chiefs of police were indicted.   Henry Wlekinski, the chief of police of Calumet City, indicted for malfeasance in office, admitted to the jury that gambling was rampant in the city.   He defended his action on the grounds that the license fees from illegal taverns were supporting the town and were responsible for the low tax rate enjoyed by its citizens. On the basis of this defense, he was acquitted of the charges and remains in office as chief of police.   Gambling operations appeared to be unimpeded when this committee visited Calumet City.

A similar situation existed in Melrose Park where Rocco de Grazia, Capone mobster, has operated the famous Lumber Gardens and other wide-open establishments for years.   The chief of police was notified of these operations by the State's attorney's office, but took no action to stop or curtail this wide-open gambling operation.   He was indicted for nonfeasance but acquitted, and is still in office.   The pattern is repeated in Cicero, which has had three chiefs of police in recent years, but which is still the seat of lucrative gambling operations by a number of members of the Capone syndicate.   The records of the chiefs of police in these towns, where gambling joints could be identified merely by walking down the street, are records of neglect of official duty and shocking indifference to violations of law.   Equally shocking is the acquiescence of the people of the towns, as evidenced by the acquittal of these men and their continuation in office.

A reason for lack of conscientious enforcement of gambling laws was disclosed by the testimony of Police Capt. Dan Gilbert, known as the world's richest cop and for many years chief investigator for the office of the State's attorney for Cook County.   Gilbert, democratic candidate for sheriff of Cook County, testified before the committee that he placed bets himself with a well-known Chicago betting commissioner.   He admitted this was not legal betting.   In explanation, he testified, "I have been a gambler at heart."   Although agreeing that raids could be initiated by his office on bookies in the city, Gilbert admitted it had not been done since 1939, despite the fact that practically every bookmaking establishment in the city of Chicago was listed in the recently published hearings before the McFarland subcommittee of the Senate Interstate and Foreign Commerce Committee.

Grundy and La Salle Counties.—The story of local corruption and indifference which was repeated many times in testimony before the committee, is not confined to the locality of Cook County.   In 1950, at the direction of Governor Stevenson, the State police made a number of raids on known gambling joints.   Among the places raided was the Seven Gables Tavern in Grundy County, which contained a bookie operation with a play of about $200,000 a year, a crap table, a roulette wheel, and slot machines which were repaired by the father of the State's attorney for Grundy County.   The gambling operations were apparently wide open, but William Spellisy, proprietor of the tavern, testified that he had never been bothered by the police before the 1950 raid.

The committee also heard testimony regarding large-scale bookie and slot machine operations in neighboring La Salle County.

Thomas Cawley admitted in his testimony that he had operated two books, roulette and a crap table for about 15 years in the towns of La Salle and Streator.   Cawley testified that his large gambling operations were generally known, but that he had never been disturbed by the sheriff or the chief of police. Cawley denied that he had paid money for protection, but admitted making political contributions, and a close friendship with Mike Welter, ex-sheriff of La Salle County who was frequently visited by Francis Currie and Claude Maddox, old-time members of the Capone syndicate. Cawley testified before this committee that he received occasional orders to close operations, but that such orders were overlooked in a short time and operations resumed. When Mr. Cawley first testified before the committee in October 1950, he stated that operations in the county had been slowed down in the preceding 3 months, but by the time of his second appearance in December, gambling was proceeding as usual in La Salle County. Cawley told the committee that his operations were possible because 90 percent of the people in the county wanted it that way, and his point was proved by the election as sheriff of a man who openly supported gambling in La Salle County.

Madison and St. Clair Counties.—The committee heard from a number of citizens who stated that slot machines could be found "in such places as drug stores, confectioneries and even grocery stores" at all times since 1927 to the present. A notorious vice district known as the Valley ran without interference until closed by Federal military authorities. A grand jury in 1946, although plagued by lack of cooperation from prosecuting officials, found appalling vice and gambling conditions in St. Clair County. The committee heard testimony about similar wide-open conditions in Madison County.

Most shocking in Madison and St. Clair Counties was the utter blindness of law-enforcement officials and the evidence of their unexplained income. The testimony of John English, commissioner of public safety of East St. Louis, that he knew of no major law violations in his city seemed to the committee to verge on the incredible. He testified that he had never done anything to disturb the operations of Carroll and Mooney and did not know that they were among the biggest bookmakers in the country although this has been notorious on a Nation-wide basis for a long time. He stated that the first time he knew anything about Mooney's operations was when he read it in the papers. He also told the committee that it was his understanding that Carroll was violating no Federal or Illinois law. The committee asked him about a number of other well-known bookmakers whose operations were common knowledge in his area, but the commissioner asserted he knew nothing about them. He admitted having stated publicly that in his opinion "it was all right to bet any place else if they wanted to make a bet." With this kind of an attitude, it is no wonder that law was flagrantly disregarded in East St. Louis.

The committee had no better impression of the law-enforcement activities of Adolph Fisher who testified that he had been sheriff of St. Clair County from 1946 until 1950. Although the operations of C. J. Rich & Co. and of the Carroll-Mooney partnership were notorious throughout the United States, Sheriff Fisher, in whose county they were operating, told the committee he knew nothing about them. In fact, he testified that he first learned about Mooney and Carroll when this committee's investigation started. When it was pointed out to him that it had been a matter of public record as a result of Carroll's own testimony before the Senate Committee on Interstate and Foreign Commerce some months earlier, Sheriff Fisher corrected his testimony to say that at that time he sent a deputy down to the establishment but found nothing going on. He could not recall whether he sent the deputy in the daytime or nighttime or whether any efforts were made to follow up the investigation. This committee's investigators, however, had no difficulty whatever discovering the Carroll-Mooney operation going at full steam.

A similar picture was presented through the testimony of Mr. Dallas Harrell who had been sheriff of Madison County from 1946 to 1950. His very frank answer to a question of why he took no action in putting out of business large gambling establishments such as the 200 Club was that he left that up to the cities and "if the mayor and the chief of police and the citizens of Madison, the city of Madison, were satisfied with it, it suited me."

Although Sheriff Harrell testified that there were no commercial slot machines in Madison County while he was sheriff, the committee learned that the Bureau of Internal Revenue's list of persons who had paid the $100-per-annum tax on establishments in which slot machines were maintained had been published in the newspapers of St. Louis. Sheriff Harrell stated that he knew this; nevertheless no action was taken against slot machines.

There can be little doubt in the minds of the committee that "wide open" conditions flourish in Madison and St. Clair Counties because of protection and "payoffs." Commissioner English, for example, never gave a satisfactory explanation of his large accumulation of assets since he became commissioner of public safety, nor the nature of the so-called "political contributions" which he reported as income. Chief of Police John Vickery, of Fairmont City, Ill., who had previously been a coal miner, first began to sport a Cadillac car and a $1,200 diamond ring when he became police chief. Perhaps his attitude toward bookmaking explains his sudden wealth. When asked why he permitted a bookmaking establishment to operate within a block of his police station, his answer was "I just never had had no complaint about it."

TAMPA

The committee hearings in Tampa were conducted against a backdrop of gangland violence and vengeance pointed up by a sordid record of more than a dozen racket killings and six attempted assassinations in less than two decades.

Through this bloody history runs the obscure but sinister shadow of Mafia operations, with its accompanying links between the criminal overlords of Tampa and their counterparts in other sections of the country. The committee could not make an adequate investigation of the Mafia background of these murders because all suspected Mafia adherents vanished from their homes and usual haunts when it became known that the committee intended to investigate their activities. Months have passed since the committee's visit to Tampa, but these men have continued to evade process. It is freely stated in the particular circles in which they operate that they intend to remain in secret refuges until the life of this committee expires.

In Tampa, as in other cities visited by the committee, there was found the same dismal pattern of corruption of public officials by entrenched gambling interests which the committee has found in other cities. There is testimony in the committee's record showing that these interests have resorted to the customary policy of outright bribery and have channeled substantial amounts of money into political campaigns, manifestly for the control they can exercise over law-enforcement officers. The committee's findings in Tampa led to the inescapable conclusion that the gambling element over a long period of years has throttled any and all efforts to secure an adequate degree of law enforcement in this community.

BOLITA GAMES THRIVE IN TAMPA

The principal source of revenue for the gambling fraternity in Tampa is a variation of the numbers racket known as bolita. The pattern of operations is similar to the numbers racket in other parts of the country but with some variation in the systems of drawing the numbers. The committee has also established that the system of distributing the bolita business among the existing bolita bankers is different from the methods employed in other cities in arriving at an equitable division of the spoils.

The committee found elsewhere that those engaged in the numbers racket were inclined to establish territorial limitations within which numbers banks could operate. In Tampa the bolita operators were free to operate anywhere within the territory. However, each banker received an assignment of men who were charged with the obligation of picking up the day's play and these men in turn were furnished with the names of specific places where bolita was sold. Thus the operations of any particular bank were limited to a specific number of selling points and an adequate number of pick-up men to cover these points, regardless of geographical location.

Apparently bolita operations do not run smoothly in Tampa. The last two gangland killings involved leading principals in the operation of the bolita racket. Jimmy Velasco was killed on December 12, 1948, and Jimmy Lumia on June 5, 1950. No one was convicted of either murder nor of any of the other Tampa gangland slayings, with one exception in 1932.

Admittedly, the participation of the Mafia in Tampa's series of murders and attempted assassinations is predicated on inferences. As is well known, intimidation and threats of retaliation operate to silence witnesses of homicides traceable to this organization. However, an analysis of the existing information produces some enlightening facts which are susceptible of being woven into an easily recognizable pattern. Connections with other cities are clearly shown by the record. One of the fugitives from the committee's process was Santo Trafficante, Sr., reputed Mafia leader in Tampa for more than 20 years. It is an undisputed fact that a search of the effects of Jack Dragna, one of the alleged Mafia leaders on the Pacific coast, yielded the telephone number of Trafficante and also that of the late Jimmy Lumia.

The lamentable state of the files of Tampa killings, kept by the Tampa Police Department, was emphasized by the testimony of Chief of Police M. C. Beasley. In fairness to Chief Beasley, it must be pointed out that he had occupied his position only 5 months prior to the time he was called to testify before the committee and the responsibility for the condition of the department's records was not attributable to him.

Requested to produce the files concerning the gangland killings in which the committee was interested, Chief Beasley was forced to admit that in many of the cases there were no files at all, and that in most of the remainder the information was extremely sparse. Whether the disappearance of the records was a matter of accident, carelessness, or design was not readily discernible.

POLICE FILES ON MURDERS MISSING

One of the missing files dealt with a character known as George "Saturday" Zerrate, twice made a target of gangland vengeance. On November 10, 1936, he was shot at Eighth Avenue and Fourteenth Street in Tampa by two gunmen in a car, firing sawed-off shotguns. He was also attacked by gunfire on another occasion at his home in the 2100 block of Nebraska Avenue. Zerrate's career was marked by an arrest in New York as a suspect in dope trafficking with Charles "Lucky" Luciano. The only murder conviction in Tampa during the past two decades was that involving Zerrate's brother, Mario, who was given a life sentence for the killing of Armando Valdez, a wholesale produce dealer, in 1932. Oddly enough, the records in the Valdez slaying also were missing from the police department files.

Another significant tie-up with the Mafia appeared in the murder of Joe Vaglichi, alias Joe Vaglichio. He died in a hail of shots poured from shotguns wielded by assassins in a passing car outside his sandwich stand early on the morning of July 29, 1937. There were no arrests and Vaglichi's past history caused police at the time to credit his death to Mafia internal conflict. Vaglichi was one of 23 Italian gansters rounded up by the Cleveland Police Department in a hotel in that city in December 1928 after the Cleveland police had been tipped off that Mafia leaders were congregating there for a meeting. Thirteen revolvers were found among the 23 prisoners, who also included Ignazio Italiano of Tampa. Vaglichi also had been tabbed by authorities in subsequent years as a killer in the pay of the Mafia for jobs in New York, Chicago, Detroit, and New York, although never convicted. He also was reported to have had a brother in the Chicago rackets who had been a bodyguard for Al Capone. The Tampa police file on the Vaglichi slaying was limited to a newspaper report of the murder, Vaglichi's criminal record, and a statement about the killing. There were no investigative reports of any kind.

Indications of a New Orleans connection with the Tampa killings were found in the circumstances surrounding the murder of Ignacio Antinori, slain by a masked gunman in a suburban tavern in October of 1940. Information in the hands of the committee was to the effect that the murder weapon was traced to a New Orleans store where it had been purchased by a man who gave the obviously false name of John Adams. The date of the purchase was October 7, 1939, which was only 5 days before the murder of Mario Perla. Whether the same gun figured in both murders was not made clear. Antinori had been at odds with the syndicate controlling Tampa gambling for 3 years before he was slain. He was the father of Paul and Joe Antinori who have been involved in narcotics activities.

Chief Beasley, with nearly a quarter of a century of police experience in Tampa except for the period between 1942 and 1946 when he served in the Armed Forces, gave the committee his views on the existence of the Mafia in the following testimony:

Question. Do you believe there is a Mafia or syndicate?
Answer. I absolutely do; yes.
Question. Do you believe—you do?
Answer. I believe it does exist.
Question. Would you like to tell us what your concept of the Mafia is and its effect on these murders and witnesses?
Answer. My concept of the Mafia is that—well, I believe it consists of Italian people who have come from the southern part of Italy, Sicily—I believe they are known as Sicilians—that have immigrated into this country through the immigration channels in the early part of Mussolini's regime.   There were criminal bands, as I have read the history of it, running wild and rampant over Italy and Sicily especially, that came over here and, as a result, we have the Al Capones and other different people that organize into a crime syndicate.   I believe that those people got themselves into this crime syndicate through a lot of political influence, higher than I am and higher than—I think I would be small fry to the contacts that they have.
Question. From your investigation of these various murders, do you feel that any of those were perpetrated as a direct result of a Mafia order?
Answer. I can only assume that it was, because of the circumstances that surrounded each one of them.   I have not had the direct testimony that we could convict in court on.
Question. We appreciate that.   We did not ask, would not ask you for an opinion on something like that.   As to the actual triggerman, the gunman, in some of these killings, do you feel that they are local members of the Mafia, or that they are imported gunmen?
Answer. I always judged that they were imported, because they had far-reaching activities, just like you show in your chart there, and they have—it would be foolish for one of them who is well known in the city of Tampa to go out on the street, even in the day or night, and perpetrate a shooting there.   Then there has been evidence that you will find in these records that will trace some of the actual implements of death, trace it back to different cities out of Tampa.

NOBODY GOES TO JAIL FOR GAMBLING

Law-enforcement officials in Tampa have been unable to cope with violence stemming from organized crime.   They have also been unable to enforce the gambling laws of the State.   In the city of Tampa and Hillsborough County for the period of January 1 to September 1, 1950, only 96 arrests for gambling violations were made and not one of those apprehended landed in jail.   Forty-five of those arrested forfeited bonds and the charges against 43 others were dismissed.   Only six defendants were fined and there were two cases pending as of September 1, 1950.

It should be noted that much of the violence in Tampa arises out of the failure on the part of the police department to enforce the gambling laws.   Antinori, Lumia, and Velasco, three victims of gangland killings, all had at one time or another before their deaths held the tenuous title of king of Tampa gambling.

The close alliance between gambling and violence in Tampa is also illustrated by the testimony of Charles M. Wall, a recognized power in gambling activities in the Tampa area for nearly a half century. Over a 14-year period, Wall was the target of three attempts on his life.   Wall, who managed to escape on all three occasions, blandly insisted that he knew of no reason why anyone would try to murder him and admitted that no one had ever been arrested for these abortive attempts to kill him.

A large portion of the testimony in Tampa dealt with the impact of unchecked gambling on the community. The committee's investigations have conclusively demonstrated that illegal gambling cannot thrive without protection from law-enforcement officials. The Tampa testimony bristles with allegations of bribes to law-enforcement officials and categorical denials from such officials.

The central figures in this welter of confusing testimony are Sheriff Hugh L. Culbreath, State attorney J. Rex Farrior, and retired Chief of Police J. L. Eddings. Sheriff Culbreath had his opportunity to refute the accusations of graft and official misconduct at the Tampa hearing and again in Washington. Farrior appeared in Washington and denied that he was the recipient of graft payments. The committee has no way to establish the truth or falsity of these denials. Nevertheless, when Farrior was questioned about the lax enforcement of the gambling laws in the Tampa area, he took refuge in double talk and attempted to evade responsibility by blaming others for his failures. Eddings was invited by the committee to appear in Washington but declined the opportunity to answer the allegations of misconduct voiced by several witnesses at the Tampa hearings.

It should be noted that after his appearance before this committee, Sheriff Culbreath was indicted by the grand jury of Hillsborough County, Fla., for taking bribes and for acts of nonfeasance and misconduct in office.

The committee does not wish to usurp the function of a trial jury and pass judgment on Culbreath. However, it should be noted that Culbreath has never satisfactorily explained to this committee how his net worth grew from approximately $30,000 to more than $100,000 during his years as sheriff of Hillsborough County. Nor did Sheriff Culbreath satisfactorily explain his association and business relationships with Salvatore "Red" Italiano, a notorious gang leader in the Tampa area, who has consistently evaded the subpena of this committee.

Difficult to understand also is the real estate deal between Culbreath and John Torrio, Capone's predecessor in Chicago. Finally, the committee must continue to wonder at how a sheriff sworn to uphold the law could permit his brother and one of his employees to carry on bookmaking operations, right in the county jail.

CLEVELAND

Organized crime in the Cleveland area presents the familiar pattern of a mob that had grown rich and powerful during prohibition days in the illicit liquor business and which transferred its activities after repeal to the even more lucrative field of gambling. The Cleveland gambling syndicate consists primarily of the following individuals: Morris Kleinman, Samuel "Gameboy" Miller, Moe Dalitz (alias Davis), Louis Rothkopf (alias Rhody and Zarumba), Samuel Tucker, and Thomas J. McGinty. Affiliated with the syndicate is an accountant, Alvin Giesey, who also functioned as secretary for certain corporations owned by the syndicate. The attorney for many of the operations of the syndicate is Samuel T. Haas. Haas was sought by the committee for questioning but has until recently evaded service of a subpena by going to Jamaica, British West Indies. This group has enjoyed close relationships and associations with certain gangsters and musclemen, who also participated in enterprises conducted by the gambling syndicate. Included in this latter group are the two Polizzis, Alfred and Albert ("Chuck"), John and George Angersola (alias King), James Licavoli, Jerry Milano, Joseph DiCarlo, and others.

The syndicate's major field of operations has been the conduct of gambling casinos at which all forms of gambling were provided, from roulette to craps, from chuckaluck to horse bets and slot machines. However, in the many different communities in which the syndicate penetrated, it never had the monopoly which one has come to associate with syndicate operations. Thus local mobs ran competing gambling enterprises. It should be noted, however, that in certain instances competing local enterprises were eventually absorbed by the syndicate and, in other cases, arrangements were entered into by which the plushier enterprises were operated by the syndicate in conjunction with local partners, while the less expensively appointed places catering to the average citizens were run by local characters.

GAMBLERS MOVE TO ADJACENT COUNTIES

The story of the Cleveland syndicate's gambling operations begins in the city of Cleveland itself. For many years gambling casinos like the Harvard Club, the Ohio Villa, and the Thomas Club ran wide open in the city of Cleveland. Governor Lausche, then a judge; Safety Director Eliot Ness, and Prosecutor F. T. Cullitan, acting in concert, closed these places in the early 1940's and they stayed closed. Prior to this time, however, the Cleveland syndicate had begun to expand into the counties outside of Cleveland itself. Apparently the heads of the Cleveland syndicate knew that their days in Cleveland itself were numbered and they had previously decided upon various hedging operations which took them and their illicit businesses into the outlying counties of Geauga, Lake, Trumbull, and Lawrence, where local sheriffs, prosecutors, and other persons charged with law enforcement were more susceptible to gangland influences. The Pettibone Club in Geauga County, the Mounds Club in Lake County, the Jungle Inn in Trumbull County, the Colony Club and the Continental Club in Lawrence County, and the Colonial Inn in Green County were among the most notorious establishments conducted by the Cleveland syndicate. These gambling clubs operated in open defiance of the law. Transportation was arranged for out-of-town and out-of-State participants in the gambling games. Players were brought to these clubs from West Virginia, Michigan, Illinois, Indiana, Kentucky, and other States. These gambling operations were finally shut down by the vigorous action of Gov. Frank J. Lausche, who used powers available to him under the State liquor and fire laws to enforce compliance with the State's gambling statutes.

The Cleveland syndicate, however, is resourceful, and is ever alert for opportunities to stay in business. Even prior to the shut-down of the various clubs in Ohio, plans were laid for an extension of syndicate operations into the wide-open communities of Campbell and Kenton Counties of northern Kentucky. Again the syndicate ran into local competition. In this area, the syndicate and the local talent operated such gambling enterprises as the Look-Out Club, the Beverly Hills Club, the Yorkshire Club, the Merchants Club, the Flamingo Club, the Latin Quarter, and the Kentucky Club.

A MILLION LOAN FOR DESERT INN

So rich did the Cleveland syndicate become from its operations that when Wilbur Clark needed over a million dollars to complete the plush Desert Inn at Las Vegas, he applied to the syndicate and obtained the money in return for which the syndicate acquired over 59 percent of this gambling enterprise. In addition, syndicate members also obtained interests in some of the gambling casinos in the Miami area, such as the Island Club, in which Samuel "Gameboy" Miller is a principal partner.

In the Ohio-Kentucky communities in which wide-open gambling has been carried on by the syndicate and by local hoodlums, officials are strangely afflicted with the inability to see the obvious, a disease which seems to afflict law-enforcement officials in wide-open communities everywhere. The police chief of Newport, Ky., was probably the only adult in the city who did not know that there were wide-open gambling houses in his community. Any taxi driver could have taken him to them. The casinos were so unconcerned with the possibility of interference with their operations that they advertised openly in the Cincinnati papers. In addition, streamers advertising the attractions at these places were placed on the windshields of automobiles. It should be noted that the gambling rooms of the establishments run by the syndicate in Campbell and Kenton Counties, Ky., shut down just before the committee hearings in Cleveland on January 17, 1951. It is significant that an advertising card has been circulated stating that Beverly Hills Country Club in Southgate, Ky., one of the syndicate establishments, advertised that it would reopen on April 1, 1951, which by a strange coincidence was 1 day after the anticipated expiration of the committee.

The failure of law-enforcement officials to enforce the gambling laws is the primary reason for the existence of the gambling casinos in Campbell and Kenton Counties. The failure is not accidental nor is it due to the mere inefficiency of local law-enforcement officials. As in other areas, the committee found a close financial and personal relationship between law-enforcement officials and the gambling interests. For example, the sheriff of Lawrence County guaranteed the water and gas bills of the Continental Club, a notorious gambling casino which was run by a convicted killer. The sheriff of Lucas County explained his sudden acquisition of wealth by stating that he had won considerable money in betting, although he had never made such sums prior to attaining the sheriff's office. A proprietor of electrical appliance stores, who also ran gambling casinos, supplied the sheriff of Trumbull County with various electrical appliances, including an $850 television set.

TAX ACCOUNTANT RACKETS PARTNER

Of particular interest in the Cleveland hearings are the relationships of Alvin Giesey to his racketeering employers. Alvin Giesey presents the familiar pattern of an accountant who had numerous gangster and racketeering clients. The cream of the Cleveland underworld had their tax returns prepared by Giesey. Giesey actually had a share in the illegal enterprises of his clients. He was an officer of two corporations which owned the land upon which gambling operations were conducted and he was also an officer in a corporation that operated the gambling casino itself.   In addition, he had a share of certain jukebox companies which did a considerable business in slot machines.

It was Giesey who gave the committee one of the clearest demonstrations of how the Federal Government may be defrauded of hundreds of thousands of dollars in taxes from the operations of gambling enterprises.   There was absolutely no way of guaranteeing the accuracy for tax purposes of the figures submitted to Giesey by the gambling enterprises.   Adequate books and records were not kept. Before the figures of income and outlay were submitted to Giesey, hundreds of thousands of dollars were probably taken off the top of the bank roll.   Giesey, like so many of the other accountants who serve gangsters, merely used the figures submitted and prepared the tax returns.   Although he was an experienced public accountant, he made no effort to verify any of the figures submitted to him.   Since the major portion of a gambling casino's business is in cash, no adequate check can be made to determine the accuracy of reported figures of income and outlay.

Two other matters brought out at the Cleveland hearings are significant.   The first relates to the typical muscling-in operation which took place in Youngstown, Ohio, and which was described in detail to the committee by Police Chief Allen.

Through the testimony of Chief Allen, and evidence before the committee in the case of Joseph Di Carlo, a typical enforcement operation was described.   Di Carlo was a criminal with a long and unsavory record in Buffalo, N. Y.   For reasons unknown, he decided to transfer his operations to Ohio, coming first to Cleveland and finally settling in Youngstown.   Shortly after his arrival in Youngstown, Di Carlo and his partners, Aiello and Caputo, made their rounds of the local bookies and advised them that as of a certain time, the partnership was going to take 50 percent of the gross receipts of the local bookies. Statements to this effect given to Chief Allen in 1948 by Manley, Alpern, Cavallaro, and Melik revealed two basic means of intimidation used by the Di Carlo partnership to effectuate its orders to the bookies.   First, the partnership threatened to use political influence to drive the bookies out if they did not succumb to the enforced arrangement and, second, they threatened physical violence.   These familiar muscling-in tactics resulted in a complete surrender on the part of the bookies.   This was the same Di Carlo who openly and contemptuously defied the committee when he was asked questions concerning his business operations and the sources of his livelihood.

The other situation relates to the wire service.   Arthur B. McBride, whose son is the nominal owner of Continental Press, described in some detail at the Cleveland hearing his key position in the distribution of gambling information to bookmakers for over a score of years through the wire service.   His testimony will be considered in the section of this report dealing with the wire service.   It should be noted here, however, that one of McBride's "tough boys" upon whom he depended during the days when he was involved in newspaper circulation and taxicab wars, was Morris "Mushy" Wexler.   Mushy, like so many of McBride's former musclemen, now holds a key position in the distribution of wire service for Continental Press in the Ohio area through his ownership of the Empire News Service.   Wexler could not be questioned as he evaded the service of a subpena, but in Ohio as elsewhere, although there is an attempted facade of respectability, the Empire News Service is primarily engaged in the distribution of gambling information to bookmakers.

DETROIT

The committee chose the Ford Motor Co.'s River Rouge plant as a laboratory in which to investigate the problem of large-scale, organized in-plant gambling, which disturbs the operations of many industrial centers throughout the country. The sole reason for focusing attention on the River Rouge plant was that it is believed to be the largest single manufacturing establishment in the world and no other significance should be attached to the choice of this plant. A Ford Motor Co. official stated that 69,000 persons were employed in an area which covers 1,212 acres. For this reason it was believed that there was probably a larger amount of in-plant gambling going on within the perimeter fence of this plant than anywhere else. The committee, however, did not find that there was more gambling going on per capita in this plant than in any other.

The Ford management, the union, the chief of police and an individual worker were in agreement that the practice of gambling was very widespread and that the principal problem was the numbers game or policy racket, but no one was able to give the committee exact figures. Gordon L. Walker, chief of the security department of the Ford Motor Co., stated that estimates of the annual amount gambled within the plant ran all the way from one to one hundred million dollars. He told the committee that he could not give any more informed estimate. It seems clear, however, that the figure is much in excess of the lower of the two figures suggested above. Saul A. Glazer testified that he had worked in the foundry at the River Rouge plant and that gambling was going on virtually everywhere. He stated that he knew of particular closets or rooms which were regularly used for gambling purposes, that many suppliers of parts or equipment who had counters would openly take bets or make numbers wagers over their counters and that it went so far that operators of overhead cranes would roll their cranes up and down buildings lowering buckets with their cranes into which wagers and money would be put.

One of the most interesting, although discouraging, aspects of this problem is that there appears to be a determined effort on the part of both management and labor to pass the responsibility from one to the other. The committee heard that on some occasions organized gamblers would throw very large funds into union elections in major locals in the Detroit area in the hopes of securing the election of officials who would tolerate in-plant gambling. Their use of money by gangsters to influence the outcome of union elections is unquestionably a perversion of the labor-union movement.

GAMBLING IN MOTOR PLANTS

It is the committee's belief that the numbers racket in Detroit plants is very highly organized. The bets are picked up by one group. The actual numbers are carried out of the plant by a second group. If this second group is arrested, they have no money in their possession and prosecution is difficult. A third group takes the money out and if these men are arrested they have nothing on them but currency which makes prosecution difficult. The money and the bets go to collectors and then on up to bankers. The committee was told by the police officials of the city that it was extremely difficult to press a case on anyone in the upper levels of the hierarchy of numbers. The committee notes with satisfaction, however, that one entire numbers system, or "Snoozy House," as it is called in Detroit, was recently successfully prosecuted.

In this connection the committee finds that not only in Detroit, but throughout the country, the members of the lower echelons in the numbers racket, who are not major criminals, are arrested, plead guilty, and receive fines. These fines are not paid by the persons convicted but are paid as a part of the cost of doing business by the big-scale numbers racket. These fines are purely a business expense to the major operators. They have no deterrent effect on the latter, nor on the minor characters in the racket, since they do not pay the fines. Jail for the minor operators appears to be the only way to effectively curb their operations.

As noted above, both labor and management shifted to each other the responsibility for plant gambling. It is the committee's opinion that neither management nor labor can be charged with the entire burden of suppressing plant gambling and that both should redouble their efforts to cooperate with law-enforcement officers. An agreement between labor and management that any person should be discharged after a fair hearing who is caught in gambling activities by either his shop steward, his foreman, the plant police or the city police, would go a long way toward terminating the evil.

GANGSTERS CONTROL HAUL-AWAY CONTRACTS

The committee, in its New York investigation, learned that the sole motor carrier hauling away Ford motorcars from the Edgewater, N. J., plant (under license of the Interstate Commerce Commission) was Automotive Conveying Co., of New Jersey, Inc., of which Joe Adonis was a very important stockholder as well as an officer. The committee therefore looked with especial interest into the relationship between the Ford Motor Co.'s Detroit area plants and their haul-away operators. It appeared that the sole haul-away operator was the E. & L. Transport Co. One Anthony D'Anna appeared to be a 50-percent stockholder of this corporation and it further appeared that he received a salary of $27,000 a year for which he did nothing so far as the committee was able to discover. The history of D'Anna's relation to the Ford Motor Co. is most obscure. D'Anna was of Sicilian birth. His father and two uncles died in what appeared to the committee to be Mafia-type murders. His father's slayer had in turn been murdered in a similar killing. D'Anna himself had been sentenced to prison for the attempted bribing of witnesses in connection with another Mafia-type rub-out. D'Anna testified that he was in the sugar business from 1925 until around 1930 and that he was selling sugar to persons whom he knew to be bootleggers. He also engaged in bootlegging with Joseph Massei, said to be chief emeritus of the Detroit underworld.

GANGSTERS STILL RETAIN LUSH CONTRACTS

The relationship between D'Anna and the Ford Motor Co. began in 1931. According to the testimony of the chief of police, whom the committee believed, Harry Bennett, then a very high official of the Ford Motor Co., telephoned to the chief and asked him to get hold of D'Anna and stated that he, Bennett, would meet him any place D'Anna chose. The chief of police then did find D'Anna, who agreed to go to Bennett's office. The chief drove D'Anna to Bennett's office at the Rouge plant. The committee heard privately but was unable to prove that Bennett said that he had sent for D'Anna to instruct him not to murder Joseph Tocco, who had a food concession at a Ford plant. The story which the committee heard but was unable to prove was that Bennett entered into an agreement that D'Anna would refrain from murdering Tocco for 5 years in return for the Ford agency at Wyandotte. As a matter of record, Joseph Tocco was not murdered until 7 years after this meeting. Also as a matter of record, D'Anna did become a 50-percent owner in the Ford agency at Wyandotte within a matter of weeks after the meeting. He remained in that position, although he put up only $6,000 and did substantially nothing in connection with the agency, until 1939 when it was transferred to his brother.

The story of Harry Bennett has been so thoroughly explored in the hearings of the National Labor Relations Board, in the press, and in published books that the committee will not once again go over the extraordinary and sordid story of a man who was certainly chief of staff to Henry Ford (although he described himself before this committee as his valet), who employed virtually a private army recruited from ex-convicts and criminals to engage in battles against labor and in other antisocial activities. The committee, however, called Bennett for the special purpose of asking him how it happened that a company in which Doto, alias Adonis, of New York, was an officer and large stockholder had received the Edgewater, N. J., haul-away contract and that D'Anna had received first the Ford agency at Wyandotte, Mich., and had then been allowed to act as a 50-percent stockholder and an officer in the carrier having the Detroit haul-away contract. Bennett testified, and the committee disbelieved him, that he had no knowledge of the Edgewater negotiations and that some official in New York must have attended to it. Bennett also could give the committee no satisfactory explanation of Ford's relationship to D'Anna. Bennett's testimony is also extraordinary from another point of view. He states that he made it a practice, although he was obviously in command of one of the largest corporations in the United States, not to keep files or records or memoranda of any kind. How D'Anna and Joe Adonis obtained such profitable relationships to Ford must therefore remain shrouded in mystery. The question which remains unanswered, however, is why, nearly 6 years after Bennett was removed from command of the Ford Motor Co., these two mobsters remain in lucrative relationships with this organization.

In fairness to Ford Motor Co., it should be noted that it is taking vigorous steps to disassociate itself from these racketeer-held contracts.

RACKETEER ASSOCIATIONS WITH MANUFACTURERS

The most important fact uncovered in the Detroit hearings of this committee was that some manufacturers have entered into and are today continuing intimate business relationships with racketeers for the purpose of affecting their labor relationships. The sad story uncovered by the committee is somewhat complicated because it operates in two stages. The first stage is that in which the Detroit, Mich., Stove Works, the president of which is John A. Fry, whose social respectability in the city of Detroit is beyond any question, entered into a relationship with one Santo Perrone, the obvious effect of which was to enlist the assistance of Perrone's gangster friends in Fry's labor problems. Perrone is an Italian-born naturalized citizen who has a criminal record including a 6-year sentence for violation of the prohibition laws. The second stage is that in which Fry's close friend, William Dean Robinson, likewise socially impeccable and a high official and now president of the Briggs Manufacturing Co., concocted a legal fiction whereby Perrone's son-in-law, Carl Renda, obtained a contract for doing nothing which has given him since 1946 an income ranging between fifty and one hundred thousand dollars a year, the real purpose of which was to have Perrone exert his and gangdom's influence in the Briggs Manufacturing Co.'s labor problems.

The Detroit, Mich., Stove Works is one of the largest of the non-automotive manufacturing plants in the Detroit area, and perhaps the largest nonunion plant in the Detroit area. Santo Perrone testified that he had worked for more than 40 years for the Detroit, Mich., Stove Works. It appeared that his education was such that he could barely read and write English and that he had difficulty in reading street signs. He could read simple names but could not read difficult street names. Although Perrone testified that he had never heard of any labor difficulty, a serious strike had occurred some years previously which required 75 or 80 policemen to guard the plant. Mr. Fry testified that approximately 25 percent of his employees observed the picket line during this strike. Fry, upon being pressed by the counsel of this committee, admitted that Perrone must have committed perjury when he stated that he had worked for 40 years at the plant and had never seen any labor trouble. He further admitted that he had asked various persons, including Perrone and his brothers, to bring in a lot of strikebreakers and that they had done so.

Shortly after this violent strike at the Detroit, Mich., Stove Works, Santo Perrone was given a contract to purchase and haul away scrap from the Detroit, Mich., Stove Works. Insofar as the committee was able to ascertain, this contract remains in effect today. Santo Perrone, also known as Sam Perrone, an illiterate manual laborer, thus acquired an income sufficient to permit him to live in a luxurious mansion in the Grosse Pointe area and to enjoy an income which in recent years has run between forty and sixty-five thousand dollars a year.

FICTION EMPLOYED TO INCREASE INCOME

Shortly after the scrap contract was awarded to Perrone, he and his brother Gaspar engaged in the illegal manufacture of whisky, which caused them to be sentenced to 6 years in the Federal penitentiary.

Gaspar, meanwhile, had also been taken care of by the stove works. He was by occupation a sand-core maker. At approximately the same time that his brother Santo received a lucrative contract to buy and haul away scrap, the stove works so arranged its operations that the coremaking department of the stove works was changed from an ordinary department of a manufacturing establishment to a subcontractorship, so that Gaspar employed his fellow core makers. Using the same equipment that he had been using for over 25 years and using company materials, he theoretically was the contractor who supplied the stove works with sand cores. Thus, a manual laborer in one of the departments of the stove works became, through some legal machinations, a contractor which in turn resulted in his receiving a very much higher income.

Shortly after the Perrone brothers went to prison, the United Auto Workers were able temporarily to organize the Detroit, Mich., stove workers. After the Perrones were released from prison, the organization disintegrated. It is not the function of this committee to inquire into labor disputes, but the committee must point out the sinister relationship between the lucrative contracts granted to the gangster Perrones and the ability of the Detroit, Mich., Stove Works to keep labor unions out of its plant.

SON-IN-LAW ALSO HAS CONTRACT

All of this is prefatory to the more striking story of the Briggs Manufacturing Co. John A. Fry and William Dean Robinson are close friends. They are the presidents, respectively, of the Detroit, Mich., Stove Works and the Briggs Manufacturing Co. Santo Peronne, who has the scrap contract with the stove company, is the father-in-law of Carl Renda; the latter acquired the scrap contract at the Briggs Manufacturing Co. The inference is permissible from the evidence before the committee that the officials of the Briggs Manufacturing Co. deliberately intended to follow the pattern of the Detroit, Mich., Stove Works in connection with labor relations.

The purchase, removal, and resale of scrap from a company as large as Briggs requires the following: Loading equipment with which to pick up scrap at the plant; trucks with which to haul the scrap out of the plant into a yard; a yard sufficiently large to unload, sort, and process scrap; equipment with which to bale, shear, or otherwise process scrap into usable units; a railroad siding at the yard; and further equipment with which to reload the scrap onto railroad cars or, in some cases, trucks.

Their testimony further was that the scrap-metal business was an intricate one which could not be quickly learned but which required very extensive experience. For approximately 18 years prior to the advent of Renda, the Woodmere Scrap Iron & Metal Co. had been engaged in the business of removing ferrous scrap from the Briggs plant in Detroit, using assets of about $500,000 in this operation. The contract to haul scrap was taken away from Woodmere and awarded to Renda despite the following facts:

1. Renda had left college within less than 1 year before he applied for the scrap contract.

2. He had no knowledge whatever of the scrap business.

3. He had no loading machinery with which to load the scrap.

4. He had no trucks with which to haul the scrap after it was loaded.

5. He had no yard in which to deposit the scrap upon delivery by trucks.

6. He had no machinery whatever to process the scrap.

7. He had no knowledge or skill whatever as to how the scrap should be processed or sorted.

8. He had no railroad siding where the scrap could be loaded.

9. He had no capital whatever to employ in the business.

10. He had no telephone at which he could be called to do business.

11. He had no office other than his hat in which business could be conducted.

BUT FORMER CONTRACTOR STILL HANDLES SCRAP

Nevertheless, Renda in April 1946 received a contract to haul ferrous scrap out of Briggs. This, however, did not disturb the operations of Woodmere. Since Renda, who had the contract to remove ferrous scrap from the largest independent auto-body manufacturer in the world, had no equipment, know-how, or capital whatsoever or any other qualification for this arrangement, it quickly became apparent to Briggs and to Renda himself that something had to be done to carry on the physical removal of scrap from Briggs to some appropriate yard. The upshot was that Renda contracted with Woodmere and other contractors who for many years had been removing the scrap. Renda had no economic function whatsoever in the operation. He did nothing. He was paid for doing nothing in connection with scrap. He was merely inserted in this operation so that he could receive an income which has ranged as high as $100,000 a year.

The committee regards it as obvious that Renda was being paid for something. While it was not proved by judicially admissible evidence, the inference is inescapable that what Renda, the entirely unequipped college student, was being paid for, was the service of his father-in-law, the "muscle" man, Sam Perrone.

The granting of the Renda scrap contract preceded the first of the notorious Briggs beatings by a little more than a week. The committee's records indicated that approximately six prominent labor officers of the Briggs Manufacturing Co. were beaten in a most inhuman fashion by unknown persons in the year that followed the granting of the otherwise inexplicable Renda contract.

The committee heard both Fry, the president of the Detroit, Mich., Stove Works, and William Dean Robinson, the present president of the Briggs Manufacturing Co. It is the opinion of the committee that neither Fry nor Robinson testified frankly concerning their relationships to gangsters. This committee believes that these two presidents knew of the underworld relationships which their companies had entered into in connection with their labor relations; that they had been questioned about this before a grand jury of State of Michigan, in the course of which they did not speak frankly and that they also failed to speak frankly before this committee.

NEW ORLEANS

Louisiana presents a complete case history on how national gambling and racketeering elements align themselves with local operators in a metropolitan area, Mayor DeLesseps S. Morrison told the committee at its first open hearing in New Orleans. Information offered by Mayor Morrison, businessmen, ministers, other citizens, and local law-enforcement officials, supplemented by the reluctant testimony of a parade of gamblers, wire-service and slot-machine operators, and narcotics peddlers, traced for the committee the nature, extent, and history of this alliance.

The activities of organized crime covered by the committee in this area were mainly four: Slot-machine operation, the conduct of gambling casinos of varying degrees of luxury, the extensive wire services which supported the bookmaking operations throughout the area, and the narcotics traffic.

The interstate nature of all four activities was made perfectly clear: They made extensive use of equipment or supplies brought in from the outside on common carriers. They depended extensively on interstate facilities of communication. They were operated wholly or in part by men from other sections of the country. Illegal in themselves, these activities were carried on by men with criminal records who had close and frequent associations with gangsters all over the country. And, finally, their operations depended in large measure on the negligence, the active support, or the participation of some local law-enforcement officials, who in large measure could nullify the efforts of diligent officials and public-spirited citizens in their own or nearby jurisdictions.

I. The slot-machine story

Huey Long's welcome to Costello and his slot machines when they were banished from New York gave the impetus to the present alignment of interstate and local operators in slot machines, gambling houses, bookmaking, and related activities, Mayor Morrison testified. From 1936 to 1946, the successive companies of the transplanted New Yorker, Phil Kastel, and his New York partners, Frank Costello, Jake Lansky, in cooperation with local gentry such as the narcotics vendor, Carlos Marcello, operated slot machines illegally and openly throughout New Orleans. They created a monopolistic arrangement whereby only the machines of their syndicate were permitted. They built up a business with a profit in the millions. Costello and Kastel were tried in 1939 on charges of trying to evade payment of $500,000 in Federal income taxes on 1936–37 income from the slot machines approaching $3,000,000, but were acquitted.

Just before his election in 1946, Morrison said, the Costello-Kastel syndicate withdrew their slot-machine and other operations into the adjoining parishes. They continued to use the city as a storage and distribution point until, in 1947, the city police raided the warehouses of their company, the Louisiana Mint Co., and confiscated 1,000 machines. Three hundred and ninety were destroyed before Costello and Kastel filed suit for damages and enjoined the city from destroying the remaining 600. The courts sustained the city's contention that, although the Costello-Kastel machines dispensed mints, they were still slot machines and illegal, and therefore could be destroyed.

This action ended the activity of the Louisiana Mint Co. in New Orleans, but not the presence of coin machines. Certain types of pinball machines known locally as "one-ball bandits" operate legally in the State and are licensed. The city issues about 2,000 of these licenses annually at $50 per machine. But Morrison was of the opinion that these, while they showed no automatic payoff when they were inspected for licensing, could easily be changed thereafter or could register free games for which payment would be made over the counter in the location where the machines were placed. Detection by watching every machine was obviously difficult.

The city was seeking to determine whether it could refuse to license machines of companies operating legal pinball devices in New Orleans, but illegal slot machines elsewhere. He listed for the committee some eight companies, holding licenses for about 75 machines in the city, among whose owners were Phil Kastel; Costello's brother-in-law, Theodore Geigerman; and Carlos Marcello, or known personal or business associates of Marcello, or owners of record known to be acting as a front for him.

1,000 UNLICENSED PIN-BALL MACHINES

From the president of the trade association of coin-machine operators, John Bosch, the committee learned that the licensed pinball machines do not represent the entire number operated in the city. Bosch estimated that the members of his association number about 45 and operate about 1,200 machines—all presumably licensed. Another 60 or 70 operators, he said, were not in his association. In all, he thought, there were at least 3,000 machines in the city, 1,000 above the number Morrison knew to be licensed.

The rules of his association and Mr. Bosch's explanation hinted that all these machines were not operating legally. One rule allowed the collection of $3 per machine from every operator for various miscellaneous expenses. Another rule stated that unless a machine was tagged with the association membership card and the name of the company, it would not be represented by the association when it was picked up. Pressed for an explanation, Bosch could not avoid the inference that "picked up" meant picked up for paying off. Bosch admitted that the association had lawyers on retainer; one of them getting over $300 a month was also the city attorney whose duty it was to prosecute pin-ball machine violations. Bosch would not estimate what the $3 per machine brought the association annually; he rejected the committee estimate of $100,000 as far out of line. Nor could be explain the uses of the fund or what was included in miscellaneous expenses.

Outside of New Orleans, slot machines operated openly in public places in flagrant violation of the law. The sheriff of Jefferson Parish would not dispute the committee counsel's estimate of 5,000 machines in his jurisdiction. Two ministers from Harrison County in Mississippi said there was one slot machine to every 25 inhabitants—operating in restaurants, barber shops, filling stations, and various other business or gambling places. The sheriff and town marshal of New Iberia, and the sheriff of St. Bernard Parish gave similar testimony concerning the wide-open operation of slot machines in their parishes.

Questioned about where he bought his machines, Kastel refused to confirm that they came from Mills Bros. in Chicago, nor would he explain transfers of vast sums of money, $75,000 in one case and $50,000 in another, from them to him, or from him to them, as slot-machine transactions. But the Jefferson Parish sheriff knew the machines operating in his area came from that company. Warren Moity, a young man who went into the slot-machine business in New Iberia to get first-hand evidence, said the rebuilt machines he bought were originally from the same company.

Until recently a member of the executive committee of the pin-ball association was Angelo Gemelli, a full-time New Orleans police officer assigned to the duty of "checking" pin ball operations and arresting operators who paid off. Obviously, Gemelli was in a most favorable position to "persuade" nonmembers to join and pay the heavy dues assessed. Gemelli received as "expenses" 10 percent of all amounts he collected for the association for "campaigns."

Nor was Costello the only out-of-State man involved. John Bertucci, another witness, testified he owned an interest in a pinball and phonograph machine company which was a Mississippi corporation and the company he operated in New Orleans was a branch of it. Moity, when he let it be known that he wished to enter the slot-machine business, was contacted by a man from Florida, who became his partner and brought his machines in from that State.

II. The gambling casinos

The parishes of Jefferson and St. Bernard, Mayor Morrison told the committee, have one of America's largest concentrations of gambling houses, wide open in violation of the law. Typical of the swank casinos was the Club Forest, whose activities early in 1951 were described to the committee. The club had a restaurant, bar, and grill. It had a casino, open to the public for day and night operation.

The daytime operation included the "big game"—the dice game—for which there were three tables, another small dice table, two roulette wheels, two blackjack games, a football pool and a race-horse book. The club paid $378 a week for its wire service.

The night operation included a keno game, six roulette wheels, small dice games, four tables of blackjack, from two to five tables for the big dice game. Customers of the gambling casino could have drinks and cigarettes on the house. If they ran out of money they could cash checks or get loans on their jewelry. The casino had approximately 48 slot machines—5-, 10-, 25-, 50-cent and $1 machines, and also a horse-race machine.

The club reported its assets at the end of the fiscal year November 30, 1949, as $718,904, and its gross receipts for the casino and other games including the slot machines as $2,008,796. This information was elicited from underlings and the records they brought in. The club owners, the three Mills brothers, Frank, Arthur, and Henry, and their partners, Edwin Litolf, Alfred B. Schorling, Gonzales Azcona, Lawrence Luke, and Vic Gallo, remained in hiding throughout the investigation.

Equally elaborate and boasting in addition expensive night-club entertainment was the Beverly Club establishment opened in the same parish late in 1945, just in time to provide Kastel and Costello with a refuge for their New Orleans enterprises. His original partners,

Kastel told the committee, were Costello, A. A. Rickefors, from whom they first rented and later bought the grounds and building, Carlos Marcello, and Lansky. When the latter sold his 20-percent interest he received $100,000 for it. Costello, admitted to a 20-percent interest in the club, also received first $1,000 a month and then $1,500 a month salary to act as a good-will agent and talent scout for its night-club shows.

The Jefferson Parish town seat of Gretna with its population of 14,000 had at least 6 large gambling clubs with horse parlors, the town marshal told the committee. The sheriff of Iberia Parish knew of at least four, and the sheriff of St. Bernard recognized the names of half a dozen others. The committee heard the names of many others, small and large, operated in the unincorporated parts of the parishes. In Harrison County, Mississippi, the committee was told, gambling rooms were marked by signs overhead indicating "No Minors Allowed." Such signs were commonly seen in connection with public restaurants and grills.

III. The wire services

With an important race track in the area, with handbooks running openly throughout the parishes, and with horse rooms figuring sub-stantially in the activities of the luxurious gambling casinos, New Orleans was an important focal point for the wire services of the Continental Press Service One of its lines ended in a building just outside the Fair Grounds race track and operated only during the racing season. Obviously this was Continental's means of getting information from the track for dissemination throughout the Nation. Other Continental lines went to the Gretna and New Orleans offices of the Daily Sports News which published racing results and forms.

During the struggle of the Capone group in Chicago to take over Continental, the New Orleans wire installation became the object of a typical, successful, and mysterious attempt at muscling in. The attempt involved setting up a branch of Trans-American, the Capone news service, as a rival to the local branch of Continental by men with criminal records and connections with the Capone gang. Typi-cally, the rival service lured employees from the local service and created an eventual merger of the two with the Chicago group or its local representatives holding the lions share of the participation. Everybody involved in the struggle—the owners of the services and their employees, or law-enforcement agents with an intimate know-ledge of the wire services in other respects—refused to testify at all or gave meager information with extreme reluctance. The picture had to be pieced together from meager admissions, court documents, Western Union records, and committee investigative reports.

John J. Fogarty, owner with his son of the Daily Sports News, had been publishing racing results and forms in New Orleans for nearly 30 years. He received his information over a direct wire from Conti-nental Press from Chicago. He insisted he was an independent owner, not an agent of Continental. But he had a characteristic agreement, made personally and orally in Chicago, with the manager, Tom Kelly, requiring him to pay $4,000 a week when he could, as much as possible in weeks when that sum was too large.

Shortly after Mayor Morrison came to office, he found that another wire service outlet, the Southern News Publishing Co., had been set up a short distance from an office of the Daily Sports News.   On two successive days, the police raided both on a charge of conspiracy; while they were not violating the handbook laws of the State in their own parish, they were the instruments of violation in other parishes. The raids and the subsequent proceedings revealed that Southern News had been set up by a native son named Joseph Poretto, whose criminal record caused the chairman to brand him one of the worst characters to appear before this committee.   He had connections with the Capone gang established in Cicero, and connections with their Trans-American Service, for which he had evidently tried and failed to set up a bootleg wire service in Houston.   Among Poretto's associates in Southern News Publishing Co. were Ralph Emory, son of an old associate of Al Capone, several former employees of Fogarty, and two brothers of Carlos Marcello.

Within a short time, a new service, ostensibly the Daily Sports News, opened in Gretna.   Neither Fogarty nor Poretto would discuss what happened in the interval, nor would they admit any association. But the idea of a merger was supported by the Western Union records. The wire service Western Union rented to Southern News in New Orleans was transferred to the Daily Sports News address in Gretna, and shortly thereafter discontinued while the service to the Daily Sports News went on uninterrupted.   The committee also had information that, before the raids, Fogarty and his son owned the Daily Sports News outright, and that when business was resumed afterward, the Marcellos figured largely in the ownership.

The key position the Daily Sports News held in the bookmaking business in the area was also revealed by the records of the Western Union.   From the same address at which it received the news from Continental, the Daily News paid monthly rentals on 66 so-called unequipped wires, with terminal points in as many different locations in Louisiana, Mississippi, and Alabama.   These were electrified, dormant wires, without transmission or receiving equipment, installed for service at some time, then when service was discontinued, presumably not removed to save the cost of a possible reinstallation. Admittedly equipment could be attached without the knowledge of the Western Union.   An agent of the company verified the fact that the rental on one such wire, to Pass Christian, Miss., was $186 a month. Some 20 other wires with terminal points in New Orleans were paid for at prices varying from $10 to $33 a month.   Mayor Morrison testified that it was over some of these wires that his police department found the only direct service to bookmakers in New Orleans after the two raids.

For the rest, bookmakers in New Orleans as in the outlying parishes relied on getting their information and placing their bets through telephones which connected with the horse rooms and bookie parlors serviced by these wires.   Every telephone in New Orleans, Mayor Morrison stated in emphasizing the need for over-all metropolitan enforcement of bookmaking laws, is a possible source of handbook violations so long as wide-open gambling goes on in the outskirts of the city.

IV. *The narcotics traffic*

From Thomas McGuire, agent in charge of the Bureau of Narcotics in New Orleans, the committee learned that the drug traffic here

ranked in importance with that of other metropolitan port areas.
The bulk of heroin, major item in the traffic, he said came from New
York by common carrier, plane, ship, or train.   Its price at the time
was up to $300 an ounce, higher than it had been up to the previous
month.   Marijuana, which came into the area in greater than normal
quantities, came from the Mexican border via Galveston and Laredo,
Tex.   His unit, he said, was investigating the participation of Mafia
members in the narcotics traffic.   Their tightly knit organization
made them difficult to deal with.   Any place which operates wide
open, McGuire said, tolerating prostitution, gambling, and so forth,
is the perfect field for narcotic peddlers who are frequently involved
in other types of rackets.   Of his own knowledge, McGuire knew
that peddlers came in for supplies from other States; he had recently
arrested a former resident in from California in search of supplies in
the area in which he had previously worked and with which consequently he felt familiar.   Other peddlers, friends of a recent deportee
named Sam Carollo, move in and out from Kansas City.
    The sheriff of Jefferson Parish minimized the dope traffic in his
own jurisdiction.   He knew and took pride in the part one of his own
men had played in a recent haul of narcotics supplies worth $21,000.
But he was sure that Carlos Marcello, who had served time for narcotics peddling and was a resident of Jefferson Parish, was never caught
in his jurisdiction.   The committee had information that Carlos and
his brother Anthony owned a boat used in running narcotics into the
port of New Orleans.   Both, when questioned, refused to answer
questions as to their narcotics activities, as well as practically every
other question except their local address, on the grounds of self-
incrimination.

V. The importance of Carlos Marcello in New Orleans rackets

    In every line of inquiry, the committee found the trail of Carlos
Marcello.   Kastel stated that Marcello was an original partner in the
Beverly Club; from another witness, it was learned that he was its
registered agent.   Several witnesses testified that he had an interest in
another luxurious club, the Old Southport, in which his associates
were two of his seven brothers and a brother-in-law.   He was rumored
to have bought this club outright for $160,000.   Marcello's brothers
were found in the raid on the Southern News Service, and figured in
the partnership of the Daily Sports News.   Marcello owned interests
in horse parlors and bookie joints such as the Bank Club and the
Billionaire Club.   He had an interest in Kastel and Costello's
Louisiana Mint Co., in the L. & B. Amusement Co. with his brother-
in-law, and in half a dozen other slot-machine companies operating
in and around New Orleans.   In addition, according to the sheriff of
Jefferson Parish, Marcello advanced money to people who were
building business establishments of one kind or another, and put his
slot machines in these locations.   Whether or not he and his brother
Anthony had boats running narcotics into New Orleans, it is a fact
that Marcello had served time for dope peddling among other things
and had asked and been refused a Presidential pardon.   Toll calls
connected Marcello with Harry Brooks, close associate of Mickey
Cohen, Joe Civello, narcotics violator, and Sam Yarras, brother of
Chicago hoodlum Dave Yarras, a prominent figure in the fight between
the "mob" wire service and Continental Press.   Also in touch with

Marcello was Charles Gordon, a main cog in a national football betting syndicate. Carlos talked over the phone to one Vincent Vallone just before the latter was murdered in Houston, Tex., in a Mafia-type killing. Among the many bars, restaurants, and inns in which Carlos Marcello had a financial interest was the Willswood Tavern, declared to be a hang-out for Mafia members. His legitimate business interests include all kinds of food concerns, particularly sea foods and frozen foods.

Marcello was born in Tunis, Africa, of Sicilian parents and came here in October 1910. He has never become a citizen. In view of this fact and in view of his record which the chairman stated made him one of the leading criminals in the United States today, the question was raised as to why he had not been deported.

VI. Typical bookkeeping of gambling enterprises

Proof of long suspected juggling of figures and keeping of books which did not accurately reflect the facts was found in the New Orleans testimony of Vernile Cavalier, a former dice man and cashier at the elaborate Club Forest. The books and records of the Club Forest, as produced by the public accountants who maintained them, were a model of bookkeeping practice, but Cavalier's story raised serious doubts as to the true situation. Cavalier said that on occasions when Deputy Sheriff Cassagne came into the club, one of the managers would instruct him to withdraw sums of over $1,000 for "ice," or protection. It was Cavalier's impression that the sum so drained off was merely taken off one of the dice tables as a loss, just as if one of the players had won the sum with a lucky streak. Committee investigators were unable to find any account or record of expense in the Club Forest's books which might relate to the "ice."

Then too, there was found the extremely questionable practice of charging off, as an expense or loss against the club's gross, the astronomical sum of $372,000 in 1 year with the explanation that this represented moneys lent to players and customers which was not repaid, or for bad debts resulting from "rubber" checks tendered by customers. Even granting the incredulous theory that many would be so bold as to hand these case hardened operators bad checks, the fact that much of the money so advanced was immediately lost by the customers at the tables without leaving the casino would render this theory of loss to the club somewhat paradoxical. Notwithstanding, equally amazing sums have been charged off through the years without apparent action by the tax authorities to question or disallow.

Having found such evidence of withdrawals of funds for the purchase of official tolerance going unrecorded, the question is immediately raised and the issue apparent—how much more money is drained off the top by those in control of the various gambling operations which never gets into the books?

VII. The frustrated attempts of citizens' groups to get court and official action

Outside of the city of New Orleans, citizens' attempts to bring about local official action met with frustration. Rev. Dana Dawson, a pastor of a Metairie church, organized a citizens' league in Jefferson Parish to close up the gambling casinos. They brought a padlock suit against the Club Beverly and the Club Forest. Dawson testified he was approached first by Pete Perez, the dice foreman at the Club

Forest, and was promised funds for the new Sunday-school building if the suit were dropped. Then it was suggested that Dawson might be satisfied if gambling was closed up in the Metairie district of the parish.

Sheriff Clancy took part in some of these conversations with Perez and Dawson. He told the pastor what a nuisance it was for him as sheriff to have to get jobs in these clubs for his friends. He boasted that he had placed about 2,000 people there, and stressed the economic value of the clubs to the district because of the jobs they provided. Perez and Clancy continued to make contributions to the church from the owners of several gambling casinos.

But the padlock suits were pressed. Both the Reverend Dawson and the attorney for the group, Mr. James McCain, recounted that they were in the courts for 4 years. The suits were fought on the ground that the act under which they were brought was unconstitutional, because it permitted legal action to be taken in any part of the State. The suits were in fact brought in the district in which the clubs were located. Despite two unanimous decisions of the State supreme court directing the lower court to try the case on its merits, the case was never tried and the act under which the suit was brought was finally declared unconstitutional by a 4-to-3 decision.

In Harrison County, Mississippi, ministers and public-spirited citizens had similar experiences. Rev. Douglas Carroll and Rev. Thomas Carruth recounted their concern about the concentration of 21,000 boys at Keesler Field, the biggest radar school in the world, some of whom came to their spiritual advisers in great distress because they had been unable to resist the temptation of the slot machines or had been unable to resist the temptation of the slot machines or blackjack games and had dropped their entire pay on the day they received it. The ministers went around, took pictures of the slot machines in restaurants, filling stations, grocery stores, and other places. They told about the mass meetings they held in protest against official inactivity. Through a Presidential order, the machines were finally removed from Keesler Field. But the Reverend Carroll and the Reverend Carruth testified they could never get convictions in the courts of the city for the craps, blackjack, and other games which were run wide open in Biloxi and other parts of the coast. When their attorney laid the matter before the Governor, the ministers said, he refused to do anything, presumably because it was a county matter.

In Iberia Parish, a young defeated candidate for mayor, Warren Moity, was shocked to have friends tell him they were in the slot-machine business but that they could operate only if the marshal and the sheriff were paid off. Sufficient interest was stirred up to start a grand-jury investigation; but, under a foreman who himself played the slot machines, no true bill was returned. Moity then tried a newspaper campaign. The papers would not even take his paid advertisements. At that point, Moity decided he would go into the business himself. He told his own partner, who was a brother of the conniving marshal, Howard LaBauve. Within a few days, Moity testified, he was contacted through a slot-machine distributing company, by a former Florida slot-machine operator named William Webster. Just to "front" for the machines, Moity was to get 25 percent of the business; his partner another 25 percent, and Webster 50 percent. When Moity went to obtain locations, he found there were no good ones left; those were held by the son-in-law of Sheriff Ozenne and by the brother-in-law of Marshal LaBauve.

Moity was promptly approached, he said, by LaBauve and was told that his machines would be destroyed unless LaBauve and Ozenne were paid off. After 3 months Webster and Moity broke up. They weren't making any money above the Federal and State licenses and the payments to the marshal, the sheriff, and the trade association. Webster took his machines back to Florida.

Moity then bought machines of his own. When he refused to pay protection, he and the owners of the locations were threatened. At least once he was shot at. He was threatened when it became known that he was going to Washington to ask the assistance of this Senate committee. Having done so, Moity tried to sell his slot-machine business. By putting an advertisement in a magazine, he got a prospect and a $750 deposit from a prospective purchaser. But the latter couldn't come to terms with LaBauve and Ozenne and withdrew. Consequently, at the time he testified in New Orleans, Moity said he was still in the business, with 25 machines on location in public places, paying off in cash strictly against the law. Urging the committee to do something to compel local officials to enforce the laws or resign, Moity said he realized how difficult it was for people with families and businesses to stand up, as he had done, against threats and against the knowledge that the legally constituted bodies would not help.

VII. Official inactivity

The committee heard the testimony of the sheriffs of four parishes and the town marshals of two incorporated towns. Every one of them stated that he knew slot machines, handbooks, gambling, and in some instances prostitution went on openly in his jurisdiction, although most of them added that they had seen none of these activities themselves.

Rowley, the sheriff of St. Bernard Parish since 1939, observed that back in the 1870's the constable and justice of peace were paid out of gambling funds. He pointed to the present-day anomaly of the State and the United States collecting taxes on slot machines, which are illegal, and then subjecting the owner to the danger of the seizure of machines whose existence is revealed by the tax payment. Sheriff Ozenne of New Iberia Parish made the same point through his attorney—the existence of the tax on these machines creates a hiatus; they are illegal, but they have them all over the State.

In New Orleans, the sheriff of Jefferson County, "King" Clancy, a graduate lawyer, arrogantly declined to answer, on the grounds that it would incriminate him, the question whether gambling was against the law in his parish and whether he had ever made any effort to enforce the antigambling laws. But, when he later came to Washington to purge himself of contempt, he admitted that he had done nothing. He justified his failure to keep his oath of office on the ground that upward of 1,000 people, most of them old or underprivileged, were employed in the five or six big casinos in his parish and for their sake gambling had been condoned.

Beauregard Miller, the town marshal of Gretna, which is the Jefferson Parish seat, also used the economic argument. He said flatly: "Without gambling, the town would be dead. It has a population of 14,000 and its main business is gambling." He added that anybody who closed the town up would be defeated at elections. Marshal LaBauve of New Iberia said that slot machines ran openly, and prostitution had gone on in restricted districts of the city all his life. Nobody objected. The health department examined the girls to see that they were not infected with venereal disease.

There was much evidence that these and other law-enforcement officials were not only neutral toward but obstructive to law enforcement. Sheriff Clancy admitted in Washington that he had accompanied the Club Forest dice dealer on his visit to the Reverend Dawson and had made every effort to persuade Dawson to drop the suits against the casinos.

Some of the officials had relatives engaged in the gambling and slot-machine activities. Sheriff Ozenne's son-in-law, in addition to his slot-machine interests, owned a night club and gambling casino. LaBauve's brother-in-law had slot machines. Sheriff Rowley denied knowing that his 40-year-old nephew was a gambler, and insisted he did not know what business he was in. There were other evidences of participation in gambling enterprises by police officers.

A former superintendent of police in New Orleans, George Reyer, who had once been president of the International Association of Police Chiefs, admitted that shortly after he left the force in 1946 he took his present job with the Daily Sports News, checking for wire taps. He also admitted that he was not a wire expert and that in 4 years he had never found a tap. But he had a salary of $100 a week. Reyer also had an interest in several gambling casinos which linked him with the owners of the Club Forest, but the committee could not definitely establish that these interests extended back into the time of his police service.

There was also definite evidence of direct bribery before the committee. Moity testified that Marshal LaBauve called him personally to demand a payoff for himself and Sheriff Ozenne if he intended to stay in the slot-machine business. Moity said that on LaBauve's instructions he did in fact pay one Amer Rodrigue $50 a month for 3 months. Both Ozenne and LaBauve denied anything more than casual conversations with Moity, and denied getting money from Rodrigue. They knew Rodrigue as a gambler and a slot-machine mechanic.

DEPUTY SHERIFF FREQUENTED GAMBLING CLUBS

Clancy, too, was reported to have a collector of protection money, one Cassagne, a deputy, who, Clancy admitted in Washington, was the man who made the arrangements for finding jobs for people in the casinos. Cassagne was admittedly seen around the clubs by Kastel at the Beverly, and by the night dice supervisor at the Forest. The latter testified that, after one of his night bosses had followed his customary procedure of taking a sum of money from the bank for "ice," he had seen Cassagne enter a private room with him. In New Orleans, Clancy refused to state on the grounds that it might incriminate him whether he had ever received any money from Cassagne. In Washington he denied it flatly but admitted that Cassagne made collections, and might possibly have taken a cut himself. Cassagne's collections were for charity, Clancy said, and the people who wanted them accompanied him when the collections were made.

Kastel admitted that Cy Ernst, one of Clancy's deputies, drove him home from the Beverly casino. At times he was carrying large sums of money with him.

While a committee investigator was serving a subpena at the Beverly club on January 18, 1951, a uniformed officer of the Louisiana State police entered the gambling club and delivered a set of license plates to Kastel's private office, passing through the gaming room to do so.

Outright payments for protection were most clearly established in the case of Sheriff Grosch of Orleans County. His divorced wife testified that in the last 6 years of their life together, ending in 1940, while he was chief of New Orleans detectives he had accumulated $150,000 in a safety box which she had bought on his instructions under an assumed name, using a false address. She had seen him receive money every week from a man named Julius Pace, identified elsewhere as a slot-machine and music-box dealer. She had herself received $39 every week in an envelope handed her by one Larry Copeland, also a slot-machine operator. A man whom she understood to be running a house of prostitution came every Saturday night and brought them their food for the week.

Grosch handed her other sums of money in small bills for her to change at one bank or another into large ones, to put in the safety box in the attic.

Today a woman of responsibility, the supervisor of nurse's aides in the hospital operated by Tulane University, Mrs. Grosch's testimony was corroborated by documents and witnesses. An employee of the Rolland Lock Co., from which Mrs. Grosch said she bought the box, produced records which jibed in every particular with her story. And finally Mrs. Grosch produced two written agreements made at the time of her divorce, one for the record which gave her $5,000, and another, a secret agreement, which made a settlement of $35,000. It indicated that Sheriff Grosch's wealth 10 years ago was far larger than could be explained by his salary of $186 a month.

The sheriffs and town marshals denied ever receiving any campaign contributions from gamblers, slot-machine operators, and bookmakers. But Bosch, head of the Association of Coin-Machine Operators in New Orleans, confronted with a check for $100 to one L. Scanlon, admitted it was for his campaign as civil sheriff. The members made contributions through the association. They decided what they would give in some fashion about which Bosch was vague. It depended on the office and what they collected. Usually they gave to both sides. They contributed some $8,000 to Morrison's campaign, Bosch said; about $5,000 to one of his opponents, and a small sum to still a third candidate.

Evidences of unexplained wealth were not confined to Sheriff Grosch. Rowley, sheriff of St. Bernard Parish, who knew of no trial for a gambling offense in his district since 1940 and could recall no conviction at all, admitted to a supplementary income of from $6,000 to $8,000 within the past 3 years. He owned a 1949 Ford, financed partly by a trade-in, and a 1949 Cadillac which he had bought for cash extracted from his own strongbox in his bedroom at home. At the time of the committee's hearing in New Orleans, the box contained between $15,000 and $20,000. Asked the source of his funds, the sheriff refused to answer on the grounds of self-incrimination.

SHERIFF'S SALARY, $5,700; INCOME, $20,000

Questioned about his income, Sheriff Clancy estimated before the Washington hearing that it was about $20,000 annually over the past 4 years. Yet, it must have been considerably more than that by his own figures. While his salary was never more than $5,700, he admitted to an annual income of nearly $5,000 in an oil interest with Judge McCune and others, which he had not reported to the Committee in the papers requested under subpena. In addition, Clancy said he had made $78,000 through betting at the races or through bookmakers. The only records he had, he said, were his bank deposits. He attributed his extraordinary success to his restraint in playing only the last two races on any day, and to the advice he received from jockeys and owners who felt indebted to him because they knew they could always come to him for a loan if they were broke.

Just as the connection of the local mobsters with the out-of-town gamblers and racketeers can be summarized in the activities of Carlos Marcello, the involvement of a local law-enforcement officer was epitomized in "King" Clancy. That all these gambling and racketeering operations were illegal, and that in law and in fact he had the power to close them up tight, Clancy admitted to the committee in Washington, in contrast to his New Orleans refusals to answer. Clancy told the committee that since his New Orleans appearance he had actually closed down the slot machines. Asked about the lush gambling clubs in the towns, Clancy first insisted that policing them was the job of the city police department but admitted he had jurisdiction to close them up, and promised he would do so.

Clancy admitted that Kastel had consulted him about opening up the Beverly Club. At the time there was a casino there, but the operators were not making any money. Kastel asked him, Clancy said, whether he would have any objection to his taking over. Clancy told Kastel he would have no objection, so long as other people didn't complain, and Kastel gave people jobs. When the committee ventured that the other clubs couldn't have been happy about it, Clancy averred they said nothing to him. At that point, Clancy conceded to the committee that he was the high power who gives clearances; they opened when he said they could, and when he said they should close, they closed.

In Washington, Clancy displayed a considerable knowledge of all these illegal operations which high lighted his equally considerable professions of ignorance. He knew that Marcello was partner of Kastel and Costello in the Beverly Club. He wouldn't admit that any deputies were employed by the casinos, but admitted he couldn't tell whom he had made honorary deputies without the records before him, and such persons might be employed at the casinos and be misusing their badges.

He had not only gone to the Reverend Dawson about the padlock suits; he knew that four separate gangster groups continued to give money to the Dawson church, and said they gave money to other churches also. He conceded that the committee would be justified in saying that his office was actually running an employment agency for the gambling casinos.

Just as he knew and could testify to many of Marcello's activities and interests in the gambling casinos, Clancy knew of his activities in

connection with slot machines.   He said that the Dixie Finance Corp.,
in which he had an interest, might be loaning money to slot-machine
distributors.

Clancy knew that the large casinos had horse rooms, wire service,
and facilities for laying off bets throughout the country.   He knew
that the headquarters of the Daily Sports News was the fan-out point
for all the handbooks in the area.   He knew there had been a merger
of two rival wire services, but didn't know anything about the
muscling-in procedure.   Clancy denied in New Orleans that there
were two telephones listed in his name at the Daily Sports News address, just a block away from his office as sheriff.   In Washington he
confirmed it and said it must have been a mistake which the telephone
company would have to straighten out.

Clancy knew Kastel, but no more about his criminal record than
he had read in the papers.   He did not know Kastel's friend Costello.
Clancy knew of no alleged Mafia meetings, operations, or hang-outs.
He was sure the recent narcotics haul in his parish had not been
intended for sale there but for the preparation of cigarettes to be
sold in New Orleans.   Marcello, a Jefferson Parish resident, though
not a desirable character, had never been apprehended in his and
Clancy's home territory on narcotics charges, the sheriff admitted.

Clancy knew that slot machines were bought from Mills Bros. in
Chicago, but not that negotiations were in progress for a proposed slot-
machine factory in his parish to defeat the purpose of the recent law
against interstate shipment.   He knew there was a State law ordering
officers to seize and destroy slot machines on penalty of removal from
office, and admitted that his failure to do so was a flagrant violation of
his oath of office.

PATHS OF CRIMINALS EASED BY OFFICIALS

Thus "King" Clancy, in his history and attitudes, his personal and
business associations with flagrant lawbreakers, posed flatly and
succinctly for the committee the problem of the admittedly negligent
local official who eases the path for organized crime and its use of
interstate facilities, but who can be dealt with personally only by local
action.

He typified in effect the foundation on which the whole structure
of organized gambling and racketeering rests.   Without conniving
and participating officials like him, neither the wire services and
bookmaking interests emanating from Chicago nor the gambling and
racketeering elements allied with Costello of New York nor the local
criminals like Carlos Marcello and Joseph Poretto could have used
the interstate facilities of communication and transportation to
further their illegal enterprises alone or in concert with other racketeers
from all over the country.

It is apparent from the foregoing that the following patterns of
organized crime and gambling are present in New Orleans:

1. The association of native gamblers and gangsters with outside racketeers, particularly those from the Costello-Lansky-Adonis
syndicate.

2. A deep-seated aversion on the part of the lawfully elected law-
enforcement officials to enforce the laws which they have sworn to
uphold.

3. The personal enrichment of sheriffs, marshals, and other law-enforcement officials because of their failure to enforce the gambling laws and other statutes relating to vice.

4. The interference with attempts of civic and religious groups to improve law enforcement in particular communities.

5. The attempt to justify "wide open" conditions by the so-called benefits they confer through employment opportunities and by the fact that the "people" (who are never asked) want it that way.

6. The failure to see that the apology for wide-open conditions is colored by the self-interest of the officials who have a vested stake in the maintenance of the status quo.

7. The brazenness of law-enforcement officials, who in gangster style refuse to answer questions, concerning their law-enforcement activities on the ground of self-incrimination.

8. The failure of the central State government to take effective steps to compel local law-enforcement officials to enforce gambling and vice laws.

LAS VEGAS, NEV.

In the course of its investigations throughout the country, the committee was repeatedly struck by the magnitude of the gambling business and by the pattern of domination of this business by an interlocking group of gangsters, racketeers, and hoodlums. In all of the localities previously discussed in this report, gambling, except for pari-mutuel betting at race tracks, is prohibited by State and/or local law. Although some of the participants in this tremendous illegal business of gambling were relatively frank about their operations, the majority of the witnesses on this subject before the committee exhibited an extreme unwillingness to reveal information about their gambling activities.

With the exception of those States which permit on-track betting and a few which permit certain special and relatively insignificant forms of gambling, Nevada is the only State which presently legalizes gambling within the framework of a State and local licensing system.

In an effort to obtain reliable information about the size and methods of operation of top-flight professional gamblers and to investigate further the interstate ramifications of the gambling underworld, while still conforming to the letter and spirit of its original authorizing resolution, the committee heard testimony on gambling operations in the State of Nevada.

The basic law legalizing gambling in Nevada was enacted in 1931. This law permitted gambling operations by persons who paid a license fee and received a license from the county authorities. Since that date, a number of changes have been made in the licensing system and the law, which was last amended in 1949, now requires that all persons who engage in gambling operations, including the operation of handbooks, must be licensed by the State as well as by the county or city in which they operate. State licenses are issued by the Nevada State Tax Commission which is empowered to hold hearings and to grant and revoke licenses on the basis of the qualifications of the applicants or licensees.

The committee was told by Clifford Jones, lieutenant governor of Nevada, and William J. Moore, member of the State tax commission, that prior to 1949 little or no effort was made to screen the applicants for State licenses.   Lieutenant Governor Jones and Mr. Moore both testified that since 1949 an effort has been made to keep out persons known to have criminal records or strong affiliations with out-of-State gambling syndicates.   No attempt had been made, however, to eliminate the undesirable persons who had been operating in the State before that time.   Both the lieutenant governor and Mr. Moore themselves participated in the operation of hotels which included more or less large-scale gambling casinos.   Gambling is a legalized business in Nevada and there is no question as to the character of these gentlemen, who were most cooperative in their testimony before the committee.   However, the committee's inquiries revealed that the caliber of the men who dominate the business of gambling in the State of Nevada is on a par with that of professional gamblers operating illegal gambling establishments throughout the country.

"BUGSY" SIEGEL WAS LAS VEGAS RACKET CZAR

Before he was shot to death in 1947, Benjamin "Bugsy" Siegel was undoubtedly the gambling boss of Las Vegas, Nev.   Siegel, who had carried on gaming operations in California and elsewhere before coming to Nevada, had been associated with "Lucky" Luciano, Frank Costello, Joe Adonis, Meyer Lansky, and other influential members of the eastern underworld.   From about 1942 until the time of his death, Siegel controlled the race-wire service in Las Vegas through Moe Sedway, an ex-convict, gambler, and long-time associate of many New York mobsters whom Siegel brought to Las Vegas.   Through a control of the wire service, Siegel controlled the operation of all handbooks operating in Las Vegas.   He refused wire service to any book unless he or his agents actually operated and managed it.   During the period of the Trans-American-Continental fight over control of the race-wire service, Siegel, who was closely connected with members of the Capone mob, dispensed the Trans-American service and in some cases, serviced bookies who were also receiving the Continental service.   Siegel was shot to death in California a few days after Trans-American went out of business.

Until his death by violence, Siegel had a controlling interest in the Flamingo Hotel at Las Vegas, one of the country's most elaborate gambling establishments.   Associated with Siegel in the hotel and its gambling enterprises were Moe Sedway, Allan Smiley, a gambler with a long criminal record who came to Las Vegas with Siegel, Meyer Lansky, and Morris Rosen also old-time associates of the New York mob.

After Siegel's death the operation of the Flamingo was taken over by Sanford Adler, a gambler with a long record of arrests, and a number of his associates.   Adler entered into an agreement with Sedway, Rosen, and Gus Greenbaum who controlled the wire service in Phoenix.   Under the agreement, Adler was to have control over the operation of the hotel, although Rosen, Sedway, and Greenbaum held the controlling number of shares in the hotel.   After a violent disagreement with Greenbaum, Adler suddenly sold out his interest and retired to his gambling clubs in Reno and Tahoe, leaving Greenbaum, Rosen, and Sedway in undisputed possession of the lucrative Flamingo operation.

With Siegel removed from the scene, Sedway and Rosen attempted to carry on Siegel's monopoly over the race wire. Trouble over the wire service came to a head when service to the Santa Anita Turf Club was cut off. The Santa Anita Club, owned and operated by the Stearns brothers, adjoined the Frontier Turf Club, a former Sedway-Siegel operation, in which Rosen had succeeded to Siegel's interest. Sedway attempted to negotiate a merger with the Stearns, but instead they tapped the Frontier Club wire service and continued to operate independently.

At this point, Robert Jones, county district attorney of Clark County, and a partner of the lieutenant governor, became alarmed about the situation in connection with the distribution of the wire service in the State. He addressed a letter to the Nevada Tax Commission expressing grave concern over the situation prevailing in Las Vegas as a result of the monopoly of the race-wire service, and stated that the "situation was fraught with danger to the public peace." In accordance with Mr. Jones' suggestion, a hearing on the wire service was held in Las Vegas late in 1948. The testimony given in these hearings revealed that although Connie Hurley nominally held the race-wire contract for Las Vegas, arrangements for the distribution of the service to Las Vegas bookmakers were actually made by Rosen and Sedway. As a result of the hearings, Rosen was forbidden to carry on gambling operations in Nevada. He has continued to hold a controlling interest in the Flamingo Hotel, however.

OLD-TIME RACKETEERS STILL OPERATE

Another million-dollar gambling operation in Las Vegas is the famous Desert Inn run by Wilbur Clark, an old-time gambler, who at one time worked on the gambling boats off the coast of California. Clark's associates in the construction and operation of the Desert Inn include Sam Tucker and Thomas J. McGinty, Cleveland gamblers; Moe Dalitz, an old-time bootlegger and gambler, and Morris Kleinman, a gambler and bootlegger who for many years has been associated with the biggest gambling operations in Ohio.

The Bank Club in Reno is owned and operated by William Graham and James McKay, who were convicted of mail fraud in New York, but who returned to Nevada after the expiration of their prison terms. At one time, Graham and McKay sold a one-third interest in the Bank Club to Joseph Stacher, a well-known eastern gambler. Stacher was reputed to be willing to spend as much as $250,000 to elect city officials who would license him to operate as a partner in the club. His application for a license was, as a matter of fact, denied by the Nevada Tax Commission before any action was taken on his application for a city license.

Also operating in Reno are Mert Wertheimer, a big-time Michigan gambler who has been in partnership in Florida with such notorious gangsters as Joe Adonis, the Lanskys, and Frank Erickson, and with Lincoln Fitzgerald and Daniel Sullivan, members of the Michigan gambling syndicate.

Benny Binion, one-time king of the rackets in Dallas, Tex., has also been involved in gambling operations in Reno.

It is also clear to the committee that the gambling operations in Nevada are inextricably tied to interstate commerce. The bookmakers receive bets from many out-of-State sources and lay off bets with bookmakers outside the State of Nevada; as a daily practice, they use telephone wires and other facilities of interstate commerce. Part of these transactions are cleared by use of the mails. Several of the gambling syndicates are financed to a very substantial extent and exist largely on money from outside States. Most of the gambling public comes to Las Vegas from places beyond the borders of Nevada.

It seems clear to the committee that too many of the men running gambling operations in Nevada are either members of existing out-of-State gambling syndicates or have had histories of close association with the underworld characters who operate those syndicates. The licensing system which is in effect in the State has not resulted in excluding the undesirables from the State but has merely served to give their activities a seeming cloak of respectability.

The reform of the race-wire service which was hoped for as a result of the legislation enacted after the 1948 Las Vegas hearings seems to have been equally unimpressive. The 1948 act requires the impartial distribution of the wire service to all licensed bookmakers, and gives the tax commission power to fix rates and inquire into the operation of the wire service.

William Moore, a member of the tax commission, told the committee that although the commission must pass on any increases over the rates charged in 1948, the commission has made no attempt to fix rates, or to eliminate the practice of fixing rates on the basis of a percentage of the bookmaker's take. It is this practice of charging for the wire service on the basis of a percentage of take which effectually makes the distributor of the wire service a partner in every bookie operation, and which inevitably leads to violent competition for control of the wire service.

Mr. Moore also told the committee that the commission had confined itself to passing on complaints from bookmakers—which, strangely enough, had been limited to one complaint in 3 years—and had undertaken no independent scrutiny of the wire service operation.

The profits which have been taken from gambling operations are far greater than those which can be earned quickly in any other business. The availability of huge sums of cash and the incentive to control political action result in gamblers and racketeers too often taking part in government.

In States where gambling is illegal, this alliance of gamblers, gangsters, and government will yield to the spotlight of publicity and the pressure of public opinion, but where gambling receives a cloak of respectability through legalization, there is no weapon which can be used to keep the gamblers and their money out of politics.

Taking Lt. Gov. Clifford Jones as a particular instance: 2½ percent of the Pioneer Club had been sold to him for $5,000 in the year 1941. Thereafter, his annual income from this operation was $14,000. Jones is also a member of a law firm, and one of his partners is Robert Jones, district attorney of Clark County.

As a member of the State tax commission, William Moore's particular function is to deal with licensees engaging in bookmaking and gambling operations. Mr. Moore also has a gambling operation of his own, being a part owner of the Last Frontier. He recently made a deal for wire service and received a rate which in the opinion of the committee gives him a considerable financial advantage over his com-

petitors. Mr. Moore explained the reason for the comparatively low
rate was that his operation was a new one, but the committee found at
least one other similarly new operation which had not been given the
same low rate.

The conditions above described are not healthful. Gambling is the
big business in the cities of Las Vegas and Reno, the two largest cities
of the State of Nevada. A short tour of either of these cities suffices
to show that gambling is the major preoccupation of the residents in
both places. As a case history of legalized gambling, Nevada speaks
eloquently in the negative.

WEST COAST

I. Racket pattern

The racket pattern in California was found to be similar in general
to that in other sections of the country, in that various forms of gambling furnished the backbone for other rackets by reason of its heavy
profit. It was noteworthy, however, that—probably because of an
awakening brought about by the activities of the California Crime
Commission—law-enforcement officers, grand juries, and prosecutors
had combined to accomplish certain results. The committee found
that the race wire service had been outlawed in California, although
it was obviously obtainable on a sneak basis. Many major gambling
figures have utilized neighboring Nevada to base their activities, pre-
ferring the less hazardous operation by telephone with their customers
in California.

Other indications of the increased vigilance of law-enforcement
agencies were found in testimony that table gambling casinos were
practicaly nonexistent, but the gamblers had devised collapsible crap
tables which could be hauled about in the rear of an automobile for
use in sneak games.

Further evidence of resistance to the shut-down was disclosed in
the testimony of Mayor Fletcher Bowron of Los Angeles, one of the
leaders in the war on crime, that the racket element had combined in
an abortive effort to reopen his area to the rackets by forcing a recall
election. For a time there were many establishments running "bridgo-
bingo." This is a type of gambling similar to bingo except that the
participant is required to demonstrate his ability to engage in the
bingo game by engaging in a so-called game of skill beforehand.
These games of skill were but a mockery and subterfuge, as a child
of tender years could readily accomplish the skill portion of the game.
Between the first inquiry by the committee into these games in November 1950, and the committee hearings in February 1951, it was
found that the bridgo-bingo games had virtually disappeared because
of police activity and the disclosures that, almost without exception,
the games were operated by known racketeers hiding behind an individual without a criminal record who fronted for them.

As in other localities, the "lay-off" system in handbooks was found.
California bookies were found to be in close touch with "lay-off"
establishments as far away as Shreveport, La., and Florida where
John O'Rourke testified he received bets over the telephone from
Mickey Cohen in Los Angeles, resulting in a loss to O'Rourke of some
$50,000 in a short period of time

II. The "vice squad pattern" and diffusion of police responsibility are of material assistance to organized crime

As found nearly everywhere, jurisdictional difficulties of law-enforcement agencies materially assisted the criminal element to operate with a minimum of harassment.   The fact that the investigative and police jurisdiction of law-enforcement agencies stopped at a city, county, or State line was used to advantage by the underworld figures who consistently sought refuge in the area where they found more "official tolerance" but, by penetrating the better policed areas by telephone and by a continuously moving operation which never tarried long enough to invite police action, they found themselves able to defeat the law.   For instance, the Guarantee Finance Co. case disclosed headquarters in one county which was actually the nerve center of operation but the customers in large measure being serviced by this gambling organization were located across the county line.   There was also the peculiar geographic set-up whereby the area known as the Sunset Strip, an island in the midst of Los Angeles, not subject to the law enforcement jurisdiction of the Los Angeles police, became an natural haven for those engaged in activities offensive to the Los Angeles police.

As was the case with Mayor Fletcher Bowron, the vigorous opposition to the racket pattern by Chief of Police William H. Parker of Los Angeles met with resistance.   Testimony adduced disclosed the detection and prevention of an attempt on Chief Parker's life.

Meanwhile, in Los Angeles County where officials seem to be more "tolerant," sheriff's deputies from time to time were charged with nonfeasance and even more serious collaboration with criminal figures. Sheriff Eugene Warren Biscailuz of Los Angeles County testified that he questioned the officers involved but they denied the allegations, and he conducted no further investigation of the charges.

As elsewhere in the country, there were interesting examples of accumulation of wealth in the hands of law enforcement officers. William Robertson, a former police officer in Los Angeles, could not remember his net worth but admitted that it was over $100,000.   He resigned from the police force when an investigation into sources of his income was pending.   In the Guarantee Finance case, the books disclosed an item of $108,000 referred to as "juice," the California term for "protection."   In Florida it is "ice."   In view of the fact that the Guarantee Finance was a "50–50 book" with participating bookmakers sharing the expense, a payoff of $216,000 was indicated. Investigation and testimony thus far have failed to develop the identity of the recipients of this "juice."   Further, there were found a number of instances where law enforcement officers profited handsomely from business deals made easy for them.   For instance, former Capt. Al Guasti of the Los Angeles sheriff's office, was able to purchase a liquor license for $525 and within a short time sell the license, taken in his wife's name, for about $12,000.   Other officers participated in similar liquor license deals, realizing quick profits.

In this connection the "vice squad pattern" was again found. This is a device used in many cities where the rackets thrive.   The police department bosses set up a vice squad composed of a chosen few directly accountable to them.   They instruct the remaining law-enforcement officers to stay away from gambling and vice and to channel any complaints to the vice squad for action or, in most cases, inaction. By this device, a small clique frequently controls the collection of the protection pay-off. It directs police activity against operations that conflict with those who are "in" or those slow to recognize their responsibilities to purchase "official tolerance" to operate. As an example of how this pattern works, it was found that in Los Angeles County even the vice squad "didn't move freely without instructions from Captain Pearson." In the case of one raid, Captain Pearson wrote a note to the sergeant in charge of the squad saying:

> Make your raids specifically at 10 o'clock. At that time, the gambling tables will be covered. Observe the girl show and then leave. During that time, there will be no gambling conducted so your officers will not be embarrassed.

Captain Pearson admitted that the note was in his own handwriting.

Evidence of obstruction of justice by violence and the tendency of the criminal to take the law into his own hands was found in the shocking shotgun murder of Attorney Sam Rummel. His voice was forever silenced on December 11, 1950, the day following a conference with Sheriff's Officers Guasti and Pearson. At the time that a grand jury was probing the bookmaking and protection of the Guarantee Finance syndicate, Rummel called on Guasti on Sunday, December 10, 1950. Guasti arranged for a clandestine meeting in an automobile between Rummel, Pearson, and Guasti. Guasti admitted to the committee that Rummel said he was going to discuss the Guarantee Finance case before the grand jury and that he "had some information." Further testimony developed that Pearson met Rummel later in the evening and made available records about the investigation, obtained in his official capacity. It was the following morning that Rummel was "removed permanently" from consideration as a witness who might shed some light upon the corruption that was evident in the Guarantee Finance syndicate. Guasti admitted to the committee that he did not bother to advise the Los Angeles police, who were investigating the murder, of the events on the day prior to the shooting.

In another case, law-enforcement officers found their path toward conviction for narcotic violations of the notorious Sica brothers blocked by the gang murder of Abraham Davidian, the man considered by the prosecution to be the key witness and "sine que non" to conviction. Needless to say, Davidian's death completely stultified their efforts and the Sicas went free. Perhaps the lesson learned from the death of Abe "Kid Twist" Reles, whose untimely demise in New York prevented the prosecution of the triggerman in the Murder, Inc., case, served the California hoodlums well.

Further manifestation of the disregard for the processes of justice was found in the revealing recording adduced in the Los Angeles hearing of the committee in which the unguarded conversation of underworld figures was brought to light. In Dallas, Tex., Herbert Noble, who has just survived the eleventh attempt to take his life by dynamiting his automobile and airplane, among other things, was engaging in a war for control of the Dallas racket with Benny Binion. So many attempts have been made on Noble's life that he is called the Clay Pigeon. Binion left Dallas after Noble's wife was murdered. Her last act was to step on the starter of the automobile usually used by Noble, thereby detonating the dynamite placed in the car by those who wished to eliminate Noble. According to the story brought out in the testimony, Binion moved to Nevada but continued to maintain an interest in the lucrative Dallas rackets and sent an emissary, Harold Shimley, to Dallas in an effort to make peace with Noble.

Vigilant Dallas police learned of the move and recorded the ensuing conversation between Shimley and Noble which took place in a tourist cabin near Dallas. The conversation furnished a graphic insight into the tactics of these lawless elements. Shimley made an effort to convince Noble that Binion did not want trouble and was not responsible for the murder of Noble's wife. Shimley maintained that Binion had spent thousands of dollars of his own to track down the perpetrator of this shocking crime and claimed that he had found the individual who had purchased the dynamite and intended to arrange to square matters by gangland methods. The alleged purchaser of the dynamite had been arrested and incarcerated. Shimley told Noble that he (Binion) said, "I can get the ———— killed in the penitentiary." Noble replied, "Well, that's good enough for me." During the conversation a telephone call was made to Binion, who remained in Nevada, from the men in the tourist cabin in furtherance of the peace effort. There is no record of these individuals ever advising law-enforcement officials of the information they insisted had been developed concerning the killings.

III. The persuasive Mickey Cohen and magnetic William Bonnelli

No discussion of the California crime picture would be complete without reference to the notorious Mickey Cohen. Although the recent police surveillance and publicity attendant to Cohen's activities have undoubtedly exerted a deterrent effect on Cohen's activities, his name is inescapably woven into the pattern of rackets in southern California. Cohen is frequently mentioned in connection with gambling enterprises and has been known in handbook circles as a lay-off man for Nation-wide horse bets. Cohen's tendency toward strong-arm tactics is evidenced by the treatment he administered to Jimmy Utley in broad daylight in a Los Angeles restaurant. It has been related how Cohen pistol-whipped Utley in the presence of numerous patrons of the place but none of them, including Utley, would testify about what they had seen. Again, Cohen accompanied Joe Sica when the latter called upon Russell Brophy, the race wire service distributor in California, to find out why Brophy had declared Sica "out." Sica was unable to persuade Brophy that he was "in" and, in the ensuing fight, Brophy was administered a bad beating. Cohen's enthusiasm mounted and he tore the telephones out of the place.

Cohen has explained that in recent years he spent money in excess of his reported income by reason of loans made to him by various individuals. These "loans" amounted to over $140,000 and Cohen admitted he was in no position to repay them. In one instance Hyman Miller, a bookmaker, "lent" Cohen $5,000 which Cohen had never repaid. Cohen apparently added insult to injury by administering a beating to Miller after they had "harsh words." On another occasion Cohen successfully "borrowed" more than $20,000 from the then president of the Hollywood State Bank on a completely unsecured basis. Cohen claimed he was able to arrange this loan merely by talking to the president of the bank, without posting collateral or security, and without giving any promissory note. It was emphasized that the loan was from the personal funds of the bank official and did not involve the bank's funds.

William G. Bonelli, a member of the California State Board of Equalization which controls the issuance of liquor licenses, proved to be an interesting witness. Previous testimony had developed that Bonelli's campaigns for office had shown a number of law-enforcement officers and racketeers to be prominent supporters. William Robertson, operator of a gambling establishment and former Los Angeles policeman, made collections for Bonelli's campaign totaling $15,000 to $17,000.

Another admitted backer of Bonelli was Capt. Al Guasti of the Los Angeles County sheriff's office who, as previously related, was able to purchase a liquor license for less than $600 which subsequently sold for $12,000. The individual who arranged for Guasti to obtain the liquor license was William J. Cook, who is one of the principals in Bonelli's campaign. Cook appeared as a partner with Bonelli in a venture known as the Hillview Oil Co., which later became a corporation in which both held stock. Bonelli testified that the stock which he bought at $1 per share was to date a losing proposition. Notwithstanding, Cook was able to sell one share of the Hillview Oil Co. stock which cost him $1 to the operator of the Rainbow Room, a liquor licensee, for $2,000. Another licensee paid $1,000 for half a share of stock which cost Mr. Cook 50 cents.

WIRE SERVICE IN CALIFORNIA

Under California law the race wire service has been outlawed. Notwithstanding, the bookies seem to be able to circumvent the law to obtain the information so vital to their existence. Although there is no evidence of direct wire outlets in the State, there have been at least four occasions of "tapping" Western Union cables which parallel the Southern Pacific tracks and carry Continental Press racing news through California to Mexico. On one occasion the tapping, obviously for gambling purposes, was so crudely done that it threw off the entire block signals system of the railroad.

Russell Brophy, who controlled the distribution of the racing news, testified in the hearing of the Interstate and Foreign Commerce Committee that he was receiving racing information by short-wave radio from Mexico and disseminating it in California. There was no testimony as to how he paid for the information but Edward McGoldrick, of the General News Service in Chicago, a Continental distributor, testified before this committee that his service was receiving $500 per week from Stanley Cohen in San Francisco under an oral agreement that McGoldrick would furnish Cohen with wire service to San Francisco if and when it became legal to run wires into California again. The $500 per week payment closely approximated the amount paid for the racing news in San Francisco when the wire was legal. McGoldrick was unable to explain how Cohen could be assured of exclusive representation of the wire service in San Francisco and it seemed highly incredible that Cohen would be paying $500 per week ad infinitum merely to protect a franchise to obtain news service which could not be transmitted into the State legally. Although there appeared to be no business relationship between Continental Press in Chicago and Stanley Cohen from the record, Cohen's 1949 tax return disclosed an expense item of $46,300 for "Continental Press Service." A further interesting item was an expense of $23,909.24 for "telephone."

When the committee sought to question Cohen about his obvious wire-service activities he refused to give any information and has been cited for contempt. Thus there remains the paradoxical situation in California in 1949 where Brophy, son-in-law of the late James Ragen, murdered Continental Press principal, claimed California wire service was obtained by radio from Mexico, which incidentally has a Continental Press drop, and McGoldrick, of General News, a Continental subdistributor in Chicago, claimed that Stanley Cohen was paying General News $500 per week for a very nebulous consideration. But Cohen's books failed to support these payments and, on the contrary, disclosed $46,000 paid to Continental Press, all of which took place during a year when the wire service was outlawed in the State. The inescapable conclusion again appears that the Continental Press Service subdistributors are merely dummies along the path which the racing news travels from Continental to the bookie, and that the funds extracted from the bookies for the service wind up in the coffers of Continental.

IV. Corruption among internal-revenue employees

A new technique for extracting money from taxpayers was developed by several Internal Revenue Bureau employees in the west coast area. Patrick Mooney, formerly chief field deputy at the Bureau of Internal Revenue at Reno, Nev., for a number of years was an officer in the Mountain City Consolidated Copper Co., which seemed to be nothing more than a "shadow mine." In other words, there is no record of the mine ever producing anything of value and it was not worked. For many years Mooney prepared the tax returns for Elmer "Bones" Remer, a prominent California gambler. Remer had a tax deficiency of $773,535 for the years 1941 to 1946. In 1946, Mooney testified, he had an income-tax warrant against Remer calling for the payment of about $7,000 or $8,000. Remer had a check ready to pay the tax assessment but, after talking with Mooney, instead bought $2,400 worth of the copper company stock and deducted $2,400 from the check to the Government. According to Mooney "it was all adjusted anyhow." Apparently Remer was not bothered further by tax difficulties at this time.

In addition to Remer, several hundred others, most of whom were having tax troubles, bought stock in the mine. Many of them have been identified as gamblers and gambling-house operators in that area. Apparently a participant in the scheme with Mooney was Ernest Mike Schino, the former chief field deputy, office of the collector of the northern district of California. Schino was the recipient of 5,000 shares of the stock from Mooney and, as "it would not be right to put it in Mooney's name" according to Mooney, it was put in the name of Schino's sister.

There was evidence that Gertrude Jenkins, a convicted abortionist who was having tax difficulties, paid $5,000 to Mooney, half of which was to go to Schino to "fix" her case. On the other hand, Robert J. Kaltenborn, the owner of a large wholesale automobile-parts store in Las Vegas, was recently convicted of violation of the internal revenue laws. During the time he was under investigation he was approached by Martin Hartmann, who purported to be a stock salesman for the Mountain City Consolidated Copper Co., with the suggestion that Kaltenborn buy $3,500 worth of M. C. C. C. stock for the purpose of taking a short-term loss to charge off on his income tax.   He explained that Mooney, of the internal revenue in Nevada, and secretary-treasurer of the copper company, would show him how to do it to evade prosecution.   Kaltenborn did not play ball and subsequently was convicted.   There were other incidents of unusual relationships between internal-revenue employees and those under investigation, such as a case where an internal-revenue employee was instrumental in bringing together a taxpayer under investigation with the madam of a house of prostitution also under investigation, for the purpose of establishing a new house of assignation near a military installation.

Subsequent to the committee hearings most of the employees involved have been removed from the service and a Federal grand jury is considering the entire matter.

V. The role of Arthur H. Samish

The strange tale of the part played by an almost unbelievable character, Arthur H. Samish, in the California picture nearly defies description.   Mr. Samish can safely be called "Mr. Big" in California.   His physical weight, around 300 pounds, can be calculated fairly accurately but the weight of his influence in the affairs of that State would be most difficult to estimate.   Mr. Samish describes himself as a "public relations counsel" or a "policy consultant" and has declared on at least one occasion, "I am the legislature."   His forte is representation of organizations and associations as a lobbyist before the California Legislature.   Prior to the actual arrival of the chairman of the committee for the hearings in California, committee investigators were rebuffed in their attempts to examine Mr. Samish's records; thus it was necessary to explore his methods in open hearing and the revelations were startling.

For many years one of Mr. Samish's clients has been the California State Brewers Institute, a trade association composed of 11 of the 14 breweries in California which accounts for 86 percent of the beer production there.   The officers of the institute testified that the organization was a nonprofit association, the stated purposes of which were to "educate and elevate the minds of men" and to "encourage civic enterprises with a view of attaining the maximum benefits for all concerned."   The dues of the association were established on a per-barrel basis according to the production of beer by the member breweries.   An assessment of 4 cents per barrel produced by the member breweries was turned over to the institute and placed in a bank account to be disbursed under the authority of the directors of the institute.   This assessment amounted to a very substantial sum when it is considered that in 6 years the total sum paid into this fund by the breweries amounted to well over $500,000.   According to the testimony, the practice of the brewers, some of whom testified, has been to deduct this entire assessment for tax purposes on their books as "an operating expense."   The members also pay another 5 cents per barrel to the institute, which money is deposited in a special account in the Crocker First National Bank of San Francisco.   Mr. Samish is a virtual dictator over the disbursement of funds from this account.   Deposits from the 5-cent assessment in the last 6 years from the brewers to the institute aggregated $935,943.19.   It has been the practice of the member breweries, according to the testimony, to deduct again as "an operating expense" 50 percent of this additional assessment.   The other 50 percent is considered nondeductible as an operating expense on the theory that half of the fund is used for nondeductible purposes.   Thus the member brewers contribute a total of 9 cents per barrel of beer to the institute.   Under this agreement nearly $2,000,000 has been paid in during the past 6 years with the brewers charging off, as an "operating expense," 6½ cents on each barrel as a tax deduction.   But examination of the record to determine if this, in fact, is "operating expense" is in order.

The committee labored through a lengthy interrogation of the institute officers, member brewers, Samish's bookkeepers and Samish himself in an effort to find out what became of this tremendous sum of money.   In connection with the $1,000,000 "Samish fund", Mr. James G. Hamilton, Secretary of the California State Brewers Institute, testified that the checks are drawn at the request of either Mr. Samish or his representatives in his office.   From the record:

Question. So, that Mr. Samish directs these three gentlemen to draw the checks.   Would you say that he is in complete control of that account?
The CHAIRMAN. For practical purposes.
Answer: For practical purposes; yes.
Question. Now, who keeps the books and records as to that account?
Answer. I don't know

Mr. Hamilton, who is a full-time paid employee handling the administrative affairs of the institute, appeared strangely uninformed with respect to what became of the bank statements and canceled checks of the account.   He advised that the statements and checks were sent to Mr. Samish's office and that the institute had no record of the expenditures; that the institute "acts merely as an agent in the collection and deposit of the funds."

Mr. Samish's function, as described by Mr. Hamilton, was summed up by Senator Kefauver in this question: "For practical purposes he makes the legislative and political decisions for the brewers of California?"   Mr. Hamilton answered "Yes."

Further it was estimated that members of the institute, persons connected with organizations and their families, wholesalers, and retailers who would be affected by the Samish influence would number around 500,000 in California.   Senator Kefauver inquired of Mr. Hamilton: "Now, when it comes up as to whether a proposed referendum is to be good or bad for the brewing industry, whether an election of a State Senator, a member of the legislature or the passage of a bill in the legislature will be good or bad, that decision is made exclusively and wholly by Mr. Samish?"   Mr. Hamilton said, "That is my understanding; yes."

The examination of William P. Baker, president of the California State Brewers Institute and also president of the Regal-Amber Brewing Co., was very enlightening.   Mr. Baker was one of the three individuals authorized to draw checks on the "Samish account" of the institute.   He testified that he did not question the checks which were presented to him for signature.   He "imagined" they came from Samish's office but he had never had occasion to refuse to sign any checks and "supposed" that Samish kept a record of the checks;

further that the only checks he remembered signing were to Mr. Samish and these took up all of the fund. The net result of that interrogation of the members of the Brewers Institute with respect to the disbursement of the funds from the special account was, "See Mr. Samish."

Mr. Samish proved to be not at all disturbed by his inability to account for expenditures traced to him and deducted by the brewers as expense to save themselves many thousands of dollars in Federal taxes. After considerable fencing, Mr. Samish finally testified that the checks on the "Samish fund" were made up in his office and sent to the institute for signature and returned to his office. When the canceled checks were returned by the bank with the monthly statement, the canceled checks and the statement and a handwritten record of the checks drawn for the month were delivered to his office by the institute. In answer to a question as to what became of the statement and canceled checks, Mr. Samish testified:

> I take the recapitulation, the bank statement, and the canceled checks and I throw them in the wastebasket.

From time to time Mr. Samish referred to a written agreement he had with the institute. It was pointed out that, under its terms concerning expenditures, there was to be a "report made." He was asked how a report was made in the light of his testimony that he destroyed all records and the testimony from the institute officials was that they kept no records. Mr. Samish replied, "I don't work on that end of it." The agreement further provided that Mr. Samish should have no authority to incur expenditures until the institute authorized them. He was asked how this could be reconciled with the statement he made that he drew checks upon his own authority. He said, "I just do it." He was asked if this did not breach his contract. He answered, "I haven't even given that any consideration."

During the interrogation Mr. Samish produced a handwritten notation of a number of checks drawn in the past year. It was noted that on October 3, 1950, a check was drawn to cash in the amount of $15,000. Mr. Samish was asked where the cash went. He explained that during the general election period many "cash" checks were drawn looking toward seeing that—

> honest, outstanding officials that subscribe to the temperate use of beer, wine, spirits and other things are returned to office.

This colloquy followed:

> Question. And where does the money go, sir?
> Answer. It is expended.
> Question. It is expended?
> Answer (nodding affirmatively).
> Question. And what does that mean?
> Answer. Well, it is expended in connection with campaigns.
> Question. And who gets it?
> Answer. The cash is handled through me.
> Question. You get the cash, then?
> Answer. Yes.
> Question. And what do you do with the cash?
> Answer. We spend it. Make contributions and distributions.
> * * * * * *
> Question. Well, sir, we are not arguing policy with you. We are trying to find out where the money went, physically; whose hands it got into.
> Answer. Well, it comes into mine.

Question. And then where does it go from yours?
Answer. It is given in contributions.
Question. To whom?
Answer. To different campaigns.
Question. Name one.
Answer. Well, I don't keep a record of that. I would be glad to see if—to see if I can find it for you.

*   *   *   *   *   *   *

Question. Now you have the money in your hand; you have $10,000; you are going to give it to the campaign committee. How do you do it?
Answer. I handle it. I have been doing it for a great many years.
Question. Do you handle it in cash?
Answer. Well, we pay bills sometimes. Sometimes we may handle it in cash.
Question. What is wrong with writing a little check to the campaign committee?
Answer. I tell you what I decided after this situation: I told Mr. Hoertkorn [his bookkeeper], "For your information, starting March 1, [1951] everything in that fund is going to be by check."
The CHAIRMAN. May I ask a question at that point. Mr. Samish, just looking here at one month—for instance in May of 1950—you have "contributions $10,000," "$10,000," "$10,000," "$10,000"—four of them definitely marked "contributions" there; others here, "liquor," and somebody is a trustee, and "Louis Lurie Company"—I guess that is printing. But anyway, there is $40,000 in "contributions" that I assume that you handle by paying some bills or giving to the candidates, or whatever it may be.
Question. Is there a distinction between "cash" and "contributions"?
The CHAIRMAN. Is that the same thing?
Answer. "Cash" and "contributions" are the same thing.
Question. Who decides whether it is going to be a contribution or cash?
Answer. All of our contributions, with rare exceptions—once in a while we may make a check out if I don't happen to be around, or for what reason I don't know. But I would say 95 percent of it is in cash.

In view of the prohibitions in the Federal Corrupt Practices Act, the disbursements by Samish of substantial sums "in connection with campaigns" indicate that there is a strong possibility of a violation of this act by the Samish group. Among other things, the act prohibits campaign contributions by corporations. Samish was found to have issued a circular letter to the brewers discussing "all candidates" and admitted that they had been called upon by some of the national parties to make contributions to their candidates. The Attorney General of the United States has been asked to look into the matter.

Samish testified that about $153,000 per year was received into the special account to be disbursed according to his direction. In the 1-year period of 1950 at least $105,000 of this sum was checked out for "cash." Samish claimed in his books that the money was spent for "contributions." Notwithstanding, he was unable to tell the committee during his testimony exactly where as much as $1 of this sum was spent. An interesting example of his vagueness and indefiniteness was a passage which took place about an item of $13,-317.94 which Samish reported in his personal income-tax return for the year 1949 under "rentals." Samish said the money came from "a little oil venture." He said he owned oil properties in Indiana and Texas and he didn't know which one—"really I don't."

Question: A "little" item you can't remember?
Answer: Oh, it's small. That's right. I can't remember.
Question: All right, sir. See if you can remember this one: Another $13,000 in your expense for 1949 for entertaining—$13,899.35. What is that for?
Answer: Oh, I can't give you any details.

*   *   *   *   *   *   *

Question: In general, who is entertained $13,000 worth?
Answer: I can't tell you. If you want to ask or inquire about those things, I think our tax consultant, or our tax counsel, will explain everything to your satisfaction.
Question: Is he the one who spends the money?
Answer: That isn't a question of that.
Question: Yes; it is the question.
Answer: Well, I don't know. I just don't know, Mr. Rice.

The light regard with which Samish holds money is further illustrated by his statement about some of his fees. Samish related that he received a yearly income from a number of accounts, one of which was Schenley Industries of New York. He said, "I get $36,000 flat fee from Schenley Industries." Senator Kefauver said, "You must do a lot of work for them for $36,000." Samish replied, "Well, I do at times, Senator, I do but not always. I mean I am 'callable' when they want me." Samish testified that he had previously been paid as much as $46,000 by Schenley but the amount of his fee was reduced to $36,000, the reason being that "I was earning too much money."

Apparently Samish has been none too discriminating in his choice of friends and associates. For instance, he testified he had on several occasions gone to Hot Springs, Ark., for the baths there. While there he talked with the notorious Joe Adonis, alias Joseph Doto, one of the major racket figures in the country. He said, in answer to a question about meeting Adonis any place outside of Hot Springs, "Oh, I might have seen him around New York." While in Hot Springs there was a telephone call placed from his room to the Beverly Country Club in New Orleans, which at that time was one of the best known gambling casinos in the country. The committee testimony has reflected that the club is operated principally by "Dandy Phil" Kastel and that Frank Costello has an interest in the place. When asked the reason for his call to the Beverly Club from Hot Springs in April of 1950, Samish replied, "Well, I couldn't tell you. Maybe I wanted to say, 'Hello', to Mr. Kastel or Mrs. Kastel." Pressed further about the conversation, he said, "I don't recall. I really can't say. I just can't say. I don't know. I don't know the nature of the conversation." It was also indicated to Samish that while at Hot Springs he had made numerous calls to Chicago to a telephone listed to the Jack Stone Cigar Store, 217 North Clark Street. He was asked what the calls were for, and answered that he probably was looking for a tip on "a horse or anything."

An example of another type of Samish influence and accomplishment was brought out through the testimony of C. H. Palmer, counsel for the Alfred Hart Distilleries, of Los Angeles, Calif. In 1943, Alfred Hart was anxious to open a new liquor distributorship in San Bernardino County, one of the largest counties in the United States. A partnership with Edward Seeman was formed in 1943 for this purpose. Seeman, according to Sheriff James Stocker, was operating slot machines and pinball machines in that section. After about 2 months, there were some negotiations between Arthur Samish, State Senator Ralph Swing, Alfred Hart, and his attorney. Mr. Palmer, the attorney, advised that "Mr. Seeman was in some sense representing Mr. Ralph Swing." A new arrangement was made and a new partnership formed with Alfred Hart retaining 51 percent of the interest and the balance distributed to Ralph Swing, Edward Seeman, and Miss Edith Mack identified as a friend of Samish. The testimony reflected that almost immediately the enterprise flourished. Seeman's investment was said to be $100, Senator Swing's $500, and Edith Mack $100 or $200. Within the first 3 months of the operation, Miss Mack's share of the profits was at least $2,700.

When there was a reorganization in 1948, Hart purchased the interest of Seeman and Swing. In addition to his dividends over the years, Senator Swing received $16,000 in cash, plus 6,000 shares of stock which were sold for $24,000. In addition to his substantial dividends, Seeman received $16,000 cash and 8,000 shares which were sold for $48,000. Miss Mack retained her interest. In discussing Samish's participation in bringing these people together, Senator Kefauver commented to Mr. Palmer, "It was very pleasing to Mr. Samish to have some participation in getting Mr. Swing a good business deal like that?" Palmer answered, "Well, I think it is fair to say that it was a feather in his cap." Senator Kefauver went on to say, "I suppose it would be helpful to Mr. Samish to have Senator Swing on his side," to which Mr. Palmer agreed. Thus, we find an apt illustration of Samish's ability to accomplish a very profitable financial arrangement for a State senator, although there would be no record traceable to Samish.

What makes the Samish story even more incredible is the fact that many of the disclosures of questionable practices made during the committee hearings of 1951 had been exposed in part as long ago as 1938 when there was a legislative investigation in California. The results were incorporated in a report prepared by Howard R. Philbrick made September 28, 1938. Strangely enough, the report, after being made a part of the record of the California Legislature, was almost immediately expunged from the record and copies disappeared to the extent that the report became a virtual collector's item. The report was a work of several former FBI agents and extremely exhaustive. Parts were read into the committee record. Among other things, charged in its summary findings were:

> The principal source of corruption has been money pressure. The principal offender among lobbyists has been Arthur H. Samish of San Francisco, through whose accounts has passed at least a total of $496,138.62 during the years 1935 to 1938. * * * Lobbying of the type represented by Mr. Samish as distinguished from open legislative representation has been a major corrupting influence. * * * Mr. Samish from one client industry obtained a political fund in excess of $97,000 between 1935 and 1938—quite distinct from Mr. Samish's own compensation fund from the client. He could spend the political fund without accounting and in fact kept no disbursement records.

In that report, Samish was quoted as saying, "I am the governor of the legislature. To hell with the Governor of the State." As far back as 1938, the investigators encountered the same difficulties in dealing with Mr. Samish's record as had the Senate committee representatives. Those predecessor investigators said that, "Mr. Samish's records were not records as a bookkeeper would understand the term. They were notations of income items and check-stub records of bank-account withdrawals. Further, there was no itemization of Samish's expense deduction. * * * Mr. Samish's return to the Federal Government in 1937 is not in compliance with rules and regulations of the United States Treasury Department and does not attempt to set up figures which actually reveal Mr. Samish's true income."

In view of the findings of this committee, recommendations have been made to both the Commissioner of Internal Revenue and the Attorney General of the United States that Arthur Samish's practices and those of the California Brewers Institute and the brewer members thereof be examined with a view to:

1. Disallowing the deductions of the brewers as "operating expense" in the 9-cent assessment fund, amounting to nearly $2,000,000 in the past 6 years. This fund has obviously been expended principally by Arthur H. Samish for purposes almost entirely unexplained.

2. Assessing Samish for additional income in view of the fact that Samish admitted personally receiving, in the past 6 years, nearly $1,000,000 in cash from the brewers. This sum should be considered income to him and taxable accordingly, unless he is able to show that the money was expended for properly deductible purposes. In other words, from the record it could be said that the money went into Samish's own pocket and stopped there.

VI. Attempt to circumvent new Federal law against shipment of slot machines

During the hearing in San Francisco early in March 1951 there was brought into the hearing room a new contraption just shipped to California from Chicago. Testimony of Allen Krause showed that despite the very recent passage of Federal legislation prohibiting the interstate shipment of slot machines, at least one company, the Buckley Manufacturing Co. of Chicago, had already produced a machine which was said to be a non-coin-operated device but appeared to be very similar to a console slot machine and had already shipped a pilot model to California. Mr. Krause had ordered one of the machines and explained that the machine would operate after the bartender or operator of the establishment had thrown a switch which would permit the playing of the machine. Obviously it was intended that any coins which changed hands would go to the bartender and the pay-off as indicated after the turning of the wheels would be made by the bartender. Thus, it was intended by the operators to argue that although the machine might be adapted to accomplish the same purpose as a slot machine, "it was not coin-operated." It appears that the racket element has no intention of abandoning the lucrative slot-machine business even though recent Federal legislation has been designed to paralyze this illicit industry.

SARATOGA COUNTY, N. Y.

The testimony before this committee clearly established that sometime toward the end of July or beginning of August 1947, Superintendent of State Police John A. Gaffney requested a survey to be made of gambling in Saratoga County. This order was transmitted to Inspector Charles LaForge, who made the survey assisted by several troopers. Their findings were incorporated in a report which Inspector LaForge made on August 4, 1947. This report describes in detail six separate gambling establishments, namely, the Chicago Club, Delmonicos, Smith's Interlochen, Piping Rock, Arrowhead, and Newman's Lake House. Each report indicates by whom the establishment is operated, a description of the property, and its location, together with the gambling equipment observed therein.

A typical example of such description is the following: Club Arrowhead, operated by Joe Adonis of Brooklyn, Charley Manny, New York City, J. A. Coakley, alias O. K. Coakley, Lefty Clark, Detroit; description, frame building, outskirts of city, consisting of bar, restaurant, and casino all on first floor; gambling equipment, five roulette wheels, one large wheel, five card tables, two crap tables, two bird cages.

All of the establishments described in the LaForge report in addition to having open gambling, sold food and liquor, and were all duly licensed by the State Liquor Authority. This LaForge report was forwarded by Inspector LaForge to Chief Inspector Francis S. McGarvey, who prepared a condensed memorandum bearing the same date, August 6, 1947, covering 1½ pages, listing each of the clubs.

The LaForge report and the McGarvey memorandum were transmitted to Superintendent of State Police Gaffney on the same date, August 6, 1947. Up to this point police action was more than prompt. The report was completed and personally delivered to Gaffney with unusual expedition, not being permitted to go through the usual channels.

Despite the great hurry to complete the report and deliver it to Gaffney, Gaffney testified that he merely read the report and immediately filed it away. He only remarked to Chief Inspector McGarvey, who had delivered it in person that, "This looks like a sizable operation." He took no further action although both Chief Inspector McGarvey and Inspector LaForge were awaiting orders to close the gambling joints, an order which never came. Superintendent Gaffney stated that the report submitted to him through his own organization made him aware of the fact that there was a very substantial operation going on in Saratoga which was run by some well-known and unsavory characters with national criminal reputations, such as Joe Adonis, Lefty Clark, and others. He further testified that the only reason he took no action was because he received no request from the local authorities to intervene and that the Governor had failed to give him orders to do so.

According to Superintendent Gaffney State troopers can only take action in cities at the request of local authorities or at the order of the Governor. He based his opinion on section 97 of the executive law. This provision of law was read to him and it was pointed out that this statute grants to the State troopers the powers of peace officers anywhere in the State. The only limitation on State police activities within cities is contained in the last sentence of section 97, which reads:

but they, the State police, shall not exercise their powers within the limits of any city to suppress riots and disorder except by direction of the Governor, or upon request of the mayor of the city, with the approval of the Governor.

Thus, the sole restriction on the activity of the State troopers within cities relates to the suppression of riots and disorder. This has no application to the subject of gambling. When this was pointed out to Superintendent Gaffney, he shifted his position and stated that State police did not intervene in cities without express order or request, because of policy and not because of any statute.

LEAVE GAMBLING IN SARATOGA ALONE, UNLESS—

Superintendent Gaffney testified that neither he nor anybody on his behalf took the matter of gambling in Saratoga up with the Governor, or with any member of his staff.   When pressed as to the cause of his failure to inform the Governor or his staff, Gaffney stated that he felt that they knew about it since, "It's been going on for 25 years to my knowledge."   In this connection, it should be stated that one of the committee's investigators testified that LaForge told him the report had been ordered by the Governor's office and was delivered to the Governor's office.   LaForge denied having said this and he and the other members of the State police denied it to be the fact.

When the chairman asked, "In other words, you just knew you just weren't supposed to do anything about it," Mr. Gaffney answered in the affirmative.   He also stated that when one gets to be the superintendent of the State police he is supposed to have enough savvy or understanding to leave gambling in Saratoga alone unless he is told to go in.

Gaffney also testified that if he brought the matter to the Governor's attention on his own initiative, he would be "out on the sidewalk."   But he took the opposite position when pressed by Senator Tobey who asked Gaffney, "Well, if you saw Tom Dewey and said, 'This is a rotten condition, what shall I do, Mr. Governor,' what do you suppose he would say."   Superintendent Gaffney answered, "Go in and clean it up."   These two answers are irreconcilable.

Subsequent to the testimony of Superintendent Gaffney, this committee received from Hon. Thomas E. Dewey, Governor of the State of New York, a report made to him by his counsel, Lawrence E. Walsh, together with a statement from the Governor himself.   The report is a substantial whitewash of Superintendent Gaffney, going so far as to state, "At several points during Superintendent Gaffney's examination, he was victimized by complicated questions which assumed facts not proven but even facts contrary to those proven." Nevertheless the report concludes:

Since September 1949 weekly inspections by the State police have completely eliminated organized gambling in the city of Saratoga.

Even this conclusion is at variance with the facts.   The undisputed testimony shows that gambling was going full blast in August 1949, during the racing season when the gambling houses are wide open. The season ends at the beginning of September.   When the racing season of 1950 began in August of that year, the State Police closed down gambling.   Right up to the beginning of the season, the gamblers made preparations to open.   There was no general understanding that the city was closed down.   The Walsh report fails to explain why the State police acted to prevent organized gambling during the racing season of 1950 but did not take any action during any prior years.

It should also be noted that Superintendent Gaffney, as well as his subordinates, testified that all of the gambling establishments referred to in the LaForge report, were licensed by the State liquor authority. These witnesses stated that it was a ground for revocation of the liquor license, if gambling were permitted on licensed premises.   No valid explanation was given for the failure of these State officials to report these conditions to the liquor authority or of the failure of the latter agency to take any action.   Mr. Walsh's report is also significantly silent on this subject.

Walter A'Hearn, one of two detectives on the Saratoga Police force, testified that in the 19 years he had been a member of the force, he never made an arrest for gambling and his general practice on going into the various clubs in Saratoga was to go as far as the lobby but not to go into the gaming rooms.   He would not go beyond the dining room.   He also testified he never had orders to go into the gaming rooms, and that it was his opinion that if he had gone in he would have been out of a job.

A study of this witness' savings bank account showed the significant fact that in the years when gambling was permitted in Saratoga, he made substantial deposits at the end of the gambling season.   In the years when there was no gambling, he made no such deposits.   The witness testified that he and his partner earned extra income by escorting the cash to some of the gambling establishments from the bank, for which he was paid at the rate of $10 a night.   For this purpose, a police automobile was used.   This practice was carried on with the knowledge of Chief of Police Patrick F. Rox.   It is apparent from the testimony in executive session of both Chief of Police Rox and Sheriff Hathorn, that they knew of the gambling conditions in Saratoga, Chief of Police Rox like Detective A'Hearn, felt that it was to his own best interest to take no action and to issue no instructions for taking of action in connection with the gambling. Sheriff Hathorn took a similar position.

It is gratifying to note that on the basis of the disclosures of this committee, the Governor has ordered a special investigation in Saratoga.   Despite the critical tone of Mr. Walsh's report the Governor's statement is most complimentary, pointing out the "great positive contributions made by the Senate subcommittee   *   *   *."

It is apparent to this committee that open gambling in Saratoga has existed for many years with the knowledge of the New York State police and of public officials and the local political organizations that control such public officials.   It is the opinion of the committee that these public officials and political organizations profited from the flagrant disregard of criminal statutes.   But what is equally disturbing to the committee is that these Saratoga operations contributed enormous sums to the coffers of some of the most notorious hoodlums in the country.

NEW YORK CITY

INTRODUCTION

Public concern over organized crime was at a high point, when this committee held its hearings in New York City.   A Brooklyn grand jury was inquiring into the ramifications of a bookmaking empire that was reputed to have done a $20,000,000 business and to have paid over $1,000,000 a year to the police for protection.   Grand juries in New York County had under consideration the misuse of firemen's funds and the heartbreaking degradation of our college students through basketball fixes, arranged by professional gamblers.   There was public apprehension over the increased narcotics traffic and its mounting toll among teen-agers.

In contrast to other cities visited by the committee, however, some of the principal law-enforcement officials in New York City were keenly alert to the menace of organized crime. The struggle against organized crime, with its deep roots in gambling, received tremendous impetus from the prompt and effective action of New York County District Attorney Frank Hogan against Frank Erickson following his confession of bookmaking activity before the McFarland Committee in Washington last year. Erickson's incarceration on a gambling charge was remarkable in that a top-flight gambler had suffered a sizable penalty for flouting the law. Hogan has been waging a courageous war against Costello and the crime syndicate for many years. Miles McDonald, district attorney of Kings County, deserves great credit for the tireless way in which he has been digging into the operations of the Gross bookmaking empire, despite repeated attempts to discourage their investigations.

Both District Attorney Hogan and District Attorney McDonald, and many able members of their staffs, were extremely cooperative with the committee in making available to it data from current and prior investigations. These data were of great assistance to the committee in its task of following the ramifications of organized crime in interstate commerce.

The New York hearings were vital to the committee for a number of reasons. New York City, because of its size, location, dominance in the country, complexity of its population and governmental problems, is one of the major centers of organized crime. It is, in fact, the headquarters of the Costello-Adonis-Lansky crime syndicate which is in close and cordial relationship with the country's other major criminal syndicate, the Accardo-Guzik-Fischetti group based on Chicago. The committee wished to determine what there was in the local situation that fostered the illegal operations of the Costello-Adonis-Lansky criminal syndicate in New York City as well as in other States.

In its 8 days of public hearings and 3 days of private hearings in 1951, following 2 private hearings held in 1950, the committee heard a total of 89 witnesses in addition to interviews and conferences with approximately 500 others. There were 40 at the open hearings and 49 at the closed hearings. These witnesses included public officials, political leaders, law-enforcement officials, Federal officials, including those of the Bureau of Narcotics, the Bureau of Internal Revenue, the Bureau of Immigration, and others. The committee heard from former Mayor William O'Dwyer; from two of his chief aides and intimate friends, Frank Bals and James F. Moran; from another former O'Dwyer aide, John Murtagh, who was former commissioner of investigation, and now chief magistrate of the city, having been appointed to that position by O'Dwyer. The committee heard considerable testimony concerning water-front conditions from such witnesses as Mr. Philip Stephens, business manager of the New York Daily News; Mr. Walter Hedden of the Port Authority of New York; and from various water-front racketeers, including Albert Anastasia, who was heard at a closed hearing, and his brother Anthony, who was heard at the open hearings.

District Attorney Miles McDonald and his able assistant, Julius Helfand, appeared to testify about police corruption in Brooklyn and to portray for the committee the gambling operations they had uncovered and the ramifications of these operations in New Jersey and in other States. The chairman of the newly formed New York City Crime Commission, former Assistant Secretary of State Spruille Braden, appeared to give his views. At a later hearing in Washington, Judge Samuel Leibowitz, who had played a prominent part in connection with the grand jury investigation in Brooklyn, also testified and gave the committee the benefit of its factual knowledge and its views.

The New York hearings covered many facets, including the links between crime and politics, crime on the waterfront, large scale bookmaking and gambling operations, narcotics racketeering, operations at the Roosevelt Raceway, gambling conditions in Saratoga, and links between gambling in New York and New Jersey. It particularly stressed both the personnel and the form of the huge crime syndicate which is primarily directed by Costello, Adonis, and Lansky. Not all of these subjects were explored at the open hearings, but all of them were covered either at closed hearings, open hearings, or in the committee's investigations. Most of the subject matter, however, revolved around the testimony of two major witnesses, Frank Costello and William O'Dwyer. Both of these witnesses were questioned on a wide variety of subjects bearing on organized crime and its links with politics with the result that practically all of the information developed in the New York hearings could most expeditiously be related by reference to the testimony of these two witnesses.

FRANK COSTELLO

A simple point illustrates the stature of Frank Costello in New York City. According to Ambassador O'Dwyer, when he was an Army officer attached to the Air Force in 1942 with orders "to keep Wright Field clean," he found it necessary to obtain some information from Frank Costello. Despite the obvious disinclination which the former prosecutor of Murder, Inc., must have had to go into the home of Costello, O'Dwyer did not even think of calling Costello to the offices of the Army Air Corps; he went to Costello's home. The record is complete with evidence of persons in high political positions going to Costello's home at Costello's call. In fact, one former judge, during the regime of Tammany leader Hugo Rogers, as recently as 1948, was known to be the man behind the throne. Hugo Rogers stated on private examination, "If Costello wanted me, he would send for me."

I. Costello—The legitimate businessman

What manner of man exercises this power and has this prestige? Both Costello and his counsel, George Wolf, protested at the executive and public hearings that Costello was falsely charged with being the leader of a national crime syndicate. They were thankful for the opportunity to testify so that they could dispose of the fantastically untrue stories about Costello.

Costello stressed his legitimate business interests in real estate, oil, and other things. According to Costello, he is not a politician, but only a friend of politicians. His political influence goes no further than that of any man who has lived in one neighborhood for many years. He maintains an apartment in one of the most fashionable buildings on the West Side of New York, has a summer home in Sands Point, and travels regularly to Florida, New Orleans, and Hot Springs. He claimed that he had no connection with bookmakers. His associations with known racketeers were purely out of friendship and when he met them in other States, it was purely by chance.

This picture of Costello as a legitimate businessman, which he and his counsel were trying to create, was blurred considerably by additional testimony. His legitimate interests, it was shown, were slight, taking little of his time. From 1944 to 1950, he had owned a parcel of land and the buildings thereon at 79 Wall Street. A management company managed it for him. He had recently invested in a company making infra-red ray broilers, but until his counsel told him, he could not answer the committee's question as to the characteristic feature of his product. While Costello testified that his counsel, Wolf, was his principal adviser on business interests, Costello had invested on the advice and casual conversation of his good friend, Frank Erickson, $4,000 in cash in oil, which he increased through the years to a total of $41,000. He admitted he didn't know anything about the oil business, had made the additional investments solely by playing hunches. He also was an investor for a time in Consolidated Television Co., in which Meyer Lansky and Joe Adonis also had investments. Apart from real-estate investments, Costello admitted, his last previous legitimate business had been a company manufacturing chocolate-covered ice-cream sticks in 1920. Before that, he had had other real-estate ventures, had manufactured kewpie dolls as punchboard prizes, and, prior to his arrest and incarceration on a charge of carrying a gun, had been employed in a piano factory.

On detailed examination of Costello, it became perfectly apparent that his legitimate business consisted of a very few investments about which, on examination, he had practically no knowledge himself and which required practically no time or attention from him. The characterization which he gave himself as being a legitimate businessman simply cannot be sustained.

II. Illegal activities of Costello

Costello's illegal enterprises were neither so quickly ascertained nor so easily described. He admitted a present 20-percent interest in the Beverly Club from which he received first $1,000 and more recently $1,500 a month for acting as a good-will agent and talent scout. The Beverly Club has one of the most elaborate gambling casinos in the New Orleans area, operating all kinds of gaming devices in clear violation of Louisiana law. With some reluctance, Costello also admitted to an interest in the Piping Rock Casino in Saratoga in 1943, but he claimed that he was not personally responsible for this operation, sharing only in the profits because he financed a man who was interested in it. A letter from Meyer Lansky to his accountant, however, indicates that Costello had an outright 30-percent interest in the casino and that Meyer's brother Jack and Joe Adonis also shared in it.

Costello was in the slot machine business in the early thirties in New York City. He admitted that it was in partnership with his present New Orleans partner, Phil Kastel. Mayor Fiorello LaGuardia put him out of business in New York City. In the mid-thirties, the late Huey Long invited him and his slot-machine business into Louisiana, intending, Costello stated, to legalize them and tax them for various State enterprises. Before he saw Long again, Costello said, Long was assassinated and the plan failed of accomplishment. But Costello's illegal slot-machine business remained under the management of Phil Kastel and flourished. Costello admitted that his income from this slot-machine operation was over $70,000 in 1946. Costello insisted that he left the active management of the slot-machine business wholly to Kastel since the time of the survey made at Long's request. Legally made telephone taps in 1943, raised considerable doubt as to this contention. They show Costello giving specific orders with respect to the purchase price and makes of machines. Costello, moreover, visited New Orleans every year for about 30 days. However, he denied that his annual visits to New Orleans were in connection with the slot machines or Beverly Club business. He denied that Kastel or the Louisiana businesses in which he was interested paid his expenses. While the hotel bill was listed in Kastel's name, Costello said he always reimbursed him.

Costello's testimony that he left the management of the slot machine business to Kastel, and that he had nothing to do with purchasing machines was manifestly untrue. It should be examined to see whether it is actually perjurious.

111. Costello and bookmaking

That Costello had been involved in the bookmaking business at one time was apparent from the fact that in 1943 he testified that he took bets on commission, handing them over to other bookmakers and receiving 5 percent of the total bet during the 1920's.

To this committee as to the Senate Committee on Interstate and Foreign Commerce, headed by Senator Ernest W. McFarland, a year ago, Costello wanted it known that he had no connection with bookmakers and had had none for 15 years or more. His own and other testimony make it difficult for the committee to accept this contention. Apart from the former mayor's statement that at the time he sought Costello out in 1942, he knew him by reputation as an outstanding bookmaker, there were two episodes which indicated that Costello's relationships to bookmakers were a great deal closer than that of the average bettor. George Morton Levy, attorney for the Roosevelt Raceway with an extensive financial interest in the track himself, testified that for 4 years ending in 1949, he had paid Costello $15,000 annually, out of his own personal funds, to have Costello keep bookies away from the track. The arrangement started in 1946, Mr. Levy testified, when the racing commissioner, Mr. Benjamin Downing, said that if the track were not cleared of bookies, its license would be withdrawn. To satisfy Downing, Levy called Costello and asked his assistance. Costello stated that he told Levy he didn't think he could do anything, but he would talk around at the bars—at the Waldorf, Gallagher's, Moore's, etc. Complaints stopped at once, Levy testified. Downing was satisfied, and a year later, Levy insisted on giving Costello payment for his service, although Costello assured him he hadn't done a thing and didn't want payment. But $60,000 was paid over and received, the last payment being made more than a year after Downing's death. Levy stopped payments when the Bureau of Internal Revenue refused to allow him to deduct them as a business expense. Both Costello and Levy testified that before 1946 Levy never consulted Costello about his trotting track affairs. On cross-examination, Levy stated that the private race-track police apparently could not satisfy Commissioner Downing. He pointed out that the private race-track police were not Pinkertons, but asserted that he did not have and never had had any personal objection to the Pinkerton men at the track.

Both the testimony of Levy and that of Costello is seriously contradicted by a telephone conversation between Costello and Levy. The telephone call made in 1943 was intercepted by agents in District Attorney Hogan's office pursuant to a legal authorization for wire tapping.

The conversation reads as follows:

LEVY. "Hello, Frank. This is George Levy. I tried to get you yesterday. Can you be up there today?"

COSTELLO. "I don't think so. Any day you can, give me a ring."

LEVY. "Have you got a minute, Frank?"

COSTELLO. "Sure."

LEVY. "In Downey's, or Dewey's presence, we were told not to have Mahoney or Walger, but to have Pinkertons. Pinkerton sent us a contract and it is the god-damnedest thing you ever saw. They can refuse to let in anyone that they choose. John Rogus is all steamed up. Yesterday, we had a meeting in Mineola and Downing said he could see no reason for convicting a man without a fair trial. I called Empire City for a conference with O'Brien and asked him if we could get our own agency. O'Brien turned it down. So you see, Frank, all Bleakley would have to do is call in the local police and he could stop the meet. We did not think we would open today. We saved the thing by putting in a 24-hour cancellation clause—which I see is in there. If we could only get O'Brien to budge an inch. We can't jeopardize the bookmakers. They are just as liable to arrest President Roosevelt's wife for prostitution, as not. It's like holding up a gun against you. They may have enough pride to step out."

COSTELLO. "If they make any errors, you are subject to a suit."

LEVY. "As boss, you should be able to tell them. The way it stands now you better tell George. As for Pete, he does not want to go into the pari-mutuel department. I will have to create something for him."

"I can't play golf Sunday. I ran a pencil into my hand, and I can't hold a club. Dunnigan stood up swell. All three did."

COSTELLO. "I will probably see you Sunday. We can sit on your front lawn and cut up your business."

Both Costello and Levy had previously, when confronted with this testimony, denied that Costello had ever recommended any of his friends or relatives for positions on the track, but on being confronted with this telephone conversation, both recalled that one Pete, who called Costello, "Uncle Frank," had been given a job at the track at Levy's request.

Both Levy and Costello claimed that the conversation was impossible and that there would be no reason for keeping the bookmakers off the track, but on a previous occasion, when testifying before the grand jury of New York County in 1943, Costello said that there would be every reason to assure that the bookmakers could stay on the track. Costello testified that the telephone conversation might be explained because it was necessary to have bookmakers on the track in order to keep the large bettors from upsetting the odds on the pari-mutuel machines.

Levy's explanation of the above conversation is in effect that the Pinkertons did not want to allow Costello to attend the opening of the Yonker's track, and that he was explaining this to Costello. A simple reading of the telephone conversation in connection with Levy's later explanation is determinative of this question.

The "George" referred to in this conversation was unquestionably George Uffner who has had close connections with Costello. He was a known bookmaker for years though Costello denied knowing this fact. When the committee asked why the telephone at Costello's Sands Point home was in Uffner's name, Costello explained that when he bought the place he could not obtain a phone unless he could persuade a friend to give his up. Uffner obliged him by giving Costello his phone. The testimony of both Costello and Levy is not only highly improbable, but inconsistent with the 1943 wire tap and with Costello's explanation of it to the grand jury in 1943. The question remains one for the prosecuting authorities whether perjury has been committed.

IV. Costello and liquor

Costello has frequently admitted having been a bootlegger during prohibition days. In his testimony, in the appeal proceedings in 1933, he stated under oath that he had been in this business in the early 1920's, prior to 1925, and he so stated also in sworn testimony before the New York State Liquor Authority given in 1947.

The precise date of Costello's bootlegging activities is important because in 1925, he took an oath of allegiance to the United States in connection with receiving his final citizenship. At that time, he swore to upholding the laws of the United States. Since he admitted that thereafter he engaged in bootlegging, it would appear that his oath was false. In fact, he engaged in bootlegging before 1925 as well.

There is ample evidence in the files of the Immigration authorities to correlate Costello's admission that he was in fact in the bootlegging business prior to 1925. In fact, Costello was indicted for bootlegging together with Bill Dwyer, the bootlegger king, and 61 other persons in December of 1925, but this indictment was dismissed against Costello after many of the others were tried and convicted.

Further evidence that Costello was active in the bootlegging business at the time he received his citizenship appears on his application for citizenship in which he gave the names of two character witnesses as sponsoring citizens, who were in fact at that time engaged in the bootlegging business with him. Before this committee, Costello vigorously denied that his two sponsors were in the bootlegging business with him, particularly since they were described in the citizenship application as being in the real-estate business. Under cross-examination, Costello insisted that one of these witnesses, Harry Sausser, had never been known to him as a bootlegger, but only as a legitimate real-estate man. At this point, Costello was confronted with his testimony in 1947 before the New York State Liquor Authority in which he stated that one Harry Sausser was the person through whom he arranged the importation of liquor from Canada. Costello admitted to fraud by asserting under oath that he had never arranged for bringing of liquor in from Canada despite the fact that he admitted to this activity, not only to the New York State Liquor Authority, but also before the New York State grand jury. Finally, he admitted that a Harry Sausser had been in the bootlegging business with him. At this point, he asserted that he knew two or possibly three Harry Saussers, and that the Harry Sausser who was in the bootlegging business with him was a wholly different person from the Harry Sausser who he knew to be a legitimate real-estate man and who had been his sponsor in the citizenship application. At the hearing, Senator Tobey appropriately referred to this story as "the tale of the flying saucers."

Little credibility can be attached to Costello's contentions, particularly in view of the circumstances under which the admissions were wrested from him after repeated self-contradictory stories. In fact, Costello testified that he understood the legitimate Sausser to be a railroad man and not even to be in the real-estate business as appeared on the naturalization application.

Costello's testimony concerning his relations with Johnny Torrio, Capone's predecessor in Chicago, was an equally contradictory story. He testified before this committee that he had met Johnny Torrio once or twice and knew his reputation only through the newspapers and did not have any dealings with him. When he was confronted with his testimony before a Federal Treasury agent in 1938, that at the request of Irving Haim, he contacted Torrio and had at least two conversations with Torrio about the sale of a large liquor company which Torrio owned. He retreated to the position that he just did not remember what his testimony might have been. On two occasions, subsequent to 1938 and prior to his testimony before this committee, he had been asked about his relationships with Johnny Torrio, and on both of these occasions, he denied under oath that he knew Torrio at all. These were the grand jury Aurelio disbarment proceedings in 1943 and testimony before the State liquor authority in 1947.

It might here be stated parenthetically that Costello's answers with relation to Torrio are typical of his answers with relation to practically every other matter. He admits as much as he thinks he has to and does not hesitate to change his story to suit the occasion.

Another transaction involving the liquor business and Costello in the late thirties engaged the attention of the committee. In the spring of 1938, as Costello admitted, he endorsed a note of a Mr. William Helis for $325,000 so that Helis, Kastel, and Haim could buy out the English liquor company, Whitely Distributors, for which Haim, at the time, was the American distributor and Kastel the good-will man. Costello insisted he backed the note out of pure friendship. In executive session, he had not mentioned the simultaneous negotiations that Haim and Kastel were conducting to have Costello take over as American good-will man, an operation which would have given Costello at least $30,000 a year and $25,000 in expenses, to act as promoter for the products of this company. The deal fell through, Costello stated, because of the objections of the attorney for Helis to the Costello connection. Costello insisted to the committee that thereafter he had no further interest in Whitely Distributors, even though Haim and Helis did eventually buy the concern. If he told a Federal agent in 1938 that he had an interest in Whitely, he might have been "optimistic," Costello explained. He denied that he ever received any money or income from Whitely. He couldn't recall a telephone conversation in which, early in a morning in June of 1943, he had called his wife to tell her that an envelope would come from Irving Haim at 5 o'clock, that if she were not planning to be home he would have to make other arrangements, and that she knew where to put it. He denied flatly that it could have been money. Confronted with the fact that two of his friends,

Judge Aurelio and Abe Rosenthal, Aurelio's district leader, had testified in 1943 that Costello told them when they were in his house that the liquor he was serving was one in which he had an interest, Costello said that he must have been boasting or that what he meant was he had an interest in Kastel who had an interest in the business. Committee counsel pointed out that Kastel had left the business in 1940. Confronted with the fact that in applying for the lease on his present apartment, Costello had put himself down as general manager of the distributing company for Whitely, Costello said he was anxious for a place to live and his statement was just a white lie. Asked why Sam Haas, an attorney in hiding from a subpena in connection with gambling operations in Ohio, would have had Costello down in his telephone book as available at the office of this liquor company, Costello said that maybe he told him he could get him there through Kastel. He could not remember the telephone calls to him there from Haas, of which the committee had evidence.

All of the above reeks of perjury and it should be carefully examined by the United States Attorney to see if the crime of perjury, as technically defined, was committed by Costello.

V. Costello's naturalization

Costello was naturalized in 1925. In the last section, reference was made to apparently untrue statements in his application for naturalization and to his patently false oath to uphold the constitution and laws of the United States taken when he became a citizen.

In addition, Costello admitted under examination by the committee that in his application for citizenship, he failed to reveal that he had used alias "Frank Severio" because had he done so, the Immigration authorities would have learned that he had been convicted of illegal possession of a gun under this name, and it was his understanding that his citizenship application would have been delayed. He admitted having revealed in his citizenship application other aliases which were innocuous because he had not been convicted of crime under these names.

The committee understands that the New York office of the Bureau of Immigration and Naturalization at least once recommended the revocation of Costello's naturalization because of fraud. The committee heartily agrees with this recommendation and urges that prompt attention be given to this matter. Costello has also admitted that, since becoming a citizen, he has engaged in illegal bootlegging and illegal slot machine and gambling operations. The committee believes that he is an outstanding gambling operator. There is no question that he has been a strong and evil influence on New York politics. On the other hand, by his own admission, he has never taken the trouble to exercise his duty as a citizen to cast a vote in an election.

The question of whether or not Costello could or should be deported after his naturalization has been revoked is open to some question. It is probable that under existing laws, he could not be deported as his record now stands, but there is every reason to believe that if he is convicted for perjury he has committed before this committee, and if he is convicted for his present illegal gambling activities in the State of Louisiana, that he will probably be subject to deportation. This matter requires careful study and aggressive action.

VI. The "net worth" of Costello

When Senator Tobey asked O'Dwyer what he considered the basis of Costello's appeal to politicians, O'Dwyer replied, "It doesn't matter whether it is a banker, a businessman, or a gangster, his pocketbook is always attractive." The committee made strenuous efforts to find out what was in Costello's pocketbook. In executive session, his counsel had promised to produce a statement of net worth within 2 weeks. This was in the form of a stipulation made in Costello's presence and with his consent. At the open hearings he refused it on the grounds that the interim report of the committee was so prejudicial to the witness as to make any reply to the question of net worth incriminatory. On this point as on others, after considerable questioning and continued refusals to answer, Costello has been cited for contempt.

The committee brought out whatever indications of his wealth it could find. His affluent mode of living has already been mentioned. He had made oil investments of over $40,000. He made a profit of approximately $119,000 on his sale of 79 Wall Street in 1950. His wife owned the house at Sands Point purchased 7 years ago for about $30,000. She owned a few lots in Florida valued at $7,500. In 1949, Costello had reported an income of some $16,000 in bets out of a total reported of $29,000. His receipt of $60,000 from Levy has already been commented upon. Costello admitted to having in a strong box in his home some $40,000 in cash; and another $5,000 in cash secreted in his summer place. He had bank accounts of about $100,000. His annual income from the Louisiana Mint Co. had run around $70,000 a year. That his name was acceptable on a note of $325,000 in 1938 was an indication that he was held to be a man of wealth even then. He receives an apparently unearned monthly salary of $1,000 or $1,500 from the Beverly Club. The $27,000 he had lost in a taxicab a few years ago, he stated, represented the return of moneys Kastel owed him, plus a loan in cash of $15,000 from his brother-in-law which he might have needed for a real-estate deal. Costello explained that this money was taken in cash because he might not have been able to get a check cashed quickly, although he had $100,000 in the bank. Costello admitted that he now owes Erickson, the big bookmaker, $30,000. He also had borrowed $50,000 in two installments from Erickson at about the time he purchased the 79 Wall Street parcel for $55,000 cash over the $250,000 mortgage. He denied knowing whether or not this loan from Erickson had anything to do with Erickson's borrowing at about the same time $100,000 from a Mr. Gallagher, president of the Pennsylvania Exchange Bank, an acquaintance of his of many years. The committee received no satisfactory reply to the question why he borrowed so much money from Erickson at a time when he seemed to have ample funds of his own and when he disclaimed any interest in Erickson's operations. Costello's only reply was he did not want to leave himself short.

VII. Costello's relations with gangsters and racketeers

The New York syndicate is headed by Frank Costello, Meyer Lansky, and Joe Adonis. Willie Moretti and others, including Abner ("Longie") Zwillman, Vito Genovese, and Joseph Profaci figure in the picture. Others might be mentioned with these, but the recital of additional names would add little to the outline.

The one most important exception is Charley "Lucky" Luciano, who together with Costello succeeded to the leadership of the New York gang during the prohibition era. Luciano was convicted during the 1930's by present Governor, Thomas E. Dewey, but while in prison apparently continued to maintain his contacts with the mob. Meyer Lansky, in particular, worked to effect Luciano's release on parole which took place in 1946. The parole itself has been subject to much question, having originally been primarily justified in the public eyes by assertions that Luciano had rendered unusually valuable service to this country during the war. On an investigation by this committee, it appeared that Meyer Lansky had arranged for the transmission of certain information from Luciano to the Intelligence Service of the United States Navy. There was no evaluation of this information whatsoever. One Charles R. Haffenden, who wrote a letter supporting the parole and stating that the services were of great value, testified before the committee that he had no knowledge at all as to the value of the services, but that he had written a letter while in a hospital recuperating from war wounds and had simply attempted to be generous at the request of Luciano's counsel. It now appears that the parole must be justified on some basis other than that of Luciano's contribution to the war effort.

On Luciano's release from prison, Lansky and Costello went to Ellis Island to say good-by to him. They were alone with him for at least a half hour. Two years later, when Luciano managed to enter Cuba, Costello met him there; Lansky actually went to Italy and saw Luciano in that country. Luciano was visited by practically every top hoodlum while he was in Cuba.

Moreover, the night before Luciano sailed, while he was still being held under guard for deportation, his friends were permitted to come aboard and hold a party for him bringing with them tubs of food and wines. Although the Immigration guards remained at a discreet distance while the party was in progress, the Immigration authorities were never able thereafter to prove that such a party had been held, and in fact, their records show that no party was held. Since then, the committee has obtained evidence satisfactory to itself that there was such a party and that the boat was protected during this period by a group of longshoremen who refused to let outsiders, including newspapermen, aboard.

Costello, Lansky, and Adonis were in the television business together in 1949. They are all admittedly close friends. They were all in the Piping Rock Casino together in 1933. Lansky and Adonis were in the gambling business together in the Colonial Inn in Florida, and Lansky and Costello were partners in the Beverly Club in New Orleans. As recently as the summer of 1950, Adonis spent several weeks at Hot Springs with Ed McGrath, a notorious water-front racketeer, occupying the same suite. McGrath is the brother-in-law of James "Cock Eye" Dunn, who was recently electrocuted for a water-front murder. Shortly before Dunn's apprehension for this murder, he vacationed in Miami with Lansky. Anastasia, who was the head of the enforcement division of Murder, Inc., was stated by William O'Dwyer to have been an underling of Adonis. Albert Anastasia, and his brother Anthony, are leading powers on the water front, and Albert Anastasia has moved into a mansion located only five blocks from Adonis's home in New Jersey. These interrelationships will give some idea of the close ties between the various members of the New York mob in the various rackets.

With men of known criminal and racketeering records, Costello had close business and personal relationships. Frank Erickson was a close friend. He was a third member of the golf foursome in which Costello and Levy played regularly. The fourth was an internal revenue agent who now enjoys a $4,000 annual income on a $200 investment in the raceway in which Levy was interested. Erickson admitted they played once a week up to the time of his conviction. While most of his legitimate business deals were through his counsel, George Wolf, Costello admitted that his oil investments were made on the casual invitation of Erickson. When Costello needed large sums of money, he borrowed from Erickson.

Costello's relationship to Willie Moretti, one of New Jersey's gambling overlords, seems to the committee to be that of boss and follower although Costello denied they were anything but close intimate friends of such long standing that he was godfather to Moretti's oldest child. A series of telephone conversations to and about Moretti indicates much more than a purely social relationship. According to grand-jury testimony, Moretti called Costello 130 times in 5 months ending in 1943. When Moretti became ill, began to have hallucinations and talk too much, Costello admitted he might have suggested as a friend that he go away. That Moretti called him "Chief" when he telephoned, was nothing, Costello said; they called each other that. But the committee had no record of any calls in which Costello called Moretti "Chief." In one conversation, Costello reported to a friend, "I will keep him out there at least a month more." When Moretti's brother Solly called to say Willie wanted to come home to take his wife to a doctor, Costello replied that he had to stay out there. Costello called a doctor to ask him to telephone Moretti in California and see what he thought of his conversation and let him know.

Meyer Lansky had an interest in the Beverly Club when it first opened; his brother Jack was a partner of Costello's in the Louisiana Mint Co. in New Orleans and in the Piping Rock Casino in Saratoga Springs. Before the committee in Washington, Longie Zwillman confirmed Costello's testimony that they knew each other very well. Costello admitted that Jerry Catena, another New Jersey gambler associate of Moretti, had been with him in New Orleans and Habana on a visit. Joe Adonis, Costello stated, was a very good friend of his. "Socks" Lanza, another notorious New York racketeer, had visited his home. Costello had told a 1943 grand jury that Lucky Luciano was an acquaintance. He admitted to the committee that he knew Luciano very well. He went with Luciano's attorney, Mr. Polakoff, and with Meyer Lansky to see him off, on the day of his deportation in 1946. Another witness, George White, narcotics agent, stated that in their company at the time was Albert Anastasia. Costello also admitted that he saw Luciano about a year later in Havana.

His out-of-town acquaintanceship and relations with gangsters and racketeers was equally extensive. Costello maintained that he did not know that Carlos Marcello, one of the worst criminals in the country, was in the Beverly Club partnership until after the club opened. The articles of incorporation of this club, however, showed that Marcello was not only one of the incorporators but was also the registered agent for the club.   Kastel himself, as Costello finally admitted, had a criminal record for stock fraud.   Bugsy Siegel, Costello said, he knew from New York.   He knew the two Fischettis, Tony Accardo, and Jacob Guzik, of the Chicago mob, but denied any business dealings with them.   He knew Tony Gizzo, characterized as the traveling secretary of the Kansas mob, but none of the other members. He had spent time with Arthur Samish of California in Hot Springs; their meetings were by chance.   It was just accident that he knew all these people, Costello told the committee.   Many of these gangsters and racketeers were in Florida at the same time as Costello last year.   Costello denied having seen any of them except Moretti and a New Jersey gangster named Nick Delmore.   He denied there was a convention there, and branded as ridiculous the statement that there was a convention in Atlantic City at which the territory for gambling throughout the United States was divided up.

VIII. Costello's influence in politics

Questioning revealed that Costello is now friendly with many Democratic district leaders in New York City.   He stated that he knows the leader of Tammany, Carmine DeSapio, very well.   Of the 16 districts in Manhattan, Costello knows, with varying degrees of intimacy, leaders, coleaders, or both, in at least 10 districts.   Some like Sam Cantor and Frank Mancuso he had known over a period of 30 years or more; they were intimate friends who came to his home for dinner.   In another district, the leader was Louis De Salvio, not only a friend but the son of a former leader and long-time friend, the late Jimmie Kelly, and the brother-in-law of Little Augie Pisano, a well-known mobster.   Another acquaintance of 4 or 5 years was the leader of the second district, Vincent Viggiano, cousin of "Socks" Lanza, the fishpier extortionist, and cousin of the former leader, Dr. Paul Sarubbi. Al Toplitz, until recently both a district leader and chief clerk of the board of elections, had been, like Cantor, a guest of Costello's at his home for Thanksgiving dinner in 1950, and was an old friend.   One of his predecessors in the board of elections, Abe Rosenthal, had likewise been a good friend of Costello's.   Mancuso, in addition to being a district leader, had held an executive position in Tammany Hall.

While James Moran testified that he met Costello only casually, bumping into him here and there by accident, Costello characterized him as a friend, intimate enough to drop in to see him for cocktails. Irving Sherman, Costello testified, he saw with great frequency.   He knew that Sherman worked for O'Dwyer's election.

Asked what was the basis of his ability to influence these politicians Costello said it was hard to explain.   He thought it stemmed from the fact that he had lived all his life in Manhattan.   "I know them, know them well, and maybe they got a little confidence in me."   He had never voted, Costello testified, never made a political contribution; never belonged to any political organization.   He denied that his influence was based on fear; that he was in a position one way or another to defeat a candidate in the primaries.   Nor would his help be enough to elect anyone.   He disclaimed any modesty; he was simply not a politician, just a friend of some politicians.

Costello denied that he had had any part in defeating Paddy Sullivan in a primary campaign.   He had asked Sullivan's support in 1942, when he tried to put over Fay as leader, and Sullivan had refused to commit himself on the ground that he did not wish to support anyone who had the support of Neal, one of the leaders close to Costello. Some time later, Sullivan was defeated in a primary fight. Costello would not deny that he might have offered to help Sullivan in his primary campaign in return for his support, but denied any share in Sullivan's defeat.

Costello reached the height of his power in New York politics in 1942 when he unquestionably had complete domination over Tammany Hall. At that time, Costello supported Kennedy for leader of the hall. Kennedy was Costello's second choice as Costello originally favored Neal's candidate, Fay. However, Costello and Neal decided that they could not bring about Fay's election, and then Costello brought Kennedy into the picture. Without Costello's support, Kennedy would not have had a chance, Costello being able to control the votes of Abe Rosenthal, Dr. Sarubbi, Jimmy Kelly, and Neal and being able to influence the votes of several others, provided a nucleus which he was able to use to bring about Kennedy's election. Costello admitted that Kennedy "might be obligated to him." The fact is that Kennedy was Costello's man.

So close was the relationship between Costello and Kennedy that when Dr. Sarubbi and Abe Rosenthal sought to bring about the nomination of Thomas Aurelio for the supreme court, they went to Costello rather than to Kennedy. Costello asked Kennedy to support the nomination and Kennedy agreed. In the following months, Aurelio's supporters among the leaders at least twice felt that Kennedy might weaken in his determination and swing his support to another candidate. Both times they called upon Costello for help. Both times Costello went to Kennedy and reminded him of his promise. On one occasion, he said to Kennedy:

> My word is as good as my bond. You gave me a commitment. Are you a man or a mouse?

Aurelio received the nomination and was reelected to the supreme court.

It is well known that Aurelio telephoned Costello to thank him and pledged his undying loyalty. It is equally well known that the district attorney of New York County, Frank Hogan, at that time had a legal wire tap on Costello's phone. As a result, Hogan was able to conduct a very extensive grand jury investigation, and also conducted disbarment proceedings against Aurelio which resulted in findings in Aurelio's favor. The testimony in these proceedings and the wire taps themselves were extremely helpful to the committee. The wire taps in particular gave a vivid picture of Frank Costello as a political boss and an underworld emperor. They reveal him as a busy man conducting his affairs on the telephone from 8 to 10 in the morning, talking to people all over the country about business relating primarily to slot machines and numerous other matters in which the conversation reeks of criminality. They reveal him as a king maker who received calls not only from Judge Aurelio, but also from Judge Savarese, from Loscalso, whom O'Dwyer later appointed a judge, and a large assortment of other political figures. All showed the utmost deference for the ruler.

When Costello finished his telephoning, he leisurely went to the barber shop at the Waldorf-Astoria Hotel where those in the know could meet him and arrange their business. Then he would proceed to lunch at one or another of the large hotels. In the afternoon, if he did not play golf, he would eventually go to the bar at the Copacabana night club, at the Waldorf, at the Hotel Madison, or some other expensive place. There he would meet those who had been told they could find him. After the Copacabana night club was opened, arrangements to meet Costello at one or another of these places, would be made by phoning the Copacabana where one of the employees was kept informed of such matters and was able to advise the proper people.

A typical example of Costello's excellent arrangements along these lines was a little dinner arranged with Judge Aurelio who informed him that Kennedy had definitely committed himself. Aurelio and Rosenthal were to proceed to dinner and to meet Costello there, but first Costello arranged to meet Kennedy and some of the leaders at a nearby bar. With everything settled, Costello proceeded to his dinner date to tell the news to Aurelio. He graciously remarked that he would like to know Aurelio better and would be willing to have him to dinner at his apartment.

When Kennedy decided that Dr. Sarubbi was becoming too ill to handle his duties as a leader, he asked Costello to talk to Sarubbi. When Sarubbi wanted his son-in-law appointed to the bench, which later occurred, he apparently talked to Costello about it because Costello remarked on one telephone call that Sarubbi wanted his son-in-law made a judge. When Loscalzo was an up and coming assistant district attorney in Queens, he took a trip out to Costello's golf club in order to meet Costello in the hope that Costello would put a good word in for him with Kennedy.

Costello's influence certainly did not end when Kennedy left the leadership of Tammany Hall. He has testified that he was on very friendly terms with James Moran, Costello's close friend and appointee, and that he was on very intimate terms with Irving Sherman. During the Tammany leadership of Hugo Rogers, Costello again rode very high. Despite Costello's assertion that the Aurelio revelations drove him out of politics, the fact remains that Hugo Rogers came to Costello's home for breakfast after the election of 1945. Costello testified that they did not talk politics, but when Rogers was leader of Tammany, as recently as 1948, Frank Mancuso was admittedly the man to see in order to accomplish anything with Rogers. Costello did not hesitate to admit that Frank Mancuso was his very intimate friend. During the Roger's regime at Tammany Hall, four members of the Tammany steering committee were all very good friends of Costello; Mancuso, Harry Brickman, Sidney Moses, and DeSapio.

Costello told the committee that after the public furor over the Aurelio revelations, he absolutely divorced himself from any participation in politics. If he meets his political friends, they talk and have a drink but if the talk goes to politics, Costello said, he pays no attention. While he admitted that district leaders usually talk politics when they get together, "With me they sort of curb their conversation because they know I am against it, I don't want to hear about it no more, since 1943."

That was his explanation for having heard nothing from Irving Sherman about his assistance to O'Dwyer from 1943 to 1945 except that he was for him. Even if he did invite Hugo Rogers to his house for breakfast after Rogers' election in 1945, Costello was sure they didn't talk politics.   Nor was there any politics at his Thanksgiving Day gathering last year when two of his guests were a leader from the Harlem district and the former chief clerk of the board of elections, now in the corporation counsel's office.

He denied having said a kind word for Loscalzo whom O'Dwyer later appointed judge, although he admitted that Loscalzo had come all the way out to a golf course to see him and ask him to put in a good word and introduce him to Kennedy.   Nor had he had any-thing to do with proposing Louis Valente as candidate for surrogate. The luncheon which he attended with Mancuso, Generoso Pope, Sr., DeSapio, and Judge Valente was to plan their part in a charity drive in which Pope was interested.   But Costello couldn't remember what the charity was.   The drive had never taken place; nor could Costello remember what part he was supposed to have taken in it, or what assignments the other political leaders had.   Driven to admitting that this was contrary to his executive session testimony, Costello finally would not deny specifically that the subject of the Valente candidacy had ever come up.   He simply couldn't remember.   Nor would Costello admit that he had ever said a kind word for Judge Lupiano, a son-in-law of his friend, the late Dr. Sarubbi.   He con-ceded that he might have said over the telephone that he thought maybe Sarubbi wanted to make a judge out of him.

That Costello's influence has continued down to the present day was the impression of Charles Lipsky, a friend of O'Dwyer, who testified that when O'Dwyer said he would not run in 1949, he got Sherman to take him out to see Costello in an attempt to win Costello's support for his candidate for mayor.   The following year when O'Dwyer resigned and there was to be a special election, Lipsky stated, he tried to get Adonis to see Costello on the same errand.

It is apparent to the committee that despite Costello's protestations, his sinister influence is still strong in the councils of the Democratic Party organization of New York County.

THE TESTIMONY OF WILLIAM O'DWYER

I. His career and views on crime

In an hour-long statement Ambassador O'Dwyer outlined for the committee his qualifications for speaking as an expert on the matters under the committee's consideration.   He testified that he had been a member of the New York City police force from 1917 to 1924—the years of upheaval and the serious problems of prohibition following the First World War.   Before 1917, Mr. O'Dwyer stated, crime was localized and without honor.   But the disrespect for law which pro-hibition created, made criminals acceptable to many people and, therefore, respectable.   The lush living the bootleggers enjoyed as the result of their illicit liquor traffic, made them enviable, especially in the slum districts from which they recruited their helpers.   Even the Nation-wide syndication of crime as we know it today, Mr. O'Dwyer traced to the exigencies of the liquor traffic.   Every boot-legger who took a load of liquor from one place to another, was in danger of hijacking by another bootlegger.   They organized armed gangs to protect their trucks.   Rather than shoot each other up, they soon formed alliances.   Necessarily, these were wholly in the hands of law violators.   But there had to be some rules, and an enforcement agency in the underworld.   In addition, the bootleggers corrupted the police.   These were changes which took place before O'Dwyer left the police force in 1924.

He left the police department in order to practice law, having studied law at night while still a patrolman.   For the next 7 years O'Dwyer practiced law.   Then Mayor McKee appointed him to the magistrate's court, where among the other troubles of the ill-housed, ill-fed, ill-clad slum dwellers who came before him, he had an opportunity to observe the evil effects of the slot-machine, which he said, he wholly eliminated when he later became mayor.   After reviewing his efforts to alleviate some of the evils revealed to him during his service as magistrate, O'Dwyer pointed out that he was appointed a county court judge late in 1937 by Governor Lehman, and was elected a year later for a full 14-year term.   Two years later, he was elected district attorney of King's County.   He took office on January 1, 1940, at a time when racketeering conditions were so notorious that a special prosecutor John Harlan Amen, had already been assigned to study rackets in Brooklyn, including gambling.   After 2½ years as district attorney, O'Dwyer left to enter the Army.   He returned to the district attorney's office briefly in 1945 while he served simultaneously on the war-refugee board.   He resigned in 1945 to become the Democratic candidate for mayor.   He served as mayor for 5 years, resigning less than a year after his second election to take his present post as Ambassador to Mexico.

O'Dwyer testified at considerable length, and also presented voluminous and interesting documentary material concerning his accomplishments as mayor.   The committee does not have jurisdiction to go into the merits of the many social and community contributions to which O'Dwyer alluded, but it has carefully noted them and unquestionably he accomplished many noteworthy achievements.   Certainly it would be unfair to give the impression that the matters in which this committee is interested give anything like a complete picture of O'Dwyer's accomplishments in public office.

II. Murder, Inc.

O'Dwyer had spent 2½ years as Kings County district attorney tracking down and prosecuting the group of notorious killers known as Murder, Inc.   His office had managed to indict a number of young gangsters for stealing cars which were later used in the commission of murders, of which about 20 had been committed in 1 year.   One of these gangsters was Abe Reles who was induced to turn State's evidence. From him and other witnesses O'Dwyer's office learned that there was a clear-cut well-planned criminal organization covering the entire country.   Jurisdiction of various criminal enterprises was allocated to certain individuals.   There was a judicial set-up, a kangaroo court holding trials at various places all over the country concerning violations of jurisdictional rules and regulations at various places.   In certain sections of the country the "combination" had men to carry out the one order these kangaroo courts issued, namely, death.   The executioners were organized into "troops" and only one person was authorized to direct them in carrying out any killings.   O'Dwyer learned that the organization was ruled by what the underworld termed the "combination."   There was no chief man in charge.

There was a mutual understanding among the members of the underworld in various cities throughout the United States. They agreed to things among themselves. Payment to the "troops" O'Dwyer stated was not in money, but in jurisdiction of specific illegal activities in particular areas, from which they collected enough money to keep them going. In return for this privilege, the individual members of the "troops" were required to carry out any orders they might receive. According to O'Dwyer, the man who directed all the killings done by the Brooklyn group and the leader of the Brooklyn "troops" was Albert Anastasia.

O'Dwyer had told a grand jury in 1945, which had investigated the conduct of his offiec, that Anastasia's boss was Joe Adonis. O'Dwyer said Reles had told him Adonis was one of the six big bosses of the combination. O'Dwyer stated that besides Adonis, who had the gambling concession, the other big men were Bugsy Siegel, who had the west coast; his partner, Meyer Lansky, who, in addition to gambling, went in for such things as narcotics; Luciano, who was regarded as very big; Longie Zwillman, and Willie Moretti. Costello, O'Dwyer said, was never mentioned in connection with murders in Brooklyn. He was only mentioned along with several other persons in connection with the turning in of Lepke, narcotics king and killer who was later tried and executed.

Of the men whom O'Dwyer identified as the big six, all were friends or associates of Costello. Adonis, Zwillman, Moretti, and Lansky appeared at one time or another before the committee as did Albert Anastasia. Luciano is in Italy, a deportee since 1946, following a 9-year incarceration here. Bugsy Siegel was murdered in typical gangland fashion on the west coast.

Despite the excellent positive accomplishments of the Murder, Inc., prosecutions, it became apparent when the work was examined in retrospect that there were many glaring deficiencies. None of the top six were prosecuted or even touched in the investigation, with the exception of Bugsy Siegel who was indicted in California and in whose case, O'Dwyer refused to produce Reles as a witness at the trial although he did produce him before the grand jury in California. As a result, Siegel never was tried.

Even Albert Anastasia, described by O'Dwyer as the boss murderer, below the top six, was not indicted. Several other major characters appear to have escaped prosecution, and the very promising investigation of the water front in Brooklyn, then controlled by Anastasia, was allowed to die. Although O'Dwyer had explanations for all of these matters, a grand jury was convened in Kings County in 1945 to discover the reasons for these failures. The grand jury handed down two presentments, the first in October just before the November election at which O'Dwyer won the mayoralty, and the second late in December. The October presentment strongly condemned the conduct of the district attorney's office and made serious charges in connection with the failure to prosecute Anastasia and to proceed with the water-front investigation. Between the first presentment and the second presentment, but after the election, O'Dwyer testified before the grand jury. He stated:

Question by the grand jury. You have heard the evidence, Mr. O'Dwyer, which we have heard and known for many weeks and which was the basis for our presentment?
Answer. Yes.

Question. Now will you agree with us that we were right in handing up the presentment?

Answer. Yes. I agree that the presentment was fully justified and I will say so at any time.

The grand jury found in its second presentment:

1. We find that every case against Anastasia was abandoned, neglected, or pigeon-holed.

2. We find that William O'Dwyer, as district attorney, and Edward A. Heffernan, chief of staff, failed and neglected to complete a single prosecution against Anastasia.

3. We find that there admittedly was available competent legal evidence, sufficient to warrant the indictment, conviction, and punishment of Anastasia for murder in a case described by William O'Dwyer, himself, as "a perfect murder case."

The grand jury attributed this to "negligence, incompetence, and flagrant irresponsibility" and stated that there was no satisfactory explanation.

O'Dwyer has branded the grand jury presentments as political documents, inspired by a mayoralty campaign, although the second presentment was handed down a month and a half after election. He asserts that the presentments were expunged from the record and that the judge who expunged them referred to their political inspiration. While these matters as stated are true, they do not represent the whole facts. The presentments were expunged on the technical ground that they contained recitations of evidence, but behind the presentments are many volumes of sworn grand jury testimony, including that of O'Dwyer and this testimony stands on the record and fully supports the grand jury conclusions. In fact, O'Dwyer agrees that there was a serious failure, but he asserts that the fault is not his but should be attributed to his subordinates and the acting district attorney who took over when O'Dwyer entered the Army in 1942.

The foreman and acting foreman of the grand jury have written to this committee stating that 22 public-spirited citizens, carefully selected and without ulterior motives, acted only on sworn testimony and that they resent any inference that they were influenced by anything but the testimony before them, including that of O'Dwyer.

III. *The failure to prosecute Albert Anastasia*

Mr. O'Dwyer told the committee that he had had only one case against Albert Anastasia, the murder of Diamond, in which the independent witnesses required by law were available. One of these witnesses was a small sickly boy, who actually saw Jack Parisi shoot Diamond. The other was Reles who said he had been with Anastasia when the details of the murder were planned and could place him in the murder car at the corner some distance away from the actual crime. This was the "perfect case" to which he had referred, when he testified before the grand jury.

But in the 20 months Reles was held under guard, consisting of six policemen at the Half Moon Hotel on the theory that he would be safer from gang retaliation there, than in prison, O'Dwyer admitted he had not prosecuted Anastasia nor had he even sought an indictment against him.

As soon as it became known that an investigation was under way and could not be stopped Anastasia and Parisi disappeared, according to O'Dwyer. Fearing that the gangsters might endanger the life of the young witness or his parents, O'Dwyer stated that he did not seek an indictment, since the child would have to be used as a witness. Asked why he did not indict Anastasia alone since for that he needed only Reles and the driver of the murder car, Julie Catalano, who was also available, O'Dwyer explained that where two men are involved in a crime, it is impractical to indict and try them separately. Furthermore, he said he was very busy with other murder cases and even if Anastasia was one of the worst criminals in America "you don't stop prosecuting other murders that are ready to proceed while you are waiting to get him."

Reles, O'Dwyer admitted, did implicate Adonis in one case. Asked why he didn't proceed against Adonis, O'Dwyer explained that Amen had arrested Adonis, and had talked to Reles. Furthermore, the idea of getting Reles before the grand jury and asking him what he had to say about Adonis was one of the things that had never occurred to him.

Reles was also a witness in a murder charged against Bugsy Siegel. The first time Reles was brought out to testify, O'Dwyer explained, something was wrong with the indictment and Siegel was released. O'Dwyer said he thought Reles was there when the second indictment was returned. But a newspaper account indicated that O'Dwyer appeared before the California judge himself, justifying his refusal to bring Reles to California because his primary obligation was to the people of his own jurisdiction. He was reported as saying that he did not want to risk having his Brooklyn cases discredited by the failure of the testimony to convict Siegel in California. With the collaboration of the local district attorney according to the newspaper report, O'Dwyer argued for Siegel's dismissal. However, O'Dwyer told the committee, that the reason Siegel could not be convicted in California was because of Reles' death.

O'Dwyer's perfect case against Anastasia became imperfect when Reles died. Shortly after 5 one morning in November of 1941, Reles body was found, fully clothed, on a balcony of the Half Moon Hotel, five stories beneath his room. A sheet on which presumably he had lowered himself dangled against the wall. According to O'Dwyer, Reles died trying to escape, although at another point he testified that Reles was terrified of gang retribution.

According to Frank Bals, who was the chief investigator in the district attorney's office, and the immediate superior of the police guard, Reles was trying to play a joke on his guard. He was attempting to reach the lower floor, re-enter the hotel, climb back upstairs, and confound the policemen outside his door. Asked how Reles could have made his preparations without the guards hearing anything, Bals explained to the committee they must all have fallen asleep. O'Dwyer rejected the contention that Reles was thrown out the window, based on pictures showing that the body fell farther from the building than it would have, if Reles went out of the building on his own power. O'Dwyer also rejected Bals' theory.

Asked what he did to establish responsibility for the loss of his most important witness against a top-ranking murderer, O'Dwyer explained that he and the police commissioner considered it a pure case of negligence on the part of the police officers. The best that could be done was to provide a departmental trial for the six police guards. O'Dwyer conceded he had appeared as a voluntary witness on behalf of the men at the trial, stating they were blameless.   Nevertheless, they were demoted.

If the men were blameless, O'Dwyer was asked, was not their superior responsible for setting up a faulty system of protecting the witness?   He had reviewed the set-up at the beginning, O'Dwyer said, and thought it adequate.   He did not learn until afterward that Reles was assigned alone to a room at the end of a corridor and that guarding him consisted of having a policeman walk down the corridor once an hour and look at him.   But he insisted that Bals, who was in charge of the detail, could not be held responsible for something which happened in the dead of night, when he was not there, even though he was the one who assigned the men to their task and supervised the arrangements.

O'Dwyer told the committee he could not have gotten an indictment against Anastasia after Reles death which would have stood up. If, as the grand jury presentment stated, he had not issued instructions to his successors about the case, it was because it was wholly unnecessary.   The man who was taking over was an experienced lawyer who had been practicing 20 years longer than O'Dwyer himself.   He had been in the office a year and a half and knew what was going on.   Moreover, the other three men who with O'Dwyer had been in complete charge of the Murder, Inc., cases—Moran, Bals, and Heffernan—continued in the district attorney's office. If nothing was done after he left the office, it must have been because their superiors gave them no orders.   Before he left, O'Dwyer stated, he had had Burton Turkus, the indictment lawyer, prepare a review of the case, and his report on file indicated that while there was no case against Anastasia at the time, the man's record was such that the investigation should be carried on.

Nor would O'Dwyer concede to the committee that the removal apparently on Moran's order of the wanted cards on Anastasia, Romeo, and several other racketeers from the police files condemned in the grand jury presentment, was of any significance.   Yet within a short time after the removal of the cards, Anastasia and Romeo returned to Brooklyn.   Anastasia entered the United States Army. Everybody knew, O'Dwyer said, that the men were wanted, cards or no cards.   The grand jury was wrong in asserting that their removal indicated to those whom he left in the office that there was no case against the men.   Nor, according to O'Dwyer, was the removal of the cards responsible for the release without questioning of Romeo (who could have been an important witness against Anastasia) when he was held in the magistrate's court on another charge.   Romeo was found dead in a river near Wilmington, Del., 2 weeks later.   Since the removal of the cards was unimportant there was no reason for reprimanding Moran when O'Dwyer returned to his office in 1945.

During his Army service, O'Dwyer stated, he couldn't be expected to find time to make any inquiries about the conduct of the case against Anastasia, which he admitted was the most important in his career. He had no recollection of a busy conference (6 hours), in the district attorney's office, 6 months after he left, which a newspaper account characterized as "making the office hum" and looked almost like old times, when O'Dwyer was in the thick of the Murder, Inc., prosecutions.   Nor did he recollect that he stated that he had reviewed the work of the office and that he highly praised the work of the acting district attorney.

It was apparent to the committee that O'Dwyer held no grudge against either Bals or Moran for their respective roles in the death of Reles and the inactivity against Anastasia. Moran, without any legal training, had been O'Dwyer's personal choice for chief clerk of the district attorney's office. He had brought him in from the county court where he had served as the court attendant. He had the power to open and close investigations and was one of three persons authorized to begin grand jury investigations. All during O'Dwyer's Army service Moran handled O'Dwyer's personal financial affairs.

He had such regard for Moran's ability, intelligence, and loyalty, O'Dwyer said, that when he became mayor he made Moran a deputy fire commissioner and, shortly before his resignation, gave him a life job as commissioner of the board of water supply, where, though he had no engineering training, he could, by virtue of his position, over-rule decisions made by engineers.

This is the same Moran who was visited regularly in his office in the fire department by Louis Weber, a well-known policy racketeer.

When O'Dwyer was asked whether he could think of any proper reason which Moran could have for seeing Weber at regular intervals, he said that he could not. Both Moran and Weber are now under indictment for perjury before this committee. Moran denied that Weber had visited him between three and six times in the 4 years he was in the fire department. Weber denied that he even knew Moran. In addition to the contradictions between the stories of Moran and Weber, both were contradicted by the fireman who was on duty outside of Moran's office and who testified that Weber visited Moran much more often and on a regular basis, approximately once a month. The testimony of this fireman has since been corroborated by the committee. This is the same Moran to whom John Crane, president of the Uniformed Firemen's Association, said he gave $55,000 of the funds of the association as a gift, because it was necessary to do so in order to keep Moran's friendship and to obtain justice for the firemen from Moran. The entire matter of Crane's testimony is discussed below.

Bals, similarly, was so close a friend that, as Bals himself testified, the day O'Dwyer returned from California to take up his duties as the newly elected mayor of New York City, Bals met him at the airport, and they discussed what his function in the new administration should be. The day after O'Dwyer took his oath of office, Bals was appointed seventh deputy police commissioner. He was able to resign less than 2 years later, with a pension of $6,000, an income $1,000 larger than any he had earned in any previous position on the police force. Bal's history in the post of seventh deputy police commissioner is discussed below.

IV. *O'Dwyer and the water front*

"There was never any doubt in my mind," stated O'Dwyer, "that Anastasia really owned that water front and had strong henchmen, too." It is obvious that one of the ways of breaking Anastasia's stranglehold on the water front was through a prosecution for the larcenies, extortions, and shake-downs in which he was involved. No such prosecution was instituted against Anastasia.

The Brooklyn grand jury found in its December 1945 presentment:

14. We find that the proof against Anastasia was neglected, disregarded, and deposited in the office files and vaults until prosecution was barred by the Statute of Limitations.[1]

John Harlan Amen, who had been appointed special prosecutor to inquire into corruption in Kings County, had started a water-front investigation into the affairs of the six racketeering unions that Anastasia controlled (the so-called Camarda unions). Amen had to institute court proceedings in order to get possession of the books of these unions.

On April 30, 1940, the day after the Supreme Court directed the production of the books and records, but before the order could be signed, Mr. O'Dwyer instituted his own investigation of the water front. The books and records for which Amen had been fighting were brought directly to O'Dwyer's office. There was an intensive 3-day investigation by his staff; in 1 night over 100 witnesses were questioned.

From these witnesses, O'Dwyer stated to the committee it was learned that Anastasia and Romeo and other gangsters had been stealing hundreds of thousands of dollars from unions and had destroyed their original books.

Three days later, Heffernan, one of Mr. O'Dwyer's assistants, began grand-jury proceedings, and testimony before it showed crimes of extortion, larceny of union funds, destruction of union books and falsification of new ones, kick-backs in wages for the benefit of the racketeers. When O'Dwyer started his investigation, Amen suspended his own and turned all his records over to O'Dwyer's office. Two weeks later the O'Dwyer investigation was suspended.

They had, O'Dwyer said, as much information as they needed on the extortion cases. With his small staff he couldn't handle everything at once. He felt the emphasis should be on the murder cases. There would be 2 or 3 years left before the statute of limitations ran out on the extortion cases.

O'Dwyer admitted that he had never ordered the water-front investigation reopened and that in consequence his suspension resulted in a complete discontinuance. While he was in the office before he went into the Army, he said, he had no time; he was busy with the murder cases. O'Dwyer told both this committee and the grand jury that he had a right to expect that the acting district attorney would reopen the prosecution of the water-front rackets.

But the grand jury found, and the evidence shows:

"12. We find that William O'Dwyer himself did nothing further about these prosecutions and investigations, nor did he instruct anyone else to do anything about them."

In this connection O'Dwyer made the point that he should not have had to give specific instructions since several of his assistants knew about the cases. O'Dwyer intimated further that Amen could have resumed the investigation and denied the contention that a special prosecutor in New York State is not supposed to take jurisdiction where a regularly constituted district attorney is doing the job.

Asked what he had done while he was mayor about water-front conditions, O'Dwyer referred to a police shake-up and various investi-

---

[1] On crimes other than those for murder. (The "perfect murder case" was abandoned.)

gations that he had ordered. But he could point to no accomplishments from these investigations except the shifting around of police officials assigned to the docks.

The committee did not have sufficient time to present in detail the evidence resulting from its own water-front investigations. But it is apparent to the committee that racketeers are firmly entrenched along New York City's water front with the resulting extortions, shakedowns, kick-backs from wages, payroll padding, gangster infiltration of unions, and large-scale gambling. The committee was impressed by the story of Mr. Philip Stephens, business manager of the Daily News, who told of the attempt to shake the Daily News down for $100,000 in connection with the unloading of newsprint. The inevitable results of racketeer domination of the water front were also presented to the committee by Mr. Walter Hedden, of the New York Port Authority, who told of the increasing diversion of freight from New York ports by shippers who refuse to put up with racketeering conditions. Most significant to the committee is that the gangster who still appears to be the key to water-front racketeering in New York is the same Albert Anastasia.

V. O'Dwyer and police corruption

Miles McDonald, district attorney of Brooklyn, and his assistant, Jules Helfand, outlined for the committee the magnitude of the gambling operations and the accompanying police corruption which they were currently in the process of investigating with the aid of a grand jury. Mr. Helfand estimated for the committee that, on the basis of the number of scratch sheets sold in New York City, a minimum of $300,000,000 a year was bet with bookmakers alone, a figure he considered to be an extremely low estimate in consideration of the fact that one bookmaker alone, Harry Gross, had taken in $20,000,000 in a year. In addition, Mr. Helfand stated, other fantastic sums were bet annually by professional bookmakers in lay-off bets, that is, in interstate gambling among the bookmakers themselves. Mr. Helfand described the interstate tie-up of gamblers in New York who phone their bets to New Jersey wire rooms, operated in many instances by New York gamblers. Mr. McDonald asserted that no large-scale gambling operation can be conducted without the knowledge and consent of at least that segment of the police department charged with the enforcement of the gambling laws, namely, the plain-clothes division. For large-scale gambling to be going on, they have both to know it and to be involved in it. He was of the opinion that the original charge that about $250,000 was being paid weekly to police in protection money was not far wrong. Mr. Helfand added that it is impossible for a bookmaker to operate more than 48 hours anywhere without the protection of police. Where raids were made and bookmakers arrested, in Brooklyn, Mr. Helfand said, they found notations in their records and accounts of "ice" payments, which give some indication of the amounts paid for police protection. At an Army base luncheonette, for instance, a notation of $1,200 a month for "ice" was found for that one place alone.

Mr. O'Dwyer agreed with Mr. McDonald and Mr. Helfand that bookmaking cannot exist on a large scale without police protection. He also agreed that the Brooklyn investigation and Erickson's indictment indicate bookmaking was going on on a large scale during his administration. Erickson's, he thought, was the largest scale there is, but he insisted he did not know where Erickson's operations took place nor how he operated.

After prolonged questioning as to whether former Police Commissioner O'Brien could have failed at least to have sensed the condition now being uncovered in Brooklyn, Mr. O'Dwyer finally agreed that he should have known about it. But Mr. O'Dwyer insisted that former Chief of Detectives Whalen, a policeman who had come on the force with him, had absolutely nothing to do with gambling conditions; that that was the responsibility of the plain-clothes division. Although Whalen was the head of the detective force, he could not have been expected to know the situation which the Brooklyn investigation was now uncovering, according to O'Dwyer.

Questioned concerning special investigations into police corruption he himself had instigated, Mr. O'Dwyer stated that he had actually ordered only one. Immediately after taking office as mayor, he appointed Frank Bals seventh deputy police commissioner. Bals, as chief investigator for O'Dwyer in the Kings County district attorney's office, had been in charge of the police detail guarding Reles.

Bals, O'Dwyer said, was not there to investigate police corruption, but to organize information about the identity, habits, associates, and hang-outs of the prosperous hoodlums whose influence on the adolescents of the slum areas both he and Bals had come to deplore during their work on Murder, Inc. O'Dwyer admitted that gathering of data on movements of criminals is a normal police function, but he said it was not being done properly. The police rarely knew about criminals outside their own precincts, and Bals had been sent in to correct the situation.

According to Bals, however, this was not his job at all. He had an information squad of six detectives and six plain-clothes men assigned to him to gather information about gambling. While Bals denied ever telling our staff that the plain-clothes men were the money men in the police force, that they were paid by the gamblers and had a list as to how much to collect from each one, he admitted saying that he believed some top brass in the police department were crooked. Bals said that he had been relieved of his function, and his squad was abolished, because he got into the hair of the top brass.

That there were objections to Bals from the police officials O'Dwyer readily admitted. Commissioner Wallander, O'Dwyer stated, complained that Bals' activities were disturbing the commands throughout the city to the point where police morale was affected. Relying on Wallander, whom he knew as a good commissioner, inherited from the LaGuardia regime, O'Dwyer said he didn't pursue the question further, but permitted Wallander to do what he thought best. As a result, Bals' squad was taken away from him after 2 months; he was left with one man. Bals may have passed on some information but never submitted any reports, and O'Dwyer conceded he had accomplished nothing. O'Dwyer had not heard, he said, the charge that, with the advent of Bals' squad, Bals was the person to see in regard to police protection of gamblers. Bals himself said charges that his men were involved with bookmakers were never substantiated.

Although defending Bals' record against the contention of committee counsel that Bals was a man whom he should have known was incompetent, from his failure in the Reles case, and should not have been appointed a seventh deputy commissioner with a job cutting across police department lines, O'Dwyer at last conceded that this appointment was a mistake. But O'Dwyer claimed he corrected it after 2 months. However, Bals remained a seventh deputy for nearly a year longer, with almost no duties beyond reporting daily to the commissioner. There was nothing in his job which required him to be made a deputy commissioner; the seventh deputy commissionership was a post which had been vacant for some time and had no essential function. Bals' appointment gave him the benefit of a clause in the city charter which made it mandatory to give a retiring commissioner a pension no smaller than that of any other deputy commissioner, no matter what his previous earnings and consequent pension rights had been.

Late in 1946, Mr. O'Dwyer told the committee, despite his confidence in Arthur Wallander, then police commissioner, and his chief inspector, Martin Brown, he felt that not everything was being done which should be done in connection with curbing gambling. He, therefore, ordered John J. Murtagh, commissioner of investigations, to have his department make a running study of how gambling was being enforced by the police department. Mr. O'Dwyer asked the committee to have Judge Murtagh tell what he did about Erickson and Adonis and Costello. The committee granted the request, although it had been unable to find any reports on gambling and corruption in the department of investigation files, and had been told by Judge Murtagh that he had made none, because what he had done had been in the nature of an operation to jazz up the police department and not an investigation.

Claiming before the committee that his was the most methodical, thorough investigation of bookmaking that has been made by any office, Judge Murtagh described the accumulation of information about the telephone calls to and from known bookies, made through subpenaing records of the New York Telephone Co. and the cooperation of the New Jersey Telephone Co. Asked what prominent bookmakers were caught by the system and who they were, Murtagh said thousands of telephone wires were pulled out in New York, but the main lay-off points were in New Jersey, outside of his jurisdiction. Although he gave information to the New Jersey authorities about Erickson, Adonis, and Moretti, in 1947, Murtagh claimed they did not act until 3 years later. In contradistinction to committee counsel's observation that Federal prosecutors had long ago told New Jersey of the gambling operations in that State, over which they, as Federal agents, could do nothing, Murtagh insisted that it was his information which resulted in Erickson's testimony before the McFarland committee that he was a bookmaker, and enabled Hogan to move in on his New York office, arrest and convict him. Asked why in 3 years he could not have moved against Erickson, Murtagh claimed first that he didn't believe Erickson had a New York office until the wire-room information to New Jersey forced him to move to the city; furthermore, prosecution was the district attorney's job, not his, Murtagh stated.

Asked whether the wire room had turned up any evidence of the $20 million Gross bookmaking operations in Brooklyn, Murtagh said, "Not to my knowledge, but if Gross was active, * * * there unquestionably is a good deal of information there regarding his activities." He couldn't recall what had happened in connection with the Dugout Cafe, which an anonymous letter called to his attention in 1948, as being the scene of wide-open bookmaking, and was later identified as the place where Gross paid off. But Murtagh was sure it had been referred to the proper person in the police department.

Asked about his investigation of corruption in the police department, Murtagh stated the only corruption he found was that which existed under LaGuardia, as revealed in the records of a Harlem policy banker, who had methodically set down in code, which Federal agencies helped him to break, the amount of protection money paid to members of the police department by rank. Asked whether he had instituted any new investigation into this graft in the police department, Murtagh said it was 3 years old by the time he got it. When it was pointed out that there seems to be the same kind of graft in the police department now, Murtagh remarked, "unfortunately the enforcement of the gambling laws do tend to corrupt men called upon to enforce them." Asked whether his conclusion, therefore, was that he didn't bother to enforce the laws, Murtagh insisted this was a misinterpretation.

He had continuously, since he took office, investigated the connection of bookmaking and the police department, Murtagh stated; he had questioned every ranking police officer under oath, but had made no analysis of their testimony. He had questioned 500 cops upon their financial status on the basis of a form he worked out and which McDonald is now using for police called before the grand jury. Murtagh told the committee, "I don't believe the cops are honest, but nothing turned up." These same financial statements have since been subpenaed for perusal before the Brooklyn grand jury, which has been reported to include the activities of the department of investigation, during O'Dwyer's regime, in its inquiry.

Back on the stand, Mr. O'Dwyer reiterated that Murtagh had made an important contribution in passing on to the New Jersey authorities information about Adonis and Erickson. He conceded that the value of the wire room would be to find the police corruption which enabled bookies to operate and to catch the big bookies. On the basis of McDonald's investigations and the evidence of scratch-sheet sales, which in 1946 to 1949 were far greater than in other years, O'Dwyer admitted, bookmaking went on on a large scale in the years 1946 through 1949; there had to be local bookmakers to bet with and Gross was one of them. O'Dwyer protested the questioning about the action of his administration in closing up one bookmaker named Katz in 1949, said to be one of the biggest bookmakers in Brooklyn. He assured the committee it had nothing to do with his political feud with Abe Stark, Katz's landlord, and an opponent of O'Dwyer's candidate for the borough presidency in 1949.

Asked why, if Erickson was jailed in 1950 and Gross indicted in 1951, his investigators had been unable to produce results, O'Dwyer replied that there is a big difference between investigation by a police or an investigation department and the powers of a court and a grand jury. If that were understood, he said, his recommendation for a grand jury once a year in every county would win support.

In the light of this recommendation, O'Dwyer was asked what his position was in reference to the investigations just before he resigned as mayor. O'Dwyer said he always favored investigations of complaints of corruption. His characterization of the Brooklyn investigation as a "witch hunt" was due to emotion over the realization that the few conniving grafters on the force would be taken as typical of the 18,000 men on the force, rather than the policeman who had just been killed in the performance of his duty, when he had rushed to someone's defense. His statement that the investigation was interfering seriously with the efficiency of the department and blackening the police force simply described what always happened, O'Dwyer said. The action of his commissioner of investigation, in investigating the chief investigator on McDonald's staff, had been undertaken because two of the policemen were supposed to have been derelict in their duty. The committee pointed out, however, that after departmental trial, the two policemen were exonerated and sent back to work, and that the episode had been interpreted as an attempt to impede the work of the Brooklyn district attorneys. Asked whether he had ever talked over with McDonald what he was doing before he termed it a "witch hunt," O'Dwyer said he had not because he was so sure the police department was clean, he had such absolute faith in the commissioners and in Murtagh, who assured him everything was all right, he could not imagine such things could happen as McDonald's investigation was disclosing.

On the witness stand O'Dwyer admitted that subsequent events proved McDonald to be right and that he had apologized to McDonald for the "witch hunt" statement.

VI. O'Dwyer and Costello

For over 4 years, O'Dwyer issued public statements deploring sinister influences in Tammany Hall. O'Dwyer insisted that this not only meant Costello, but also the venal people that are leaders. He admitted, however, that Costello was a dominating influence behind these venal figures.

O'Dwyer stated that he had never found an occasion to say publicly that he had seen the leader of Tammany (Kennedy) in Costello's home. Kennedy's debt to Costello also did not stop O'Dwyer from supporting him in a leadership fight on the West Side, after Kennedy had been forced out of the Tammany leadership by the Aurelio revelations. O'Dwyer said in this fight he made a choice between two evils, and Kennedy was the lesser.

O'Dwyer was questioned about some of his appointments of men who were known to be friends of Costello. O'Dwyer appointed Hugo Rogers to the traffic board, "because of his special knowledge of the subject," although he had heard that Rogers, as leader of Tammany Hall, was a close friend of Costello, and was dominated by Mancuso, Costello's pal. O'Dwyer denied knowing that Rogers' assistant in the borough president's office, Philip Zichiello, was a brother-in-law of Willie Moretti, the New Jersey racketeer and big-time gambler. When Zichiello was ousted from his position in the borough president's office by Rogers' successor, Wagner, O'Dwyer appointed him as deputy commissioner of the department of hospitals. When asked whether he could not have found someone else for the hospital job, O'Dwyer replied, "There are things you have to do politically if you want cooperation." He had rested on the bar association's approval of Loscalzo as judge, O'Dwyer stated, although he knew that he was the "Joe" referred to in the telephone tap when Aurelio thanked Costello, and said, "Now we have to take care of Joe." He had not known that Loscalzo sought out Costello to ask him to say a good word for him with Kennedy. O'Dwyer remembered appointing Rosenthal, another good friend of Costello and a district leader, to a job, although he could not remember that it was as assistant corporation counsel. He didn't know until he read it in the papers, said O'Dwyer, that Lawrence Austin, whom he appointed city marshal, was a cousin of Irving Sherman, another Costello intimate. Loscalzo is the judge who disqualified himself in the Erickson case.

In 1945, O'Dwyer testified before the grand jury in Brooklyn that he had had two meetings with Frank Costello. Testifying before our committee, O'Dwyer could recall only one meeting and Costello also testified that they had had only one.

The occasion of this meeting, according to both O'Dwyer and Costello, was an investigation being conducted by O'Dwyer in the latter part of 1942 when he was a major in the Army Air Forces. O'Dwyer was attached to Air Procurement with orders "to keep Wright Field clean." According to O'Dwyer, an anonymous letter was received at the district attorney's office in Brooklyn, charging certain contract frauds at Wright Field by a Joe Baker and mentioning that he was a friend of Frank Costello. O'Dwyer testified that he had Irving Sherman, who was a close friend of both his and Costello's, arrange for the meeting with Costello. O'Dwyer took Moran with him. In this connection, it may be of some significance that Moran's recollection was that it was Moran who arranged the appointment, and that he did it through Mike Kennedy, leader of Tammany Hall, because he had never previously met Costello. Costello, however, testified that he had met Moran previously.

O'Dwyer did not ask Costello to come to any Army office because he was "no longer a district attorney with a fistful of subpenas, but just a little major or maybe a lieutenant colonel." O'Dwyer testified that Costello told him that he knew a Joe Baker, but did not know whether this Joe Baker had an interest in Air Force contracts and that Costello himself had no interest in Air Force contracts. O'Dwyer never attempted to see the Joe Baker whom Costello knew to check further on the letter, nor did he ask anyone else to do so at this time. Although O'Dwyer thought the entire matter important enough so that he personally went to Costello's home, he did not follow up the Costello meeting in any way until several months later when another letter came to Wright Field about Joe Baker. This second letter was referred to other investigators, who followed through.

The committee had before it at the hearing the Army file on the Joe Baker matter. There is no reference in it whatsoever to O'Dwyer's meeting with Costello, There is certain information from O'Dwyer but none relating in any way to Costello or suggesting a relationship between Baker and Costello. O'Dwyer states that he did give such information to his superiors.

In the course of the Army investigation, the record discloses, the relationship was discovered between Baker and Costello.

No action was ever taken by the Air Corps barring Baker from Wright Field, although an associate of Joe Baker was barred. Baker himself is a close associate of Costello and Phil Kastel and lives in luxurious quarters at the Hotel Madison in New York City, which at one period was a favorite meeting place of Costello. Baker has no legitimate source of income to account for his mode of living.

At Costello's home, when O'Dwyer was there, were also Michael Kennedy, then leader of Tammany Hall, Judge Savarese, Bert Stand, formerly secretary of Tammany Hall, Irving Sherman, as well as Moran.

O'Dwyer testified that he had a private conversation with Costello and then some little amenities with the other persons present. Bert Stand testified that he had met Kennedy on the afternoon of the meeting and that Kennedy asked him to come along to Costello's apartment and said there was to be a cocktail party there. Stand did not remember any private conversation between Costello and O'Dwyer. He said that the conversation was general and that there was some talk about the 1941 election campaign, primarily between O'Dwyer and Savarese.

O'Dwyer stated to the committee that he was very surprised to find Mike Kennedy in Costello's apartment at the time when O'Dwyer had an appointment to be there to discuss official business. He testified that the presence of the leader of Tammany Hall in Costello's apartment made a very strong and lasting impression upon him, one which he never forgot.

For many years, O'Dwyer has issued public statements deploring sinister influences in Tammany Hall. O'Dwyer first insisted before this committee that he had reference to certain venal leaders of Tammany and not specifically to Costello. Later in his testimony, however, he stated that Costello was a dominating influence behind these venal figures and was, in fact, one of the sinister influences in Tammany Hall. Despite this, he had never found an occasion to say publicly that he had seen the leader of Tammany in Costello's home, or to make public this concrete evidence of the relationship between Tammany Hall and Costello. Although he never forgot Kennedy's presence in Costello's apartment, he publicly supported Kennedy in 1948 in a leadership fight on the West Side, in which Kennedy was seeking to regain the position he held prior to the Aurelio revelations. O'Dwyer publicly characterized this move to support Kennedy as a clean-up of Tammany and he advanced Kennedy as a clean leader. He stated to the committee that as between Kennedy and incumbents, he made a choice of the lesser evil.

VII. O'Dwyer's friends

All during the war, O'Dwyer told the committee, he saw a good deal of Irving Sherman, a known gambler and intimate of racketeers. He did help him in a big way, O'Dwyer said, referring to inquiries Sherman made for him for his Army work. O'Dwyer knew that Sherman was a good friend of Costello and a good friend of Adonis. He knew Sherman was a shirt manufacturer, doing business with the Navy, but not that he was also engaged in getting contracts for other persons on a 5-percent basis. He told the 1945 grand jury that he wouldn't be surprised to know that Sherman had been a collector for Adonis and Costello and Lepke. While he heard that Sherman had had a dining room and gambling casino in New York's garment district, he said that McLaughlin, a former telephone man, who claimed to have seen him there, must have been mistaken. Nor did he know that this same witness, at the request of Sherman, had tested his wire for possible taps. McLaughlin testified that at Sherman's request he had also tested wires for Kastel, Nat Herzfeld, and Costello, and that Costello personally paid him. Costello denied this.

All during his Army service, O'Dwyer told the committee he sought Sherman out every time he came to Washington. They kept in touch by long-distance phone all over the country. Once, at least, he agreed he, Sherman, and Marcantonio had met together, but the occasion was purely social; he was not seeking political assistance from them. Sherman, he admitted, did help him throughout his 1945 campaign, as Costello, Moran, and Charles Lipsky had testified. He had utilized what help he could give.

There was also testimony that Moran and Sherman kept in touch with each other. The fire department receptionist stated that Sherman came frequently to Moran's office, announcing himself as Dr. Cooper. He found out his real name only when Moran was out one day, and his caller asked the receptionist to announce him to Commissioner Quayle as Irving Sherman. Moran admitted these visits of Sherman, and said the alias was just a joke between them.

O'Dwyer denied that his friendship with Sherman and the aid Sherman rendered in the 1945 campaign in any way tainted him with the Costello influence. Sherman, according to O'Dwyer, never asked for anything in return; never asked him to go easy on bookmakers, even though Sherman's business partner is the brother of one of New York's biggest bookmakers.

Questioned about friendships he shared with Joe Adonis, O'Dwyer said he recalled meeting him casually years ago; he could not remember where. He was sure that witnesses who had told the committee they had seen him in Adonis' restaurant were mistaken. However, Judge George Joyce, his law associate of 6 months, and one of his dearest friends, was and is a friend of Adonis. Quayle, whom O'Dwyer appointed to the fire department commissionership, is a good friend of Adonis. Kenneth Sutherland, the district leader who recommended O'Dwyer for appointment as a magistrate, was also close to Adonis. Lipsky, in whose house O'Dwyer spent many evenings and who was very close to O'Dwyer in 1945, was a good friend of Adonis. Lipsky used to make investments for Adonis. O'Dwyer told the Brooklyn grand jury in 1945 that Anastasia, Romeo, and other water-front characters frequented the City Democratic Club in Brooklyn, which was run by a good friend of his, Dr. Tom Longo, and had as its president another good friend, Dr. Thomas. But he stated that no friends of Adonis had ever brought pressure on him so that he would not prosecute Adonis.

The committee heard testimony from Charles Lipsky, and Jerome Ambro, an undersheriff when Frank Quayle, O'Dwyer's appointee in the fire department, was sheriff, about the political popularity of the restaurant Adonis ran in the thirties. It was in a poor district, a good distance from the borough hall, yet it attracted with considerable regularity the prominent Brooklyn Democratic political figures of the day. During prohibition it was a speakeasy and had a reputation for good liquor as well as good food. Though he denied any political activity, Adonis admitted that prominent politicians came to his restaurant and he met them there. Among them were, he said, Frank Quayle and Judge Joyce. Adonis admitted that he knew

Kenneth Sutherland, Irwin Steingut, Anthony DiGiovanni, Bill O'Dwyer, and Jim Moran, all of whom Ambro said he had seen at the restaurant. Adonis admitted that he went to a lot of political dinners because he felt he was obligated; if a fellow was close to him and asked him to go to a dinner, he would go.

Adonis refused to answer, on the grounds that he would incriminate himself, the question whether he ever gave his political friends any money to help in a primary campaign. But both Jerome Ambro, with obvious reluctance and an attempt to hedge on his executive session testimony, and Charles Lipsky, freely testified to his active assistance to various political leaders.

Lipsky testified that anybody who had a primary fight on the Democratic end came into Adonis' restaurant. Adonis had a lot of friends, and he was free with his money in support of his candidate. Lipsky described Adonis as a fellow who would hardly refuse to help most people who contacted him, particularly leaders in primary fights, and as a result, a great many of the leaders in Brooklyn, Lipsky felt, were under obligation to him. When Ambro ran the campaign of Sam Liebowitz, against the organization candidate Francis Geoghan for Kings County district attorney, Quayle asked him either to support the organization candidate or resign. Ambro resigned. He stopped frequenting Adonis' restaurant. Three years later, he was deposed as leader, and Ambro gave the committee a vivid picture of how he thought it was done; by the use of floaters brought into the district to vote illegally under the eyes of bribed election inspectors, both Republican and Democratic. He testified in both executive and public sessions that he thought about $30,000 was spent to defeat him; in executive session where he was also under oath, Ambro left the impression with the committee that this money could be traced at least in part to Adonis; hearsay, he said it was, or whatever you want to call it. In open session, he insisted that he never mentioned Adonis, and stated with some emphasis that he did not believe Adonis had any political influence.

VIII. The testimony of John P. Crane

John P. Crane, president of Local 94, International Association of Fire Fighters, testified before the committee on two separate days. On the first occasion, he refused to testify on the ground that his testimony would incriminate him. The committee thereafter obtained a court order for the production of certain testimony Crane had given before the New York County grand jury. Crane was recalled and testified that he had made certain withdrawals from the bank account of his association, that these withdrawals were made by check countersigned by two other officers of the association, that Crane had received cash for the amounts of the checks and had turned over this sum to certain persons. They included $55,000 turned over to Moran, $35,000 of which was stated by Crane to have been gifts and $20,000 of which was a campaign contribution in the 1949 mayoralty campaign. Crane testified that he also made a campaign contribution in cash of $10,000 to O'Dwyer, and one of $3,500 to John Crews for Dewey's Oregon primary. Moran and O'Dwyer have denied receiving these moneys. It is understood that Crews publicly stated that he did receive a contribution of $3,500 from Crane.

Crane testified before the grand jury and told our committee:

Some time in 1946—and this is what you want to know, Mr. Hogan—Mr. Moran was appointed Deputy Fire Commissioner, and I want to say that I admire Mr. Moran. But at least he was a man that had some basis you could work with. Moran allegedly was strong enough in his position in the O'Dwyer administration that if he said "no," nobody could move O'Dwyer to say "yes."

Crane stated to this committee:

Senator TOBEY. Then why did you give him the money?
Mr. CRANE. Because in my experience—which is limited—when I find a man such as Mr. Moran and whose influence is such that a word from him can help or hurt us, I want him on my side.
Senator TOBEY. So you underwrote Jim Moran; is that it?
Mr. CRANE. I underwrote what?
Senator TOBEY. You underwrote him $35,000 in the expectation, or the hope— either one you want to use—that he would come across and be kind to the men you serve in the Fire Department; is that it?
Mr. CRANE. That's right, sir.

According to Crane, he went to the Gracie Mansion sometime around October 12, 1949, and saw Mayor O'Dwyer alone on the porch at Gracie Mansion. Crane states that he told the mayor at that time that he had promised him the support of the firemen and that he offered him some evidence of that support on the occasion, in the form of $10,000 in cash in a red manila envelope. Crane states that O'Dwyer took the envelope, thanked him, but did not look inside the envelope.

O'Dwyer specifically denied that he met Crane on the porch of Gracie Mansion, that he saw Crane alone at the Gracie Mansion in October 1949, or that he ever received any cash moneys or any campaign contribution from Crane.

O'Dwyer also testified before the grand jury, where he waived his immunity. Crane did not waive immunity before the grand jury.

As the matter now stands, the committee does not have sufficient evidence to form a conclusion concerning the transactions alleged by Crane to have occurred. It is hoped that the continued investigation by the district attorney of New York County will produce concrete evidence to establish the truth.

The committee felt that Crane's testimony was of such importance that public inquiry had to be made of Crane, Moran, and O'Dwyer.

IX. The patterns of O'Dwyer's conduct

A single pattern of conduct emerges from O'Dwyer's official activities in regard to the gambling and water-front rackets, murders, and police corruption, from his days as district attorney through his term as mayor. No matter what the motivation of his choice, action or inaction, it often seemed to result favorably for men suspected of being high up in the rackets. Although he admitted he could have indicted Anastasia alone for at least one murder, he did not do so on the ground that it is a poor practice to indict only one defendant for a crime in which two are involved. When he could have indicted both Anastasia and his companion Parisi, he did not, again, this time on the ground that to do so would endanger the health and possibly the life of a small boy. He failed to indict Anastasia or any of his companions on extortion charges because he was busy with the murder cases; but the investigation of the water-front rackets which

Amen started, and O'Dwyer took over, was never resumed in the 2 years before he entered the Army or at any time thereafter. Despite the admitted importance of Reles to what he conceded was the most important murder case his office had, O'Dwyer was content to label his escape through death as the result of negligence; he never fixed the responsibility. He personally appeared to absolve the six policemen guarding Reles from blame at their departmental trial, and he rewarded their superior, Bals, as well as Moran who apparently ordered the removal of the "wanted cards" which in effect closed up the investigation on Anastasia and his associates, with intimate personal friendship and financial preferment through lucrative city positions.

Toward other official agencies engaged in law enforcement or investigation, Mr. O'Dwyer exhibited a sometimes antagonistic attitude. He characterized the 1945 grand jury presentments upon the work of his own office, as having been inspired by political bias. Five years later, he branded District Attorney McDonald's grand jury inquiry into gambling and police corruption a "witch hunt." Though he denied that the action of his commissioner of investigation, in investigating two policemen, attached to McDonald's investigating staff, for dereliction of duty, was designed to hamper the Brooklyn investigation, it did, in effect, delay its operations for several weeks, although in the end the men were exonerated in a departmental trial and sent back to work.

The tendency to blame others for the ineffectualness of official efforts to curb the rackets and the ensuing corruption has also turned up very often at every stage in O'Dwyer's career. California was to blame for not turning up sufficient evidence against Siegel. Amen had Adonis under arrest and had access to Reles; why didn't he act? Why didn't Amen resume the water-front investigation after he, O'Dwyer, suspended it? Why did not his successor, the acting district attorney, move against the water-front rackets? As mayor he depended upon his subordinates; if there was any laxity, they were at fault.

The committee found it necessary to present the stories of O'Dwyer and Costello in detail, because they illustrate so dramatically one of the major factors that must be overcome before substantial progress can be made in dealing with organized crime. When racketeers and gangsters have great influence in selecting public officials, they can paralyze law enforcement. Unless such influence is eliminated, gangsterism and racketeering will flourish in any community.

X. Gambling in New Jersey

Scratch sheet statistics and other specific evidence indicate that during the LaGuardia administration vigorous action against gamblers forced many of them to transfer their major operations to New Jersey, although relying on patrons in New York City for their support. During the O'Dwyer administration, bookmaking in New York increased but many of those who had moved to New Jersey continued their interstate operations.

Among the most prominent of these was Frank Erickson, who, however, conducted a sufficient amount of business in New York City that District Attorney Hogan was able to convict him for bookmaking in 1950. Many other bookmakers conducted similar interstate business operations with seeming impunity in New Jersey, particularly in Bergen County.

Emboldened by the success of the bookmakers, operators of gambling houses began to conduct operations across the Hudson River from New York, relying primarily on a New York City clientele. The committee held hearings concerning a series of gambling houses operated by Joe Adonis, Salvatore Moretti (Willie Moretti's brother), Anthony Guarino (whom the committee questioned in the New Jersey State penitentiary at Trenton, N. J.), James Lynch, Arthur Longano, James Rutkin, and Jerry Catena. Some of these same operators had gambling houses in other places, including Saratoga, N. Y., and Florida. All of them have close associations with notorious racketeers, and several were very close associates of Frank Costello, who at least on one occasion visited New Orleans with Jerry Catena, and who, as has been previously pointed out, was extremely close to Joe Adonis, Salvatore and Willie Moretti.

These gambling houses employed persons who appeared to ride a circuit traveling from Florida to New Jersey, to Saratoga, and even to Nevada.

The customers were transported from New York free of charge in automobiles provided by the house. They were given all they wished to eat and drink of the very best in food and liquor, but the minimum bet at the crap tables was $5, and in practice, few bets were made under $20. In 5 months during which this operation cashed checks in a New York City bank, they totaled $1,000,000 a month in checks of customers. The practice of banking gambling checks in New York City was stopped by District Attorney Hogan, who convicted Max Stark, the individual who brought the checks to New York and cashed them. Following this conviction, Guarino was indicted and pleaded guilty in New Jersey. No others were indicted in New Jersey, despite the fact that the name of James Lynch appeared on the back of almost every check as endorser. After Guarino "took the rap" for the entire group, the houses continued to operate in New Jersey until the early part of 1950 when they closed down. There were no further prosecutions in New Jersey until after this committee publicly aired the situation. Then Adonis and others were indicted.

Although the various gambling houses reported profits of from $100,000 to $250,000 annually for income-tax purposes, it is obvious that the profits must have run to many millions of dollars a year. A study of the operations of gambling houses indicates that if $1,000,000 a month was cashed in checks, the monthly profits must have been close to this amount. The reason for this is that most of the customers brought cash with them as a general rule, and the few who won back their losses would redeem the check before leaving.

There is great suspicion that some of the individuals who appeared on the record as partners in these gambling operations were simply dummies for others, and that the huge profits made between 1945 and 1950 were used to finance many of the top members of the eastern crime syndicate.

CONCLUSIONS FROM THE NEW YORK HEARINGS

The New York City hearings demonstrated to the committee that:
1. Frank Costello has close personal friendships, working relationships, and mutual financial interests with leading racketeers in the city, State, and Nation, confirming the opinion obtained elsewhere

that he, Joe Adonis, and Meyer Lansky formed the eastern axis of a combination of racketeers working throughout the Nation.

2. The extortion rackets on the water front of today and 10 years ago, the bookmaking rackets in New Jersey and New York, the gambling casinos in New Jersey and Saratoga, the narcotics traffic, and even the wave of murders in the late thirties and early forties, were not and are not isolated enterprises. They were and are the work of men whose personal friendships, working acquaintanceships and mutual financial interests were established by the testimony, and represent different aspects of the far-flung illegal operations of the eastern crime syndicate.

3. There can be no question that Frank Costello has exercised a major influence upon the New York County Democratic organization, Tammany Hall, because of his personal friendships and working relationships with its officers, and with Democratic district leaders even today in 10 of the 16 Manhattan districts. Costello also had relationships with some Republican political leaders.

4. Despite Mr. O'Dwyer's frequent public castigations of Tammany Hall, and his acknowledgment that Frank Costello was a sinister influence therein, he has been on terms of intimate friendship with persons who were close friends of Costello. Many of his intimate friends were also close friends of racketeer Joe Adonis. He has appointed friends of both Costello and Adonis to high public office.

5. During Mr. O'Dwyer's term of office as district attorney of Kings County, between 1940 and 1942, and his occupancy of the mayoralty from 1946 to 1950, neither he nor his appointees took any effective action against the top echelons of the gambling, narcotics, water-front, murder, or bookmaking rackets. In fact, his actions impeded promising investigations of such rackets. His defense of public officials who were derelict in their duties, and his actions in investigations of corruption, and his failure to follow up concrete evidence of organized crime, particularly in the case of Murder, Inc., and the water front, have contributed to the growth of organized crime, racketeering, and gangsterism in New York City.

6. The pattern of connections between crime and politics is well established in New York City, certain counties of northern New Jersey, and Saratoga. A great deal remains to be done by public officials and the citizens of these areas to alter the basic pattern.

ANALYSIS OF THE CITY STORIES

THE SYNDICATION OF CRIME AND THE MAFIA

The structure of organized crime today is far different from what it was many years ago. Its power for evil is infinitely greater. The unit of organized crime used to be an individual gang consisting of a number of hoodlums, whose activities were obviously predatory in character. Individual gangs tended to specialize in specific types of criminal activity such as payroll, or bank robbery, loft, or safe burglary, pocket picking, etc. These gangs normally confined their activities to particular areas of the country or particular communities. Occasionally their activities were aided and abetted by law-enforcement officials. The crooked sheriff who aids the outlaws is as much of a stock character as the fearless "law man" who makes justice triumph.

New types of criminal gangs have emerged during prohibition. The huge profits earned in that era together with the development of twentieth century transportation and communication, made possible larger and much more powerful gangs, covering much greater territory. Organized crime in the last 30 years has taken on new characteristics. The most dangerous criminal gangs today are not specialists in one type of predatory crime, but engage in many and varied forms of criminality. Criminal groups today are multipurpose in character engaging in any racket wherever there is money to be made. The modern gang, moreover, does not rely for its primary source of income on frankly predatory forms of crime such as robbery, burglary, or larceny. Instead the more dangerous criminal elements draw most of their revenues from various forms of gambling, the sale and distribution of narcotics, prostitution, various forms of business and labor racketeering, black-market practices, bootlegging into dry areas, etc.

The key to successful gang operation is monopoly of illicit enterprises or illegal operations, for monopoly guarantees huge profits. In cities that gangland has organized very well, the syndicate or the combination in control of the rackets decides which mobsters are to have what rackets. In cities which have not been well organized, the attempt by one mobster to take over the territory or racket from another mobster inevitably breeds trouble, for modern gangs and criminal syndicates rely on "muscle" and murder to a far greater degree than formerly to eliminate competitors, compel cooperation from reluctant victims, silence informers, and to enforce gangland edicts.

CRIMINAL ORGANIZATION LIKE BUSINESS ORGANIZATION

Modern crime syndicates and criminal gangs have copied some of the organizational methods found in modern business. They seek to expand their activities in many different fields and in many different geographic areas, wherever profits may be made. We have seen evidence of the operation of the Costello-Adonis-Lansky crime syndicate, whose headquarters is in New York, in such places as Bergen County, N. J., Saratoga, N. Y., Miami, Fla., New Orleans, Nevada, the west coast and Havana, Cuba. We have seen evidences of operations of the other major crime syndicate, that of Accardo-Guzik-Fischetti, whose headquarters is in Chicago, in such places as Kansas City, East St. Louis, Miami, Nevada, and the west coast.

Some indication of how modern crime syndicates operate and how they open new territory is apparent from the facts described under the city story of Chicago elsewhere in this report in relation to the extraordinary testimony of Lt. George Butler of the police department of Dallas, Tex. Lieutenant Butler was approached by a member of the Chicago mob by the name of Paul Jones. According to Butler, Jones stated that he was an advance agent of the Chicago crime syndicate and was prepared to offer the district attorney and the sheriff $1,000 a week each or a 12½-percent cut on the profits if the syndicate were permitted to operate in Dallas under "complete protection." Jones also stated that syndicate operations were conducted by local people who "front" for the Chicago mob. The syndicate, according to Jones, controlled such cities as St. Louis, Kansas City, New Orleans, and Little Rock. In addition the syndicate had connections in every large city, and if Jones ran into trouble anywhere, money and help would be forthcoming.

Lieutenant Butler advised his superiors, and on instructions, played along with Jones and indicated that the Dallas police were interested in his propositions. Jones, therefore, brought Pat Manno, a notorious Chicago syndicate mobster and a partner of Guzik and Accardo, who was labeled as the fifth man in the syndicate, to Dallas to talk matters over with Butler and Sheriff Guthrie, who had been apprised of the situation. Recordings of the conversation between Lieutenant Butler, Sheriff Guthrie, Manno, and Jones were made. Manno stated that he had been in the policy business in Chicago for 17 years and was interested in opening up operations in Dallas. He stated that the Chicago syndicate was definitely interested in coming into Dallas and that he, as representative of the syndicate, was looking the town over to see if they could operate it in collaboration with the police. The work of the Dallas Police in this connection was most commendable.

There are many other criminal gangs and criminal groups throughout the country that have more than a local importance. For instance, the Kleinman-Rothkopf-Polizzi group has operated in many different Ohio counties as well as in the Newport and the Covington area of Kentucky, in Nevada, and in Miami, Fla. Members of the Detroit gang have operated in Miami, Saratoga, and Kentucky. Individual gangsters and gangs in different parts of the country have also frequently worked in close and profitable relationship with each other, particularly in gambling casinos where often members of several gangs participate on a systematic basis. Outside gangs coming into an area will often use local hoodlums and local gangs.

It is apparent, as Narcotics Commissioner Anslinger testified before the committee, that the leading figures in organized crime do business with each other, get together in places like Miami and Hot Springs and on occasion do each other's dirty work, when a competitor must be eliminated and an informer silenced, or a victim persuaded. Commissioner Anslinger did not think that the activities in one part of the country occur as a result of instructions given in other parts of the country as a general rule. In some cases "it is pretty well organized in that particular way but I wouldn't say that one section of the country controls another section." What happens, Mr. Anslinger testified, is that leading mobsters throughout the country "confer together or talk to each other, deal with each other." He agreed with Mr. Halley's characterization that "they confine their dealings pretty well to the family."

As we have seen one of the major areas in which leading gangs cooperate is in enforcing each other's edict, silencing informers, persuading potential victims through intimidation, violence, and murder. It is obviously far more difficult for local law enforcement officials to detect the work of outside gangsters than the products of their local talent.

Modern gangland operations on any sizable scale cannot be carried on without protection. The gangs have unbelievable cash assets available for this purpose, moreover. Much of the moneys of criminal gangs and syndicates are invested in legitimate enterprises which presents special dangers to our economy and our people.

The Mafia, the committee is convinced, has an important part in binding together into a loose association the two major criminal syndicates as well as many minor gangs and individual hoodlums throughout the country. Wherever the committee has gone it has run into the trail of this elusive, shadowy, and sinister organization. Because of its importance to organized crime in this country, data on the Mafia will be presented in some detail.

MAFIA ORIGINALLY HAD HIGH PURPOSE

The Mafia was originally one of many secret societies organized in Sicily to free the island of foreign domination. The methods used for securing secrecy of operations, unity of command, intimidation and murder, and the silencing of informers, were adopted by a criminal group that became the Mafia after the Bourbons were driven from Sicily.

According to historians and the most authentic research material available, the following is the history of the Mafia:

The various secret organizations in Sicily were fused into a single group known as the Fratellanza or the "Brotherhood" which sometime later became known as the Mafia. Initiates and new members of this organization took solemn oaths never to reveal the secrets of the group under any circumstances and never to divulge the names of fellow members, even under torture. This secret association was organized in groups of 10 members. Each group had a leader. The group leaders were known to each other but not to the members of the various groups. The group leaders reported to the provincial chief who in turn reported to the supreme chief in Palermo, a very wealthy and influential man.

This organization grew enormously in Sicily after 1860. Smuggling, cattle stealing, extortion, and shake-downs were its major criminal activities. The administration of justice was so openly defied by this organization that many attempts were made by law-enforcement agencies in Sicily to deal with it. Although many arrests were made, law-enforcement agencies found it extremely difficult to break the power of the Mafia. The arrested members of this organization would not talk. Witnesses of various crimes committed by members of the Mafia were intimidated and were afraid to testify. Political influence was used to protect Mafia members charged with crime. Good legal talent was always available for their defense. The various drives against the Mafia in Sicily which were made by Italian Governments from the 1870's down to Mussolini's time, were therefore largely ineffective in destroying the Mafia. However these drives had the effect of causing large numbers of Mafia members to migrate to the New World and many of them came to this country.

As early as the 1880's, New Orleans was the focal point of Mafia activity. According to Pasquale Corte, the Italian consul in New Orleans, large numbers of escaped Italian criminals settled there. These and other desperados grew rich and powerful upon the profits of robbery, extortion, assassination. Most of the victims were fellow countrymen who failed to pay the sums demanded by Mafia leaders.

The Mafia in New Orleans overreached itself when it ordered the murder of a popular police officer, David Hennessy. After he was murdered, a dozen Mafia leaders were arrested. None were convicted after a trial marred by the intimidation of witnesses and jury fixing. The defendants, however, who had been held in jail on other charges, were lynched by a mob of aroused New Orleans citizens. After these lynchings the power of the Mafia in New Orleans was temporarily broken.

The Mafia became established in other cities besides New Orleans. Moreover, like many other underworld organizations, it grew rich and powerful during prohibition in the sale and distribution of alcoholic beverages. In addition both during prohibition and since that time this organization has entered every racket promising easy money. Narcotics, pinball machines, slot machines, gambling in every form and description are some of its major activities at the present time.

MAFIA OPERATES BEHIND LEGITIMATE FRONTS

Many of the individuals suspected of connection with the Mafia operate behind legitimate fronts. The olive oil, cheese, and the export and import businesses are some of the favorite fronts for Mafia operations. They offer a cover, particularly, for narcotics operations. They also help explain interstate and international contacts between persons suspected of Mafia connections.

Mafia operations in this country have been described by the Narcotics Bureau as follows:

It is almost inevitable that the Mafia should take an important part in American criminal rackets. Here is a Nation-wide organization of outlaws in a sort of oath-bound, blood-cemented brotherhood dedicated to complete defiance of the law. Where personal advantage or interests are concerned, here is a more or less permanently established network, an organized maze of underground conduits, always ready and available when racket enterprise is to be furthered. The organization is such that a member in one part of the country can, with perfect confidence, engage in any sort of illicit business with members in any other section of the country. Most helpful to the Mafia has been the attitude on the part of many law-enforcement officers in connection with its murders. These are sometimes passed over lightly on the theory these cases are just hoodlums killing off one another and that it is not a matter on which to waste police time and energy.

The ruthless elimination of competitors from enterprises which Mafia leaders decide to take over, the ruthless elimination of persons who have weakened in their Mafia loyalties, failed to carry out Mafia orders, or who have informed against the Mafia, has left a trail of murder from Tampa to San Francisco. This is well illustrated by the following comments of the Narcotics Bureau:

Joseph Sica and Alfred Sica of California are satellites of Anthony Rizzoti, alias Jack Dragna, and closely allied to members in New York and New Jersey from where they went to California several years ago. In 1949, a narcotics case was developed against the Sicas, principally upon the testimony of one Abraham Davidian who made purchases of narcotics from them, sometimes in lots costing more than $15,000. Early this year, while the case was pending for trial, Davidian was shot to death while asleep in his mother's home in Fresno.

Another west coast case of great importance was developed in 1944. This concerned a New York-California-Mexico smuggling ring in which Salvatore Maugeri and others were convicted. During the course of the investigation, a narcotics agent working undercover learned that one of the ring with whom he was negotiating, Charles "Big Nose" LaGaipa, of Santa Cruz, Calif., was in bad odor with some of his criminal Mafia associates. LaGaipa disappeared. He never has been found. His car was recovered with blood on the seat and brain tissue on the dashboard.

One Nick DeJohn, active in the narcotics traffic in Chicago, and Thomas Buffa, active in the narcotics traffic in St. Louis, transferred their activities to California. A short time later, evidently for trying to muscle in, both were killed. Buffa died from shotgun fire. DeJohn's body was found in an automobile with wire twisted around the neck.

A member of this combine named Ignazio Antinori went to Havana frequently to obtain narcotics for middle western members of this organization. The leader was Joseph DeLuca * * *. On one occasion, Antinori, in return for $25,000, delivered a poor grade of narcotic. The middle western group gave him 2 weeks in which to return the money. At the end of that period, having failed to make good, he was killed in Tampa by shotgun fire in 1940. Evidently the middle western group ordered the Tampa leader to do this job. Thereafter his two sons continued in the traffic. After considerable investigation, we arrested DeLuca, Antinori's two sons, Paul and Joseph, and many others involved in 1942. The testimony of one of the defendants, Carl Carramusa, served to assure conviction of all defendants. The sentences meted out to these vicious murderers were shockingly low. In the case of Joseph DeLuca, who got 3 years, the court ordered that he not be deported on recommendation of the district attorney. After the leader, DeLuca, had served 1 year, he was paroled. Carramusa had moved to Chicago to escape vengeance by the combine. One morning, in 1945, as he was repairing a tire in front of his home, he was killed by a shotgun blast before the eyes of his 15-year-old daughter. His murder remains unsolved, but it unquestionably was the work of the Chicago members of the combine on orders from the Kansas City group. The neighbors of Carramusa who could have furnished information remained silent because of fear. This is the same pattern which follows all of their activities. Witnesses in narcotic cases against members of this combine refuse to testify knowing that they will be marked for death.

DIFFICULT TO OBTAIN RELIABLE MAFIA EVIDENCE

The committee found it difficult to obtain reliable data concerning the extent of Mafia operation, the nature of the Mafia organization, and the way it presently operates. One notable concrete piece of evidence is a photograph of 23 alleged Mafia leaders from all over the United States, arrested in a hotel in Cleveland in 1928. When arrested, the group possessed numerous firearms. Among those arrested were Joseph Profaci of New York, Vincent Mangano of New York, and "Red" Italiano of Tampa. Profaci, who is considered by the experts to be one of the top leaders of the Mafia, was questioned about this meeting at a closed committee hearing. At first, he asserted that he was in Cleveland in connection with his olive-oil business. Then after admitting that he had no olive-oil business in Cleveland before 1935 or 1936, he was unable to give a satisfactory explanation of his presence at the Cleveland convention.

Almost all the witnesses who appeared before the committee and who were suspected of Mafia membership, either denied that they had ever heard of the Mafia, which is patently absurd, or denied membership in the Mafia. However, many of these witnesses readily admitted knowledge of and associations and friendships with suspected Mafia characters in other parts of the country. A notable exception is Tony Gizzo, who testified in a closed hearing that he had heard that James Balestrere was the leader of the Mafia in Kansas City. Gizzo changed his testimony at the open hearing. Another notable exception is Philip D'Andrea who said that the Mafia was freely discussed in his home when he was a child, and that he understood it to be a widely feared extortion gang. On the basis of all the evidence before it, plus the off-the-record but convincing statements of certain informants who must remain anonymous, the committee is inclined to agree with the opinion of experienced police officers and narcotics agents who believe:

1. There is a Nation-wide crime syndicate known as the Mafia, whose tentacles are found in many large cities. It has international ramifications which appear most clearly in connection with the narcotics traffic.

2. Its leaders are usually found in control of the most lucrative rackets in their cities.

3. There are indications of a centralized direction and control of these rackets, but leadership appears to be in a group rather than in a single individual.

4. The Mafia is the cement that helps to bind the Costello-Adonis-Lansky syndicate of New York and the Accardo-Guzik-Fischetti syndicate of Chicago as well as smaller criminal gangs and individual criminals throughout the country. These groups have kept in touch with Luciano since his deportation from this country.

5. The domination of the Mafia is based fundamentally on "muscle" and "murder." The Mafia is a secret conspiracy against law and order which will ruthlessly eliminate anyone who stands in the way of its success in any criminal enterprise in which it is interested. It will destroy anyone who betrays its secrets. It will use any means available — political influence, bribery, intimidation, etc., to defeat any attempt on the part of law-enforcement to touch its top figures or to interfere with its operations.

The Mafia today acts closely with many persons who are not of Sicilian descent. Moreover, it must be pointed out most strongly that the Mafia group comprises only a very small fraction of a percentage even of Sicilians. It would be most unfortunate if any inferences were erroneously drawn in any way derogatory to the vast majority of fine law-abiding citizens of Sicilian and Italian extraction.

THE ROLE OF THE WIRE SERVICE IN ORGANIZED CRIME

In our second interim report we stressed the great importance of the race wire service as a lever which makes it possible for organized criminal syndicates to gain a foothold in every community in the country. Bookmaking provides the richest source of revenue from gambling operations and the wire service, which transmits up-to-minute information about racing news, is essential to big-time bookmakers. A bookmaker who does not have the wire service cannot compete with one who has. The wire service is as essential to a bookmaker as the stock ticker to a stockbroker. It is because of this importance of the wire service to the bookmakers that the organization which controls the wire service can, in effect, control bookmaking operations. It has bookmakers at its mercy and it can charge what the traffic will bear. Thus, the characteristic of wire service distribution is the great disparities in the prices charged for similar types of service. Bookmakers are charged vastly different rates than the few legitimate users of the wire service, such as the newspapers. Bookmakers are frequently compelled to pay a fixed percentage of their profits to distributors of the wire service, whereas the few legitimate users pay only nominal sums.

In view of the great importance of the wire service to bookmaking operations, throughout the country, and in view of the fact that the wire service is one of the means whereby organized crime siphons off the lush returns from bookmaking, the committee feels that it is necessary to retell the story of the Capone mob's influence on the wire service which appears in its second interim report.

CONTINENTAL PRESS SERVICE A MONOPOLY

As stated in that report, the committee is of the opinion that the Continental Press, which has a monopoly of the transmission of gambling news throughout the country, is not fully controlled by Edward McBride, its nominal owner, or by Thomas Kelly, its general manager, but is substantially influenced by the gangsters who constitute the Capone crime syndicate. As a corollary, the Capone syndicate has the power to dominate bookmaking operations of any size throughout the country.

The racing wire news service first assumed importance under the ownership of M. L. Annenberg, some 30 years ago. Annenberg had been circulation manager for several large metropolitan newspapers and had likewise interested himself in the distribution of racing news publications known as scratch sheets. These scratch sheets contained information with respect to various aspects of horse racing which was intended to guide prospective bettors.

He conceived the idea of establishing a telegraphic news service which would carry over the wires fast and accurate information on racing for bookmakers and, with the big daily news distribution loops as his model, set up his own method of racing news coverage.

In the days when Annenberg, now deceased, was building newspaper circulations, competition between daily papers in metropolitan areas was intense. It was the era when newspapers were numerous. Since then many have become defunct and many others have been merged. The fight for circulation was a rough-and-tumble affair. Often violence was resorted to in order to cut down the circulation of a rival journal. Obviously many of those who participated in the circulation wars were strong-arm individuals to whom street brawls for control of newsstands and distribution outlets were everyday affairs.

To obtain the news from race tracks was the first problem of the new wire service. Some track owners were willing to sell the exclusive privilege of reporting from their enclosures to the news service which Annenberg named Nationwide News Service. However, some tracks were unwilling to cooperate and here it was necessary for the news to be purloined. For this purpose it was only natural for Annenberg to employ some of the individuals who had been associated with him in the newspaper-circulation wars. Crews were formed to telegraph racing information from some point near the track, if not inside it, to a central location in Chicago, whence it was relayed to other distribution points in the various States. From these latter subcenters of distribution local distributors furnished it to bookmakers.

Annenberg and his principal associates, including James A. Ragen, Sr., not only controlled Nationwide in Chicago, they also apparently owned controlling interests in the suboutlets which in turn purveyed the racing information to the bookmakers. The profits accruing to the owners of this system were enormous.

ONE SUBDISTRIBUTOR TYPICAL OF ALL

In view of its limited time and facilities, this committee was unable to study exhaustively the various subcenters that constituted the provincial capitals of the old Annenberg empire but to complete its study it was considered necessary to make a detailed investigation of one typical point and for this purpose the committee selected the Pioneer News Co. of St. Louis, a relict of the old Annenberg distributorship.

The testimony shows that Annenberg, Ragen, and one Al Kruse of Chicago owned 50 percent of the stock of Pioneer News Co. when the latter was an affiliate of Nationwide.

Their participation in the business was not active but another Nationwide associate, William Molasky, who then lived and still lives in St. Louis, was their respresentative on the spot. There came a time in 1939 when Annenberg divested himself of all his interest in the racing wire news service, at about the time when the Internal Revenue Bureau opened an investigation into his income tax returns, and the Department of Justice began investigating his monopolistic control of the wire service. Molasky purchased the entire Annenberg interest in Pioneer News Co. for $1; its actual value had no relation to the nominal purchase price.

Annenberg's dissociation with the racing wire news service was complete. He did not attempt to sell it to anyone or to realize any salvage from it; he simply walked out.

At that same time Ragen was also under indictment for violation of income-tax regulations. Ragen turned to an old friend, an associate of the newspaper war days, Arthur B. McBride of Cleveland. McBride was, like Ragen, a veteran of the vicious street battles for newspaper circulation. Moreover, Ragen's man Friday, Thomas Kelly, had been married to McBride's deceased sister.

It is one of the amazing aspects of this whole story that without any break in the service, without any dislocation of the facilities used in the entire process of obtaining racing information, legitimately or illegitimately, from the race tracks and without any disruption in its distribution, one man stepped out of this complicated business and another man took it over without any formal transfer or without the passing of a single dollar.

It is hardly believable that no one else made any attempt to acquire the race news wire service either by purchase or by force. It happened just that way. The old management closed the door and a new management walked in and sat down and started operating.

ARTHUR B. M'BRIDE TAKES OVER

McBride, in his testimony before the committee, said he believed that without him the organization would have fallen apart. But his testimony is also on record to the effect that when he went into the wire service he knew nothing about it, had no time to devote to it and that if, at Kelly's asserted plea, he did go into the business, it would have to be run by Kelly and Ragen.

From McBride's testimony, the committee finds it hard to discern just how he was indispensable to the conduct of the racing wire service. McBride said that it was necessary for him to provide the original working capital of $20,000 but this does not appear to be convincing because $20,000 in the operation of the new racing wire service which was given the appellation Continental Press Service appears to have been small money. As a matter of fact, McBride got his $20,000 back out of net profits before 2 weeks had elapsed. It was also apparent that Ragen could have put that amount up out of his own pocket or could have borrowed it without any difficulty whatsoever.

McBride testified that the only reason he went into the business was to help his brother-in-law, Kelly, and another old friend, Ragen. It was suggested by counsel for the committee that he could have loaned Kelly $20,000 and allowed Kelly to become the owner of the business but McBride said that he did not feel Kelly was sufficiently seasoned in business to be trusted with a loan of that size—this despite the fact that McBride had loaned similar amounts to known gangsters on at least two occasions and also despite the fact that when he did take the business over he had to trust Kelly to run it.

McBride stayed in Continental until 1941. Then he sold out to Ragen.

The story continues with Ragen and Kelly operating Continental until 1943 when McBride says Ragen came to him and said that he simply had to have McBride or a member of McBride's family in the organization. Nobody has given a clear reason for this because McBride, in his testimony before the committee, said that he had not learned anything further about the business up to that time and he had neither the energy nor available time to give to it.

McBride had a son, Edward, who at that time was overseas with the Armed Forces. Obviously Edward could not give any attention to the business. But for him McBride purchased a one-third interest for $50,000 which was paid out of McBride's share of the profits. Why McBride had to be brought into a business which was operating successfully and did not need capital is obscure unless it was to make available to the business such advantages as might result from McBride's powerful connections with John Angersola (King) and other important leaders of the underworld in Cleveland.

Continental Press Service continued to operate without serious trouble until about 1946. During this period Ragen and McBride operated it as partners and there is no indication on the record that during this period it was dominated by any out-and-out gangster element although, beyond any doubt, Continental Press enjoyed amicable relations with the gangsters who were building up large-scale bookmaking operations in the bigger cities of the country.

CAPONE GANG STARTS MUSCLING IN

It was in 1946 that trouble began.

The first eruption came in California where Mickey Cohen and Joe Sica, undoubtedly acting on behalf of Jack I. Dragna, a leader of the Mafia in California, entered the premises of Russell Brophy, who was in charge of the local distribution agency for Continental. Brophy, incidentally, is Ragen's son-in-law. Sica is a reputed member of the Mafia under indictment on a narcotics charge; his trial has been delayed because the chief witness against him was recently mysteriously murdered. Brophy took a beating from the two hoodlums. At about the same time, back in Chicago, Ragen himself was having serious trouble with the R. & H. Publishing Co., a subdistributor of the racing news service controlled by the local Capone syndicate which was stealing news from Midwest News Service, a controlled distributor of Continental. R. & H. serviced several hundred bookmakers from Chicago. R. & H., which was operated by Hymie Levin, Phil Katz, and Ray Jones was actually controlled by Tony Accardo, Jacob Guzik, and the Chicago syndicate.

Ragen threatened to tell what he knew about the Chicago mob to the Federal Bureau of Investigation and also threatened to report R. & H. to the Federal Communications Commission so that the subdistributor would be forced out of business. He made a number of attempts to get R. & H. out of the business, saying that the wire service could not tolerate the gangster element or it would itself be put out of business.

Ragen offered to buy out R. & H. but he would not pay the enormous price that the gang set as the consideration for their elimination. The syndicate in turn appears to have been anxious to ease Ragen out and to take over the entire wire service, and thereby gain control over every handbook in the country.

Then, from nowhere, suddenly appeared a new racing information distribution service known as Trans-American Publishing & News Service, Inc.

One of Trans-American's first customers was R. & H. which withdrew from the Continental Press set-up. Heading Trans-American were three nonentities, not one of whom had any address or stature in gangdom. Two of them, Pat Burns and his son, Andrew, were former employees of Continental who had been lured away by Trans-American for the new set-up. One of the three was Ralph O'Hara, a minor gangster of Chicago. All were officers and stockholders of the new corporation but none had the capital necessary to embark on this costly venture. O'Hara was a witness before the committee in Chicago. The books and records of Trans-American were supposed to be in his custody, but many of them proved to be missing. But from those that were available it would appear that in its first year's operation Trans-American lost about $200,000, most of which was put up by R. & H. Publishing Co. Other gangster-dominated customers provided financial support by loans or advances for service.

In addition to the huge "loans" from R. & H., Trans-American received a "loan" of $12,000 from Benjamin (Bugsy) Siegel, who at that time had a monopoly of the bookmaking and wire-news service in Las Vegas. Hoodlums in various parts of the country furnished support to Trans-American's operation, and among those who provided money was William (Butsy) O'Brien, who had formerly controlled the racing-news service for Continental in the State of Florida and who continued throughout Trans-American's operations to give support to Continental, thus playing both ends against the middle. Many handbooks hedged by subscribing and paying for service from both the Continental and Trans-American systems.

TRANS-AMERICAN EXPANDS ITS ACTIVITIES

Trans-American made no attempt to operate directly in St. Louis; it utilized one of the partners in Pioneer News Service to work from the

Illinois side of the Mississippi in East St. Louis, thus competing directly with Pioneer. In Kansas City, Trans-American was directed and operated by four of Binaggio's henchmen, who included two notorious Mafia members with outstanding records for violence. They operated independently for a few days and then moved into the office of Continental which they took over lock, stock, barrel, and personnel. The Kansas City group spread its wire-service tentacles out into a number of neighboring States, including Iowa, Nebraska, and Colorado, taking with it Continental wire outlets and utilizing them for Trans-American set-up.

Police officials in the cities involved confidently anticipated that there would be considerable violence but the outburst did not reach the height which they expected. It is possible that the reason for this is that before local violence became too acute Ragen, the head of Continental Press Service, was assassinated in Chicago in a fashion typical of gangland.

A few weeks prior to his slaying, he had gone to the district attorney of Cook County, Ill., and had made a very lengthy statement saying that his life had been threatened and he fully expected the threats to be carried out. If he were killed, he said the probable killers would be Accardo, Guzik, and Murray ("The Camel") Humphreys, the top echelon of the Capone syndicate. Ragen said that the Capone syndicate wanted to be cut in on Continental and that he was resisting with all his might even though his life was thereby endangered. Ragen's statement to the district attorney of Cook County is a part of the record of this committee. It is corroborated, at least in part, by the testimony of Dan Serritella, Jake Guzik's partner in the Capone syndicate's scratch sheet.

After Ragen's death, active management of Continental was taken over by Tom Kelly; Kelly and McBride arranged to buy the two-thirds interest in Continental which belonged to the estate of Ragen and the latter's son. Title was taken in the name of Edward McBride, Arthur McBride's son, but Edward had no part in the negotiations and was not present except when the papers were executed. Edward McBride thus became the sole owner of Continental. He remained in Florida where he was attending law school and had absolutely nothing to do with the management of the company. When questioned at a committee hearing he could not even recite elementary facts about the important personnel of his news transmission system but had to refer to his uncle or to his counsel for the replies. It is obvious that, although he now owns Continental Press of record, he knows nothing whatever about its operation or management.

The acquisition of Continental by McBride's son had a mysterious paralyzing effect on the hostilities between Continental and Trans-American. Like the Arabs in the poem, Trans-American quietly folded its tents and silently withdrew from the scene—just at the point, according to the testimony of Kelly of Continental Press, where the latter seemed doomed to be forced out of business.

As an illustration of the effects of the wire service warfare, it is interesting to note that John J. Fogarty, Continental distributor in New Orleans, was forced into a partnership with two brothers of Carlos Marcello, reputed Mafia leader in Louisiana, who was an associate of Joe Poretto, Trans-American's representative.

TRANS-AMERICAN MOBSTERS DODGE SUBPENAS

Although the most diligent efforts were made, the committee was unable to serve subpenas on any of the persons connected with R. & H. Publishing Co. It did obtain the presence of Ralph O'Hara, the head of Trans-American, but he refused to answer any questions whatsoever about the business on the ground that his answers would tend to incriminate him. He did not change his attitude when it was pointed out to him that the McBrides and their counsel insisted that the Continental operation, parallel in all respects to that of Trans-American, was wholly legitimate and in no way in violation of any law. Kelly and McBride insisted in their testimony that Trans-American discontinued doing business on its own initiative and not as a result of any deal.

After Trans-American folded, Continental's distributor, Illinois Sports News, took back into its employ one Pat Burns and his son and daughter, both of whom had walked out on Continental to take jobs with Trans-American. Why Continental gave reemployment to these persons, with substantial salaries, and others who had left to go into the employ of its competitor has not been satisfactorily answered. Nor has any convincing explanation been given as to why Continental then gave racing wire service in Kansas City to the same group who in effect had stolen the local outlets of Continental for Trans-American. In fact, the Mafia operators who took over the Reliable News Service in Kansas City received much better terms than the old wire service in that city had received from Continental before the fight and certainly got better terms than other distributors in various cities who had not fought Continental but who are not connected with the Mafia or the Capone gang. R. & H. in Chicago encountered no difficulty in contracting for service with Illinois Sports News on terms far more profitable than those given to another racing service distributor in Chicago who had no connection with either Mafia or the Caponites. R. & H. paid $750 a week for its service, whereas its competitor, Midwest News Service, a long-time and loyal subscriber of Illinois Sports News, for precisely the same service, paid between $4,000 and $5,000 a week. The owners of Illinois Sports News failed to give convincing testimony to the committee in explanation of the reason why R. & H. was given such a preferential rate in the light of their statements that for years R. & H. had stolen news from the Continental system. The owners of Illinois implied that the theft of news was a costly expense to R. & H. and after the cessation of the Trans-American Co., Illinois would have a great competitive advantage over R. & H. if they had refused to sell R. & H. service. It is of further significance that the usual practice of Illinois Sports News to investigate into the volume of business of its customers for the purpose of fixing the service rate was not resorted to in establishing the rate for R. & H. No satisfactory explanation was advanced by the owners of Illinois Sports News as to why it failed to request information from R. & H. as to the number of handbook customers R. & H. intended to service and the rate R. & H. was to receive from these customers. In New Orleans, Continental made Marcello its distributor; on the west coast, Dragna was rewarded for his part in the fight with Continental by being given a contract at

$25,000 a year to steal news from the race tracks and send it into Continental's headquarters for interstate distribution.

In Florida, "Butsy" O'Brien held on to his distributorship for Continental. The testimony taken by the committee in Florida shows particularly that it was not until after Trans-American took itself out of the picture that the Capone henchmen infiltrated the racing news service in that State.

SERVICE TURNED OFF AND ON FOR S. & G.

One of the most significant aspects of the racing-wire story in Florida was the manner in which service from Chicago was cut off from the S. & G. bookmaking syndicate and its operatives in order to force that syndicate to take into partnership the Capone gang whose front man was Harry Russell, a Chicago gambler and former partner of Tony Accardo. A representative of the Western Union Telegraph Co., over whose wires the racing news to Miami Beach was carried, testified that the cut-off was ordered by William (Butsy) O'Brien.

Continental Press claimed that if all these things occurred, they were done by independent news-distributing companies to whom Continental sells the news, but over whom it has no control. Continental, it is claimed, stands simon pure as a central news-distributing agency which does not steal news or deal with bookmakers or characters of the underworld.

The facade of legality which Continental Press has erected for itself on the advice of eminent and learned counsel is a sham. In a court of law, as a corporate structure, it might stand up. But this is all the more reason why the true facts must be called to the attention of the Senate.

Continental Press is said to be owned by Edward McBride, a young man in his early twenties studying law in Miami, Fla. He knows nothing of its operations. Continental Press is operated by young McBride's uncle, Tom Kelly, who says he simply sells a news service to Illinois Sports News, Inc., and he does not know, he says, what Illinois Sports News does with it thereafter. It is significant that Illinois Sports News hired Pat Burns and the other dissident Continental employees back after Trans-American went out of business. It was Illinois Sports News that resumed business with R. & H. after Ragen was shot. Strangely enough, Illinois Sports News is operated by two other Kellys, the brother and son of Tom Kelly of Continental. The brother, George, admitted he knew little about the wire service and depended on Tom for advice and guidance.

On the business side, Illinois Sports News does not keep the considerable profits that it earns but it remits to Continental all of its net profit beyond a certain amount which has been agreed upon as a fair payment to Kelly's relatives for their services for running the outfit.

CONTINENTAL PULLS THE STRINGS

Illinois Sports News is a dummy. It is a typical dummy, but it is not the only one of its kind. Everywhere this committee looked among the subdistributors of Continental it found other dummies which are captained and manned by former long-time affiliates of the wire service chiefs and the Capone mob. They go through the fiction of stockholders' meetings, of meetings of board of directors, of voting themselves salaries which, in terms of the huge returns that roll in from the wire service, are picayune—they pay themselves $90 or $100 a week sometimes—and each year, by a solemn vote of the board of directors, arrange to pay into either Illinois Sports News or Continental Press everything that has come in over and above their actual operating expenses and these peanut salaries so that the subdistributors make no profit and pay no dividends. There is nothing left, after Continental Press gets its share, from which to pay any dividends. The wire rooms of both Continental and Illinois are in the same building. The news is stolen from some tracks by track crews of Illinois Sports with equipment supplied by Continental. On other tracks, the news is stolen by crews of Continental. The entire wire service system is centered in the headquarters of Illinois Sports News in Chicago.

Continental's operators and counsel contended in the face of all this that these subdistributing companies are independent operators and that their actions are their own. On its face, this contention is almost insulting and can be rejected out of hand. In every case investigated by the committee the purpose of attempting to insulate Continental Press was clearly obvious. As an example, in the case of Howard Sports News, which operates out of Baltimore and is one of the most flagrant of Continental's dummies, Continental wants to be isolated because Howard Sports News has for one of its functions the procurement of news from most of the race tracks. By the admission of its manager, Kelly, and the assertion of its lawyers, Continental has been very careful to divorce itself by every legal maneuver from any possible connection with activities as sordid as the stealing of news or selling the same to bookmakers who it cannot deny are engaged in an illegitimate business.

In fact, the testimony is uncontroverted that Continental deliberately set out to erect a business structure of such a kind that if its activities were ever questioned it would be able to defend itself with the half-truth that its news is sold only for a legitimate purpose. This fictional attempt at legality was attempted to be supported by distributors at the second level of the Continental set-up who had the temerity in their testimony before the committee to assert that they did not know they were selling their service to bookmakers.

SELL NEWS TO BOOKMAKERS—AND KNOW IT

The efforts of the subdistributors to keep up the legal fiction sought to be established by Continental collapsed under persistent questioning before the committee. The various distributors finally admitted that they sell racing news service to bookmakers and that they are fully aware that they are doing so. James Ragen told the State's attorney that the sole purpose of the legal fiction was to give Continental the appearance of not having too close a touch with the "undesirable ones."

Typical of the legal sham is the method by which the General News Service at Chicago was created. Prior to 1949 the Midwest News Service, a customer of Illinois Sports News, was owned and operated by James Frestel and Sylvester Farrell former employees of Annenberg and minions of James Ragen. In 1947 Illinois and Midwest merged to combat R. & H., George Kelly becoming a partner in the new company. As Midwest had always done, the Midwest-Illinois continued to service handbooks in the State of Illinois. In addition it enjoyed a profitable interstate business, subdistributing to handbooks and smaller distributors in many States. In January of 1949 the merger was dissolved by the sale of George Kelly's partnership interest to John Scanlon who had influential connections with the syndicate. The other partners Farrell and Frestel became silent. All three avoided service of committee subpena. As part of the same transaction Midwest decided to dispose of its lucrative interstate business. Edward McGoldrick, a $70-a-week employee decided to buy. Being without funds he negotiated a loan for the purchase price of $3,000 from the house counsel of Continental without interest. To assist this young entrepreneur, Illinois Sports News granted him 2 weeks' free service, the rate being $1,000 weekly. Net profit from the interstate customers was $1,500 to $1,800 per week. In no time the loan was repaid. Continental and Illinois provided the technical assistance and advice needed for operation of the new distributor.

These second-level outfits also groped for a pretense at legality by offering highly favorable rates to any legitimate publication which would buy their services. For example, a New York newspaper with one of the largest circulations in the country pays no more than $30 a week for Continental's news service, although other customers are billed as much as $5,000 a week for the same identical service.

Here is another typical example testified to by William P. Brown, manager, operator, and owner of the controlling interest in the Pioneer News Service of St. Louis:

Brown stated in his testimony that some customers pay about $100 a week for service and other customers of Pioneer pay as much as $350 a week for service. He was then asked, "What is the difference between the service given a $100 a week customer and the service given a $350 a week customer?", to which Brown replied, "Really none."

Question: "Really no difference whatsoever? Can you justify that difference?" Answer by Brown: "No; I can't."

FACADE OF LEGALITY A SHAM

The committee believes that the facade of legality which was set up by Continental's counsel with such great particularity must be rejected. It must also reject the insulation erected between McBride and the ultimate customers of Continental's service, the bookmakers, and, having rejected both of these factors, the inference becomes inescapable that Arthur B. McBride created a machine in which Edward McBride, through his agents, operates a racing wire service which is an integral part of a Nation-wide system employing discrimination in service and price against various persons seeking to purchase a commodity.

The conclusion is also inescapable that through agents and subagents McBride's organization steals news from race tracks and supplies this news through direct and indirect channels to bookmakers operating in violation of the law throughout the country. Whether this constitutes violation of local laws on the part of McBride is a matter for the determination of the courts in the respective States. The sole function of this committee in respect to the circumstances is to ascertain the facts and to determine whether or not any Federal legislation or regulation is required.

It also becomes inescapable, once the fiction of the divorce of Continental Press and McBride from the various distributors of Continental's news service, particularly in Chicago, has been rubbed out, that Arthur McBride is deliberately making a gift to the Mafia-affiliated Capone mob in Chicago of about $4,000 a week, which represents the difference in price paid by the Capone-controlled R. & H. service and the price paid by their competitors in the same city. In Kansas City, the Mafia group operating the wire service receives largesse of several hundred dollars a week on the same comparative basis. It is also clear that in many other cities the Capone affiliates and the Mafia are now in control of the distribution of racing wire news with a resultant source of enormous profits and power over bookmaking.

One final incidental fact may be noted at this point in connection with McBride: his interest in a Florida radio station whose license is now up for renewal by the Federal Communications Commission.

As late as March 1951 when the attorney general of Florida released an interim report on the Florida "antibookie" law, interesting indications of the continuing influence of the Chicago gangs were disclosed in Florida phases of the wire service. When an investigator checked into the activities of William "Butsy" O'Brien, Continental's Florida distributor for many years, he found none other than Alphonse "Sonny" Capone, son of the late "Scarface" Al Capone, printing bookie wall charts at O'Brien's Graham Press in Miami.

SYNDICATED BASKETBALL, FOOTBALL AND BASEBALL BETTING

That horse race betting was not alone in the field of big-time gambling was emphatically brought out in the testimony of Sydney A. Brodson of Milwaukee, Wis., who appeared before the committee in Washington. Brodson is a sharp-eyed college graduate, with a law degree. His luck at picking winners on cards distributed by operators of football and basketball pools diminished his interest in the practice of law until, some 7 years ago, he engaged in the betting business on a full-time basis.

Brodson established a small office in Milwaukee, setting himself up as a "food broker." With the help of several assistants, he read as many as 100 newspapers per day for information which might have a bearing on the outcome of college football and basketball games. Brodson frankly admitted placing bets with bookies or other gamblers in some 20 States to the amount of $1,000,000 per year, dealing almost exclusively over the telephone. He used three phones in his office, one of which was listed under the name, "Get the Vote Committee." Brodson readily conceded that in fact, this meant "get the bets." Long-distance telephone calls cost Brodson $15,000 yearly. After deducting such expenses as the cost of his newspapers and an athletic handicapping service somewhat comparable to the wire service in horse racing, known as Gorham Press, in St. Paul, Minn., Brodson nets some $80,000 per year and has amassed an admitted net worth of $250,000. Although Brodson maintained that he was not a "bookie," it was evident from his description of his activities that there was little to distinguish between his practice of betting man to man after negotiating as to points given or taken and the practice of handbook betting where the odds are set at the track.

Brodson explained that he maintained a lengthy list of individuals throughout the country who could be called and who would either accept his bets or channel them to bookies who would. Investigation established that Brodson himself could be called by individuals who wished to bet and would accept their play. Brodson had never met many of the individuals with whom he was betting daily but, through the mysterious grapevine of the gambling fraternity, was able to get in touch with them, determine their financial reliability and reputation as to paying off, and thus, participate in a veritable network of athletic betting on a Nation-wide basis. In addition to his knowledge that these individuals were betting with him, Brodson knew that they were betting with one another.

In straightening out their accounts at agreed periods, Brodson and those with whom he bet exchanged checks or cash through the United States mail and used Western Union wires. He said that sometimes he received as much as $1,000 in cash through the mail and had won as much as $20,000 on one bet.

Of particular interest to the committee was the fact that the Milwaukee Police Department was aware that Brodson was gambling on a full-time basis and vigorously explored his activities, but was unable to establish—and Brodson verified the fact—that he made any bets with anyone in Wisconsin, thus avoiding prosecution at the local level. It seemed that Brodson thus had the correct legal answer to successful operation without fear of police interference without the necessity of arranging "protection." Brodson betrayed what must have been a sense of self-degradation when he said:

My wife has always brought pressure on me to get out of this thing and perhaps I should have abided by her advice.

Brodson explained the "spread system" of basketball betting under which it is possible for a bookie to win both ends of bets on college basketball games if one team beats another by a score falling within the spread which may run from 2 to 7 points. Brodson readily conceded that this practice unquestionably contributed toward the corruption of college basketball players who could be talked into controlling the score of a game so that it ended within the spread and yet won the game for the school they represented. The transition from this stage of moral destruction in youth to the point where a player would accept money to throw the game completely became, thereafter, relatively simple.

COMEBACK MONEY

As part of every major interstate bookmaking syndicate's operation there is the apparent necessity to maintain agents in the vicinity of the major race tracks to handle the syndicate's last-minute bets at the tracks. This practice is commonly referred to as the betting of "comeback money" possibly because some of the off-track, or illegal, handle is coming in to the mutuel machines. There are probably two reasons for these transactions:

1. The "comeback money" may represent large bets which illegal bookmakers are unable to "lay off" among themselves, bets which no one in the bookmaking organization desires to hold.

2. Sending of large bets to the tracks reduces the odds on the horse involved so that if it should win the odds which the illegal bookmaker would have to pay would be considerably less than if the "comeback money" had not been placed and, too, such a bettor collects on the winning tickets at the track. Paradoxical as it may seem, these bookies' bookies maintain that they hope that the horse selected by them for the betting of "comeback money" will lose. They explain that the procedure is merely a "balancing of their books" and, in many cases, because of the much larger amounts bet on other horses in the race, they maneuver themselves into a position where they cannot lose, no matter which horse wins.

Those race tracks which are members of the Thoroughbred Racing Association frown on the handling of "comeback money" and refuse cooperation and use of track facilities to the agents of these betting commissioners.

An official of the Thoroughbred Racing Protective Bureau explained the practice in terms of money this way:

Let's say a man goes to his bookie and bets $200 on a horse. The bookie knows that man normally is a $10 bettor, so he's suspicious and to protect himself against a large loss he "lays off" part of that bet with a bigger bookie.

The big bookie, in turn, might have an unusual amount of play on that same horse. He distributes some of his risk to commission houses in St. Louis, Chicago, Cincinnati, or Miami. The commission house is loaded with $20,000 worth of bets on one horse, let's say. The horse is 10 to 1 and if it wins the commission house will lose $200,000.

The commission house phones an agent at a gas station near the track and instructs him to bet $5,000 on the horse. The odds promptly are knocked down to 3 to 1. If the horse wins the payoff on a $2 ticket will be $8 instead of $22, in addition to which the commission house collects on its $5,000 bet to help pay off on the $15,000 worth of bets it held. And, of course, they have all the money bet on other horses in the race.

Naturally, they don't lay off all the money because gambling is their business. If the horse loses they pocket the $15,000 they held minus the $5,000 they bet and meanwhile they've insured themselves against taking a terrific beating.

In Washington hearings, three "comeback" men were heard: Fred Cogan, Richard Remer, and Joseph Uvanni. The first two were agents for Louis "Rosy" Rosenbaum, Newport, Ky., gambling mogul. Uvanni claimed to be an "independent contractor," working for the James Carroll-John Mooney betting commission organization in the St. Louis area.

Cogan explained that Rosenbaum paid him $150 a week to station himself at a telephone near a race track. Throughout the afternoon, he would remain in contact with Rosenbaum by telephoning collect to Rosenbaum's Kentucky headquarters. Cogan received money from Rosenbaum by Western Union money order and followed Rosenbaum's telephonic instructions each race by going into the track and placing the amount of money ordered on the horse specified. Cogan admitted that it was necessary to replenish his funds frequently in view of the fact that, over any period of time, the come-back operation was a loss.

Remer testified to similar operations for Rosenbaum with the notable exception that at one track on his circuit, Bowie, Md., special arrangements were made with some of the track officials. Remer was able to obtain the use of a telephone in the track office and thus save the leg work of running from an outside telephone into the track for each race. At Bowie, too, it was possible to deposit a bank roll with the mutuel clerk against which he could bet until it was depleted. Remer also advised that the replenishment of this bank roll was necessary from time to time, indicating that the procedure was a constantly losing proposition.

When Rosenbaum testified, he admitted that he used five telephones in a small office occupied by him in the name of the Northern Kentucky Hospitalization Insurance Agency. Asked if it wasn't a fraud to do business under the name of such an agency and not to sell hospitalization insurance, he retorted that it would be a fraud if he did sell the insurance. Rosenbaum estimated his telephone bill at $3,000 to $3,500 per month and the committee found, from telephone company records, that as many as 1,053 long-distance calls were charged to his telephones in 1 month.

In 1947 and 1948, Rosenbaum admitted that he paid Federal income tax of approximately $200,000. He claimed that he had never been arrested in the Cincinnati-northern Kentucky area. He admitted taking lay-off bets from numerous bookies and also laid off himself occasionally to other large operators such as John Mooney in St. Louis. In order to accomplish the payment of the bets he maintained a checking account in the name of a relative who was directed to send out checks as required through the mails and deposit the incoming money in the account.

The Carroll-Mooney come-back man, Joseph Uvauni, covered a circuit of race tracks including those at New Orleans, Detroit, New Jersey, Nebraska, Colorado, and Kentucky. He said his operating bankroll was sent to him by Mooney, sometimes in the form of cash in registered letters, sometimes by cashiers' checks, and sometimes by Western Union money orders. His expense arrangements were such that he had wide latitude in financing the facilities arranged by him for his operations near the tracks. In New Orleans, he paid the owner of a house near the Fairgrounds race track for an ostensibly private phone. The committee found that it was listed under the name of Munez Collection Agency.

L. Edward O'Hara, general manager of the Bowie race track, presented an interesting version of the Bowie race track attitude toward the comeback problem. He readily conceded that Bowie, under his direction, permitted the comeback men to operate with the blessing of management. He thought the comeback system was very similar to the practice of insurance companies in letting out their policies to other insurance companies. From the figures presented by Mr. O'Hara, it is possible to estimate roughly the scope of operation of these bookies' bookies. Although Bowie is considered a minor track in racing circles, Norman Helwig, the comeback man of the Carroll-Mooney group, bet as much as $23,000 in a day. Helwig bet a total of $143,691 at the 10-day race meeting from November 18 to December 2, 1950. O'Hara estimated that the total comeback money taken in by the track from all of the comeback men there during this period was probably $500,000. O'Hara identified a check made out to John Mooney in the amount of $20,105 on the track account, which he said represented the money forwarded to Mooney at the conclusion of the 1950 season which Mooney had left on deposit. O'Hara thought that stopping the comeback operations would put a "crimp" in the operations of the big commissioners but would not make their operations impossible.

There are these conclusions of great import to be drawn from this exposé of the technique of these big betting commissioners in transmitting their wagers to the tracks:

1. It has been advanced that the major bookmaking syndicates would be seriously hampered, if not forced out of business, if the practice were effectively fought, either on a local level or by Federal intervention.

2. The frequent, and in some cases almost exclusive, use of the channels of interstate commerce by the betting commissioners' entire operation, including the transmission and reception of the original lay-off bets, messages, transmission of money, brands the practice as one which is somewhat insulated from attack by local law enforcement and possible fertile field for Federal help in policing those channels of interstate commerce.

ILLICIT TRAFFIC IN NARCOTIC DRUGS

The illicit narcotic drug traffic is an excellent example of a type of organized crime which is interstate and even international in nature. Considerations of time prevented the committee from giving to this problem the intensive attention which might be desired. However, sufficient testimony was obtained to give some indication of the nature and magnitude of this racket.

In recognition of a serious and rapidly developing narcotic-addiction situation in this country, the first comprehensive Federal narcotic law was enacted in 1914. That was the so-called Harrison Act. This law uses the taxing power of the Federal Government to legalize the commerce in medicinal and other legitimate narcotics. By the same means it seeks to outlaw illicit traffic in opium and its derivatives and in the coca leaf and its derivatives (cocaine, etc.)

Another important Federal law known as the Jones-Miller Act, or the Import and Export Act, was passed in 1922. This law sets up a system of import and export permits and limits import of raw material to medical needs; also by amendment in 1924, it outlawed the very dangerous opiate heroin in that it prohibited the importation of opium for the manufacture of this derivative.

The Opium Poppy Act of 1942 was passed to insure against any practice of growing opium poppies here.

Since, like the opium poppy, coca leaves are not grown in this country it is obvious that the raw material, both for the legitimate and for the illicit traffic in these narcotic drugs, must come from abroad. There is a tremendous excess of opium production throughout the world. The great bulk of this excess is consumed in Asiatic and Middle East countries where the opium habit is a form of dissipation employed by large segments of the population. Some of this excess in one form or another is directed at markets in this country.

The Federal agencies principally concerned with narcotic-law enforcement are the Bureau of Narcotics and the Bureau of Customs, both under the Treasury Department.

Enforcement of comprehensive Federal narcotic laws began about 1915 and was intensified at the close of World War I. This has been accompanied by much action at the State and local level in the way of enforcing uniform State laws and city ordinances against the traffic. Along with law enforcement on a broad front there has been an active campaign spearheaded by the Government of the United States to restrict world opium production and to take such international action in the way of exchange of information as to shut off supplies of illicit narcotics to so-called victim countries such as the United States. Under this program there has been for a generation, up to and including World War II, a steady decline in the incidence of narcotic addiction in this country according to the United States Bureau of Narcotics.

Prior to the beginning of narcotic-law enforcement in the United States it was estimated that there was one narcotic addict in every 400 or 500 of the population. Surveys made about the beginning of World War II indicated that the rate had declined to less than 1 in 3,000 and the Bureau of Narcotics reports further declines during the war years. Moreover, the Bureau estimates that the incidence is very much lower in certain localities such as Pennsylvania and Minnesota. A survey by the Bureau in Minnesota in July 1950 showed only 1 addict in each 25,000 of the population.[1]

This drop in addiction was accompanied by a general rise in prices of illicit narcotics and by an increasing relative scarcity of the amount of narcotic drugs available to illicit traffickers. Several years before World War II the cocaine traffic, for all practical purposes, disappeared. This favorable trend in narcotic-law enforcement continued until about 1948 which year was marked by a large influx of Peruvian cocaine into this country. This was coincident with the loosening of controls on cocaine in Peru. Active countermeasures in the way of convictions of several rings of smugglers in this country and corrective action by the Peruvian Government in that country have again greatly reduced the cocaine traffic.[2]

HEROIN USE INCREASES ALARMINGLY

However, coincident with the reappearance of cocaine, there began a trickle of heroin which gradually increased to stream proportions. Where heroin had been scarce it now appeared in increasing volume. In some areas where it had been absent for several years it could be found in the underworld. Much of this influx was absorbed by established narcotic addicts who were able to increase their daily intake. Some of it was used by new addicts who also commenced to appear in increasing numbers. A most disquieting feature is that in several localities, principally in large cities, a substantial proportion of the new addicts are young people, persons in their late 'teens and early 20's. At the present time this phase of the narcotic problem is a matter of acute public interest and widespread alarm. In one city alone, a civic crime-prevention group, in its study of the narcotics problem, estimated that the value of property stolen annually to provide the addicts with funds to buy dope is $60,000,000.

There can be no doubt that the narcotic traffic is highly organized crime. Early in narcotic-law enforcement there was considerable diversion from legitimate stocks. Controls which were established with the cooperation of the drug manufacturers and the medical and

[1] Files, U. S. Bureau of Narcotics.
[2] Annual reports, U. S. Bureau of Narcotics 1947–48. Files, Bureau of Narcotics.

pharmacy professions have made diversion at the higher levels virtually nonexistent. (There was a wave of robberies and burglaries of pharmacy houses during World War II.)   While there is some diversion at the addict level due to forgery and small thefts and a very few venal registrants, existing controls keep this at a stage relatively unimportant in the over-all enforcement picture.

Therefore drugs for the illicit narcotic traffic must necessarily be smuggled from abroad.   Prior to World War II, important sources for these were India, China, Japan, and Iran.   Also in the 1920's there was an enormous diversion from European drug manufacturers and drug production by clandestine plants there.   Largely on the insistence of and through the leadership of the United States this was pretty well checked by energetic enforcement and multilateral agreements among the nations involved.

Presently, a large flow of heroin is coming from Turkey where it is manufactured from excess opium production in that country and Iran. Also, a large amount of heroin has been coming from Italy lately as the result of diversion from medical stocks available by reason of allotments of heroin obviously excessive for alleged medical purposes. Cooperative American-Italian law-enforcement efforts plus action by the Italian Government in greatly reducing the amounts of heroin allotted for medical use may help solve this problem admittedly made difficult by the presence in Italy of numerous racketwise deportees from the United States now repatriated there.

Testimony before this committee of one representative of the Bureau of Narcotics [3] is to the effect that the influx of heroin from Italy coincided with activity there of Salvatore Lucania ("Lucky" Luciano) who was deported to Italy in February 1946.   The United States Bureau of Narcotics learned that this deportee had left Italy and had arrived in Cuba late in 1946, reportedly for the purpose of using Cuba as a base for narcotic and other crimes.   The Bureau asked the United States State Department to make representations to Cuba which resulted in the prompt banishment of Luciano to his native Italy in 1947, an excellent example of the necessity and value of international cooperation in narcotics control.[4]

TWO POUNDS OF DOPE MAY RETAIL FOR $100,000

The profits of the illicit narcotic business are big.   Calculated on the basis of the pure drug, a kilogram (approximately 2.2 pounds) of heroin costing the smuggler a few hundred dollars in Turkey may eventually bring approximately $50,000 to $100,000 or more at prices actually being paid in the narcotic traffic today (approximately $1,500 to $3,000 per ounce or more).   This, of course, is after the drug is adulterated to many times its volume.[5]   (Incidentally, despite the rise in addiction these fantastic prices may indicate a high effectiveness of law enforcement.)

The lure of such proceeds is attractive to the conscienceless racketeer.   At one time or another, a great many of the bigger interstate racketeers in the United States have dipped into the narcotic traffic.   This fact has made the files of the Bureau of Narcotics a veritable gold mine of information on interstate racketeers to the com-

[3] Sam Levine, New York.
[4] Files, U. S. Bureau of Narcotics.
[5] Files, U. S. Bureau of Narcotics.

mittee's investigators. In the 1920's, for example, there thrived in
Europe the Eliopoulos brothers, so-called drug barons of Europe,[6]
who had access to the narcotic production of several chemical factories
there. These men formed conspiracies with outstanding American
racketeers such as "Legs" Diamond, the Newman brothers, "Dutch"
Schultz, and others.

Narcotics were shipped to United States ports generally concealed
in cargo, sometimes in baggage, and from New York were distributed
throughout the length and breadth of the country.

In the 1930's the sinister power of "Murder, Inc." was injected into
the illicit drug traffic. The case of Louis "Lepke" Buchalter, its
leader, has often been described; however, it is so illustrative of
interstate crime operations in the narcotic field that it will bear
repeating here in brief: [7]

In the middle 1930's, Buchalter emerged as the head of an extortion
racket organization in New York. He maintained preeminence for
some time by a practice of ruthlessly killing persons who did not
accede to his racket demands. Possible witnesses to murders and
his other crimes were also mercilessly eliminated. During the time
of Buchalter's preeminence certain long-established figures in the
illicit narcotic traffic formed a conspiracy to smuggle drugs from
Tientsin, China. This gang was headed by Jasha Katzenberg, Jacob
Lvovsky, and several others. A cleverly devised scheme to introduce
narcotics was successful. These drugs were being smuggled into the
port of New York at a rate estimated sufficient to supply the current
needs of a fifth of the country's then addict population. Buchalter
had no part in the formation of this scheme, but when he heard of its
success, he promptly declared himself to be entitled to one-third of
the profits. The smugglers apparently felt they had no choice but
to agree. The arrangement was not a total loss to them since it
insured them the protection of the "muscle" of "Murder, Inc." against
competitors and hijackers.

When investigations by the Treasury's Bureaus of Narcotics and
Customs broke up this operation, Buchalter's part was disclosed. He
was placed on trial and convicted; then he pleaded guilty to additional
narcotic offenses for which he received prison sentences totaling 12
years. This blow shook the Buchalter empire. He subsequently
was to be taken from the Federal penitentiary and made available to
New York authorities for conviction on extortion charges and finally
placed on trial with his first lieutenant, Emanuel "Mendy" Weiss,
and another to be convicted for murder and electrocuted.

The case of Emanuel "Mendy" Weiss,[8] Buchalter's lieutenant, was
an interesting variation. Unlike Buchalter, he was an active organizer
of narcotic ventures. He was implicated in a smuggling case at
Rouses Point in 1937 involving a large quantity of heroin but the
case collapsed when the principal witness against him committed
suicide by hanging himself in his jail cell. In May 1940, Weiss was
indicted at Dallas, Tex., with 28 other persons comprising an organization distributing narcotics from New York to Chicago, Texas, and
other places. All except five of these persons had long criminal
records, several involving such desperate crimes as robbery and

[6] 1941 Annual Report, U. S. Bureau of Narcotics. Files, U. S. Bureau of Narcotics.
[7] Annual Report, U. S. Bureau of Narcotics, 1939, 1940, 1941, 1943, 1944.
[8] Annual Report U. S. Bureau of Narcotics, 1939, 1940, 1941.

murder.   Weiss forfeited bond on the narcotics charges and became
a fugitive when he learned of the pending murder charges against
him and Buchalter.   Later he was captured by narcotic agents and
was turned over to the State of New York for murder prosecution.
He was convicted and electrocuted with Buchalter.

During World War II some of the United States narcotic traffic
was supplied from Mexican sources where the opium poppy is illicitly
grown.   At the present time, the Mexican Government, according to
the Bureau of Narcotics, is attempting to do a good job of narcotics
policing, particularly with respect to opium.

MARIHUANA NOW COMES IN FROM MEXICO

There is, however, a tremendous flow of marihuana into this country
from Mexico.

The postwar revival of the narcotic traffic is now being carried on
by the successors to the Diamonds, Buchalters, etc.   It centers
principally in New York from which city distribution is made to all
parts of the country.   The trend of the traffic seems to be to the
smuggling of heroin in relatively small quantities.   This is carried on
either by international travelers or by seamen.   The task of inter-
cepting the drug at ports and borders is tremendously difficult due to
the small bulk and high value of the product.   (Many thousands of
dollars' worth of drugs can be readily concealed under the clothing of
the smuggler.)

This same consideration makes extremely difficult the catching of
narcotic culprits once the contraband is successfully landed.   Its small
bulk, extreme portability, and ready destructibility make the catching
of the narcotic criminal "with the goods" a task of great practical
investigative difficulty.   This, according to the Bureau of Narcotics
agents who testified, is particularly true in the light of the very
strict requirements of the Federal courts in the matter of evidence.

The Bureau of Narcotics has had particular occasion to deal with
interstate crime organizations in specialized forms.   One of these
types was the Chinese tong, ostensibly a nationalistic, family, commercial or social type of organization.   Some of these have been
found to be perverted as covers for organized crime, particularly
gambling and narcotics distribution.   The Bureau of Narcotics
reported [9] that an investigation disclosed the use of a Chinese tong
as a cover for a widespread narcotic traffic ranging through most of
the large cities in the country.

Originally most of the supplies for the tong members were obtained
in New York from Mary De Bello, reputed wife of Tommy "The
Bull" Pennachio, aide to "Lucky" Luciano.

The Bureau also reports that there are indications that some tong
organizations now are again active in the narcotic traffic.

From the available information it appears that the narcotic traffic
in this country after a slow but steady decline for a generation has
recently shown a sharp upsurge.   This is accompanied by an outbreak of youthful addiction noted in many large urban centers.   The
major traffic appears to be in the hands of some of the most astute,
wily, and desperate criminals who operate interstatewise.

[9] Annual Report 1937, U. S. Bureau of Narcotics.

The identity of the criminal groups behind this rise in the distribution and use of narcotics was the subject of testimony by field agents of the Bureau of Narcotics in Kansas City and New York.

Particularly illuminating on this score was the testimony of Agent Claude A. Follmer, of the Kansas City office of the Narcotics Bureau. In that city, he said, traffic in illicit drugs involved "for the most part persons   *   *   *   banded together in a secret society known as the Mafia." (A more detailed account of the criminal activities of the Mafia is to be found elsewhere in this report.)

Follmer detailed a long list of police characters and traced their activities and associations across State lines into various sections of the country and even across national boundaries into foreign countries where they obtained their supplies of dope.

Numerous suggestions for the suppression of the traffic in drugs were made by these agents and their Chief, Commissioner Harry Anslinger, head of the United States Bureau of Narcotics.

One of these is the proposal that more severe sentences be meted out to offenders against the narcotics laws. The average prison sentence for dope traffickers in Federal courts is under 2 years. Those charged with enforcement of the narcotics laws aver that these short sentences do not act as a sufficient deterrent. Both the United Nations and the League of Nations before its demise urged more severe sentences for offenders in this category.

It is also apparent from the testimony that the present authorized strength of the Bureau of Narcotics is too low to cope adequately with the situation. Commissioner Anslinger testified that his present force consisted of 190 agents; before the war it was approximately 250. Obviously an increase in this working force is called for.

Another phase of narcotics-law enforcement has to do with the comparative ease with which individuals known to have been associated with the dope racket and with other individuals in it are able to enter and leave the country almost at will.

It would be effective if such persons, upon proper identification by the Bureau of Narcotics, could be restricted from international travel when their obvious purpose is either to meet others engaged in the nefarious business in other countries or where they might be suspected of arranging for further importation of narcotic supplies into the United States.

The simple expedient of refusing a passport visa to such individuals would probably accomplish the purpose and would undoubtedly prevent such meetings as that Meyer Lansky testified he had with Charles "Lucky" Luciano in Cuba, and on another occasion in Italy.

Also submitted by Commissioner Anslinger as worthy of study is a proposal that some centralized agency maintain a gallery of major interstate racketeers and that it systematically collect, correlate, and disseminate information respecting them. The Treasury Department does this now with respect to major narcotic suspects.

Often the operations of modern big-time racketeers are so diverse and so extensive, geographically, that few local law-enforcement officers can carry in mind a catalog of all of them. A device of this sort which would spotlight the operations of major criminals would prove most helpful.

INFILTRATION INTO LEGITIMATE BUSINESS

One of the most perplexing problems in the field of organized crime is presented by the fact that criminals and racketeers are using the profits of organized crime to buy up and operate legitimate enterprises. This committee has no quarrel with the sincere efforts of men with criminal records who have seen the error of their ways and who now wish to earn an honest living by going into some type of legitimate business. The committee realizes that many men sow their "wild oats" in the form of crime, in their younger years, and then settle down to become decent citizens. This process of rehabilitation of offenders should be encouraged in every possible way. What the committee does object to, however, and what the committee finds is fraught with great danger to our country, is the extent to which gangsters and racketeers continue to pursue their vicious careers and invest the spoils of their illegitimate activity in legitimate enterprises.

A gangster or racketeer in a legitimate business does not suddenly become respectable. The methods which he used to achieve success in racketeering and gambling enterprises are not easily sloughed off. Thus, evidence was produced before the committee concerning the use of unscrupulous and discriminatory business practices, extortion, bombing, and other forms of violence to eliminate competitors and to compel customers to take articles sold by the mobsters. Monopoly is the key to big money in criminal activity. It is also sought by mobsters when they enter legitimate business. A racketeer who has contempt for the law and who enters legitimate business has no hesitation in engaging in black-market practices. This gives him a considerable advantage over a more timid competitor and is one of the means whereby the racketeer can push such a competitor to the wall.

There is another aspect of gangster infiltration into legitimate business which troubles the committee. The big-time gamblers and racketeers usually live a life of luxury but they must have some way of explaining their source of income to prying income-tax officials. One of the functions of investment into legitimate business enterprises is to provide a source for income which cannot be impeached by the Internal Revenue authorities. Returns from gambling and other illegitimate enterprises are extremely difficult to check. Some of the winnings may be invested in legitimate business and taxes may be paid on the income from such business. Taxes on the huge returns from gambling and other illegitimate enterprises have not been paid.

RACKETEERS PREFER BIG-TURNOVER BUSINESSES

It should be noted, however, that gangsters and racketeers have an affinity for enterprises in which there is a large turn-over and in which problems of accounting and control are difficult. Thus, even when the ill-gotten gains of a racketeer or gangster are invested in a legitimate enterprise there is no assurance that the Government will not be defrauded to a considerable degree of its taxes.

There can be little doubt that the public suffers from gangster penetration into legitimate business. It suffers because higher prices must be paid for articles and services which it must buy. This is the result of the monopoly which is often secured and because of unfair trade practices frequently applied. The public suffers because it may have to put up with shoddy and inferior merchandise in fields where gangsters have been able to obtain a monopoly.   One such olive-oil dealer, Joseph Profaci, was cited for a series of violations of the pure food and drug laws including one for which he was fined $12,000.   The tax load of the general public is increased when gangsters and racketeers fail to pay their lawful return on the enterprises in which they are engaged.   Finally, the public suffers because the vast economic resources that gangsters and racketeers control enables them to consolidate their economic and political positions.   Money, and particularly ready cash, is power in any community and over and over again this committee has found instances where racketeers' money has been used to exercise influence with Federal, State, and local officials and agencies of government.   An official who is beholden to the mob for his election or appointment thinks first of his boss and only secondarily of the people of the community that he must serve.   The money used by hoodlums to buy economic and political control is also used to induce public apathy.   The committee found that hoodlums, behind the front of their respectable enterprises, contribute enormous sums to hundreds of worthy causes.   While the committee in no way wishes to reflect on the worthiness of such causes, it has found that hoodlum contributions do tend to fool uninformed people and thus contribute to the relaxation of public vigilance.   The committee has had before it evidence of hoodlum infiltration in approximately 50 areas of business enterprise.   These include:

Advertising
Amusement industry
Appliances
Automobile industry
Baking
Ball rooms, bowling alleys, etc.
Banking
Basketball
Boxing
Cigarette distribution
Coal
Communications facilities
Construction
Drug stores and drug companies
Electrical equipment
Florists
Food (meat, sea food, dairy products, groceries, cheese, olive oil, fruit)
Football
Garment industry
Gas stations and garages
Hotels
Import-export business
Insurance
Juke box and coin-machine distribution
Laundry and dry cleaning
Liquor industry
Loan and bonding business
Manufacturing (gambling equipment, broilers, etc.)
Nevada gambling houses
News services
Newspapers
Oil industry
Paper products
Racing and race tracks
Radio stations
Ranching
Real estate
Restaurants (taverns, bars, night clubs)
Scrap business
Shipping
Steel
Surplus sales
Tailoring (haberdashery)
Television
Theaters
Transportation

While the committee has not been able in the time available to explore fully the situation in these fields, it has developed enough information to clearly indicate the problems and dangers involved in hoodlum penetration of legitimate industry.

One of the most shocking problems in this connection, and one which constitutes a black page in the history of American industry, is the indisputable evidence obtained by the committee of cooperation with major hoodlums on the part of important segments of business enterprise.   In Detroit, the committee found leading industrial concerns admittedly cooperating with notorious hoodlums for the purpose of suppressing labor difficulties. (See discussion of Detroit elsewhere in this report.) In New York, the same situation prevailed in connection with the Phelps-Dodge Co. which invited in hoodlums from the gang of Albert and Anthony Anastasia to help break a strike. Where business uses racketeers, there is a tendency for labor unions to use tactics of violence and vice versa. Finally, the committee found leading hoodlums holding valuable franchises in the liquor and automobile industries.

The specific discussions below must not be read as an index or directory of all known instances. They are rather a sampling of typical situations.

THE LIQUOR INDUSTRY

The committee found that leading hoodlums have penetrated the liquor industry, principally the distribution end of the business, due to failure of the industry to assume its proper share of responsibility and to failure of our laws and law-enforcement agencies adequately to cope with the situation.

Many of the Nation's leading hoodlums got their start as bootleggers during prohibition. Many have a history of prohibition arrests. The transition from bootlegging to the legitimate liquor business was a natural one. Unfortunately, however, many racketeers found it hard to drop the methods of operation which characterized their rum-running days and consequently, the committee was not surprised to find hoodlums involved in huge liquor black-market deals during World War II and in present-day bootlegging operations into dry areas. After the committee found the hoodlum element playing a dominant role in liquor distribution in Kansas City, it decided that this situation was serious enough to warrant further investigation since competition within the industry, at least in Kansas City, was definitely affected; the reputation of the overwhelmingly legitimate members of the liquor industry was involved and most important, the public interest was vitally concerned.

Accordingly, the committee proceeded to accumulate information on the conduct of the liquor industry in various parts of the country, questionnaires were addressed to the Nation's leading distillers and breweries; and the industry's attitude was explored in hearings before the committee.

In Kansas City, the committee found such notorious hoodlums as Joe and Vincent di Giovanni holding exclusive franchises for several leading brands of whisky including Schenley's and Seagrams. After the disclosures made by this committee, the liquor licenses of these two Mafia hoodlums were revoked by the State liquor control supervisor. However, the committee feels that the revocation was nullified by the subsequent reissuing of these licenses to the sons of these gangsters. The committee also found evidence in Kansas City that the retail liquor dealers association was mob controlled and that violence was used to force liquor dealers into the association.

In Chicago, the Manhattan Brewery was owned and controlled by the Capone mob during prohibition days. At the present time it is called the Canadian Ace Brewery and is controlled by Alexander Greenberg, who was an associate and financial backer of many Capone syndicate members. Canadian Ace Beer was sold in Kansas City by Tony Gizzo, a leading member of the Binaggio-Gargotta mob, and a suspected leader of the Mafia. He told the committee that he persuaded tavern owners that they should use Canadian Ace, but he denied using violence.

The committee found several other former Capone associates involved in a substantial manner in the wholesale and retail distribution of liquor. Joseph Fusco, an old-time bootlegger and present associate of such Capone mobsters as Pat Manno, the policy racketeer, is president of a $2,000,000 corporation which holds exclusive franchises for many leading brands of whisky. Rocco DeStefano, another Capone syndicate associate, controlled a chain of retail liquor stores in Chicago. He is also a stockholder along with Fusco in the Bohemian Brewing Co. of Joliet, Ill.

In New Jersey, Joseph Reinfeld, a leading liquor distributor, and Abner ("Longie") Zwillman owned substantial stock as late as August 1950 in the whisky distilling firm of Browne-Vintners Corp., which they controlled until 1940 when it was sold to Seagrams. Reinfeld, Zwillman and, among others, Jimmy Rutkin, an associate of Zwillman, were notorious bootleggers during prohibition, during which time they were partners in some of Bronfman's operations in Canada. Zwillman and Rutkin now claim that Reinfeld defrauded them in the Browne-Vintners sale and Rutkin is presently suing Reinfeld for $22,000,000. Since 1940, Reinfeld has been unable to obtain a liquor license in New York State, but he has a license in New Jersey. New York State, however, allows his son-in-law to operate and Reinfeld sells all of his imports of certain products to his son-in-law's company in New York. Reinfeld Importers, Ltd., of New Jersey, is the exclusive distributor in 38 States for Gordon's Gin and also is the exclusive importer for Haig and Haig and Piper Heidsick champagne.

In 1948 the State Liquor Authority of New York revoked the liquor license previously held by Irving Haim for the International Distributors Co. Haim promptly moved over to New Jersey. This company has the exclusive agency for King's Ransom and House of Lords Scotch. In 1937 Haim, an ex-bootlegger, negotiated the purchase of J. J. Turney & Sons, the holding company for William Whitely Liquors, Ltd., the distillers of King's Ransom and House of Lords Scotch. The purchase was made in the name of Haim with money obtained from a New Orleans bank with notes secured by Haim, Phil Kastel, and Frank Costello. Prior to this purchase, Phil Kastel was the "good will" man for this company and received an override commission on every case of this Scotch sold in the United States. Part of the original purchase deal was for Costello to take Kastel's place, in receiving the override, which was to be increased in amount. In 1940, according to Haim, Costello and Kastel disassociated themselves from the distribution of William Whitely Liquors at the insistence of the late William Helis, one of the partners in the enterprise. Yet, in 1943 Frank Costello was bragging that King's Ransom and House of Lords scotch were "his whiskies." And there is evidence that in 1943 Haim delivered to Costello a small package, valuable enough to have to be placed in a safe.

In Tampa, the committee found a Mafia hoodlum, Salvatore "Red" Italiano, to be the general manager of a wine and beer distributing business. The committee also found a man with a narcotics distributing record, Louis Swed, to be the principal distributor of Budweiser beer in Florida. In Des Moines, Iowa, Lew Farrell, an alleged Capone syndicate hoodlum with a considerable criminal record, who allegedly controlled the race wire in that city, and who helped get the notorious Gargotta brothers of Kansas City out of jail in 1947, distributes Blatz and Prima-Bismarck beers. Until recently he handled Canadian Ace beer. His inactive partners in the Canadian Ace distributing firm were the brother and sister of Alexander Greenberg, owner of Canadian Ace. In spite of Farrell's record and an adverse report on him by field supervisors of the Federal Alcohol Tax Unit in Des Moines and St. Paul, the ATU gave him a license in 1945 to distribute beer. His license is now up again before the ATU.

The fact that the committee has mentioned the names of certain leading distillers and brewers should not be construed to mean that they have been the only or even the worst offenders. Practically every large distillery and brewery has granted franchises to racketeer dealers, most of whom were blanketed in under the original licensing activities of the Alcohol Tax Unit after the repeal of prohibition.

Following some of these disclosures, the committee invited representatives of the major distillers to a private hearing in Washington. The committee wanted to give the industry an opportunity to review the committee's findings and to suggest measures for correcting this situation.

As a result of this meeting, the industry did make certain constructive recommendations. However, the committee found that the industry as a whole believes it is the responsibility of the Government to keep hoodlums out of the industry.

The committee feels that while no industry can control the character of those who deal in its products, any industry has a responsibility for the character of distributors holding exclusive franchises.

The attitude of the industry was further explored in the committee's hearing on March 9, 1951, with revenue and liquor commissioners from most of the Southern States. These commissioners told a sordid story of a huge bootlegging operation extending into the South out of Cairo, Ill.

This bootlegging operation is fully reminiscent of the 1920's, with its hi-jacking of trucks, camouflaging of liquor shipments, use of fictitious names, counterfeiting of Federal and State liquor stamps, violation of ICC regulations and corruption of public officials. Some of the wholesalers involved in the current ring were found by the committee to have been connected with a huge World War II liquor black-market ring.

The leading distillers were asked by a conference of southern revenue and alcohol commissioners to cancel the franchises of distributors found to be engaging in the bootlegging ring and they agreed to do so, but conditions failed to improve.

In a further effort to determine the extent of hoodlum infiltration in the liquor industry, and what was being done by the industry to correct this situation, questionnaires were addressed to the principal distillers and breweries throughout the country requesting information with respect to their distributors and their franchise policies. An analysis of replies from over 100 distillers and 240 breweries indicates that while the large majority of franchises are granted to legitimate, upstanding businessmen, all the major distillers and some of the leading breweries have granted distribution franchises to some hoodlums, including some in the top ranks of organized crime. While these distillers and brewers state that they did not know of the criminal associations at the time they granted the franchises, they were almost all vague on the question of whether they would fire a distributor upon finding he had criminal associations.

Perhaps the best summing up of the general attitude of the industry is the reply of one major distiller whose products, incidentally, were found to be involved in past black market and present-day bootlegging activities:

Since practically all wholesale distributors handle the products of many distilleries, we do not believe that any purpose would be served by our termination of the distribution franchise * * * we feel that if this criminal record were such as to make him an undesirable distributor * * * his license should be revoked by the proper authorities * * * we believe that it is the responsibility of the various governmental departments who issue these licenses to weed out undesirables.

The committee feels that the industry should share responsibility with the Federal Government for getting and keeping the hoodlum element out of the industry. The Federal Government, however, has a number of powers at its disposition which it has not used to full advantage. In addition to the need for a State license to operate in the liquor business, it is necessary to have a license from the Alcohol Tax Unit of the Treasury Department. The committee fails to understand, for example, how the Alcohol Tax Unit could grant a wholesaler's permit to hoodlums such as Joe DiGiovanni and Lew Farrell. Much can be done by stiffer application of existing regulations to correct the situation but the committee feels that additional legislation is also needed.

AUTOMOBILE AND TRUCKING BUSINESS

In many communities, gangsters have obtained valuable automobile dealer franchises. In Brooklyn, for example, Joe Adonis was able to control the distribution of a number of automobiles out of the Kings County Buick Co., which ran up an unsavory record of black-market deals during World War II. Adonis also owns stock in the Automotive Conveying Co, which hauls Fords from Edgewater, N. J., to various points in the East. He obtained his exclusive franchise during Harry Bennett's regime at Ford. Ford has publicly deplored this situation and is taking action to rid itself of Adonis.

The committee also found that Anthony D'Anna, a former Detroit bootlegger and racketeer, also received a Ford haulage franchise, and a sales agency during Harry Bennett's regime. While Ford has largely succeeded in ridding itself of the Bennett influence, D'Anna is a notorious exception. Today, his company—E. & L. Transport, Inc., of Michigan and Indiana—hauls most of the Fords produced in the Dearborn and Highland Park plants, although numerous other carriers hold ICC authority to transport this same traffic. The manner in which D'Anna, an associate of notorious hoodlums Joe Massei and Pete Licavoli, was accepted by Ford provides one of the best examples in the committee's record of how hoodlum penetration is accomplished. In 1931, after a meeting between Bennett and D'Anna, the latter went into partnership with one William Pardo. Until shortly before that time, Pardo had held a franchise from Ford. Suddenly, it was mysteriously terminated. Pardo found that if he wanted to get his franchise back it would be wise to take D'Anna in the business. In 1939, however, the partnership was dissolved on orders from one of Bennetts underlings and D'Anna turned up in a new company, Superior Motor Sales, Inc., of Wyandotte, which today is operated by his son. D'Anna received the E. & L. Transport Co. franchise in much the same manner. D'Anna seldom appears in the company's offices but nevertheless enjoys income from Ford to the extent of at least $27,000 a year.

The use of huge, illegally acquired resources to obtain strong economic and political influence is well illustrated in the case of "Longie" Zwillman. Zwillman was a leading racketeer during prohibition and made a fortune out of his illegal ventures. Today he owns a number of very profitable legitimate enterprises, including a truck sales company which holds a valuable General Motors franchise. This company does a sizable business with the city of Newark. It may be more than coincidence that the registered agent for Zwillman's truck company and most of his other legitimate businesses is also the corporation counsel for the city of Newark. It is also significant that Zwillman's control of the truck company is exercised through his accountant, I. George Goldstein, who testified that the reason he fronted for Zwillman was that Zwillman was afraid he would not obtain the General Motors franchise if his name appeared.

TRANSPORTATION

In addition to hoodlum penetration of the automobile business, they have made some inroads in other areas of interstate transportation. The twin cities of Minneapolis and St. Paul, Minn., were recently rocked by evidence showing that the hoodlum element had nearly succeeding in taking over the Twin City Rapid Transit Co. Fred Osanna, a lawyer for and a director of this company, led an almost successful fight to oust the present management. Fortunately, the company's president, Charles Green, discovered just in time that Osanna was associating with such notorious hoodlums as Kid Cann. In Cleveland, Arthur "Mickey" McBride of Continental Press operates the Yellow Cab Co. In New Jersey, an interstate trucking firm—People's Express Co.—is run by a notorious hoodlum, Jerry Catena, and an ex-bootlegger and long-time friend of "Longie" Zwillman—Philip Dameo. Dameo buys his trucks from Zwillman's company.

STEEL

Further illustration of how tremendous illegitimately obtained resources are invested in legitimate enterprises is provided in connection with the steel industry. In Detroit, the committee found that members of the notorious Cleveland syndicate invested large sums of cash to help put over a stock deal whereby the Detroit Steel Corp. was able to take over another steel company. Longie Zwillman is a heavy investor in the steel industry. He is one of the largest stockholders in the A. M. Byers Co. of Pittsburgh and furnished the chief support behind the management in a recent proxy fight. Zwillman also controls the E. & S. Trading Co. of Newark, which deals in iron and steel. This company had gross sales in 1948 of $336,000.

In Philadelphia, hoodlum penetration of a steel-fabricating concern was accomplished through political influence. A numbers racketeer by the name of Louis Crusco bought his way in to the Strunk Steel Co. by virtue of his close association with the son of Philadelphia's mayor. Until Crusco came along, the company had never been able to get any business from the city of Philadelphia but while Crusco was negotiating his stock purchase in the company it received a contract from the Philadelphia Rapid Transit Co., a local public utility, on which there were no competitive bids. The president of the company testified that this deal had been suggested to him by the mayor's grandson, who, coincidentally, was placed on the company's payroll as part of the Crusco stock deal.

OIL INDUSTRY

The committee obtained evidence that a number of hoodlums have invested heavily in the oil business, another example of how illegal gains may be invested as a cover or foil to avoid taxes. A number of Capone syndicate associates are involved in an oil venture in Wyoming, including Pat Manno, who has over $55,000 in the concern, Joe Fusco, and Rocco deStefano, together with several well-known hoodlums from St. Louis, including Louis Calcaterra and Thomas Hynes. Frank Costello has invested over $40,000 in a Texas oil company, with Frank Erickson and George Uffner while other hoodlums, including Carlos Marcello, Joe Poretto, and Moe Dalitz have also invested in the oil industry.

BANKING AND FINANCE

While the committee has evidence of hoodlum penetration of major industries by means of stock acquisition, there is actually no way in which the committee or any other group can determine the full extent of hoodlum ownership of stock in the Nation's major industries, but the few examples that the committee has unearthed leads it to believe that very large amounts of stock are owned directly or indirectly by hoodlums. The danger of such infiltration is not great where hoodlums have only a small amount of the stock outstanding of large industries. The danger arises when hoodlums control enough of the stock so as to exert influence on the management of a given industry.

It is not a healthy situation when William Molasky, a substantial stockholder of one of our largest companies, Western Union, is also a dominant figure in the gambling world which depends so heavily upon the facilities of Western Union. Molasky also tried unsuccessfully to influence the appointment of a St. Louis police commissioner by means of a campaign contribution.

It is far from reassuring that Terry Fayhe, a well-known hoodlum and associate of such racketeers as Waxey Gordon, almost succeeded in manipulating a fraudulent stock deal which would have enabled him and his associates to take control of the Follansbee Steel Co. William Gallagher, vice president of the $20,000,000 Pennsylvania Exchange Bank of New York, is reported to have assisted Fayhe in this deal by recommending him to reputable bankers as respectable and financially well off, although Fayhe had been permanently restrained from ever engaging in the securities business in New York. The president of the bank, James Miller, was also permanently enjoined from engaging in the securities business in New York following several indictments for fraudulent stock schemes, and Gallagher himself has a prohibition record. Gallagher is closely identified with Frank Erickson, who was allowed to maintain accounts in the bank under assumed names, to aid his gambling operations. The committee, incidentally, had a difficult time serving a subpena on Gallagher; when he finally was served, he refused to answer questions of committee counsel in an informal conference attended by his lawyer because no member of the committee was present; and when the committee did come to New York, he presented a doctor's certificate asserting that he was too ill to testify.

It is difficult to understand how one of New York's worst criminals, Albert Anastasia, was able to obtain a first and second mortgage totaling $30,000 on his $48,000 home in New Jersey, prior to its completion, from the president of the Fort Lee Trust Co. of New Jersey, who handled the deal personally. It is also significant that Anthony D'Anna, an ex-bootlegger and racketeer, who had lucrative Ford franchises, and who has maintained relations with notorious hoodlums in Detroit, is also a bank director.

The committee also found evidence of hoodlum infiltration into the loan and bonding business. Charles Fischetti of the Capone syndicate and Meyer Gordon (a jewel fence sentenced in 1946 to 20 years in the penitentiary) ran the Liberal Loan Co. in Chicago. Joseph DeLuca, a Kansas City hoodlum who owns three liquor stores, is a major stockholder of the Colony Finance & Loan Co.; Charles Bruno of Kansas City, a Binaggio associate with a long police record, operates the Kansas City Bonding Co. with Raymond Muller. This concern does a large business in bonding criminals in Kansas City. In Cleveland, Anthony Milano, a notorious hoodlum, owns the Brotherhood Loan Co. Milano, who did 6 years in the penitentiary for counterfeiting, was alleged by Mickey Cohen to have loaned him money. Milano admitted knowing Cohen, but denied making any loan. Arthur "Mickey" McBride testified that he once put up some money for this company.

Irving Glasser is a partner in, and fronts for many of the gambling operations in the Los Angeles area. He also has a loan business and handles the major portion of the bail bond business there, including bonds for Mickey Cohen.

THE GARMENT INDUSTRY

This industry has attracted some of the top gangsters in the country. Harry Stromberg, alias Nig Rosen, a tough Philadelphia criminal, was a partner in the Dearest Miss Dress Co. in New York City. In 1947 he was production manager of the company with a one-third interest in its profits. He also has a one-third interest in the Jay Lou Dress Co. and the Lou Jay Dress Co. in the Bronx with his brother and David Bernoff.

Irving Sherman, the gambler associate of both Costello and Mayor O'Dwyer, is a partner in Courtshire Fashions which manufactures ladies' coats and suits.

Albert Anastasia, one of New York's major criminals, has a dress business in Hazelton, Pa. Thomas Luchese, whom the Narcotics Bureau states to be associated with an important narcotics ring in New York, but who has consistently denied any gangster affiliation, is an officer in a ladies coat manufacturing concern. Frank Livorsi, whose criminal record includes a narcotics conviction and numerous arrests, and who was involved in a big black-market sugar operation during World War II, was in a dress concern with Max Edler, who also had a narcotics record. The firm dealt extensively in black-market textiles during World War II.

JUKE BOXES, CIGARETTE VENDING MACHINES, AND SLOT MACHINES

There seems to be a natural affinity of underworld characters for the distribution of these machines. The committee has found that juke box and cigarette vending machine distribution is usually the front employed by hoodlums for the illegal distribution of pinball and slot machines. Distribution methods, moreover, are often based upon the use of muscle. In Chicago, there is some evidence that certain Capone syndicate associates have muscled into the tobacco and cigarette-vending-machine business and that they have seriously affected the business of their legitimate competitors. Cigarettes have been hi-jacked and cigarette-metering machines, used to affix the Illinois tax stamp, have been stolen.

Ed Vogel, who has been known as the slot-machine king of Cook County, Illinois, and an old Capone syndicate associate, is secretary and treasurer of the Apex Cigarette Service. This company is one of the largest distributors of phonograph and cigarette machines in Cook County. Al Capone's brother, Ralph, operates the Suburban Cigarette Co. which has vending machines throughout Cook County.

Evidence of strong-arm methods in the juke-box distribution business was found by the committee in Chicago, Kansas City, and Detroit. Joe Peskin, one of the old Capone gang and a leading juke-box distributor in Chicago, admitted threatening a former associate who later became a competitor. In Kansas City, Wolf Riman, before his murder, successfully pressured tavern owners into using his juke-box machines with the help of the county sheriff. More refined methods of shake-down and extortion were found by the committee in connection with juke box distribution in Detroit. Here, a union was used as a front by underworld characters to extort money from juke-box distributors. These distributors were forced to join the union as "honorary members" and pay initiation fees and dues, or risk having a picket line thrown around their locations. Another more refined technique for forcing juke box distributors into line was found by the committee in New Orleans where Carlos Marcello, one of the worst hoodlums in the country, supplies juke boxes and slot machines to bars, night clubs, etc. He also loans money to these bars and clubs at a very low rate of interest. In return for this low rate, the proprietor agrees to use only Marcello's machines.

Most of the Nation's leading hoodlums, including Frank Costello, Jake Lansky, Joseph Stacher, Phil Kastel, Buster Wortmann, and many others, have been engaged in the distribution of juke boxes and slot machines.

LAUNDRY AND DRY CLEANING

The phenomenon of Willie Moretti, one of Costello's associates, in making a success of a large linen-supply company because "he knew a lot of people" and "got plenty of business in a polite way" (which his competitors found not so polite) is one of the darker chapters of American business.

In Detroit, Louis Riccardi, an associate of such Detroit hoodlums as Angelo Meli, and who was arrested five times for murder, operates a very profitable laundry—the Clean Linen Service Co. Riccardi made $56,000 out of this business in 1949. It is alleged that customers who drop his service may find that no other laundry will dare to accept their business.

Moe Dalitz and other members of the Cleveland gang operate laundries in both Cleveland and Detroit.

REAL ESTATE, HOTELS, RESTAURANTS, AND NIGHT CLUBS

In many large cities important real-estate holdings, hotels, office buildings, night clubs, restaurants, and taverns are acquired by gangsters and mobsters. In Miami, for example, valuable ocean-front property was acquired by the S. and G. Syndicate. In true gangster disregard of established laws and existing vested interests, the S. and G. Syndicate teamed up with Thomas McGinty of the Cleveland Syndicate in an attempt to have this property rezoned in order to triple its value. They set up a dummy corporation. By a strange coincidence, the lawyer hired by the syndicate to put through the rezoning application turned out to be Ben Shepard, the city attorney. A member of the city council, who was expected to vote on the zoning proposal, turned out to be an officer of the dummy corporation.

Al Polizzi, John Angersola, and Arthur "Mickey" McBride are associated in lucrative real-estate ventures in the Coral Gables section of Florida. The notorious Kid Cann of Minneapolis owns valuable ocean-front property in Miami Beach in addition to several hotels and apartments. T. J. McGinty, of the Cleveland syndicate, told the committee he had invested some of his gambling profits in valuable real estate in Florida, which includes the property in Miami on which Hickory House is located and certain race track property. Frank Costello recently made a large profit on the sale of a valuable office building in Wall Street. In Chicago, Rocco DeStefano owns stock in a profitable real-estate venture, and Alexander Greenberg runs a large real-estate business.

Gangsters from all over the country met in Florida at three hoodlum-run hotels: The Wofford, Grand, and Sands. The Wofford Hotel, for example, which was for a number of years operated by Abe Allenberg, Frank Erickson's front man in Florida, is now owned by Thomas Cassara, who has fronted for various Capone syndicate members in Chicago, John Angersola of the Cleveland mob, and Anthony Carfano, a Costello associate. The hotel was originally leased on funds borrowed from Frank Erickson. George Sax, the Chicago punchboard king, has a large investment in the Saxony Hotel in Miami Beach, while in Chicago, Greenberg operates the Seneca Hotel, where he was once associated with Charlie "Cherry Nose" Gioe, who still lives there along with several other Capone hoodlums. In Los Angeles, Fred Evans, a former Capone associate has an interest in the Hayward Hotel.

Among the leading hoodlums in the restaurant, night club, bar, and tavern businesses, are Frank Costello, Phil Kastel, Charles Fischetti, Carlos Marcello, Mushy Wexler, Harry Russell, and Mike Lascari.

FOOD PRODUCTS

The committee found numerous hoodlums engaged in the distribution of food products, including Big Bill Tocco, Joe Massei of Detroit, Carlos Marcello of New Orleans, Paul DiGiovanni (nephew of Joseph DiGiovanni), Emilio Georgetti in California and many others. The committee found evidence of muscle tactics in connection with the baking business in Kansas City, where a hoodlum-dominated bakery owned by the late Charlie Binaggio, Joe Cusumano, and Joe Filardo was muscling in on legitimate bakeries. The committee also found a number of hoodlums engaged in the olive oil, cheese, and other food-importing businesses, including Joe Profaci of New York, Anthony Milano in Detroit, and Jack Dragna on the west coast. There is evidence that the olive-oil business has been used as a front for narcotics operations.

UNIONS

The committee found that hoodlum penetration of labor unions has decreased steadily over the years. In the 1920's and 1930's hoodlum infiltration into the cleaning and laundry, dairy, the beverage, stage hands, and retail clerk's unions, was on such a large and violent scale that it threatened to disrupt entire industries. Today, however, the hoodlum element has been driven to the wall in all but a few important instances. One union which is still infested with hoodlums is the International Longshoremen's Union on the east coast. Here after 20 years of repeated efforts to correct conditions there still persists one of the ugliest situations in labor-union history.

BREAKDOWN OF ENFORCEMENT MACHINERY

Although the committee has seen and paid tribute to many fine, efficient, honest, and able law-enforcement officers and officials, law enforcement has broken down in many of the communities visited by the committee. Where criminal gangs and syndicates operate openly as they have done in such places as Saratoga; Bergen County, N. J.; the Newport-Covington area of Kentucky; the Miami area of Florida; many of the parishes outside of New Orleans; many of the Illinois and California counties and the area of Jackson County outside of Kansas City, to cite only the most notorious examples, it is apparent that too many local police, sheriffs, prosecutors, and courts are failing to do their sworn duty.

The committee places no stock in the professed inability of many law-enforcement officials to detect violations of the law which are apparent to any informed citizen. The blindness which afflicts many law-enforcement officials in wide-open communities is for the record only.

There can be little question that these officials know perfectly well what is going on. Nor can there be little doubt in the mind of the committee that vigorous, honest law enforcement can put an end to wide-open conditions in a very short time. The fact that Saratoga was run without open gambling in the racing season of 1950; that Sheriff "King" Clancy could give the order to shut down operations in Jefferson Parish; that Pat Perdue, the so-called "one-man vice squad" of Miami Beach, could boast that he could shut down operations in

Miami Beach in 24 hours if he were given the order to do so, is an indication of what can be accomplished where law-enforcement officials really wish to act.

It can be assumed that this failure of law-enforcement officials to suppress gambling and vice conditions in their community affects their law-enforcement responsibilities in other fields. By refusing to act against the racketeers who run bookmaking operations, slot machines, gambling casinos, and houses of prostitution, law-enforcement officials give aid and encouragement to some of the worst hoodlums and criminal gangs in this country. These hoodlums and criminal gangs do not restrict their operations to exploiting the human desire to gamble.

They also engage in activities which are even more devastating to the community and to the welfare of the people; the sale and distribution of narcotics, various forms of extortion and shake-downs, various types of business and labor-union racketeering, as well as outright robbery, burglary, and larceny. Inevitably, their operations in gambling and other fields bring in their train aggravated forms of violence against persons and property. The ultimate weapon that these mobsters have is murder and they have not hesitated to use it in communities all over the country.

Nor should it be assumed that law-emforcement agencies, which are ineffective in suppressing gambling operations, suddenly become efficient instruments of justice when confronted with other crimes. The record is clearly the other way. Police officials, sheriffs, and district attorneys who refuse to do their duty in enforcing the gambling laws because of corruption or the use of political influence do not prosecute vigorously when the racketeers and gangsters operating gambling enterprises become involved in other crimes.

If money or political influence will fix a gambling case, it will also fix a case involving a more heinous offense. The creeping paralysis of law enforcement which results from a failure to enforce the gambling laws, therefore, contributes to a breakdown in connection with other fields of crime.

It is axiomatic in the underworld that once a public official allows a case to be fixed, thereafter the underworld owns him.

One other aspect of this breakdown must be noted. Wherever organized criminal gangs are entrenched in a particular community and have been given the green light to operate, it is not unusual to see the forces of law enforcement being used against their competitors, while protected operations are left severely alone. This fact helps to explain the growth of such vast bookmaking conspiracies as the S and G Syndicate in Miami, the Guarantee Finance Co. in Los Angeles, and the Gross bookmaking empire in New York. Only too frequently, bookmakers, slot-machine operators, policy bankers and punchboard sellers have been given to understand that they must come to terms with the "syndicate" or the "combination" that has the "in" with law enforcement. The penalty for failing to come to terms is continual harassment by the police and other agencies of law enforcement. In the Miami story, we saw this weapon of inequal enforcement of the law by a State official being used against the S and G as one of the weapons to compel it to capitulate to the demands of Accardo-Guzik-Fischetti crime syndicate.

OVERLAPPING JURISDICTIONS IMPEDE ENFORCEMENT

The breakdown in law enforcement is not entirely due to corruption of law-enforcement officials or to the use of political influence to paralyze law-enforcement processes. Much of the responsibility must be placed upon the present organization of law-enforcement agencies. In metropolitan communities like Cook County, Ill.; Los Angeles County, Calif., or Bergen County, N. J., there is a congerie of independent local police forces covering the county. In addition, a sheriff's office with wide law-enforcement responsibilities and the State police with a wide jurisdiction to enforce State laws, may also operate within the county.

There is no centralized direction or control and no centralized responsibility for seeing that a single uniform law-enforcement policy is applied over the entire geographic area of a county. The situation lends itself to buck-passing and evasion of responsibility which can only inure to the benefit of gangsters and racketeers. It makes it possible for hoodlums to find those cities and towns where law enforcement is lax and to concentrate their operations there.

It is obvious that many factors contribute to the breakdown of law-enforcement agencies. No single panacea can make law-enforcement agencies more efficient and effective in dealing with organized crime. It is suggested, therefore, that each State make an over-all survey of its law-enforcement agencies to see whether or not they are adequately organized and equipped to cope with modern racketeering and gangsterism. It is obvious that a survey of this character must not only inquire into the organization and operations of law-enforcement agencies, it must also determine whether they are so beset by corruption and political influence that no matter how they were organized, they would continue to be ineffective.

Surveys in each State are necessary because of the difficulty of making suggestions which are applicable to the entire country.

The peculiar problems of each State vary and there are significant differences in the organization of their law-enforcement agencies. However, there is sufficient administrative know-how in the various States to make it possible to lay out a plan and a method for dealing with organized crime which will considerably curtail this threat to our institutions.

OFFICIAL CORRUPTION AND CONNIVANCE IN ORGANIZED CRIME

The most shocking revelations of the testimony before the committee is the extent of official corruption and connivance in facilitating and promoting organized crime. Nevertheless, it should not be assumed that our revelations cast doubt as to the integrity of the great preponderance of law enforcement and other public officials. On the contrary, our findings and conclusions relate only to a small but disturbing minority of such officials. The committee found evidence of corruption and connivance at all levels of government—Federal, State, and local. The evidence of the corruption of Federal Government officials is primarily in connection with the enforcement of the income-tax laws. Certain officials of the Bureau of Internal Revenue in California conceived the scheme of selling stock which they owned in a company that they controlled to persons who were likely to have trouble with their income taxes. The stock was worthless, but its purchase assured immunity from a too-careful scrutiny of income-tax returns. This is not an indictment of the Bureau as a whole; most of these employees have been discharged and some have been indicted by a Federal grand jury.

The evidence of corruption and connivance with organized crime in State and local government is present in four different forms:

(1) Direct bribe or protection payments are made to law-enforcement officials, so that they will not interfere with specific criminal activities.

(2) Political influence and pressure of important officials or political leaders is used to protect criminal activities or further the interests of criminal gangs.

(3) Law-enforcement officials are found in the possession of unusual and unexplained wealth.

(4) Law-enforcement officials participate directly in the business of organized crime.

Just before his death, James Ragen, head of Continental Press, told the State's attorney that over a 3-year period, the wire service had in the past paid out $600,000 in political contributions.

EVIDENCE OF DIRECT PAYMENTS TO OFFICIALS

At the local level, the committee received evidence of corruption of law-enforcement officers and connivance with criminal gangs in every city in which it held hearings. The testimony at the Tampa hearings indicates that Sheriff Culbreath, of Hillsborough County, was the center of the criminal conspiracy to violate the gambling laws. Evidence was received of direct and regular payments of protection money by gamblers to Culbreath and to other law-enforcement officials in Tampa.

The sordid story of direct payments to law-enforcement officials in return for the protection of criminals, is repeated in Philadelphia, where the "bag" man for a Captain Elwell, would come into the station house with his pockets bulging with money. Three thousand dollars to four thousand dollars a month was alleged to have been paid in each of 38 police districts or approximately $152,000 a month, not counting payments to the higher ups. In New York City it has been estimated that the Gross bookmaking empire paid over $1,000,000 a year for police protection. In Dade County, Fla., a deputy sheriff is alleged to have turned over to the wife of the sheriff seven, eight, ten, and eleven thousand dollars at a time in cash and obtained signed receipts therefor. In Jackson County, Mo. (K. C.), some deputy sheriffs were on the payrolls of slot-machine distributors and taverns that violated the liquor laws. In Los Angeles, at least half a dozen police officers "borrowed" money from the Guarantee Finance Co., a big bookmaking operation. One suspended officer worked as a collector from bookmakers for the Guarantee Finance Co. during the period of his suspension. An entry of $108,000 on the books of the Guarantee Finance Co. for "juice" undoubtedly indicates payoffs to law enforcement officials. The strong box which Sheriff Grosch of Orleans Parish, La., bought with such elaborate precautions at a time when he was a city detective, was intended to keep not his legitimate earnings but the fruits of his betrayal of the public trust—protection money from law violators. But his official behavior was similar to that of many other important law-enforcement officials in the New Orleans area. This is illustrated by the extraordinary story of Moity who discovered that he could not stay in the slot-machine business without paying "ice."

There is also the case of former Police Chief George Reyer, of New Orleans, who once was president of the International Association of Police Chiefs. Squeezed by a change in administrations, Reyer took his pension and switched to the wire service payroll at $100 a week without the loss of a payday.

Law enforcement has been an easy road to affluence for many law-enforcement officials. The case of Dan "Tubbo" Gilbert, "the richest police officer in the world," who was chief investigator in the State attorney's office in Chicago, is well known. Such officials as "King" Clancy, sheriff of Jefferson Parish, La., and Walter Clark, sheriff of Broward County, Fla., have grown rich, powerful, and arrogant from their association with the underworld elements who ran the gambling and prostitution enterprises in their jurisdictions. There are many other illustrations in the testimony before the committee. Typical of this is the fortunate economic position of John English, the city commissioner in charge of the police department of East St. Louis, who was able to obtain a $100,000 summer home, various interests in real estate in East St. Louis, interests in a restaurant and a gas station, on a salary of $4,500 to $6,000. The fact that the city was wide open for years and only two or three gambling arrests were made in 1950 may have some relation to the commissioner's wealth.

POLITICS USED TO PARALYZE POLICE

The attempt to paralyze law enforcement by political means is encountered again and again in the testimony before the committee. The success of mobster Frank Costello in exercising control over the New York County Democratic organization is typical of what one can expect from the alliance between politics and crime. Mobster Joe Adonis' influence upon the Kings County (Brooklyn, N. Y.) Democratic organization may go far to explain why neither he nor a major subordinate like Anastasia was ever subjected to prosecution and punishment. The committee developed at great length the extraordinary attempt by Binaggio, a powerful political leader to acquire control of the Police Board of Kansas City so that he could install his candidate Braun as chief of police. Binaggio finally offered a substantial bribe to one of the commissioners who had refused to go along with his program. Gene Burnett, police chief of Granite City, Ill., was apparently willing to close down the gambling places and the handbooks in his town, but the orders from the mayor were to let them operate as that is how the city council wanted it. There is more than a remote connection between the orders to Police Chief Short of Miami to "lay off" gambling, "although the city could be closed in a matter of hours," and the fact that one of Miami's councilmen had had many extremely profitable deals with Harold Salvey, a member of the S and G Syndicate. The story of Governor Fuller Warren of Florida is told elsewhere. After accepting a huge campaign contribution from William H. Johnston, who has close connections with present and past members of the Capone syndicate, Warren allowed the power of his office to be used by the Capone syndicate in its successful effort to muscle into Miami Beach gambling. Most recently Warren has reinstated Sheriff James Sullivan of Miami without any satisfactory explanation of the serious evidence and charges brought against Sullivan before this committee.

There was considerable evidence before the committee concerning contributions to political campaigns by gamblers and gangsters. For example, Molasky contributed $2,500 to the gubernatorial campaign in Missouri in the hope that he would be given the right to name a member of the St. Louis Police Board. When he was unable to do so he claimed to have been double-crossed. Pat Noonan, an associate of the mobsters in the Binaggio gang, did considerable political work in the campaign to elect Governor Smith. Much of his expenses were paid by persons involved in violations of the gambling laws. The fact that Emilio Georgetti, "the Gambling King of San Mateo County," worked "like hell" for the election of Sheriff McGrath and "accumulated a little money for the campaign," did not hurt him in his gambling operations.

Evidence has also been presented to the committee that certain law-enforcement officials or their relatives not only received protection money from gangsters but that they actually ran gambling operations themselves. The bookmaking operation which was run right in Sheriff Culbreath's office by his brother and an employee of the sheriff, may or may not have been as insignificant as the sheriff tried to show. But the same thing cannot be said for the partnership which Sheriff Clark of Broward County had in the Broward Novelty Co. This company operated bolita games (policy) and slot machines and provided the sheriff with his principal source of income. The participation of public officials in the New Orleans area in the operation of slot machines has almost come to have the status of an established institution.

It is obvious that law-enforcement officials who are themselves engaged in gambling operations will have no special desire to enforce gambling statutes.

PUBLIC RESPONSIBILITY

The committee has been most gratified by the tremendous interest which the general public has demonstrated in the hearings conducted by the committee over the past 11 months. That interest has confirmed anew the committee's fundamental faith that the heart of America is basically sound.

The active participation of an informed public is essential to the correction of the conditions which the committee's investigation has shown to exist throughout the country. The committee has emphasized time and again that organized crime cannot exist without political protection. It is the responsibility of the voting public to insure that their representative governments at all levels are made up of men who are not open to corruption or persuasion by criminals and racketeers.

In the course of its investigations, the committee has seen numerous examples of public apathy toward the operations of organized crime and its alliance with officials at various levels of government.

In the State of Florida, it seemed clear to the committee that the highest officials in the State condoned, and in some cases, affirmatively aided the operations of organized gamblers. In the State of Illinois, where there can be no question as to the honesty and integrity of the Governor and his aides, the committee found evidence that numerous local law-enforcement officials made no effort to interfere with illegal gambling operations. More shocking than the defection of individual law-enforcement officials was the testimony before the committee that many of these men were elected and re-elected by a voting public which was well aware of their tolerance of illegal gambling.

Equally shocking is the fact that efforts to remove and punish such officials for their obvious acts of malfeasance are often nullified by juries that refuse to recognize the venality of such behavior.

There is a segment of public opinion in many cities that believes that gambling, in some cases "just a little gambling," is good for business, and that strict enforcement of the antigambling laws would be a mistake. This attitude on the part of normally law-abiding citizens can only come from a failure to comprehend the violence and racketeering which inevitably accompany gambling operations, and the extent of the resulting damage to the economic and social fabric.

The theory that gambling is good for business was expounded in Kansas City, in Las Vegas, and in Miami. The fact of the matter is that the huge sums which accrue as a result of gambling are pocketed by criminals, hoodlums, and corrupt politicians, and the general public receives little or no part of the income from the milking operations carried on by the big-time gamblers.

It is established practice for big-time gamblers and gambling syndicates to contribute generously to charities, fraternal organizations, and other worthy causes as part of their program to ingratiate themselves with the community and convince the public that while more or less illegal, their activities are thoroughly moral.

In the light of the tremendous profits which gamblers enjoy so long as the public will tolerate their operations, they can well afford to expend substantial sums of money to cloak themselves with an aura of public-spiritedness.

It is the hope of this committee that as a result of its investigations and report specific legislation aimed at dealing with organized criminal activity will be enacted; that certain changes recommended by the committee will be made in Federal, State, and local law-enforcement procedures.

However, the ultimate responsibility for the success of the suggested legislation and reforms rests squarely in the hands of the public. Unless the public expresses an affirmative desire for the elimination of organized criminal operations and official corruption through the continued exercise of the vote, through active participation in the work of such organizations as local and State crime commissions, and through the careful attention to the efficiency and honesty of the men whom they employ to govern them, there can be no real and lasting progress toward the elimination of organized criminal activity in this country.

Ultimately success in the war against crime depends on the uplifting of standards of public and private morality, a rededication to basic spiritual values, which will entail righteous indignation over crime and corruption. To this end, the committee looks with confidence to the great force of religion and morality as applied in all phases of life and to sound education of the generations which follow.

ACCOMPLISHMENTS, RESULTS, AND EFFECTS OF COMMITTEE WORK

The popular misconception has existed in many circles that the committee was dedicated to a crusade against crime looking toward the jailing of every criminal in the country. As a matter of fact, the committee was—and is—properly an inquisitorial body with no prosecutive or law-enforcement functions. Nevertheless, there have been many results both directly and indirectly affecting the previously smooth path of many criminals with prison sentences presumably in store for many of them.

About the only pitfall which faced witnesses appearing before the committee which could result in legal action against them initiated by the committee, was a possibility that the witnesses by their answers or refusals to answer would be guilty of contempt of the United States Senate or, by reason of false information, would be guilty of perjury. A number of witnesses seemed unable to avoid these pitfalls and have been the subject of Senate citations and referral to the appropriate United States attorneys for prosecution. Among those cited for contempt were the following 33 individuals:

Harry Russell (acquitted)	John J. Fogarty
Joseph Doto, alias Joe Adonis	Phil Kastel
Anthony J. Accardo	Anthony Marcello
James Lynch	Mike Rubino
Arthur Longano	Joseph A. Porretto
Salvatore Moretti	Jacob Guzik
Walter Pechart	Frank Costello
Patrick Manno, alias Manning	Frank Erickson
Jack Dragna	Stanley Cohen
Joseph Aiuppa	John Doyle
Joseph DiCarlo	George Bowers
James Licavoli	William G. O'Brien
Peter Tremont	Ralph J. O'Hara
David N. Kessel	John Croft
Carlos Marcello	Morris Kleinman
Peter Licavoli	Louis Rothkopf
Russell Trilck	

Occasionally the committee found a witness contradicting another to the extent that it was apparent that one or the other was giving false testimony. A number of these situations have been referred to the proper United States attorneys for inquiry and prosecution. In other cases the testimony appeared to be false on the basis of records of sworn statements of others and these, too, have been referred for prosecution. Already indicted for perjury are James Moran and Louis Weber in New York and Sheriff John Grosch in New Orleans.

There also have been certifications to the United States attorneys of many other witnesses for investigation of possible perjury charges.

PUBLIC AWAKENING BRINGS LEGISLATIVE ACTION

Beyond any question a noteworthy effect of the committee's work has been the tremendous response in the nature of public awakening and its constructive reaction to enlightenment.   There has been a far-reaching chain reaction, the extent of wnich can only be assayed broadly because in many cases the translation of this awakening into action is only in a formulative phase at the time of this writing. Aroused citizenry has accounted for increased interest in the problem at State and local levels, as indicated by the formation in many State legislatures of little Kefauver committees with the avowed purpose of exploring, exposing, and eradicating the cancerous conditions existing in these areas.   Some of these legislative inquiries have already produced needed corrective legislation.   The State of Florida has recently sought to curb bootlegging of racing information to the bookmakers by supplementing the wire-service prohibition already on its statute books with an enforced 20-minute delay in the transmission of racing news by legitimate news-gathering organizations.

Grand juries too numerous to mention are delving into areas untouched for many years.   Reports of action by alert officials in cleaning up crimination conditions and in throwing out corrupt officeholders come from every State.   Such a racket stronghold as Cook County, Ill., has seen, within the last 3 months, 11 men indicted for conspiracy to violate the gambling laws and this investigation is continuing.   In Florida, grand juries have indicted 50 gamblers and law-enforcement officers.   Five sheriffs were removed, two of whom were later reinstated.   In Tampa, Fla., where the committee sought in vain for evidence of law-enforcement activity looking toward the prosecution of perpetrators of 15 unsolved gang-type killings, nearly all identified with the gambling rackets, the grand jury has reported more activity than at any time within 15 years.

Nearly every section of the country is experiencing a wave of grand jury activity with ensuing disclosures and indictments which are a testimonial to the American system of justice and the ability of the people to rid themselves of the scourge of the underworld by judicial process.   It is reasonable to forecast that venal politicians whose corruption has permitted the racketeers to become so firmly entrenched will in large measure be eliminated as aroused and awakened citizens go to the polls.

Outside recognized judicial channels, other potent forces in citizen crime commissions are springing up to wage war against the criminals. The committee finds that crime commissions, where established, have played an important part in focusing attention on evil conditions by giving them publicity and spurring sometimes disinterested law-enforcement agencies into action.   Where crime commissions were formed prior to the advent of this committee, it was apparent that criminal activities in those communities such as Chicago, Miami, and California were being scrutinized most carefully, resulting in the elimination of many rackets and the operation of others being made more hazardous.

Some of the places where new crime commissions have been formed or are in the making are Tampa, Fla.; Dallas, Tex.; New Orleans, La.; Des Moines, Iowa; New York, both State and city; Detroit, Mich., and in New England. It has been indicated that a California crime study commission which had expired will likely be re-created.

Trained personnel from our committee has been drawn upon to serve in important capacities in local anticrime groups.

Definite indications of increased interest and awakening, possibly due to committee activities, have been noted in law-enforcement fields both Federal and local.

GANGSTERS REVISE INCOME TAX RETURNS

Perhaps the figures will never be known but informed sources advise the committee that fear of scrutiny of their tax returns, either by this committee or other agencies having prosecutive powers, has caused a great number of racketeers, large and small, suddenly to become extremely circumspect in the filing of returns. They are being careful to report their real income more accurately, resulting in a gain of perhaps millions of dollars to the Government in taxes for income which might have gone unreported. It is strongly intimated that this tax gain to the Government has been many times the entire cost of this committee's work. Moreover, spurred by the committee's revelations, the Bureau of Internal Revenue has now set up a special Frauds Section consisting of racket squads across the Nation, which, if they realize their full constructive potentialities, may be expected to regain additional millions for the Treasury. Indictments have already been announced against racketeers and gamblers like Mickey Cohen and Washington, D. C., gamblers Emmett Waring and Sam Beard. Then, too, the various State tax coffers have benefited, not only from the increase in income taxes paid by racket figures but from such indirect sources as increased taxes received from money bet at race tracks where horse racing is permitted. For example, New York has filed tax claims amounting to $715,152 against Frank Erickson. State taxes are levied on the "handle" or volume of money bet. Because of the activity of this committee it has been found that in every area visited by the committee where racing is legal the "handle" at the race tracks was considerably higher than in precommittee times.

At the local level accelerated police activity has accounted for the complete revision of some police departments, shaking up of indifferent vice squads and formation of new, more vigilant, racket squads. Disclosures by the committee of the identity and location of gamblers in many instances resulted in immediate raids and arrests. An interesting example developed during the testimony in Washington of Sidney Brodson, a Milwaukee, Wis., betting commissioner. The Brodson hearing was televised and as he revealed the name, address and telephone number of individuals across the country with whom he placed bets, it was found that police officers viewing the televised proceedings learned for the first time of the gambling activities in their towns. They immediately visited the addresses mentioned and, before Brodson had left the stand, they had located and arrested his betting associates in cities separated by thousands of miles.

Mayor Dorothy McCullough Lee of Portland, Oreg., advised that she would follow through further in the case of Irving Hasson, a book maker mentioned by Brodson. Hasson was arrested for bookmaking immediately following Brodson's testimony. The mayor stated that she would revoke Hasson's city licenses such as those for cardroom or restaurant. In other localities, prosecutors learning of these telephone bookmaking activities have directed the telephone companies to discontinue service to the bookmakers thus removing from them the instrument which is sine qua non of their activity.

From time to time it was found that certain lawyers seemed to have overstepped the bounds of legal ethics either by actively engaging in criminal operations or by giving improper advice and counsel to the criminal that it can be only concluded that the lawyer was aiding and abetting the perpetration of the offense rather than defending his client. Disbarment proceedings by bar associations have followed. The disclosures of the activities of these lawyers have become the subject of study by a special committee of the American Bar Association which is attacking the problem with a view to purging the ranks of the profession of those who have been discredited.

NEW ACTION ON OLD CASES

Other Federal law-enforcement agencies have caught the competitive feeling and have pursued matters in many cases that have been dormant for many years. While the committee was in the New Orleans area the Immigration Service, at the insistence of a committee investigator, found a long-sought immigration violator, Sylvester (Sam) Carrollo, who had been hiding out near New Orleans, and deported him. The Department of Justice has announced an intention to make an annual survey of racketeers to determine whether any Federal laws are being violated and to concentrate on certain areas with special Federal grand juries to probe matters brought to their attention by the heads of the various Federal law-enforcement agencies and by local complainants.

Civic or citizens' groups have rallied and it is everywhere apparent that community leaders are unwilling to accept evidence of complacency or apathy on the part of their law-enforcement officers. These groups with programs of education and research into the problems of their communities will serve as an inspiration to the competent and honest law-enforcement officer and as a deterrent to the crooked. The recommendations of these groups have led to enactment of new legislation and consideration of additional legislation to tighten laws, to close loopholes and to increase the severity of penalties for the violator. In Maryland the legislature will consider a law making gambling a felony, heretofore only a misdemeanor. Judges have announced and put into practice an intention to cope with the problem by jailing offenders. Heretofore small fines paid willingly by the gamblers have been accepted, and looked upon by the criminals as a small license fee to continue their lucrative practice of milking the public.

Even during the committee's investigations those who operated outside the law were found to be constantly scheming and devising new ways to defeat law enforcement. Some of these attempts were exposed during the committee's hearings. For example, the committee found that in New Orleans a factory had been rented and dies ordered to manufacture slot machines. All slot machines are illegal in Louisiana. Obviously the enterprise was designed to defeat the recently enacted Federal law prohibiting interstate transportation of slot machines, or parts thereof. Disclosures at the committee hearing resulted in the abandonment of the project. Similarly the committee's investigators found in San Francisco a pilot model of a new slot machine which operated electrically which was not "coin operated." This device, too, was exposed and the distributor, who had imported the device from Chicago, announced an intention to abandon distribution of them.

Not the least remarkable adjunct of the activities of the committee has been a Nation-wide dislocation of principal hoodlums from their well-entrenched haunts.

Invariably the committee found that when racket leaders became fugitives from committee process, the flight may have diminished in some cases the speed of the committee's accomplishments, but unquestionably the racketeers' efforts to avoid service foreclosed to them their ability effectively to function, and temporarily at least, caused the shutdown of many criminal operations.

SHOULD GAMBLING BE LEGALIZED?

The widespread incidence of illegal gambling disclosed by the committee's investigations has resulted in the suggestion, made by many well-meaning and conscientious individuals, that the antigambling laws should be abandoned as unenforceable, and that the business of gambling should be legalized and licensed.

This suggestion appears to be premised on the dual assumptions that once gambling is legalized the crooks and the cheats will retire from the field and leave the operations of the handbooks, policy wheels and the gaming rooms to honest and upstanding businessmen, and that public officials, who have previously been persuaded to ignore or affirmatively aid illegal gambling operations, will automatically prove incorruptible when entrusted with responsibility for controlling these same operations through a licensing system.

It seems to this committee that the simple statement of these premises is sufficient to demonstrate how invalid they really are.

It is the nature of the business of gambling, and not its legality or illegality, that makes it so attractive and lucrative for gangsters and hoodlums.

Elsewhere in the report the committee has described the ways in which professional gamblers can and do protect themselves from loss, and the size of the profits which can be made from a well-run gambling operation. The tremendous profits to be made from these completely nonproductive operations offer obvious attractions to the lawless and parasitic elements in our society. Legalization of gambling in no way diminished its attractions for underworld elements, nor did it prevent them from maintaining their domination of the field through intimidation and corruption.

Proponents of legalization often argue that the urge to gamble is inherent in human nature and that the enforcement of antigambling laws is an impossible and impracticable task. It is undoubtedly true that a great number of people enjoy gambling but the investigations of this committee have disclosed ample evidence of the evils which inevitably accompany the gratification of the desire to gamble. The fact that it is undoubtedly impossible to eradicate gambling completely would not justify the abandonment of attempts to limit the operations of the professional gamblers.

The history of previous experiments in legalization of gambling has shown that legalization results in an increase in gambling, particularly in increased participation by small-wage earners—the people who are least able to bear the inevitable losses. Wherever large-scale gambling has been carried on it has been the experience of law-enforcement officials that violence and crime increase in proportion to the size of the gambling operations. The promise of income to the gambling operator is sufficient to encourage large-scale intimidation and corruption in order to maintain a monopoly of the gambling operation. The losses incurred by victims of gambling have driven them to embezzlement, robbery, and other crimes committed by men desperately attempting to recoup gambling losses they could not afford to sustain.

SITUATION IN GREAT BRITAIN COMPARED

The committee has studied with interest the scholarly report which was recently returned by the British Royal Commission on Betting, Lotteries, and Gaming. The commission stated its conclusion that gambling on the scale on which it is indulged in the British Isles at the present time, does not impose a serious strain on the national resources or manpower, or constitute a serious inducement to criminal activity.

The commission estimated that the annual turn-over in all forms of gambling for the year 1950, amounted to about 650 million pounds, or about $1.8 billion. This committee has estimated that the present annual turn-over in the United States is about $20 billion. It is the belief of this committee that the conclusion of the Royal Commission that gambling can be satisfactorily licensed and controlled, is explicable in terms of the size of the problem with which they were dealing.

Under the system presently in force in England, off-track betting is legal only if bets are credit transactions placed through phone or wire, and not by the bettor in person. The commission reported that despite the illegality of handbooks operating on a cash basis, off-track bookmakers do a flourishing cash business. The commission also reported that although it had found occasional evidences of attempted corruption of officials by persons illegally carrying on gambling operations, there was little evidence of actual corruption or violence as a result of betting and gambling. Gambling casinos and dice and roulette games are illegal in England, and the Royal Commission did not find any evidence of organized illegal operations in this field.

The investigation which our committee has carried on for the past year has shown that an entirely different situation exists in the United States. The extravagant profits to be made from the continuous operation of gambling casinos, handbooks and lotteries in this country have attracted the worst gangster and hoodlum elements. The amounts of money involved are so tremendous that the expenditure of large sums of money for corruption of enforcement officials, and officials at even higher levels, can and is absorbed as an expense of doing business.

It should be noted that the Royal Commission's conclusion that gambling in the British Isles was not necessarily accompanied by violence and corruption was based on a study of extra-legal as well as legal gambling. Their conclusion that off-track betting on a cash basis should be legalized was based on their findings that the comparatively small-scale operations carried on in the British Isles had not resulted in conditions similar to those which this committee found prevailing throughout the United States. Whatever the reasonableness of the commission's recommendations may be in terms of the situation existing in the British Isles today, there is no argument by analogy from their recommendations to the legalization of a $20 billion a year empire built on corruption.

In short, in the United States the question is not solely whether or not gambling in itself is harmful to the public. Here gambling has led to harmful byproducts that can be controlled only by continuously fighting organized professional gambling. The committee is convinced that this will produce far lesser evils than legalized gambling.

WHAT TESTIMONY IN NEVADA DISCLOSED

If legalized gambling could be successfully divorced from the evils of crime and corruption, the State of Nevada would offer the most ideal climate for its operation. Nevada is a State with a small population, where gambling operations can be policed easily and the comings and goings of undesirables can be noted, yet the State of Nevada has found it necessary substantially to increase police surveillance as a result of the legalization of gambling and the accompanying influx of hoodlums, racketeers, and the other inevitable parasites who spring up like weeds wherever gambling operations are carried on.

While it is true that the revenue received by the State of Nevada in connection with the licensing of gambling in that State contributes somewhat to the rather meager finances of the State, it should also be noted that the revenue from such operations as the Flamingo Club, which netted $400,000 in 1949, finds its way into the pockets of men like Rosen and Sedway. At the same time, the taxpaying citizens of the State must foot the bill for large expenditures for relief and police protection, expenditures which are necessary accompaniments of the wide-scale gambling operations in the State.

COMMITTEE OPPOSES LEGALIZATION OF GAMBLING

It is often argued that it is impossible effectively to outlaw the operation of handbooks, lotteries, and other forms of gambling in States where pari-mutuel betting is permitted. The fact that a number of States have considered it desirable to permit on-track betting under conditions that are most easily subject to policing and control does not furnish any basis for the legalization of other forms of gambling which are far more likely to be dominated by underworld elements and most apt to lead to violent competition and criminal activity.

Those States which have legalized pari-mutuel betting have done so in an attempt to satisfy the gambling urge in the manner which can be most closely controlled and least likely to be accompanied by the familiar evils of gambling. While race-track wagering undoubtedly results in individual personal tragedies as a result of undisciplined betting, the damage can be more or less limited to persons who can better afford to incur financial losses. The operation of handbooks and other gambling establishments in places that are easily accessible to the workingman and the nonhabitual bettor results in the spread of the evils of gambling to increasingly larger segments of the population.

In the opinion of this committee there is no sense or logic in legalizing the greater evils of off-track betting simply because it has been the considered judgment of a number of States that pari-mutuel betting can be controlled and operated without undue detriment to society.

There has not been presented to this committee any plan for the extension of controlled gambling which carries with it a substantial chance of success. On the contrary, each plan for extending legal gambling appears to play into the hands of the gangster element.

In many communities, the professional gambling element is synonymous with the gangster element. This is particularly true in the large cities which the committee investigated. In these cities, much of the propaganda for legalized gambling can be traced to organized and professional gamblers. They have attempted through public relation channels open to them to persuade legitimate businessmen that an open town is good for business. They have succeeded in many cities, primarily Miami Beach, in intimidating law-abiding citizens so that they are reluctant to enter into political campaigns against the candidates supported by the gangsters. Particularly in resort areas where wide-open gambling had the connivance of local police have these efforts been made to persuade the non-gambling businessmen to support the gamblers. But during the last year when both Miami Beach and Saratoga were closed to gambling, each of these resorts enjoyed an unusually successful season. The Miami area, in particular, has just made available reports showing the success of its 1950–51 season. Apparently, more tourists spent more money in this area than ever before, and more of the money which was spent was diverted into normal legitimate trade channels. Of course, some illegal and clandestine gambling existed, but the fact is that closing down the wide-open gambling did not adversely affect the economy of the resort. It did result in an upsurge of awareness on the part of the honest citizens and dealt a serious financial and political blow to the racketeers engaged in organized illegal gambling.

If, on the other hand, gambling were legalized in the Miami area, and the imprint of respectability placed upon the racketeers who have been controlling and corrupting law enforcement, it is the committee's opinion that they would renew and extend their efforts to control and corrupt State and local government with a resultant decay of governmental morality far in excess of that which the committee found to exist during its investigations.

O

82D CONGRESS }
1st Session }

SENATE

{ REPORT
{ No. 725

ORGANIZED CRIME IN INTERSTATE COMMERCE

FINAL REPORT

OF THE

SPECIAL COMMITTEE TO INVESTIGATE ORGANIZED CRIME IN INTERSTATE COMMERCE

UNITED STATES SENATE

PURSUANT TO

S. Res. 202
(81st Cong.)

AS AMENDED BY

S. Res. 60 and S. Res. 129
(82d Cong.)

AUGUST 31 (legislative day, AUGUST 27), 1951.—Ordered to be printed

UNITED STATES
GOVERNMENT PRINTING OFFICE
88534   WASHINGTON : 1951

SPECIAL COMMITTEE TO INVESTIGATE ORGANIZED CRIME IN INTERSTATE COMMERCE

[Pursuant to S. Res. 202, 81st Cong., as amended by S. Res. 60, 82d Cong., and S. Res. 129, 82d Cong.]

HERBERT R. O'CONOR, Maryland, *Chairman*

ESTES KEFAUVER, Tennessee   CHARLES W. TOBEY, New Hampshire
LESTER C. HUNT, Wyoming   ALEXANDER WILEY, Wisconsin

RICHARD G. MOSER, *Chief Counsel*
DOWNEY RICE, *Associate Counsel*
JAMES M. HEPBRON, *Administrative Assistant*

II

CONTENTS

FINAL REPORT OF THE SPECIAL SENATE COMMITTEE TO INVESTIGATE ORGANIZED CRIME IN INTERSTATE COMMERCE

August 31 (legislative day, August 27), 1951.—Ordered to be printed

Mr. Hunt (for Mr. O'Conor), from the Special Committee To Investigate Organized Crime in Interstate Commerce, submitted the following

FINAL REPORT

[Pursuant to S. Res. 202, 81st Cong., as amended by S. Res. 60, 82d Cong., and S. Res. 129, 82d Cong.]

I. GENERAL OBSERVATIONS

This committee has served as a powerful searchlight, exposing widespread national and local crime conditions to public gaze. Its activities have had a tremendous effect upon the whole field of law enforcement. Everywhere throughout the country citizens, made suddenly aware of the character and ramifications of organized crime, have risen up to demand greater vigilance in stamping out crime and corruption.

In the first phase of its activities ending on May 1, 1951, the committee concentrated primarily on the large cities. Since that date it has directed its attention largely to the field of narcotics and to crime in medium-size cities.

Everywhere it has turned there has followed an enormous increase in local enforcement activity.

In many cities, large and small, visited by the committee, corrupt officials have been forced to resign, grand juries and enforcement officials have doubled their vigilance, and gangsters have gone into hiding. Even Virginia and the District of Columbia, which were not themselves the subject of investigation, have felt the repercussions of the committee's work in adjacent Maryland. In Maryland itself at least four investigations not previously under way are now being conducted largely as the result of the committee's disclosures. In New York, four new investigative bodies not in existence before the committee began, are now at work.

In the field of narcotics, the committee's searchlight has created a Nation-wide awareness of the seriousness of this great evil. As a result, investigations have been started, court procedures have been modified, remedial laws have been passed, educational programs have

1

been undertaken and the despicable drug peddler has run for cover. The President of the United States only recently has been prompted to call for increased penalties in narcotics cases.

The committee's study of selected samples of medium-size cities was necessarily less spectacular than in the large cities, but a vitally important fact was established, namely, that the same pattern of crime conditions found in the large cities exists in Main Streets throughout America. Crime must be attacked at the local level and it is from the local level that the committee has received a flood of pleas for information, guidance, and help.

When the committee's life ends the man in the street in every local community will want to know what is to take its place.

II. CONCLUSIONS

A. CONSTANT VIGILANCE

As the result of the committee's activities there exists a great public awareness of the nature and extent of organized crime. The public now knows that the tentacles of organized crime reach into virtually every community throughout the country. It also knows that law enforcement is essentially a local matter calling for constant vigilance at the local level and a strengthening of public and private morality.

People everywhere are pleading for a means of keeping alert to crime conditions and avoiding a return to the state of public complacency and indifference under which gangsterism has thrived for so long. The demand for a permanent force that can, in some measure, replace this committee must be met.

With a view to answering this demand, the committee, in its Third Interim Report, proposed the establishment of a Federal Crime Commission, and a bill to accomplish this has been introduced. The Commission contemplated by this proposal is an independent Federal agency in the executive branch of the Government, organized and staffed independently of other Government agencies, and required to report to the Congress.

This bill is opposed by the Treasury Department and the Department of Justice, and Senator Wiley has expressed his dissent. Although the committee does not recede from the proposal, a realistic approach compels the committee to recognize that enactment of the bill cannot be accomplished in a short period of time.

In the meantime, it is highly desirable that some action be taken promptly to afford local communities a means of obtaining help in their attacks upon organized crime.

The answer seems to lie partly in the field of local, privately constituted crime commissions. Several of these have been in operation for a number of years and they have shown themselves to be highly effective. They are not investigative or policing agencies. Their function is to observe local crime conditions, to cooperate with civic, educational, and enforcement agencies where possible, and to report to the public any evidence of laxity or corruption.

A great step forward would be accomplished in the field of law enforcement if privately constituted crime commissions of this character could be established in every city in the United States where organized crime presents a serious problem, and if a central agency could be established which would foster the establishment of local commissions and serve as a clearing house and coordinating agency for their information and experience.

Experience has shown that the crime commission movement cannot progress unless it has a national parent body with sufficient prestige and funds to give it drive. It is believed that if Congress fosters the establishment of such an organization, funds from private foundations or philanthropists can be obtained to give it permanent life.

This report contains a recommendation for establishment of an organization of this character.

B. NARCOTICS

1. The illegal sale of narcotic drugs represents an evil of major proportions requiring for its eradication the combined efforts of law enforcement bodies, legislators, educators, and parents. It should be attacked at all levels of the Nation's social structure. If not successfully overcome in the near future, it may do lasting damage to the youth of the Nation.

2. The organized gangster syndicates will unquestionably turn to the sale of narcotic drugs when they are driven out of the presently lucrative field of gambling. As they did at the end of the prohibition era, when bootlegging no longer offered substantial profits, they will turn to another form of illegal activity. Under present conditions, narcotic drugs offer them the most profitable opening. Their protestations that they would not stoop so low are hollow in the light of the recent arrest of Waxey Gordon in New York City on a narcotics charge.

3. There has been a startling increase in the abuse of drugs by young people, many of whom are unaware of its frightful consequences. They fail to realize that they are dealing with what is, in effect, a contagious disease which brings degradation and slow death to the victim and tragedy to his family and friends.

4. There has been a tendency to shroud the subject of drug addiction in a veil of secrecy. The result is that young people learn about drugs from bad associates or from the drug peddlers in the back streets and alleys, rather than from qualified sources of information. It is for this reason that many young people have tried drugs, innocently unaware of the dangers they face.

5. Addiction is extremely difficult to cure. It is a chronic condition with a high rate of recurrence. If discovered in time, addiction may be prevented, but once it occurs the victim can overcome it only through a painful and bewildering perplexity of treatment entailing difficult physical and psychological readjustment.

6. Members of the public generally are not aware of the fact that voluntary, noncriminal patients may be treated at the United States Public Health Service Hospital at Lexington, Ky., and that patients who cannot afford to pay are treated without charge.

7. The United States Public Health Service Hospitals at Lexington, Ky., and at Forth Worth, Tex., do not have sufficient facilities for caring for all of the women patients in need of treatment. Furthermore, there is not sufficient segregation of young patients from

older, hardened addicts.   There is considerable danger that youngsters going to these institutions for the first time are retarded in their recovery by mingling with the older addicts.

If the public should become fully aware of the availability of these hospitals for voluntary patients, it is entirely possible that the demands upon them will increase materially.   In that event additional Federal facilities may be required.

At the State level, the facilities for treatment appear to be wholly inadequate.

8. The illegal sale of narcotic drugs pays enormous profits to the lowest form of criminal, namely, the peddler who is willing to wreck young lives to satisfy his greed.   No penalty is too severe for a criminal of such character.   Until recently the courts have been far too lenient toward narcotic violators.   Short sentences do not deter the potential peddler and suspended sentences are a waste of judicial effort.

9. The drug representing the greatest problem is heroin, the importation and possession of which are forbidden in the United States.   All of the heroin now used in this country is smuggled in from abroad, for the most part by passengers and seamen carrying it off ships on their persons.   Because of the ease of concealment, checking its flow through customs search is extremely difficult. Present practices and procedures for canceling the sailing papers of seamen convicted of narcotics violations are unsatisfactory.

10. The most effective means of combating the narcotics problem is through effective enforcement facilities.   The Narcotics Bureau of the Treasury Department is efficient and effective as far as it is able to go, but it is pitifully undermanned considering the enormity of the task assigned to it.   With sufficient personnel, the Narcotics Bureau could do more than any other force toward stamping out the illegal importation and sale of narcotic drugs.   Most addicts would like to see the traffic stamped out so that it will not be available to them.

At the local level, there are too few enforcement officers who have had experience in specialized fields, especially in the field of narcotics. Although the Narcotics Bureau of the Treasury Department works in close cooperation with State authorities, its manpower is not sufficient to permit it to furnish training to local agents.

11. Barbiturate drugs, such as luminal, seconol, amytol, and the other products popularly known as sleeping pills have not yet become an object of organized crime.   However, in its study of narcotics the committee learned that their addiction properties when used in large quantities are as severe as those other narcotic drugs.   Their sale should be the subject of strict regulation under both State and Federal law.

12. The Commission on Narcotics of the United Nations has made great strides in bringing about cooperation among the nations of the world regarding control of the production of opium and of the manufacture of drugs derived from opium.   The countries in which the drugs are manufactured have been fairly successful in limiting the output to the actual medical needs of the world.

On the other hand, the countries where the opium poppy is grown have found it to be impossible, in spite of strenuous efforts, to regulate the quantities planted and cultivated by the farmers. These countries grow enough opium poppy plants to produce 40 times the amount of opium needed for legitimate medical purposes.

It is believed that, whereas in the growing countries the quantity cannot be regulated, complete prohibition against the planting of opium poppy plants could be enforced.

Except in the case of cocaine, which represents a minor problem, adequate synthetic substitutes have been developed for opiate drugs, especially for morphine, which is the principal pain-relieving product. Although the synthetics are easy to produce, it is believed that their manufacture could be regulated within reasonable limits. The medical profession would not be materially handicapped if opium poppy growing were prohibited throughout the world.

C. CRIME AND CORRUPTION

1. The same pattern of organized crime found in large metropolitan areas exists in the medium-size cities with similar evidence of official sanction or protection. In some cases the protection is obtained by the payment of bribes to public officials, often on a regular basis pursuant to a carefully conceived system. In other cases, the racketeering elements make substantial contributions to political campaigns of officials who can be relied upon to tolerate their activities. Sometimes these contributions will support a whole slate of officers in more than one political party, giving the racketeers virtual control of the governing body. Democracy vanishes in a captive community because the ordinary citizen for practical purposes has nothing to say about his Government.

In many cities, large and small, there is evidence of active and often controlling participation by former bootleggers, gangsters, and hoodlums in the political affairs of the community. In some cases this participation extends to other cities and even to the government of the State. Underworld characters do not engage in politics for the good of the community or the Nation. They do so for the purpose of increasing their power and wealth and gaining greater protection for their illegal activities.

Organized crime has been able to flourish and grow largely because of the economic power wielded by gangsters. The ordinary, honest citizen cannot expect to be able to compete in either business or government with persons who obtain wealth and power through illegal means.

2. Wiretapping is a powerful tool in the hands of law-enforcement officers. Federal agents are seriously handicapped in their regular enforcement work by the legal restrictions which presently surround this valuable instrument of investigation. If properly safeguarded by the same restrictions that are imposed by law upon searches and seizures, wiretapping does not infringe upon the right of privacy of the honest citizen. Several States, notably New York, have laws which permit the use of wiretapping pursuant to court order and subject to reasonable safeguards. These laws work satisfactorily and without objection on the part of law-abiding citizens. A similar Federal law would represent an important contribution to law enforcement.

III. RECOMMENDATIONS AND SUGGESTIONS

A. RECOMMENDATIONS FOR ACTION AT THE FEDERAL LEVEL

1. Establishment of National Crime Coordinating Council

In order to keep the searchlight of public vigilance turned upon crime and corruption in a manner that leaves at the local level the basic responsibility for law enforcement and at the same time affords centralized guidance and coordination, the committee proposes the establishment of a privately constituted National Crime Coordinating Council.

The Council would be a body composed of representatives of privately established local crime commissions. Its first chairman would be designated on an interim basis by the President of the United States to serve until appointment of his successor. As soon as the organization was established it would nominate five persons from whom the President would select a chairman to succeed the interim chairman. The chairman so designated would serve for a term of not more than 2 years at which time the same procedure would be followed for selection of his successor.

Congress would appropriate the sum of $100,000 to be applied as a grant in aid to the Council for the purpose of permitting it to organize and begin its activities. It is not contemplated that the Congress would be called upon for any additional funds. Thereafter, the Council would be expected to obtain its funds from charitable foundations or other private sources.

Solely to provide the mechanics for establishing the Council at the initial stages, the Attorney General of the United States would have the responsibility of drafting its charter and bylaws, arranging for its organizational meetings, and otherwise sponsoring its creation. Local crime commissions now in existence would be invited to serve as its charter members and thereafter it would sponsor throughout the country other local crime commissions which would also become members or chapters of the national organization.

The functions of the Council would be as follows:

(a) To foster the establishment of privately constituted local crime commissions wherever needed throughout the country.

(b) To serve as a clearinghouse for information of interest to local crime commissions.

(c) To inquire into and study such new patterns or innovations in organized crime as may develop and to make the results of its studies available to appropriate agencies and to legislative bodies so that immediate deterrents may be devised.

(d) To sponsor meetings for the purpose of exchanging ideas and information regarding local crime conditions to which would be invited representatives of local social and civic organizations, religious groups, educational bodies, women's clubs, law enforcement agencies, and all other groups having an interest in crime conditions.

The committee believes that establishment of the proposed National Crime Coordinating Council would constitute a great contribution toward the cause of law enforcement because it would provide at the local level the civic vigilance without which the evil of complacency and indifference may soon return.

As previously pointed out, this plan differs substantially from the proposal for a Federal Crime Commission as described in the third interim report. The Federal Crime Commission would be an official agency in the executive branch of the Government; whereas the National Crime Coordinating Council would be a private agency serving the local, privately established crime commissions constituting its membership. If the bill now pending in the Senate for establishment of the Federal Crime Commission should be enacted, the official functions of the Commission would not be in conflict with the private activities of the Council, although a demarcation of responsibilities between them might be advisable to avoid duplication of effort.

2. Continuation of crime investigation

Section 7 of Senate Resolution 202 as added by Senate Resolution 129 provides that on or before September 1, 1951, this committee "shall transfer all of its files, papers, documents, and other pertinent data to the Senate Committee on Interstate and Foreign Commerce, which committee shall, under and by virtue of the authority of section 136 of the Legislative Reorganization Act of 1946, continue the study and surveillance of the subject matter of this resolution."

This committee hopes that the study of organized crime will continue and it is gratified that the Committee on Interstate and Foreign Commerce has already taken cognizance of the foregoing provision. It is suggested that serious consideration be given to the problem presented by the witnesses who have evaded the committee's process.

With regard to the District of Columbia, this committee has, on several occasions, received evidence that the city of Washington may be a pivotal point for gambling operations of considerable size. There is also evidence before this committee of widespread traffic in narcotic drugs within the District. The committee therefore strongly recommends that an appropriate committee of the Senate undertake a thorough investigation of crime conditions in the District of Columbia, including the relationship of such conditions to crime in adjoining areas.

3. Coordinate information regarding narcotics

It is recommended that one of the activities of the proposed National Crime Coordinating Council be to serve as a clearinghouse for information regarding local action taken in connection with the illegal sale and use of narcotic drugs.

At the present time, aside from the information on enforcement supplied by the Bureau of Narcotics, there is no central agency to which civic, educational, religious, and enforcement agencies may turn for information regarding the subject of narcotics. Each community is approaching the matter in its own way without having the benefit of experience gained in others. Duplication and waste of effort would be reduced if coordination of activities could be brought about by use of a central clearing agency.

4. Narcotics Bureau training squad

A squad should be organized in the Narcotics Bureau of the Treasury Department having as its function the training of local enforcement officers in the specialized techniques required for narcotics law enforcement. The squad should consist of at least 10 experienced Federal narcotics agents who would furnish instruction to local enforcement agencies everywhere.

Such a program would increase greatly the number of trained narcotics agents serving throughout the country on both Federal and local levels.

5. Increase staff of Narcotics Bureau

The Appropriations Committees and the Congress are to be commended for action in increasing the appropriation of the Narcotics Bureau to provide for 30 additional agents. The studies of this committee, however, indicate that the problem presented by the importation and sale of narcotic drugs has reached such magnitude that at least 40 more agents, in addition to the 30 provided for, are urgently needed. This would cover the enforcement needs as well as the local training program described in the previous recommendation.

Enforcement is the one point in the entire narcotics problem where results of a tangible nature will be evident immediately. Given the men, the Bureau, with the help of local agencies, can do much more to erase this evil than it is able to do under present conditions.

6. Promote narcotics education

A Nation-wide educational program regarding the character and effects of narcotic drugs and the nature and results of addiction should be developed by the Federal Security Agency and made available to educational institutions, civic organizations, and enforcement authorities throughout the country. The objective of the program should be to lift the veil of secrecy from the subject and to bring it out into the open where it can be dealt with in an intelligent and effective manner. The present authority and funds of the Federal Security Agency are sufficient for this purpose.

7. Increase drug peddlers' penalties

Federal laws increasing the penalties that the courts may impose upon convicted drug peddlers should be enacted without delay.

8. Increase treatment facilities

The facilities for treating drug addicts in Federal institutions should be increased to permit accommodation of more women patients and segregation of young addicts. Public awareness of the fact that the United States Public Health Service Hospital at Lexington, Ky., is open to voluntary patients and that its services are free to those who cannot pay, may result in a substantial increase in patients. In that event the facilities of that hospital should be increased to meet the needs then found to exist.

9. Require notice to seamen's and longshoremen's unions of narcotics convictions

The Narcotics Bureau should notify the appropriate national unions of all narcotics law convictions of seamen and longshoremen in order that the unions may more easily enforce their rules calling for expulsion of such cases.

10. Cancel sailing papers of narcotics violators

The Coast Guard should be empowered and required to cancel the sailing papers of any seaman convicted of a violation of the narcotics laws, irrespective of whether the violation occurred on land or at sea.

11. Prohibit opium production throughout the world

The United States representatives at the United Nations should work toward the adoption of measures that will prohibit the growing of opium poppy plants in any country of the world.

12. Attorney General's Crime Conference

The Attorney General of the United States made a substantial contribution in the effort to combat organized crime in calling an Attorney General's Crime Conference which had its meeting in Washington in February 1950. The importance of the conference was shown by the fact that it was addressed by the President of the United States. It was attended by Federal and local enforcement officers, prosecuting attorneys and by representatives of municipal, county, State, and Federal officials.

The conference made notable achievements among which were the recommendation for enactment by the Congress of legislation preventing the use for gambling purposes of interstate communication facilities and prohibiting interstate shipment of gambling devices. The legislative committee of the conference in cooperation with the Attorney General prepared bills to effectuate these recommendations. The bill preventing interstate shipment of slot machines was passed by the Eighty-first Congress.

Extensive hearings were held by the Interstate and Foreign Commerce Committee of the Senate, and the wire-service bill was unanimously reported favorably, the report being made by Senator McFarland of Arizona, now majority leader.

The committee strongly recommends that the Attorney General call annual conferences of this kind and that the legislative and other committees of the conference have more frequent sessions to study and propose legislation at both Federal and local levels to combat organized crime.

PREVIOUS RECOMMENDATIONS

In addition to the foregoing recommendations, the committee made 22 recommendations in its Third Interim Report. In order to have all of the recommendations of the committee made available in a single place, those contained in the Third Interim Report are set forth below:

I. The Congress through a continuation of this committee should for a further limited period continue to check on organized crime in interstate commerce. The basic function of the committee should be to scrutinize the efforts made by the Federal agencies to suppress interstate criminal operations, and particularly the racket squads described in later recommendations. It will also follow up the legislative recommendations made in this report.

II. A racket squad should be organized in the Justice Department.

III. Appropriate legislation should be enacted to set up an independent Federal Crime Commission in the executive branch of the Government.

IV. The establishment of the Special Fraud Squad by the Bureau of Internal Revenue of the Treasury Department is one of the most effective and useful steps taken to collect taxes from the criminal element. The committee applauds the Department for this act and recommends that it be supported with necessary appropriation and that it work in close cooperation with the special racket squad if set up by the Department of Justice as is recommended by the committee. The Bureau of Internal Revenue should maintain on a current and continuing basis a list of known gangsters, racketeers, gamblers, and criminals whose income-tax returns should receive special attention by a squad of trained experts. Procedures leading to prosecution should be streamlined and speeded up.

V. The Bureau of Internal Revenue should enforce the regulations which require taxpayers to keep adequate books and records of income and expenses, against the gamblers, gangsters, and racketeers who are continually flouting them. Violation should be made a felony.

VI. Gambling casinos should be required to maintain daily records of money won and lost to be filed with the Bureau of Internal Revenue. They also should be required to maintain such additional records as shall be prescribed by the Bureau. Officials of the Bureau of Internal Revenue should have access to the premises of gambling casinos and to their books and records at all times. Where the casino is operating illegally, in addition to the aforementioned obligations, the operators of the casino should be required to keep records of all bets and wagers.

VII. The law and the regulations of the Bureau of Internal Revenue should be amended so that no wagering losses, expenses, or disbursements of any kind, including salaries, rent, protection money, etc., incurred in or as a result of illegal gambling shall be deductible for income-tax purposes.

VIII. The transmission of gambling information across State lines by telegraph, telephone, radio, television, or other means of communication or communication facility should be regulated so as to outlaw any service devoted to a substantial extent to providing information used in illegal gambling.

IX. The internal revenue laws and regulations should be amended so as to require any person who has been engaged in an illegitimate business netting in excess of $2,500 a year for any of 5 years previously, to file a net-worth statement of all his assets, along with his income-tax returns.

X. The transmission of bets or wagers, or the transmission of moneys in payment of bets or wagers, across State lines by telegraph, telephone, or any other facilities of interstate communication, or the United States mails, should be prohibited.

XI. The prohibition against the transportation of slot machines in interstate commerce should be extended to include other gambling devices which are susceptible of gangster or racketeer control, such as punchboards, roulette wheels, etc.

XII. The penalties against the illegal sale, distribution, and smuggling of narcotic drugs should be substantially increased.

XIII. The immigration laws should be amended to facilitate deportation of criminal and other undesirable aliens. To this end, the committee recommends the adoption of the legislative proposal heretofore recommended by the Commissioner of Immigration and contained in section 241 of S. 716 (82d Cong.), now pending before the Senate Judiciary Committee.

XIV. The Immigration Act of February 5, 1917, should be amended to provide punishment for smuggling, concealing, or harboring aliens not entitled by law to enter or reside in the United States.

XV. The Attorney General should be authorized to revoke suspensions of deportation and to make such revocation ground for the cancellation of certificates of naturalization granted aliens who have succeeded in getting their immigration status recognized but who are later found to be ineligible for such relief.

XVI. The personnel of Federal law-enforcement agencies should be materially increased. Consideration should be given to eliminating inequities, in the salaries of law-enforcement officers, many of whom are woefully underpaid for the duties they perform and the risks they undertake.

XVII. The existing Federal law with respect to perjury should be tightened; the committee endorses H. R. 2260 (82d Cong.) and recommends its passage.

XVIII. The Attorney General of the United States should be given authority to grant immunity from prosecution to witnesses whose testimony may be essential to an inquiry conducted by a grand jury, or in the course of a trial or of a congressional investigation.

XIX. The committee favors the passages of legislation providing for constructive service by publication or otherwise upon a witness whose testimony is desired who evades personal service upon him.

XX. The committee favors passage of the legislation recommended by the Alcohol Tax Unit of the Treasury Department to prevent racketeering elements from entering the liquor industry and to eliminate any now in it. The committee also favors passage of legislation which will extend the same Federal protection to local-option States as is now extended to the wholly dry States against the illicit transportation of liquor into the dry areas.

XXI. The committee recommends that the present Federal regulation and application forms which require a listing of individual owners, partners, and holders of Alcohol Tax Unit permits, be amended, so that, in addition to the present requirements, the names of all beneficial owners will be stated: also that the application forms require the disclosure of all previous arrests and convictions. A report should be filed with the Alcohol Tax Unit of every change in such interests or in management as such occurs.

XXII. The committee recommends that the Interstate Commerce Commission be required by law to consider the moral fitness of applications for certificates of necessity and convenience as one of the standards in acting upon applications for such certificates or transfers of certificates.

A number of the committee's previous recommendations, above, called for administrative action by the Treasury Department and the Department of Justice. The committee is gratified to note that these have been put into effect, and commends both agencies for the constructive way in which they have acted upon both the letter and the spirit of its recommendations. Both the Secretary of the Treasury and the Attorney General, with their staffs, have been consistently helpful and cooperative in every phase of the committee's work.

B. SUGGESTIONS FOR ACTION BY STATE AND LOCAL GOVERNMENTS

1. *Revision of outmoded laws and adoption of uniform laws.*—State and local prosecutors sometimes attribute their ineffectiveness in law enforcement to the inadequacy of the laws they are called upon to enforce. The committee therefore suggests that State legislatures might reexamine their criminal laws with a view to correcting any such deficiencies, especially in the fields of gambling and the other illegal activities that have been found to constitute the basis for organized crime. The committee strongly endorses efforts to develop and promulgate uniform State laws on gambling, vice, narcotics, racketeering, and related areas of criminal activity.

2. *State legislative or executive investigations.*—State legislatures in more cases might profitably appoint legislative committees, with broad subpena and investigative powers, for the study of organized crime within their borders, perhaps patterning the duties of such committees after those of this committee. The establishment of crime investigating commissions in the executive branches of State governments is also suggested.

3. *Enact laws relating to barbiturates.*—The committee suggests that special attention be directed by States to regulation of the sale of barbiturate drugs to require that they be sold on prescription only. Some States have already enacted such laws. These laws should be so drafted as to conform to corresponding Federal legislation which is now pending and uniformity among the States is highly desirable.

4. *Provide treatment facilities for addicts.*—The committee strongly suggests that local government, civic, educational, and religious groups promptly survey the facilities available for the detection and treatment of addiction, and that, where necessary, additional facilities be provided in order that persons, especially young people, abusing drugs may be discovered at early stages and treated promptly.

5. *Conferences of local prosecutors.*—State attorneys general should take the initiative wherever possible to insure better coordination among local prosecutors. In a few States attorneys general have had conferences with district and county attorneys for the exchange of views and information and to emphasize the need for close cooperation in dealing with organized criminal activities. The committee

urges the attorneys general of other States to adopt this practice on a regular basis.

6. *Organization of State crime conferences of citizens groups.*—The interest currently being shown by public-spirited citizens, educators, religious groups, and civic organizations in the assault on organized crime should be kept alive, and fully utilized. Continuing public support of the activities of enforcement officials is of great importance. Officially sponsored crime conferences, where civic leaders can meet and exchange views with enforcement officials, might well be organized on a State-wide basis from time to time, perhaps in coordination with the activities of the National Crime Coordinating Council described in this report.

7. *Use of State income tax data.*—Much valuable information on the activities of organized crime is available in State income-tax returns. Special staffs could be organized to screen this material in order to provide local law-enforcement officers with many leads which are not presently available to them.

8. *Utilization of Federal occupational-tax data.*—Federal occupational-tax returns require disclosure of the identity and activities of liquor dealers, slot-machine operators, the possessors of gangster-type firearms and (if H. R. 4473, now pending before the Senate Finance Committee, is enacted) gamblers. These returns are available to State and local enforcement officials by a special provision of the Internal Revenue Code. They have not been widely relied upon, and the committee urges local authorities to take advantage of such information wherever it would help them in detecting violations of applicable local laws.

9. *Closer relations with Federal enforcement agencies.*—State and local enforcement units which deal with organized crime are invited to avail themselves fully of the research and training facilities and the accumulated data which are available in parallel Federal agencies, the Federal Bureau of Investigation, the Narcotics Bureau, and the Alcohol Tax Unit, and to reciprocate with assistance, and a steady flow of suggestions and information to these agencies.

10. *Prohibiting political contributions by racketeers.*—State legislation similar to that proposed in this report for Federal candidates prohibiting campaign contributions by racketeers might be considered to safeguard the democratic processes at the State level. Gangster participation in local campaign activities has been clearly exposed in a number of instances and remedial action therefore seems appropriate, especially in the case of candidates for offices which involve any aspect of law enforcement.

PREVIOUS SUGGESTIONS

In addition to these suggestions, the committee made seven suggestions in its Third Interim Report. In order to have all of the suggestions of the committee to local authorities available in a single place, those contained in the Third Interim Report are set forth below:

I. A committee might well be appointed in each State to make a thoroughgoing investigation of the problem of organized crime.

II. Grand jury investigations could well be instituted in every community in which wide-open gambling and racketeering conditions exist, so that local responsibility for such conditions can be fixed and determined.

III. It might be advantageous for each State to institute a survey of its law-enforcement agencies with a view toward bringing about greater cooperation between agencies, greater centralization of responsibility for lax enforcement of the criminal law, and greater efficiency.

IV. Organization of rackets and special purpose squads in each State with sufficient manpower and authority to make investigations and arrests in connection with organized criminal activities would be helpful. Such squads are particularly desirable on both the State and local levels, in connection with the suppression of narcotics traffic.

V. Each State would do well to analyze the provisions of its criminal law and its sentencing practices so as to make certain that deterrent sentences are imposed upon offenders engaged in criminal activities connected with organized crime.

VI. Each State should consider legislation making it possible to deprive any establishment of its license which permits gambling games or gambling operations on its premises.

VII. A citizen crime commission charged with the duty of observing the activities of local law-enforcement agencies and with the duty of observing and reporting on local crime conditions would be helpful in each large community.

IV. BACKGROUND OF THE COMMITTEE

This committee was created by Senate Resolution 202, Eighty-first Congress, which provided that the committee's authority was to terminate on March 31, 1951. By Senate Resolution 60, Eighty-second Congress, its life was extended to May 1, 1951, and by Senate Resolution 129, Eighty-second Congress, its life was further extended to September 1, 1951.

The members of the committee from its inception have consisted of Senator Estes Kefauver, Democrat, Tennessee; Senator Herbert R. O'Conor, Democrat, Maryland; Senator Lester C. Hunt, Democrat, Wyoming; Senator Charles W. Tobey, Republican, New Hampshire; and Senator Alexander Wiley, Republican, Wisconsin. For the period from the creation of the committee to May 1, 1951, Senator Kefauver acted as chairman, and Senator O'Conor has served as chairman since May 1, 1951.

The activities, findings, and proposals of the committee during Senator Kefauver's chairmanship are set forth in the Third Interim Report dated May 1, 1951. This final report covers the period of Senator O'Conor's chairmanship from May 1, 1951, to September 1, 1951.

V. STAFF AND ORGANIZATION

As of May 1, 1951, the committee's chief counsel and all but two of the members of its legal and investigative staff had resigned, having served for the periods for which they had committed themselves. It therefore became necessary for the committee to rebuild its staff anew. In view of the brief life available for the committee's work, it was necessary to create a staff large enough to do a highly concentrated job in a short period of time, tapering off as investigative projects were completed.

Richard G. Moser was appointed chief counsel on May 14, 1951, and Downey Rice remained as associate counsel. George H. Martin remained as director of information and James M. Hepbron was drafted by Senator O'Conor to serve on a voluntary basis as administrative assistant. A new staff of lawyers was selected consisting of the following: John P. Campbell, Edgar H. Farrell, Jr., Robert E. Frisch, Lawrence C. Goddard, Rufus G. King, Jr., R. P. S. McDonnell, Robert F. Morten, Roswell B. Perkins, Norman Polski, Wallace Reidt, and Nicholas John Stathis.

In addition, three lawyers who had served previously with the committee assisted it from time to time on a per diem basis. These were Joseph L. Nellis, Alfred M. Klein, and John J. Winberry. Another former associate counsel, George Robinson, now with the Army Air Force, also provided assistance on occasions.

Investigators were selected from various sources. Col. Elmer F. Munshower, superintendent of the Maryland State Police, loaned two detectives to the committee, namely, Murray E. Jackson and Thomas S. Smith. The New York City Police Department, through the co-operation of former commissioner (now United States judge) Thomas F. Murphy and later of Commissioner George Monaghan, loaned the committee four members of that force, namely, Detectives Terence J. Harvey, Jr., Ellsworth Monahan, and Sherman Willse; and Police-woman Georgette Carroll. The Department of Public Safety of Newark, N. J., through Commissioner James B. Keenan, made the Services of Detective Michael G. Jordan available to the committee for a short period of time.

The Narcotics Bureau of the United States Treasury Department, through the courtesy of Commissioner Harry J. Anslinger, supplied the committee with the services of Charles Siragusa, who acted as chief investigator, and it also made available from time to time the services of Agent John T. Cusack.

The Alcohol Tax Unit of the Bureau of Internal Revenue, through the courtesy of Mr. Dwight Avis, loaned to the committee two investigators, namely, Jacob E. Erkilla and Michael A. Pessolano.

From the Bureau of Internal Revenue, through the cooperation of Mr. George Schoeneman, former Commissioner of Internal Revenue, the services of Raymond L. Adams, an internal-revenue conferee, were made available to the committee. Mr. Edward J. FitzGerald, public-relations expert of the United States Public Health Service, served the committee on a part-time basis through the cooperation of Surgeon General Leonard A. Scheele.

In addition, the committee employed the following independent investigators: William D. Amis, Fred V. Bruch, Joseph R. Bucher, Francis X. Mulrean, and Robert Rehman.

Mr. Wayne C. Grover of the Bureau of Archives made available the services of Paul Soules, a systems expert, who undertook the difficult assignment of placing in readily usable form the large mass of documents, reports, and correspondence which the committee had accumulated during the previous year. The Department of Justice loaned the committee Mrs. Paul Soules, who served as assistant filing clerk.

The rebuilding of the entire staff on short notice presented an organizational problem of considerable difficulty falling mainly on the shoulders of the chief counsel who was engaged simultaneously in preparing for the committee a program of investigations and hearings to be completed within the then remaining period of 3½ months.

Deserved tribute is paid at this point to the extraordinarily devoted and efficient work performed by the members of the Crime Committee staff, ofttimes under the most trying conditions. In the very limited time available normal schedules were completely forgotten. No committee staff ever addressed itself more painstakingly to the duties at hand.

To the leadership of the committee's chief counsel, Richard G. Moser, must be attributed in great measure the excellent results achieved by the staff under his direction. It would not have been possible to have found a chief counsel better equipped by the standards of learning, keen insight into the vast complexity of questions involved, or a more conscientious devotion to the fulfillment of this important assignment. Mr. Moser did not seek this post but the committee records officially its unanimous conviction that his contribution to the public service has been exemplary and will have lasting beneficial results.

Mr. James M. Hepbron, who served on a voluntary basis as administrative assistant to the committee, brought to the investigation a wealth of valuable experience gained through his many years as the guiding figure of the Baltimore Criminal Justice Commission, and in the service of the United States Navy Intelligence. His mature judgment in the handling of administrative matters, and his assistance in the direction of various phases of the investigative work, were of the utmost value. He merits public commendation for his wholly satisfactory handling of vital segments of the committee's functions.

Downey Rice, associate counsel, who had been with the committee from the beginning of its activities, was an unerring source of competent advice. His investigative talents and his technique of examination of witnesses at hearings assisted immeasurably in the development of testimony of importance to this committee's program. Helpful in like manner was George H. Martin, director of information, who also served in an investigative capacity on many occasions throughout the committee's activities. The many other members of the legal staff, as well as the clerical assistants, were uniformly capable and helpful. They well merit our thorough commendation.

The committee also wishes to acknowledge the splendid cooperation accorded by August J. Bourbon, administrative assistant to Senator O'Conor, and also by Julius N. Cahn, executive assistant to Senator Wiley, of Wisconsin. Both of these gentlemen rendered invaluable assistance during the life of the committee and were of the utmost help in connection with the committee's report.

The committee likewise would be remiss in the extreme if it failed to acknowledge gratefully the very valuable and continuing assistance and advice given by Mr. J. Edgar Hoover, Director of the Federal Bureau of Investigation, and his assistant, Mr. Louis B. Nichols, and by Mr. Harry J. Anslinger, Commissioner of Narcotics of the Treasury Department, and his deputy, Mr. George W. Cunningham. The committee had the benefit of their wide knowledge of crime conditions throughout the country in the planning of its program and throughout its activities, and their unfailing courtesy and helpfulness contributed vastly to the committee's accomplishments.

The committee also acknowledges the cooperation and able assistance furnished to it by Frank S. Hogan, district attorney of New York County, N. Y., and Miles F. McDonald, district attorney of Kings County, N. Y., and the members of their staffs.

The committee again records its deep appreciation for the great contributions made to its work by the distinguished group of lawyers and judges who constitute the American Bar Association Commission on Organized Crime of which Hon. Robert P. Patterson is chairman and Judge Morris Ploscowe is executive director.

The member telephone companies of the Bell System and the American Telephone & Telegraph Co. continued to display commendable willingness to further the causes and aims of the committee by frequent and sometimes costly research into their records, the utilization of which contributed in great measure toward the unraveling of the interstate ramifications of the rackets explored.

Thousands of communications have been received from public-spirited citizens offering encouragement and constructive suggestions. The committee takes this opportunity publicly to thank these correspondents and to acknowledge their interest and support.

The newsmen who have followed the committee's career also deserve a hearty word of thanks for their courtesy and patience. Their work, as a link between the committee and the American public, has contributed immeasurably to the achievements described in this report.

VI. PROGRAM

The committee adopted as the basic program for its new staff the following subjects:

1. Illegal narcotic drugs.
2. Crime in medium-size cities.
3. Crime in large cities.
4. Local effects of national crime investigation.
5. Introduction of corrective legislation.

The selection of places to be investigated (including cities within States represented by the five members of the committee) was a decision unanimously concurred in by the members. Similar unanimity has characterized every major decision of the committee from its inception.

A summary of the committee's objective under each of the foregoing headings is set forth below.

1. *Illegal narcotic drugs.*—From every corner of the country there came rumblings of an insidious evil beginning to eat its way into the fiber of the Nation's youth. Shocking stories were reaching the committee of young people, confused and unnerved, turning to the use of narcotic drugs, either as a form of pleasure or as an escape from psychological strains they could not master. It was obvious that these young people were wholly ignorant of the disastrous effects of narcotic addicition upon their lives and their families and that they failed to realize that narcotic addiction requires long hospitalization in a secured institution withdrawn from ordinary living. Unchecked addiction and its concomitant craving result in a life of degradation and crime. These young victims were the innocent prey of the lowest form of criminal known to society, the drug peddler.

It seemed clear to the committee that if its legislative program should be successful in driving organized gangster syndicates out of the field of gambling, these racketeers would ultimately turn to other forms of illegal business activity just as they had turned from bootlegging to monopolized gambling. Many a hoodlum has stated with pride that he had never stooped to the sale of drugs, but he said that only because gambling was a sufficiently profitable source of income. Deprived of gambling, he would have no difficulty in adjusting his resilient conscience to the sale of drugs. No better example of this can be found than the case of Waxey Gordon, once a notorious boot-legger, then a racketeer gambler, and recently arrested for drug peddling.

The evils of monopolized gambling are great. Many a family has been driven to poverty and many a child has been unnecessarily deprived of life's opportunities because his parents, tempted by a distant hope of sudden wealth but ignorant of the enormity of the odds against them, have gambled away the family's pay envelope. But these evils are nothing compared with the sorrow and tragedy to individuals and families alike resulting from drug addiction.

Accordingly, the committee undertook an intensive study of the whole field of narcotic drugs, including the following:

(i) the types of narcotic drugs;
(ii) the laws restricting their importation, sale, and use;
(iii) the cause and nature of drug addiction;
(iv) the extent of drug use by young people;
(v) the methods of illegal importation and sale; and
(vi) the possible remedies.

The results of its study are set forth under an appropriate heading in this report.

2. *Crime in medium-size cities.*—The work of the committee as described in the Third Interim Report showed the existence of organized gangster syndicates exercising monopolistic control over illegal gambling operations in most of the large cities of the country. It showed that the mobs which had their beginnings in the prosperous bootlegging combines of the prohibition era had turned from the illicit liquor traffic to the equally lucrative field of illegal gambling, often operating under corrupt official sanction.

The committee decided that its work in this field would not be complete without a study of the less conspicuous but equally important field of gangster operations in medium-size cities. It had received a flood of requests from every type of community for investigation of local crime conditions. As only a small fraction of these requests could be satisfied in the short time available and in any event only those presenting interstate aspects, the committee decided to select a few medium-size cities as samples. Those selected were the resort town of Atlantic City, N. J.; the suburban towns across the river from Cincinnati, namely Newport and Covington, Ky.; the mining town of Scranton, Pa.; and the industrial city of Reading, Pa.

These cities were selected not because they are considered to be more crime ridden than other communities of their size but because they seemed to be representative samples of many other communities throughout the country and their comparative proximity to Washington made investigation more feasible in the light of the shortness of time and limited funds at the committee's disposal.

The committee's objective was to ascertain whether there exists in medium-size cities the same pattern of gambling operations as was found in the large cities.

A detailed description of the committee's activities with respect to each of these communities appears further on in this report.

3. *Unfinished investigation of large cities.*—At the conclusion of the committee's hearings in March, there remained a certain amount of unfinished business. In New York, Irving Sherman, a close friend of Ambassador William O'Dwyer, had eluded the committee's search.

The New York story was not considered complete without his testimony. Abner Zwillman, former bootlegger and underworld character of substantial importance, who had avoided appearance before the committee in March until the last minute, had testified at that time, but because of the pressure of time the whole story had not been told. Further investigation of his background, connections, and influence was considered desirable.

In Miami, Sheriff James Sullivan, who had been removed from office as the result of the charges made against him by witnesses appearing before the committee, had been reinstated. This called for further investigation of the Florida criminal picture. Seven witnesses from Chicago and Cleveland who had been arrested pursuant to Senate warrants, had not been heard.

Baltimore, Md., hub of one of the great horse-racing centers of the world, was one large city which had not been investigated, but which seemed to require study in view of its proximity to Washington, D. C., and in view of the committee's previous emphasis on the Continental News Service which has an important distributing outlet in that city. The committee decided to include in its program not only Baltimore but also Anne Arundel County and Prince Georges County of Maryland.

A summary of the results of these projects is set forth later in this report.

4. *Local effects of national crime investigation.*—It is apparent from a review of the huge mass of correspondence received by the committee that the publicity given to its hearings had profound effect upon law enforcement throughout the country. Everywhere people were rising up to demand that police and prosecutors exert greater vigilance in tracking down and convicting the criminals who thrive under the protective umbrella of official corruption. There arose a national awareness of the fact that gambling, although perhaps relatively harmless when conducted on an individual basis, could become, in the hands of monopolistic gangster syndicates operating across State lines, a cause of general breakdown in law enforcement leading not only to laxity in all branches of crime prevention but also to a decline in the quality and integrity of local government.

It was also apparent that public interest in law enforcement would continue only so long as a spotlight, such as is created by the activities of this committee, was directed at the problem. When the committee goes out of existence, there is serious danger that public complacency and indifference will take the place of the present state of vigilance. Obviously, local governments cannot be expected to turn the spotlight on themselves; the pressure must come from an outside force that is not subject to improper local influences.

In some cities the problem has been approached by establishment of crime commissions privately operated and financed. In others, existing civic organizations have attempted to place the pressure of vigilance upon public officials.

The committee felt that it should give attention to a study of this problem with a view to arriving at a solution that would be helpful from a long-range standpoint. This report sets forth a description of the Nation-wide effects of the committee's work and its studies regarding the possibility of avoiding a return to a state of public apathy toward law enforcement.

5. *Enactment of corrective legislation.*—The committee considered one of its major responsibilities to be the preparation and introduction of legislation in line with the proposals contained in its Third Interim Report, as well as such additional legislation as its further investigative work might indicate to be desirable. In spite of the heavy schedule of the Eighty-second Congress, the committee decided to proceed with its legislative program and to press for its enactment. Its progress in this regard is reported below.

VII. THE FINDINGS OF THE COMMITTEE

A. PRACTICAL RESULTS OF COMMITTEE'S WORK

The basic function of this committee was to study the interstate aspects of organized crime. However, its activities had the practical effect of turning a high-powered searchlight, not only on interstate crime conditions but also its byproduct, local crime conditions all over the Nation.

Through the medium of television, the citizens of the country for the first time had it driven home to them with dramatic and startling impact that top-ranking hoodlums and underworld leaders were in their midst and were not story-book characters.

Some controversy has arisen by reason of the committee's decision to permit televising of some of its hearings but it is undeniable that this modern medium of communication was a particularly potent factor in arousing the public from its apathy. The result has been an overwhelming demand for reform in the entire field of law enforcement.

Prosecutors and police have been rigorously prodded in areas where laxity in law enforcement had become an accepted thing. In other sectors where vigilance already had been exercised by prosecuting and policing agencies, still tighter measures were invoked against the lawbreakers.

Underworld figures who had been regarded as immune from prosecution have found it expedient to take long vacations from their usual sinister activities. Not a few of them have been impelled to take indefinite holidays in places far removed from their usual haunts.

The public reaction to exposure of the evils to which the committee devoted its attention has been exceedingly healthy.

In its Third Interim Report the committee set forth a series of seven suggestions to State and local authorities designed to promote improvement in local law-enforcement conditions. The reaction to these suggestions has been very encouraging and the committee is tremendously heartened by the splendid display of interest on the part of State and local authorities in countless areas from coast to coast.

Although the committee has found that crime and lawlessness are not confined to the larger cities of the United States, it is an inescapable fact that the larger cities are considered to be the underworld strongholds. It has been gratifying to the committee to note that in practically every State in the country where there is a city with a population in excess of 500,000, positive action has been taken along the lines suggested by the committee.

Privately constituted crime commissions have either been organized or revitalized in a vast number of communities and in those sections where such commissions have not been formed, similar activities are being undertaken by civic organizations having the same broad objective.

The American Bar Association Commission on Organized Crime will submit its report to the American Bar Association at its annual meeting in September. Its work and recommendations have already been of great assistance to the committee and to local groups and legislatures. Its report will be awaited with great interest. In the field of uniform laws and other efforts to combat crime particularly at the local level, this commission can continue to be of substantial assistance. The committee hopes greatly that it will be continued as a permanent commission of the American Bar Association.

Grand jury activity has attained a new vigor probably unknown heretofore on such a wide scale. Indictments are pouring forth in ever-increasing numbers as illicit enterprises and corruption receive closer scrutiny.

Formation of special racket squads has been reported on all levels, Federal, State, and local. The Bureau of Internal Revenue has swung into concentrated action with racket squads operating across the Nation and reports of commendable progress in investigations of tax evasion by gangsters and racketeers have already been noted.

Crime legislation received special attention in nearly every State legislature which held 1951 sessions. Eleven States have taken steps to tighten their narcotics laws; eight have imposed new controls on horse racing and other sports events; five have introduced new bookmaking laws. Ten States have revised their laws to give better control of gambling, and one, Iowa, has put into effect the Wisconsin-Minnesota type of restriction (providing for cancellation of all licenses for any public premise where gambling is allowed), which the committee specifically urged in its Third Interim Report.

Four legislatures have provided new plans for assuring better centralized control of local law enforcement; three have tightened and improved grand jury procedures. The uniform laws drafted in the 1930's to give better control over interstate activities received new impetus, and were the subject of legislative action in nine States. North Carolina and Texas, as the forty-seventh and forty-eighth States to ratify the Interstate Probation and Parole Compact, extended that excellent measure throughout the United States. Nearly a dozen States took steps to create special legislative or executive agencies to study crime problems.

In California a study committee on organized crime has been authorized by the Governor and the legislature and is scheduled to take action within a short time. Wholesome results of grand jury investigations in southern California have been high lighted by one grand jury report in Los Angeles which named 60 persons as defendants in connection with a $7,000,000 bookmaking operation.

Suspected violations of California's State income-tax laws are being given close study and demands have been forthcoming for increased penalties for narcotics violations.

Mickey Cohen, the notorious west coast hoodlum, has been convicted of income-tax evasion and has been sentenced to 5 years in prison and fined $10,000. The committee, during its California hearings, spent considerable time in an inquiry into his activities.

As a result of the committee's spotlighting of conditions in New York State, Governor Thomas E. Dewey named a five-man crime commission that has been active for months. Saratoga, to which this committee devoted considerable attention during its New York hearings in March, is the scene of a protracted investigation which already has produced some indictments and the resignation of the sheriff.

In New York City a crime commission organized under the chairmanship of Mr. Spruelle Braden, formerly Ambassador to Argentina, also is actively functioning. The attorney general of New York, like this committee, has been making a lengthy investigation of the narcotics evil and James J. Moran, close friend of former Mayor William O'Dwyer, was compelled to resign his lifetime position as water commissioner to which O'Dwyer had appointed him, and he has been convicted of perjury in connection with his testimony before this committee. Disclosures before this committee that he had chauffeured Irving Sherman, friend of O'Dwyer and Frank Costello, from LaGuardia Airport, forced Deputy Chief Police Inspector Abraham Goldman into retirement. The police department in New York City has undergone a drastic overhauling marked by the application for retirement of 505 members of the department to avoid having to comply with a new law requiring 30 days notice of intent to retire.

In New Jersey, Joseph Doto, alias Joe Adonis, labeled by this committee as a coleader with Frank Costello of the east coast underworld, has been sent to prison, along with several of his associates. Racket squads are operating at the State level. The liquor licensing authority has the power to revoke licenses where gambling is permitted, and a padlocking law has been drafted to close such places permanently.

In New England a privately constituted crime commission with branches in several States has been organized. In Maine a 5-month secret probe financed by the Governor's office had produced 146 indictments in Cumberland County, the State's most populous areas, as of May 30, 1951. The legislature adopted a new gambling law making bookmaking, lottery, numbers, and similar offenses felonies instead of misdemeanors and providing stiffer fines and prison sentences.

In Connecticut the State police commissioner and the Governor took prompt action to prevent gamblers and racketeers driven from other States from seeking refuge in Connecticut. The Connecticut Legislature stiffened the penalties for sale of narcotics to minors, and in New Britain a big-time bookie was fined and imprisoned for 1 year.

In Delaware the legislature also took prompt action and enacted measures improving the procedure for search and seizure, increasing penalties for bookmaking and gambling, and making jail sentences mandatory for second offenses.

The legislature in Florida adopted six bills designed to deal more effectively with gambling, including more stringent regulation of the wire service. Unfortunately, one bill which would have outlawed the printing of scratch sheets, wallboards, and other detailed horse-race information, was vetoed by the Governor.

Increased law-enforcement activity was reported by the attorney general of Illinois. In that State some 1,200 slot machines were seized and destroyed by the State police and two large bookmaking establishments, one grossing more than $6,000,000 a year, were raided and closed. A withdrawal of utility transmission facilities forced 28 others out of business.

In East St. Louis, Ill., scene of widespread operations in the past, gambling was dealt a terrific blow. The police commissioner who had tolerated bad conditions in the past was soundly defeated when he sought reelection and a new sheriff was elected.

Police activity in Chicago against the gambling element has proceeded on a constant and sustained basis over a period of months and the Chicago Crime Commission has won a notable victory by persuading the legislature to pass a bill permitting grand juries to stay in session for 3 months instead of 1.

Crime committees and good government commissions have been organized in several Indiana cities and slot machines that formerly were operated openly in a number of sections have been forced into storage.

In Iowa the legislature passed a law whereby any firm convicted of operating gambling slot machines, pinball machines, or punchboards, would automatically be deprived of all of its licenses to operate any type of business.

The attorney general of Kansas has made an exhaustive survey of law-enforcement machinery in the State and the legislature made an appropriation to support the peace officers school at the University of Kansas, although it killed legislation sponsored by the attorney general which would have made slot machines, punchboards, pinball, and other such machines illegal.

Citizens groups previously organized in northern Kentucky to fight organized gambling and crime continue to be active and have made their weight felt.

In Louisiana organized gambling in Jefferson Parish has ceased to exist in accordance with the promise made to this committee by the sheriff but gambling is reported to be continuing in St. Bernard Parish. Slot machines which formerly were found in practically every kind of business establishment in Louisiana continue to remain in storage. Five contempt actions grew out of the committee's hearings in New Orleans. Although the case against "Dandy Phil" Kastel, associate of Frank Costello, has been dismissed, other contempt proceedings have been more successful. John J. Fogerty, co-owner and operator of the wire service, entered a plea of nolo contendere and was given a fine while Carlos Marcello, recognized kingpin of Louisiana racketeering, has been convicted and has received a sentence of 6 months in prison and a fine of $500. The cases against Marcello's brother, Anthony, and against Joseph Poretto still remain to be tried.

The committee's investigations into conditions in Maryland drove bookmakers and other gamblers under cover, and sale of scratch sheets and other materials used by the gambling element is reported to have become almost nonexistent. A legislative committee was authorized by the legislature to set up a committee to study crime and the State prosecutor has submitted a recommendation for a new search and seizure law. In Baltimore, the Mayor set up a special committee to combat the narcotics evil and a special narcotics squad was established in the police department. The State's attorney secured a $10,000 fund for use in narcotics cases. A Baltimore police lieutenant whose dealings with a known gambler were exposed by this committee was removed from office. There was a general intensification of law-enforcement activity throughout the city and the State.

In Michigan, the legislature restored the so-called "one-man grand jury" and there have been increased activities in narcotics law enforcements.

The attorney general of Mississippi has advised that the suggestions of the committee for action on the State level will be presented to the legislature of that State when it convenes in 1952.

Reports from Missouri indicate that crime investigations have been launched by a State senate committee and by several special grand juries. In Jasper County, a grand jury investigation led to the resignation of the prosecuting attorney and a magistrate. The State senate committee looked with favor on the suggestions of this committee for centralization of responsibility for enforcement of criminal laws and for a survey of the various State law-enforcement agencies. The Kansas City Police Department now has a racket squad whose primary duty is the enforcement of the gambling laws. In both Kansas City and St. Louis, the authorities and the crime commissions concentrated their fire on the wire service, and Pioneer News Service went out of business.

The attorney general of New Hampshire sought legislation to make prison sentences mandatory in certain types of gambling cases and backed a uniform narcotics law.

In Ohio, Governor Lausche has launched a program to strike hard at those guilty of peddling drugs to school children; and in Cincinnati, the highly favorable reaction to the exposure of organized crime has revitalized an agreement with the telephone company for removal of service where gambling operations are suspected.

Grand jury investigations have been reported in several areas in North Dakota and Oregon, and in some sections of Pennsylvania. In South Carolina, the Charleston Chamber of Commerce has decided to organize a local crime commission, and activities against organized criminal elements in Texas are worthy of considerable praise. Notable among the achievements in Texas was the conference called by the attorney general in March which was attended by district and county attorneys from all parts of the State. The legislature furnished commendable cooperation by enacting practically all of the legislation recommended by the group, which included bills outlawing possession of slot machines, punchboards, and policy games. The attorney general sought and secured injunctions against both the telegraph and telephone companies, prohibiting gambling information from being disseminated over their wires. Grand juries have been active and a crime investigating committee of the legislature has been functioning. Citizens in many parts of Texas have voluntarily begun the formation of local crime commissions.

The National Junior Chamber of Commerce at its annual meeting praised this committee for its accomplishments and adopted the study of organized crime as its major project for the ensuing year.

The committee is proud of the part it has played in helping to bring about this fine record of accomplishment on the local level, although it realizes that there still remains a great deal to be done.

B. ILLEGAL NARCOTIC DRUGS

Introduction

The illegal traffic in narcotic drugs exemplifies organized crime at its devastating worst. It represents one of the great tragedies of our times, especially when it preys upon young people who are ignorant of drug addiction not only upon themselves as individuals but also upon the family and society as a whole.

Addiction resulting from an ignorant or depraved attempt to obtain temporary pleasure is an inexcusable tragedy. Drug addiction is a form of contagious disease with a high recurrence. Anyone who starts abusing a drug for whatever reason is immediately exposed to a serious danger of becoming addicted. Addiction occurs in a very short time and once it occurs there is no going back. The addict's whole life changes from one of usefulness and normalcy to one of suffering and degradation and in many cases, eventually to crime. One of the great constributions that could be made to the welfare of the young people of today would be to bring home to them the cold fact that narcotic drugs are to be avoided like the plague.

Against this backdrop of tragedy, the picture of the dope peddler promoting drug addiction in order to create new customers is nothing short of revolting.

A parade of witnesses representing every sector of the narcotics problem came before the committee. Physicians explained the properties of drugs, the course of addiction, the clinical processes of its treatment, and the psychological after-effects. Citizens of aroused communities described alarming local situations and told of efforts to stem the evil of narcotics abuse. Heartbroken parents described the tragedies that had befallen their children through drug addiction. Enforcement agents bared the workings of the international network through which illegal drugs move and the fabulous amounts of money involved in the traffic.

The committee traveled to the Maryland House of Correction, the Woman's Prison of Maryland near Baltimore, and to the United States Public Health Service Hospital, Lexington, Ky., to hear the story first-hand from prisoners serving time for narcotics violations and from patients under treatment for addiction. The professional nonaddict peddlers told of giving "for free" enough heroin to get new customers "hooked," i. e., dependent on drugs; and of employing addicts as "testers" to judge the quality of the merchandise at the wholesale level. Nervous teen-agers, still jittery following withdrawal of narcotics, spoke haltingly of the confusion and the futile misery of the drug habit. Some had suffered enough for a dozen lives, yet they were not old enough to vote.

From the testimony of these witnesses and from other data submitted for study, the committee formulated the observations that comprise the body of this report on the illegal narcotics market and the extensive many-sided problems it presents.

(a) The drugs of addiction

The drugs usually abused to the point of addiction are grouped as stimulants and depressants, according to the effects they produce on the behavior of the user.

Of the stimulants, the most common and most dangerous is cocaine, derived from the leaves of the coca plant growing in South America and Java. In large doses, cocaine incites a transient elation, followed by extreme nervous discomfort, irritability, and paranoid delusions that make the user a menace to those around him. Among the other stimulant drugs are benzedrine, dexedrine, and mescaline, a drug used by the Indians in the southwestern United States to "help them see God."

The depressants, on the other hand, relieve tension and nervous disturbance, producing a false and temporary feeling of well-being. They are used medically as pain relievers (called "analgesics") and many of them are necessary and extremely valuable for this purpose. They include opium and its derivatives such as morphine, heroin, dilaudid, codein, and metapon, to mention a few. They also include synthetic pain relievers such as demerol, methadon, and the new levo-iso-methadon. The depressants also include alcohol and marijuana. The bromides and barbiturates are classed as hypnotic drugs.

Frequently addicts take a depressant and a stimulant simultaneously, the depressant serving as an antidote for the dangerous and unpleasant effects of the stimulant. Known as a "speedball," one of these concoctions is a mixture of heroin and cocaine. The former relieves tension and anxiety; the latter furnishes the concurrent feeling of well-being and subdues fatigue. Some addicts engage in the viciously dangerous practice of spending long hours balancing the exciting effects of the cocaine with the restful euphoria of the heroin.

According to Federal law, the habit-forming drugs, those for which the Government provides addiction treatment facilities, are cocaine, coca leaves, codein, dicodid, hycodan, dilaudid, heroin, marijuana, laudanum, demerol, isonipecaine, methadon, metapon, morphine, opium, pantopon, paregoric, mescaline, and other drugs that may be designated by the President. These statutes do not encompass alcohol, the barbiturates, or the bromides.

(b) Laws relating to narcotic drugs

Recognizing the profound seriousness of the rapidly growing drug-addiction problem, Congress passed in 1914 the first comprehensive Federal narcotics law—the Harrison Act. Under the provisions of this law, commerce in medicinal and other legitimate narcotics was legalized and controlled under the Federal taxing power. By the same mechanism, illicit traffic in opium and its derivatives and in the coca leaf and its derivatives (cocaine) was outlawed.

The Miller-Jones Act, passed in 1922, established a system of import and export permits and restricted the import of raw narcotic material to medical needs. By an amendment adopted in 1924 the dangerous and currently popular heroin was forbidden entrance to this country as was also opium for use in manufacturing heroin.

The Opium Poppy Act of 1942 insures against the growing of opium poppies in the United States.

Controls on the traffic in marijuana were imposed by the Marijuana Tax Act of August 2, 1937. It provides an occupational tax on all persons legally permitted to produce, sell or deal in marijuana. There is also a heavy transfer levy when unauthorized individuals are involved in a marijuana transaction.

On the state and municipal levels, uniform laws and ordinances help to control the traffic in narcotics within their jurisdictions. Forty-two states have enacted the Uniform Narcotic Drug Act and two others have the equivalent. The only states which do not have restrictive legislation are Kansas, Massachusetts, New Hampshire and Washington. Recent enactments in Illinois and New York have stiffened the penalties for sales to minors.

(c) Cause and nature of addiction

The crux of the narcotics problem lies not in the drugs themselves but in the persons who abuse them. Addiction involves taking drugs in excessive quantities.

Some individuals by reason of their physical and psychological make-up can become addicted to drugs more easily than others. Persons easily addicted are referred to as "addiction prone." There are some individuals who are relatively immune to addiction. The difficulty is that no one knows for certain whether he is addiction prone until after he has become addicted and then it is too late.

The most a victim can expect from treatment is to be taken off the drug and furnished psychological aid to remain off it. Medicines given during treatment do no more than relieve the tortures of withdrawal. No one, however strong his psychological framework, should run the risk of ruining his life and the lives of his friends and family by using any narcotic drug except under the strictest medical control. Prescribed in proper amounts, narcotic drugs are important aid in the practice of medicine and serve the humanitarian purpose of helping to alleviate the pain of the suffering. They should not be denied those who need them merely because of their addicting qualities. Until a nonaddicting pain reliever is discovered, physicians must use narcotics. Those who divert the stream of legitimate narcotics for their own selfish gain, actually rob the sick and the injured.

Although the therapeutic use of opium traces back some 6,000 years, nonmedical addiction dates only to the latter part of the nineteenth century when the "social use" of opium for its euphoric effect became known in India and China. Many of the cure-all patent medicines so popular in the United States at the turn of the century had opium as their principal ingredient. These preparations were later banned from public sale by the Federal narcotics control legislation.

Most habitual users of narcotics have psychoneuroses and personality disorders of varying degree, ranging from those of the criminal psychopath to the immature thrill seeker who craves extraordinary excitement. Addiction prones experience difficulty adapting themselves to the ordinary pressures and tensions of living. They may be extremely dependent or unusually hostile, incapable of entering into normal human relationships. In their discomfort, they frequently suffer obscure symptoms of indeterminable origin.

The average human being has normal defenses with which to cope with life's disappointments, frustrations, and conflict. But the potential addict lacks this natural ability to battle successfully against emotional problems and the anxieties they engender. If he looks to narcotics to ease his pain, subdue his disturbance, and escape his problems, he may find in drugs the substitute for his weak defenses. The feeling that "all is well" gives him a paper crutch of power and security and he is on the way to a heavy drug habit that only a life of crime can maintain. This is the weak, irresponsible creature on whom the parasitic illicit narcotic trader feeds and grows rich.

The course of addiction is easily illustrated by the testimony of individuals who were addicted to heroin. As one 17-year-old boy described it, he was associating with boys older than he who were using drugs. They urged him to try it, telling him he would get a kick out of it. They assured him he would not become "hooked" if he merely "sniffed" or "snorted" it. He tried snorting and did not like it. Later he tried again and did not mind it so much. Then the older boys explained to him that it was cheaper to take heroin in the veins because the effect was greater with a smaller quantity. So he tried "mainlining," that is, shooting the drug directly into his veins with a hypodermic needle. He tried this a few times and one morning he awoke feeling very sick. He took a shot and felt well again. From then on he was "hooked."

The boy had developed a physical dependency on the drug and had to keep taking it in ever increasing quantities to avoid being sick. He no longer took it for pleasure, he had to have it. He became irregular and inefficient at his job and finally had to quit. Finding drugs became a full-time job. For money, he borrowed, stole and forged Government checks. He said there was nothing he would not have done for drugs. He ended up in a Federal prison where he was taken off the drug and allowed to go through the painful suffering of withdrawal.

This is not an isolated case. The same story is told by hundreds of addicts who blame their predicament on bad company and inadequate surroundings. Without exception, they say that the addict's life is one of perpetual misery and if they had realized in advance what they were headed for, they would have avoided drugs like a dangerous disease.

(d) Use of drugs by young people

In the past 24 months, America has been jolted to its foundations by the discovery that youngsters, especially in the larger cities, are using narcotic drugs, many to the point of addiction. New York, Chicago, Baltimore, and Washington, D. C., saw big increases in the number of under-age drug users coming to the attention of the police. In a large number of cases, these young people were engaging in crime for the sole purpose of supporting their drug habit.

The United States Public Health Service Hospital at Lexington, Ky., the larger of the two Federal hospitals devoted chiefly to treating addicts, compared the year 1946 when patients below the age of 21 represented 3 percent of the patients in the hospital, with the early part of 1951 when, with a higher total patient count, the proportion of young patients had climbed to 18 percent. Nearly three-quarters of these youngsters had no record of criminality or delinquency prior to addiction. Testimony from an experienced social worker on the situation in New York City revealed that the narcotics problem cuts across all social and economic lines. A young negro addict from Chicago said, "There is no segregation in the use of dope."

The committee interviewed many of these youngsters, among them a 19-year-old boy who quit school, throwing away a full scholarship in an eastern university, because of narcotics. To support his habit, he stole Government pension checks. A midwestern college freshman said he dropped out in the middle of his first semester and shortly thereafter was arrested for stealing money from the mails, all because of dope. Another collegian revealed that he and his friends grew marijuana in a yard and dried it in the oven of their apartment before rolling it into cigarettes.   Girls in their late teens with narcotic addiction lasting several years, admitted that they had resorted to prostitution rather than endure the horror of going without drugs.

While many of these boys and girls do not evidence the character and personality disorders of the veteran addict, they have proven themselves susceptible to drugs, at least enough to continue taking narcotics to the point of becoming "hooked."   Representing the carefree, thrill-seeking youth, they told the committee that they started on narcotics or "junk" as they sometimes call it, out of curiosity, because their friends were doing it and because they didn't want to be considered "square" or unsophisticated.

Youngsters place great value on "belonging" in their group.   They resent the rejection that would go with being labeled "chicken" by their associates in the playground, ice-cream parlor, or on the street corner.   So they tend to follow the leader who unfortunately turns out to be a hoodlum or emotionally twisted "bebopper", bent on introducing them to the pseudo pleasures of smoking marijuana and shooting heroin.

Mr. James R. Dumpson, consultant on correction and deliquency of New York's welfare council, described the situation in east Harlem as follows:

Social workers dealing with gangs all report that the rate of marijuana usage is at least 50 percent with this being a very conservative figure in their estimation.   These include youths 13 years of age, and you have many indications that the age of this type of addiction is lowering steadily.   In fact, one minister reported that several 9-year-old boys had been approached by peddlers attempting to have them take the drug   *   *   *.

In a social athletic club in one of the blocks with a membership of about 50 boys, at least 18 to 20 were known to be regular heroin users.

Dr. Lois Higgins, director of the crime prevention bureau in Chicago, cited statistics on the growth of the narcotic problem in her home city.   In 1948, 136 out of 738 arrests were under 21.   The following year, under-age persons accounted for 203 of 2,230 narcotic arrests.   Of the total of 4,437 narcotic arrests in 1950, 1,107 were under 21.   And for the period January 1 to late June 1951, Dr. Higgins gave a figure of 989 under-age narcotic arrests.

The path to addiction ran practically the same throughout the testimony taken from young addicts.   In their own vernacular, Mr. Dumpson put it this way: "They say they go from sneaky Pete to pot to horse to banging."   In ordinary language, this describes the popular sequence—drinking wine, smoking "reefers" or marijuana cigarettes (sometimes starting at the age of 13 or 14) then sniffing or "snorting" heroin, finally injecting it directly into the vein.

Cutting across the thousands of words of testimony, the committee concludes that these youngsters are mildly neurotic.   Addiction among our youth is a problem the seriousness of which cannot be underestimated especially in the world's present state of instability.   Many adolescents are mildly neurotic and therefore somewhat addiction prone.   Under present conditions, even post adolescent young people are under unnatural strain.   Boys of draft age and the friends who surround them feel great uncertainty as to what the future holds for them.   Their lives are engulfed in an atmosphere of crisis.

Much was said in the testimony as to the role of the parents.   The love and affection of intelligent parents does much to give a child the feeling of security that will keep him away from drugs.   Where a sense of security cannot be attained, supervision of the child's activities and immediate attention to any evidence of drug use is essential.

Medical authorities believe that most of the young people who have been exposed to drugs are sufficiently intelligent to be capable of complete rehabilitation if the problem is tackled promptly. Without exception the addicts who testified stressed the belief that if they had known the horrors of drug addiction, the suffering, the personal degradation and the crime, to say nothing of the discomfort and bewildering perplexity of treatment for addiction, they never would have played with drugs. They have learned that "It can't happen to me" is a cruel hoax.

The committee believes that drug addiction should be treated as a contagious disease and that its sufferers should be treated as patients, not as criminals. It also believes that like any disease it can be attacked with greater vigor if brought out in the open and discussed in a forthright manner. If by education the young people of the Nation can be made aware of the true character of narcotic drugs and the dangers of addiction, they will become strong fighters in the campaign against the evil.

(e) Methods of illegal importation and sale

The narcotic drugs lend themselves conveniently to illicit traffic. A fortune in narcotics can be carried in one pocket. Easy to handle, transport, and conceal, drugs slip quickly through the underworld's serpentine labyrinth, making it extremely difficult for enforcement officers to track down the carriers.

Narcotics have a ready market of insatiable consumers who keep coming back for more, often several times a day. The amount an addict will use depends solely on the amount he can get. He will "shoot" all he has available.

Narcotics move in a seller's market where the customer is always wrong. Dope peddlers charge all the money in the buyer's pocket, keeping him financially, as well as physically, enslaved. Witnesses told the committee how in Baltimore the identical quality and quantity of heroin sold for three times the amount charged in Washington. Drug sellers swindle their customers, adulterating the merchandise to almost nothing, heedless of the suffering they inflict on their victims. An addict who "squeals" to the authorities is likely to get a "hot shot" (a highly concentrated or poisoned dosage) the next time he comes to the peddler for his drug. The helpless addict struggles along from day to day a captive of the greedy criminals who have him hopelessly trapped.

Most American addicts, including practically all of the younger group, use heroin, the drug banned by law from the United States since 1924. Since heroin is the drug peddled on street corners through organized crime syndicates, its traffic presents the most serious aspect of the narcotic problem. Morphine and the opiate synthetics are more commonly diverted from legitimate channels, often by forging prescriptions and stealing from drugstores. The committee heard several addicted nurses and pharmacists tell how they obtained medicinal drugs in this manner.

Heroin is a fine white powder legitimately manufactured for medical use in several countries including Italy, Turkey, and China. However, through illegal dealings, a substantial part of this legal output, after it leaves the factory, finds its way to the United States, concealed on the persons and in the luggage of crewmen and passengers coming in from abroad.

In Italy, a kilogram (a fraction over 2 pounds) of heroin sells on the illicit market for from $1,000 to $1,500. Transported overseas and landed safely in the United States, its value leaps to $6,000 to $10,000. Once inside this country, it is divided and diluted with milk sugar, traveling many miles and the price doubling each time it changes hands. As the price soars the quality dwindles, so that the final concoction as it reaches the hands of the addict in capsule form consists of not over 2 percent pure heroin. It is handled under the crudest of conditions with no attention being given to cleanliness or antisepsis and when the addict uses it, he has no idea how much poison, contamination, or germ matter he is shooting into his blood stream.

More than a million of these capsules are made from a kilo. Thus, along the route from the back door of the factory in Italy to addicts' blood, the illicit heroin pays a dividend of at least $1,000 for every dollar invested.

Some peddlers deal in 1-ounce quantities which they can buy for as little as $50 to $100 for an ounce, depending on how good their "connection" is. On American soil, this ounce is worth over $200 and by the time it is watered down and parceled out to other peddlers, it may bring as much as $5,000.

Experienced enforcement officers believe that the present influx of heroin from abroad is managed by the Mafia with Charles "Lucky" Luciano, notorious gangster, vice king, and racketeer, deported convict, now resident in Italy, as the operating head. His chief lieutenant is believed to be an Italian resident named Joseph Pici and one of his principal contacts in the United States is believed to be Joseph Biondo, former small-time New York politician who visited Luciano a few months ago and is now a fugitive.

World-wide in scope, the Mafia is believed to derive the major source of its income from the distribution and smuggling of narcotics. An undercover agent of the Treasury Department's Bureau of Narcotics testified at length before the committee just after his return from an extended assignment in Italy. Asked whether Luciano is the kingpin of the Mafia, the agent responded that if "Lucky" isn't the kingpin, "he is one of the royal family," that he receives large sums of money from American gangsters and that he certainly wields influence in Mafia policy matters. To the question "Is Lucky Luciano the kingpin of the narcotics traffic in the United States?"— he answered, "The United States and Italy." The agent further revealed .that in Mafia circles, Luciano enjoys the honorable title "Don," a symbol of the respect and esteem the membership holds for him.

In sworn statements made by Luciano to the Italian police, he claims to be a poor man. He says he brought with him from America about $22,500 and since coming to Italy he has received from time to time other sums of money averaging a few thousands of dollars each as gifts from old friends in the United States. Since his present residence in Italy, which dates from 1947, Luciano was interested in a pastry shop in Palermo, but he claims that after 2½ years the business failed and he lost 7,500,000 lire. He says he has no other commercial activities in Italy, although he plays the horses frequently. He said, "All of the money which I brought to Italy and that which I have received subsequently from my friends in America, I have spent—about 500,000 lire a month, I expect, which comes from the United States and not from activities in Italy, because all of the business affairs I have tried to conduct in Italy have come to a bad end."

In Italy, Luciano is close to Nicolai Gentile, well known in New York rackets, who while under indictment for a narcotics charge, jumped bail and fled to Italy in the early 1940's. Gentile also enjoys the Mafia title of "Don". Joseph Pici, Luciano's narcotics lieutenant, is currently a codefendant with Luciano in a narcotics investigation being conducted by the Italian Government. Pici previously had lived in the United States, but was deported on a white slave conviction. Several years ago, he smuggled himself into the United States, bringing with him 15 kilos of heroin which he delivered to the Kansas City Mafia organization. Pici's current whereabouts are unknown.

Other deportees now in Italy who are believed to be associated with Luciano include Ralph Liguori and Gaetano Chiofalo, alias Charlie Young.

A narcotics agent testifying before the committee described a heroin transaction and the role played in it by the Mafia and Luciano's henchmen. He told of 28-year-old Frank Callace of the One Hundred Seventh Street mob in New York, sent to Italy in April of 1951 to pick up some heroin. Callace first contacted his uncle of the same name who had previously fled the United States because he was wanted by the FBI. The uncle and nephew, both of whom are considered members of the Mafia, met in Palermo and proceeded to Milan where they met in a hotel to talk quantity and price of heroin. They checked out of the hotel shortly after returning to Palermo. Then they received a telephone call from Pici, Luciano's lieutenant, and backtracked to Milan. The younger Callace was arrested in the Rome airport en route to Palermo with a suitcase containing three kilos of heroin. The police had been tipped off by an anonymous telephone call.

Internal circulation.—Mystery and secrecy enshrouds the movement of illegal narcotics within the United States. The innocent looking white powder travels hundreds of miles from dockside to consumer, usually carried by hand.

Small peddlers make periodic trips to their "connections" (mostly in other localities) buying just an ounce or two at a time in order not to keep a supply on hand. One witness, a very small-time peddler, told of making evening calls on his "connection" in another city. After the money passed, the "connection" left and would not return until the following morning with the order. So, in this case, the deal included a night's lodging.

On the high level, the "big shot" of course never enters the picture visibly, except perhaps to be seen talking to his boys. He makes no deliveries and accepts no money direct from a purchaser. He merely finances the deal, reaping the lion's share of the profits. The assistants to the big shot after seeing the customer's money and assuring themselves of his intent to buy, usually go by air to the source (usually in New York) and bring back enough stock to fill the order. Seldom are large stores cached in the city from which distribution is being made.

A narcotics agent related to the committee a fascinating story of undercover work in 1950. Posing as a peddler, he helped track down several top operators of a major narcotics syndicate of which San Antonio, Detroit, Chicago, and New York were the key cities. The agent gained the confidence of a peddler named Robert Kimball, the Texas link of the chain. Following arrest for illegal sale of narcotics, Kimball expressed willingness to cooperate with the Narcotics Bureau in bringing his associates to justice. He and the agent purported to become partners.

Kimball's practice had been to import marijuana from Mexico and sell it to connections in Detroit, Chicago, and New York, who in turn supplied him with heroin for outlets in Fort Worth, Dallas, Galveston, New Orleans, San Diego, Hollywood, and San Francisco. In an effort to buy a kilo, Kimball and the agent made nearly a dozen trips to the syndicate's headquarter cities, making ounce purchases along the way. The big shipment eluded them for weeks, but meanwhile they met other eager buyers with pipelines to Cleveland, Topeka, Kansas City. In the course of their travels, they were offered an "in" to an illegal gold transaction, but the profit wasn't big enough for them to accept. Early in December, Kimball was murdered in Texas by a former night club partner. From that point, the agent carried on alone, acting as the sole Texas contact for the syndicate. Late in December in a New York hotel room, he succeeded in arresting Anthony Pisciotta of the high echelon of the syndicate as Pisciotta was making delivery of two kilos of heroin. A half dozen other members were arrested simultaneously. The "master mind" of the syndicate is still free and one of the other leaders known as "Fat Sam" escaped to Florida where he is believed to be in hiding now.

Since the time of that testimony, newspapers all over the country have been filled with stories of further major arrests connecting the illegal dope trade with organized crime, national and international.

The July 28 papers featured the breaking up of a $30,000,000 combination narcotics and counterfeiting ring. This group made and sold bogus American currency for good money with which they bought illegal drugs. A tie-up between this group on one side and the Mafia-Luciano mob and a French underworld mob on the other, is suspected. It is believed that 50 pounds of pure heroin were smuggled into the United States each month by agents of the ring.

On August 1, 1951, narcotics agents and the New York City police closed in on Irving Wexler, more familiarly known as Waxey Gordon, former beer baron and wartime black marketeer, now turned dope dealer. The committee had known of this case but had stayed away from it to give the Narcotics Bureau a free hand. Waxey was caught with 2 pounds of heroin reportedly destined for coast-to-coast trade. It is believed that his market centered on the west coast and that he was in the process of expanding eastward. Whether his market linked with or worked in competition to the Luciano enterprises is not known to the committee.

The press painted a dramatic picture of the underworld big shot, now a fourth offender, kneeling on a sidewalk of New York, begging the arresting officer, "Please kill me, shoot me. I'm an old man and I'm through. Don't take me in for junk. * * *" Meanwhile, his minions offered the policemen $25,000 to let "Pop" go.   Gordon and his associates were held for a total of $500,000 bail.

On August 4, 1951, the story of an international combine employing couriers to carry narcotics of Italian origin on airflights from New York to Canada, broke with the arrest of five men carrying $20,000 worth of heroin.   Thought to be the biggest narcotics syndicate in Canadian history, this group is allegedly linked with the international cartel headed by Luciano.

It is of interest to observe that only two or three of the characters involved in all of these dope empires, were themselves addicts.

(f) Possible remedies

The committee has come to the conclusion that illegal narcotic drugs constitute an evil of great magnitude.   The problem calls for vigorous and effective action at all levels of our social and governmental system.

The problem should be attacked from many different angles with the hope that the combined effect will be to stop the spread of illegal drug use and perhaps eventually reduce it to controllable proportions. The committee suggests the following approaches:

(i) *Sociological approach.*—The deep-seated sense of personal insecurity which causes an individual to be addiction-prone may be the result of any one or more of a number of complex forces.   Personal tragedy, unidentified childhood frustrations, family discord, poverty, loss of employment, and similar factors contribute to this.   Perhaps the congenital character of the individual's nervous system is as important a factor as any.   The addict seldom feels that he is to blame for his predicament and in large measure he is right.   His affliction is caused by forces he cannot understand or control.   He is sick and should be treated as such.

Obviously any action which has the effect of improving living conditions, strengthening the home environment and generally contributing to the security of the individual will help eliminate the causes of drug addiction.

(ii) *Education.*—The committee does not subscribe to the theory that public discussion of drug addiction should be avoided to protect nonaddicts from being tempted to try drugs.   As in the case of venereal diseases, the attack upon which has been greatly enhanced by public knowledge, the committee believes that much will be gained by a carefully devised program of education designed to make the people of the Nation aware of the true facts regarding the excessive use of narcotic drugs.

Most of the objection to public discussion is based upon a danger which the committee believes can be avoided in a well-conceived educational program.   There is no doubt that a drug user before he is actually "hooked" experiences a temporary pleasurable sensation and it is this sensation that might tempt others to try it.   Improper emphasis on this sensation should be avoided and the true facts with regard to it should be brought out.

Actually, the sensation is extremely short-lived and is ordinarily followed by addiction within a period of from 10 days to 3 weeks of repeated use.   Once addiction sets in, the victim cannot go back and from then on he takes the drug not for pleasure but for the sole purpose of avoiding the dread sickness caused by his physical need for the drug.

The committee believes that education should start in the schools and social organizations of the country and should be carried from there to the home. The basic responsibility for such a program rests on the shoulders of the country's educational leaders who should carry it forward at the local level.

(iii) *Treatment facilities.*—Medical science has not yet found a specific for the cure for drug addiction. Much has been accomplished in this direction at the United States Public Health Service Hospitals at Lexington, Ky., and Fort Worth, Tex., but the only available treatment is to take the addict gradually off the drug and thereafter, through psychiatric treatment, to attempt to help him overcome the deep-seated weaknesses that contributed to his illness.

The Lexington and Fort Worth hospitals are minimum-secured institutions with modern hospital facilities to treat narcotic addiction and any other chronic or addict condition from which the patients may be suffering. Although these hospitals were established to receive Federal prisoners who are also addicted to drugs, they also admit nonprisoner addicts as voluntary patients. There are no separate accommodations for prisoner and nonprisoner patients. These hospitals are excellently managed under the supervision of Dr. Victor H. Vogel and Dr. Richard B. Holt, medical officers in charge at Lexington and Fort Worth, respectively.

Facilities for the treatment of addiction at State and community levels are extremely limited. The establishment of local clinical resources, at least for putting new drug users under immediate treatment, may preclude the tragedy of addiction in many cases.

Perhaps the greatest weakness in the field of treatment lies in the lack of facilities for following up patients after they leave the hospital.

Actual rehabilitation of the addict covers a span of years, not merely the 4 to 6 months spent in the controlled hospital environment. Supervision of the patient is necessary for a long period beyond the direct treatment phase. It is wasteful to spend millions of dollars each year caring for these addicts if they are to go back among people who are abusing drugs and thus be exposed to the temptation of starting again.

The United States Public Health Service has prepared and is hoping to undertake a program of local follow-up on a trial basis in New York or Chicago or both. The plan is to send teams of social workers and psychiatrists to those cities to maintain contact with former patients and assist them in using community facilities to help them rebuild their lives.

Local communities over the Nation can make real contributions toward insuring the rehabilitation of addicts—by providing adequate mental health services where they may seek and receive understanding and intelligent advice. Too often the former addict will seek the answer to his dilemma in narcotics, lacking a secure source of counsel. One worth-while utilization of community funds might consist of providing transportation for addicts to proper treatment centers.

(iv) *Increased penalties.*—Bills are now pending in Congress, two sponsored by members of this committee, proposing sharp increases in the fines and prison sentences that may be imposed for violation of the Federal narcotics laws. Efforts should be made to enact legislation along these lines.

The committee believes that casting the shadow of steep penalties over the path of the dope peddler will do much to deter him. A criminal bent upon performing an illegal act always weighs the risks against the rewards. At present the financial reward to the peddler seems to outbalance the fear of a 1- or 2-year prison term with a fair chance of having his sentence suspended.

In this connection, much can be accomplished by making judges aware of the seriousness of the crime of drug peddling. A judge passing upon an individual case is often tempted to be lenient, but if he appreciates the true relationship between the case before him and the over-all aspects of the drug evil, he will be more likely to mete out the punishment that is deserved.

(v) *Increased enforcement.*—Old-time addicts who have spent their lives struggling to escape from the drug habit say that the best solution to the problem is to kill the source of supply. They say that as long as the drug is available to them, they are not able to resist it.

The Narcotics Bureau of the Treasury Department has a staff of 180 skillful agents serving long hours in what is probably the most hazardous type of enforcement work. Under present conditions this number of men is discouragingly small. Mr. Harry J. Anslinger, head of the Bureau, is convinced that with twice the force he could stamp out the peddling of narcotic drugs. The committee believes he is right.

(vi) *Port and border control.*—The committee was impressed with the futility of attempting to stop the flow of heroin through customs search at the borders. The drug is so easy to conceal that finding it on the person of a passenger or sailor or in the many hiding places aboard ship is virtually impossible. The type of search that is required to find hidden drugs is often obnoxious to the person being searched and, even when done on a sampling basis, it gives rise to some resentment.

However, the committee feels that the present procedures of the Customs Bureau in this regard should be continued as a deterrent to drug smuggling.

It appears that one of the principal methods of smuggling heroin into the country is on the persons of sailors, especially those on ships of foreign registry. It is believed that this accounts for the present flow of drugs from abroad into the port of New York. The committee believes that customs inspection should be directed particularly at these ships and their crews, at least until the present influx has been checked.

American sailors and longshoremen for the most part belong to unions which have strict rules regarding the smuggling of drugs. A man convicted of a narcotics violation is subject to discharge from the union and the union leaders who testified before the committee said that these rules are strictly enforced. They also testified that drug smuggling is extremely repugnant to most American seamen and longshoremen and that a man known to be smuggling is likely to be forced off the job by his fellow workers.

There appears to be one step that the Coast Guard could take that would be helpful in the case of seamen. As long as a seaman has his sailing papers, it is difficult for the unions to keep him from working. If a seaman is convicted of a narcotics violation which occurred aboard ship, the Coast Guard will lift his papers. Apparently, this is not true if the violation occurred on shore.

In view of the serious character of a narcotics violation, irrespective of whether it occurs at sea or on shore, and considering the fact that seamen are believed to be an important source of importation, the committee believes that a man convicted of this crime is not fit to hold sailing papers. It believes that the Coast Guard should extend its practice in this regard to men convicted of narcotics-law violations occurring on land.

Another step that the committee believes would help in the enforcement of union rules would be for the Narcotics Bureau to inform both the appropriate national unions and the Coast Guard of all narcotic convictions involving seamen and longshoremen. In the case of the unions, this information could be passed along to the locals in the regular publications.

(vii) *Revised court procedures.*—Early in April of 1951, Chicago's chief justice of the municipal court, Edward S. Scheffler, issued an order designating a specific courtroom for the special purpose of hearing all cases in which narcotics are in any way involved. Special prosecutors were assigned to the narcotics court, the first of its kind to be created, by the State's attorney for Cook County and the corporation counsel of the city of Chicago. In addition, the Chicago Board of Health appointed a full-time psychiatrist to serve this court. There are also present a social worker and representatives of the Crime Prevention Bureau. This appears to be an experiment worth watching and studying with a view to putting similar arrangements into effect in other jurisdictions. It is a step in the direction of treating the addict as a patient rather than a criminal.

(viii) *Mexican border.*—Information has reached the committee to the effect that in towns across the Mexican border where Americans may come and go without restriction, a dangerous situation has arisen involving narcotic drugs. Many youngsters are visiting these towns for the sole purpose of obtaining drugs, including marijuana and heroin, which can be purchased on the street. Restrictions on narcotic drugs under our law are of little benefit to the citizens of border communities if their children are able and perhaps encouraged to cross freely into Mexico where the drugs are readily available.

The committee believes that the appropriate agencies of the Federal Government should study this problem with a view to finding a solution. The answer may lie in prohibiting minors to cross the border when not accompanied by their parents.

(ix) *World-wide prohibition of opium poppy growing.*—Opium, which is the raw material from which heroin, morphine, and similar drugs are manufactured, is produced in China, India, Iran, and Turkey. Experience has shown that neither the United Nations nor the nations themselves are able to control the amount of opium poppy plants grown. They grow about 40 times the amount required to satisfy medical needs of the world.

Most of the countries have been wholly cooperative, although there is some doubt as to the attitude of Communist China. When the United States representative on the Commission on Narcotic Drugs of the United Nations called attention to the large heroin manufacture in Communist China, the Russian delegate tried unsuccessfully to have his remarks stricken from the record.

Nevertheless, experience has shown that the manufacture of opiates, as distinguished from the growing of opium poppy plants, can be controlled within reasonable limits. Accordingly, a great step forward would be accomplished if the growing of these plants could be completely prohibited.

This, of course, is feasible only if there are adequate synthetic substitutes for the medicinal opiates. In this connection, the committee heard the testimony of Dr. Henry K. Beecher, of Harvard University, head of the department of anaesthesia of Massachusetts General Hospital. He told the committee that methadon and levo-isomethadon, newly developed products, are not only adequate substitutes, but in many ways superior to morphine as pain-relieving drugs. He said, "I shouldn't be worried at all if there were no morphine." Dr. Beecher said that adequate synthetic substitutes for codeine have not yet been developed but he considers codeine to be a minor problem compared with morphine.

The committee is satisfied that these synthetic substitutes make the manufacture of morphine entirely unnecessary and that nothing of importance would be lost to the medical profession or to the people of the world if the growing of opium poppy plants were wholly prohibited in every country.

The very existence of opium appears to be the root of one of the greatest evils known to man and the committee strongly urges the Department of State and the United States delegates to the Commission on Narcotics of the United Nations to make strenuous efforts to bring about a world-wide prohibition against the growing of the plant from which opium is extracted.

C. CRIME IN MEDIUM-SIZE CITIES
Introduction

As previously stated, the medium-size cities selected for investigation by the committee were Atlantic City, N. J.; Newport and Covington, Ky.; Scranton, Pa.; and Reading, Pa. These cities represent population centers of approximately 100,000.

The purpose of the study was to ascertain whether the pattern of crime found to exist in the large cities also prevailed in smaller communities. As it would have been impossible to investigate all medium-size cities, the committee selected these five as samples.

The committee found that the same crime pattern does exist in these cities as in the large metropolitan areas. The Accardos, the Guziks, and the Costellos who direct the big-city syndicates have their counterparts in the smaller cities. Territories may be more restricted, but the modus operandi of the small-town racketeers is virtually a carbon copy of that followed by the big-city mobs.

As in the larger cities, small-city organized gambling is controlled by former bootleggers, and the emphasis is on illegal bookmaking which is dependent upon the wire service emanating from Continental Press Service, controlled by the old Capone syndicate.

Gambler-politico-police alliances are readily discernible. The strong inferences of bribery of the police and marked overtones of large contributions by the mobs to political campaigns, all for the purpose of insuring noninterference with gambling operations, are the causes of the existing breakdown of law-enforcement machinery. Repeatedly the committee was told that candidates for public office who were not "liberal" toward gambling simply could not be elected.

Frequently officials said that they adopted the "liberal" policy because their constituents want to gamble; but the inference is strong that the lure of the mob's racket-financed political machine was more attractive than the vote of the ordinary law-abiding citizen.

Some public officials strongly insisted, as a point in their favor, that the presence of racketeers from other cities was never tolerated. The record does not support this claim. Such law-enforcement activity as is undertaken against these outside interests is probably more motivated by demands of the entrenched local mobs to be protected against competition than by a wholesome desire to rid the community of undesirables.

An unfortunate attitude that helps nurture organized crime is the feeling that bookmaking and other gambling violations do not warrant imprisonments. Statutes and municipal ordinances are ignored by public officials who state that their days are filled with traffic problems, paper work, complaints about mischievous boys, etc. They are also ignored by sheriffs who claim to be tax collectors only. Instead, official warnings or unofficial word that "the heat is on" are issued sporadically. In some cities, the custom has grown up of having all gambling cease when grand juries are in session.

The acute myopia which besets the duly constituted law-enforcement officials must be provocative to informed citizens, to whom wide-open gambling violations are so readily apparent. Is it any wonder that disrespect for law and constituted authority inevitably follows in the wake of continued and studied disregard of the obvious?

The committee also found in these small cities the same buckpassing of responsibility that appeared in the large cities. The district attorneys disavow responsibility for enforcement and insist that they are prosecutors only; the State police stay out of cities except under rare circumstances, while city authorities close their eyes.

Small-scale bookmaking in local communities may seem innocuous, but it is part of a huge gangster monopoly that reaches its tentacles into every corner of the Nation. A bookmaker cannot do business without prompt racing information. And this he cannot obtain except through the interstate monopoly of the mob-controlled Continental Press Service which obtains the news from the track illegally, and broadcasts it through an elaborate system of wigwag, telephone and telegraph. The $2 bet placed with a local "bookie" is a contribution to a $5,000,000,000 mobster operation.

Similar considerations apply to other types of gambling. It is believed that if local judges and prosecutors could be made aware of the interstate aspects of gambling operations and the serious effect which their sanction has upon the whole structure of law enforcement, they would view such violations more seriously. Similarly, the people of the smaller communities throughout the country should realize that the official toleration of criminal activity, however small and innocuous it may appear on the surface, contributes to interstate gangster syndicates and leads to a pervasive lowering of governmental standards and integrity.

The committee's findings with respect to each of the smaller cities investigated are set forth immediately hereinafter:

(a) ATLANTIC CITY

Atlantic City, N. J., is a resort town with a permanent population of 60,000 and a summer influx of 150,000 visitors. Its geographical isolation from the rest of the State has permitted the local machine to run it largely without interference from State-wide law-enforcement agencies.

The city is riddled with rackets, including nearly every known type of gambling operation. Its famous Boardwalk is lined with stands operating devices purporting to be games of skill but looked upon by their customers as games of chance. It contains two substantial numbers syndicates and nearly every cigar store is a front for a bookmaker.

Atlantic City also has a race track which represents an important source of revenue to the State. Anyone in Atlantic City can go to the track and bet; yet off-track bookmaking is permitted by the local police to flourish on a wide scale. Every dollar bet with a bookmaker represents a loss of tax revenue to the State, and yet the State authorities show very little interest in seeing that local gambling laws are enforced.

When this committee moved into Atlantic City at the height of the tourist season, numbers runners and "bookies" ran for cover and a storm of protest arose from the politicians and racketeers (both of whom seem to think alike in Atlantic City) to the effect that business would be ruined. To their chagrin, Atlantic City has had the biggest year in its history. The gate at the race track and the pari-mutuel betting have reached a new high.

The exposure of crime conditions in Atlantic City already has produced a movement by civic groups to free the city from the clutches of a machine which operates with amazing discipline. This machine has two heads, one the political boss of Atlantic County and the other the rackets boss of Atlantic City. The tracks showing the operating relationship between the two are cleverly concealed, but the true bosses are known to be close personal friends and they are frequently seen with their heads together at all hours of the day or night.

The political head is Frank S. Farley, State senator for Atlantic County at a salary of $3,000 a year, treasurer of Atlantic County at a salary of $6,000 a year, and chairman of the Atlantic County Republican Committee. Because of the rule of senatorial courtesy and his strong influence no judgeship or any other State office in the county can be filled without his approval of the appointee. His influence over the administration of Atlantic City is also potent. His law firm is counsel to the race-track association at a retainer of $20,000 a year, and he has been extremely active in connection with all bills in the legislature affecting race tracks.

The rackets head is Herman "Stumpy" Orman, owner of the Cosmopolitan Hotel, which has served for many years as a rendezvous for political figures and perhaps underworld characters as well.

Stumpy Orman is a gambler with former bootlegging connections who, until recently, toted a gun under a permit for which Senator Farley was once a sponsor. His only income records consist of a little black book which he produced before the committee and then suddenly snatched back, refusing thereafter to reveal its contents.

Anonymous letters received by the committee indicate that that little book would show the entire racket operation in Atlantic City, with an accounting of how much each racketeer owes for protection. Whether this is true may never be known, but it is clear that Stumpy Orman has a great deal to say about the running of the Atlantic City police force, and there was testimony before the committee to the effect that no one can run numbers, make book, or obtain a license for a Boardwalk game until he clears with Stumpy.

Stumpy Orman has the convenient type of memory. In testimony before the committee he was able to recite without hesitation the name and title of practically every public official of Atlantic City and Atlantic County. His knowledge of local government and personalities was excellent. On the other hand, with regard to financial matters, he was unable to remember transactions that had occurred only a few months before. Bank deposits sent by him from New York to Atlantic City aggregating over $40,000 during a short period in 1936 had completely vanished from his memory. When asked about bank deposits made in recent years amounting to $16,000 or more a year in excess of his gross income for tax purposes, he refused to answer on the ground that the answer might incriminate him.

There have been three large numbers operations in Atlantic City. One operated in part of the "white" area under a partnership consisting of Fred Masucci and Ben Rubenstein, with a net profit running as high as $38,000 a year. The second operated in the "colored" areas with a gross profit of about $175,000 a year. This was formerly operated by Harold Scheper, but because of illness he has had to divide the operation among several of his lieutenants. The third was operated by Harry "Cherry" Haggerty. Scheper and Haggerty are both on probation as the result of gambling convictions obtained in 1947 by a special prosecutor sent to Atlantic County by the Governor. They report to Vincent Lane, the assistant probation clerk. It is Lane's duty to ascertain whether his probationers are complying with the law, but he told the committee he never saw anything to indicate that these men were carrying on, under his very nose, numbers operations of large proportions.

The administration of the police department of Atlantic City shows definite signs of deliberate laxity, creating an almost inescapable suspicion of official alliance with law violators. The director of public safety is an elderly man who is unable to devote much time or energy to his job. The actual head is the assistant director, who is an intimate of Senator Farley and Stumpy Orman. The chief of police is a man who is obviously putty in the hands of others. He has very little to do with the administration of the police force and frequently learns of important changes after they have occurred. He professed complete ignorance of any bookmaking or other gambling in Atlantic City and claimed not to know how the numbers racket runs. The true facts known to practically every other member of the department are that there are approximately 200 bookmakers operating in Atlantic City with lay-off arrangements with bookmakers in other cities as far away as Baltimore.

The police department has a rackets squad which has orders from the chief to stamp out all gambling but which never seems to be able to find any.

The only arrests of gambling violators seem to have been made through the efforts of a group of patrolmen on the force known as the "Four Horsemen." These consist of Francis B. Gribbin, Jack Portock, and Frederick J. Warlich, plus one or more others of the younger members of the force who help out from time to time. These men have undertaken a crusade against protected gambling in Atlantic City. Although their crusade was sparked initially by reprisals practiced against them for their leadership in a policemen's and firemen's pay-raise campaign and by opposition to their campaign on the part of the city administration, the committee was deeply impressed by their honesty, sincerity, and extraordinary courage.

These men have faced underworld threats of bodily harm to themselves and their families and severe reprisals from the police department itself, all designed to compel them to refrain from making gambling arrests. But they have remained undaunted. Nothing could have been more obvious than the manner in which they were punished by their superiors for their vigor in enforcing the gambling laws. Their treatment perhaps more than anything else clarifies the close alliance between the underworld and the official administration of Atlantic City. The forces against them were working in complete harmony at every stage.

The conclusive proof occurred when Stumpy Orman personally interceded and agreed, in return for their agreement to leave the gamblers alone, to have them transferred back to their original posts from the lonely, outlying beats to which they had been shifted as punishment. On the advice of a Special Deputy Attorney General of the United States, they accepted this "deal" as a test and within a matter of 4 hours they had been restored to their posts. In the face of this uncontradicted testimony, the conclusion is inescapable that Stumpy Orman has controlled the Atlantic City Police Department in the interest of the underworld gambling fraternity.

The committee cannot too strongly express its praise of these courageous policemen for the great contribution they have made to law enforcement and good government and for their willingness to face every kind of threat, punishment, and reprisal for the good of their cause.

The committee was also favorably impressed by the testimony of Francis L. Smith, former operator of a Boardwalk game. Smith frankly admitted that he had been "in the rackets" most of his life, and there is some possibility that he was motivated by resentment at the treatment he had received when he tried to obtain a license for a new game. However, he testified before the committee twice, once in executive session and once in an open hearing, and on each occasion he testified in a forthright, unhesitating manner such as to cause the committee to believe he was telling the truth. Further credence is given to his testimony by the fact that Senator Farley, against whom Smith made serious charges, was urgently invited by the committee to appear before it to refute the charges and he failed to appear.

Smith testified that in order to obtain a license to operate a Boardwalk game he paid the license fee of $1,000 plus an additional $1,000 in cash "under the table" to Joseph McBeth, the treasurer of the Republican County Committee. He also testified to a $250 cash payment directly to Senator Farley made in Farley's kitchen in order to keep operating. Furthermore, he stated that in order to get the license in any event he had to obtain clearance from Stumpy Orman, and there was some indication that Orman resented his having gone directly to Farley in the first instance.

Although Smith's testimony might be attacked on the basis of his background as a former small-time racketeer, the committee feels that it should be given great weight, in view of the fact that it stands uncontradicted and is entirely consistent with the testimony of other witnesses whose testimony cannot be doubted. It establishes a definite link between Farley, the city administration, and Orman. If other residents of Atlantic City were willing to show the same courage as Smith in coming forward with information, the link would probably be forged in a manner that could not be questioned on any ground.

The most amazing testimony given at the Atlantic City hearings was that relating to the race-wire service. The only race-wire drop coming into Atlantic City is at radio station WOND, which broadcasts racing news received from Transradio News, a distributor for the gangster-controlled Continental News Service. Many reports were received to the effect that Lester Burdick, a salesman for the station, was receiving weekly payments from bookmakers for racing news. The question that came to mind was how Burdick could charge bookmakers for information anyone can receive over the radio.

It then appeared that Burdick was executive clerk of the State senate, appointed through the efforts of Senator Farley, and that he had been seen with Stumpy Orman. Investigation revealed that he drove two Cadillacs (one a 1951 model), owned a $20,000 home, spent $1,000 in 1950 for suits costing $200 each, and paid nearly $2,900 in 1950 toward the operating expenses of Station WOND. At the same time his 1950 income had been less than $1,900, and his average income for the last 5 years had been less than $3,000 a year.

The answer to this mystery was given through the testimony of a small cigar-store owner in Atlantic City who testified that he rented his back room to a bookmaker who told him that, if a man driving a red Cadillac came into the store and asked for a package of Philip Morris cigarettes, he should give the man a $10 bill along with the cigarettes. The man came in every Thursday while the bookmaker was operating and received the $10. He later learned that the man was Lester Burdick.

When Burdick was confronted with this testimony and asked if it was true, he refused to answer on the ground that it might incriminate him. He gave the same answer when asked whether he had not made similar collections all over town and whether he had not threatened recalcitrant bookmakers with "police visits" if they did not pay.

Shortly after the hearings Burdick was removed as executive clerk of the State senate, and the committee is informed that the matter is now under consideration by the grand jury.

(b) KENTUCKY

Campbell County, Ky., of which Newport is the county seat, is directly across the river from Cincinnati, and many residents and visitors of Cincinnati are accustomed to go there for the purpose of visiting the lush gambling casinos that have operated openly in

Campbell County for many years. Kenton County, Ky., of which Covington is the county seat, adjoins Campbell County and presents a parallel situation. At the time the committee's investigators visited this area, the gambling operations in both counties, especially Campbell, were so open that the casual visitor would gain the impression that gambling is legal in Kentucky.

The fact is that Kentucky gambling laws are very strict. It is a felony under Kentucky law to "set up, keep, manage, operate, or conduct" any gambling device or contrivance. The penalty is a $500 fine and a mandatory prison sentence of 1 to 3 years, plus permanent loss of suffrage and of the right to hold public office. However, not a single successful prosecution under this law has been reported in either of these counties and not one defendant has gone to jail.

The committee had held hearings in Cleveland on January 17, 18, and 19, 1951, at which it received testimony to the effect that the Cleveland gambling syndicate, having been driven out of Cleveland, had moved into Campbell and Kenton Counties. Accordingly, upon the extension of the committee's life until September 1, it was determined to investigate these northern Kentucky counties.

The committee found that the city of Newport under a new reform administration is making fast strides toward honest law enforcement, despite obstruction on the part of the chief of police and some of his subordinates. On the other hand, the rest of Campbell County was found to be wide open.

The committee's investigators visited the Beverly Hills Country Club, the Latin Quarter, the Yorkshire Club, and the Alexandria Club, all in Campbell County, and found them to be operating openly. At the Beverly Hills Country Club, about 150 persons were observed, in the casino where there were four dice tables, two roulette wheels, a black-jack table, and chuck-a-luck table. About 100 persons were observed in the Latin Quarter which featured three or four dice tables and two roulette wheels. An investigator for the committee was barred from the gaming room at the Yorkshire and told there were no games in progress, but he noticed in the parking lot far more cars than were needed to transport the four or five persons in the dining room. At the Alexandria he found approximately 250 persons and announcements being made on the public address system that the blackjack table was open. There was also a chuck-a-luck table in the place.

In Kenton County the situation was similar, except that the establishments were smaller and operated more surreptitiously. Those in operation were the Lookout House, the Kentucky Club, the 514 Club, the Kenton Club, the Press Club, the Gold Horseshoe, and the Turf Club.

The committee conducted open hearings in Washington on July 23, 1951, regarding conditions in Kenton and Campbell Counties and heard a graphic description of the futile efforts by church and civic groups to secure better law enforcement. It appears that Kentucky has a quaint custom under which all gambling ceases during the three periods of the year when the grand jury is in session. The grand juries purport to investigate gambling and find none taking place. Grand juries are in session for a total of about 27 days each year and the rest of the time gambling continues unhindered.

Kenton County has been flooded with slot machines for years and it was estimated on one occasion that there were 1,500 machines in operation. Gambling has been a paramount factor in a number of court cases arising out of domestic difficulties.

In March 1950, a meeting was held in Covington attended by representatives of a civic association, law enforcement officials, and the press of Kenton County. All those present subscribed to this statement:

> We who have met and conferred concerning commercialized organized gambling and law enforcement conditions in Kentucky agree to cooperate full-heartedly in the enforcement of the law. We agree that commercialized organized gambling must cease throughout the county immediately.

This pledge subsequently turned out to be meaningless as far as the public officials were concerned. Six months later, a news article reported that Covington led the State in the number of slot machine receipts issued by the Government, with 163 listed as having paid the Federal tax. Included was a payment of $5,000 by the Lookout House on 50 machines. As of May 1950, according to the report of the McFarland committee, wire service was being supplied to 111 bookmakers in Covington.

On January 22, 1951, shortly after the committee's hearings in Cleveland, the Kenton County Protestant Association sent a letter to Judge Joseph Goodenough and Commonwealth Attorney James Quill demanding a full-scale grand jury investigation of gambling. Enclosed was the list of slot machine owners and the judge was reminded of the existence of a permanent injunction outstanding against the Lookout House. The judge and the commonwealth attorney discussed the matter and agreed that it was the commonwealth attorney's responsibility to enforce the injunction. Nothing was ever done about it.

A representative of the Kenton County Protestant Association spent 55 minutes before the grand jury giving testimony about three dozen places that were violating the law. He told the grand jury he had seen slot machines and other gambling in practically all of these establishments, but the grand jury and the commonwealth attorney manifested no interest in the documentary evidence he had with him and no indictments were returned. As soon as the grand jury adjourned, gambling was resumed.

Frequent threats of bodily harm were made against a civic leader who was spearheading a campaign against the gambling interests. Also, the plate glass front door of his home twice has been the target for containers of filth. On one occasion, gamblers operating through the Tavern Owners Association which had made a pledge of $52,000 toward the local hospital building drive, to be paid at the rate of $1,500 a month, threatened to discontinue payments on the pledge unless those promoting the campaign against gambling were persuaded "to lay off."

W. Sharon Florer, executive secretary of the Kenton County Protestant Association, testified that two large industrial concerns that would have employed hundreds of persons refused to locate plants in or around Covington merely because of the community's reputation as a center of wide-open gambling.

Leonard J. Connor, sergeant at arms of the Kentucky State Senate since 1942, member of the elections commission for Kenton County, has operated the Turf Club in Covington since 1937. In his testimony before the committee, he admitted that he had carried on a book-making operation in the Turf Club since 1937 and that he paid $28.60 a week for wire service to a man he knew only as "Red." He said he had arranged for the wire service through W. R. Cullen of Cincinnati. He also admitted owning four slot machines purchased in 1940 or 1941 in Cincinnati but he said he stored them in his cellar in June 1951 when the grand jury was in session and the committee opened its inquiry. He said his brother was once arrested in connection with the bookmaking operation at the Turf Club; that after that the place had gone along undisturbed for years.

This public official·further testified that his income from gambling far exceeded that from his bar. He estimated that the handbook averaged a gross of about $1,300 a week in race-track bets and that the slot machines were good for $6,000 to $7,000 a year. Asked if he intended to open up again, Connor replied that he hadn't made up his mind, he was "just waiting."

Testimony of the most amazing character was received from Theodore Hageman, field agent for the Kentucky State Alcohol Board. Mr. Hageman insisted that operation of a gambling establishment or the commission of any other violation of law was no basis for refusing a liquor license. The form of application for a liquor license or renewal contains a question whether there are any gambling or any gambling devices on the premises. Hageman testified that "almost 100 percent" of the applicants answer this question in the affirmative.

Where gambling is found on licensed premises, Mr. Hageman said, "We are not instructed to interfere with them, and have not been doing so." He maintained that the board never suspends licenses for gambling alone, although it may sometimes be included in general charges of disorder. He does not consider it his duty to bring gambling violations to the attention of the alcoholic beverage control board.

Hageman acknowledged that he had been active in political campaigns including one in 1950 of which he was chairman. He admitted he collected between $7,500 and $8,000 from liquor licensees "who desire to make a contribution" and he estimated that 20 or 25 licensees had come through with donations.

Hageman's present salary is $3,840 a year and he testified that the most he ever earned was during his tenure as city manager of Covington when he was paid $5,000 annually. He ran twice for sheriff and was defeated, his out-of-pocket expenses in each campaign, according to his own testimony, approximating $5,000 to $6,000. Yet he fixes his net worth at $40,000, which includes a new unencumbered home which cost him $23,960 in 1948, two automobiles, Government bonds, other securities and some cash.

Hageman's testimony was especially interesting in the light of what the committee was told by John J. Moloney, who became a city commissioner in Covington in January 1950. Mr. Moloney, who is to be commended for his earnest efforts in behalf of honest law enforcement, testified that a month after he went into office he was approached by Hageman, who advised him that he was eligible to participate in a "profit-sharing plan" conducted by the gambling interests for high appointive or elective officials. Hageman said Moloney might just as well take the money because people would say he was doing it anyway. Moloney rejected this offer but was told to let Hageman know if he should change his mind.

Mr. Moloney said that he gradually became aware of the presence of the Cleveland syndicate in the Covington gambling set-up and was glad to see that the committee eventually had proved him to be right. He has made several attempts to drive organized and syndicated gambling out of Covington, but all of these attempts have been unsuccessful. In the spring of 1950 he prepared a statement that he intended to release at a commission meeting, demanding that organized gambling be driven out of Covington, and showed it to Mayor William Rolfes. The mayor became perturbed and told Moloney "this will put us all on the spot," urging him to withhold it, which he did for the time being.

Next, Mr. Moloney wrote a letter to the city manager demanding that the gamblers be forced to cease operations and to move their equipment out of the city. An order to this effect was issued by the city manager but there was only partial compliance on the day fixed for the cessation. At about the same time, Mr. Moloney was approached by a friend, who said he had been authorized to tell Moloney that he could have complete control of the police department, all hiring, firing, and promotions, and could also have the final word on all hiring and firing in the gambling establishments if he would terminate his campaign to drive out gambling.

Mr. Moloney refused and continued thereafter to try to persuade his colleagues on the commission to go along with his campaign for a clean-up. But he has been completely ignored in this effort. Mr. Moloney testified that he was told that the mayor was to receive $150 a week, the commissioners $100 a week, and the city detectives $150 a month, if they would not interfere with gambling.

Mr. Moloney also related to the committee the story of a police officer who seized two slot machines in a Covington place of business. Cliff Brown, an associate of Brink and representative of the slot machine syndicate, rushed into the police station and berated the patrolman for his act in front of his superior officer. The patrolman not long after was suspended on a charge of drinking on duty and thereafter was harassed to the point where he quit the department.

In February of this year, Mr. Moloney received another indirect approach and this time a figure of $50,000 was mentioned. Whether this was a bona fide offer Mr. Moloney was unable to determine. He frequently received telephone calls threatening him for his activities and he produced two anonymous letters which had been sent to him. One of these said, "This is a warning. You had better not close Covington gambling. You and your friends will be dead. Your body will be among the missing. Leave gambling the way it is."

Judge Joseph Goodenough of the Kenton County court was questioned about gambling in the light of a permanent injunction granted by his predecessor in 1939 against a number of gambling establishments. No judicial notice is taken of this injunction and the Commonwealth attorney never takes steps to enforce it, although it would serve as a quick basis for stopping gambling.

Judge Goodenough asserted that the crime record of Kenton County is good. But he admitted that up until January of this year gambling in Kenton County had been "openly notorious." He knew that before January, slot machines, bookmaking, and the Lookout House casino were running. The committee had no difficulty in finding that they were operating after the first of January.

Admitting that there are never any prosecutions under the felony statute for gambling, Judge Goodenough could not explain why grand juries refused to indict. He admitted that it might be possible to indict the Cleveland mobsters under the conspiracy statute and it was suggested to Judge Goodenough that the grand jury might be "inspired" to look back into operations by the syndicate. The jurist replied, "I am not so much interested in what has gone on as I am in keeping gambling out of Kenton County, as a judge. Now my conduct, of necessity, must be restricted. I am a judge, sir."

Mr. Quill, in his testimony, admitted his authorship of the report of the May grand jury. The committee found it difficult to reconcile obviously contradictory portions of the report. In one section, the grand jury observed that "gambling had gone haywire" in the county, and in another it said that "at the time of our original convening, the only gambling in the county was slot machines and handbooks." Requested to explain the grand jury's failure to do anything about conditions it recognized had existed, Mr. Quill claimed that the grand jury felt it "unjust and inequitable" to return indictments for conduct that had been acceptable for years.

The following colloquy between Senator O'Conor, chairman of the committee, and Mr. Quill throws interesting light on the attitude of this enforcement officer:

Q. Mr. Quill, you are an experienced prosecuting officer and a man of wide experience generally, having been in the legislature and otherwise. It is very apparent that you are quite conversant with conditions generally and you are a man of ability. * * * I am asking you for a simple fact, whether you do not agree with us that widespread gambling activities such as have been shown here to have existed and are admitted could not exist without the connivance and the protection of law-enforcement officials.

*   *   *   *   *   *   *

A. I would say permitted or suffered to happen. I know I tolerated a good bit of it simply because it had been there since I was born and I knew that was the way the community had grown and that is what it had all these years. I felt to improve that condition takes not only law enforcement but takes education.

*   *   *   *   *   *   *

Q. Mr. Quill, wouldn't you think also that such widespread gambling operations with a large amount of money being realized from the operations could easily lead to corruption and to graft on the part of the police and other enforcement officials?

A. I certainly think it could, sir, yes, and maybe in many cases does.

Q. And do you think it might have possibly existed in this case?

A. I would certainly say it was within the realm of possibility.

*   *   *   *   *   *   *

Mr. Quill admitted that he had never made any effort to subpena the partnership books and records of the Lookout House in Covington which is owned and operated by James H. Brink. The committee had subpenaed these records and found that for the 2-year period of 1948 and 1949, the partners' shares had been as follows: Marion Brink, wife of James H. Brink, $33,860; B. W. Brink, $16,930; Charles V. Carr, $16,935; Mitchell Meyer, $20,858; John Croft, $10,429; Samuel Schroeder, $39,583; Louis Rothkopf, $41,765; Morris Kleinman, $41,765; Moe Dalitz, $41,765; Louise Tucker, wife of Samuel Tucker, $41,765; and Charles Polizzi, $33,352. Several of these names will be recognized as those of the Cleveland mob which had moved into Covington and Newport. Brink has testified that the mob sold their interests to him as of the end of 1950.

Mr. Quill said he had no idea that the profits of this establishment ran so high until they were dug up and publicized by this committee.

Mr. Quill told the committee that when he first became common-wealth attorney "there was very little sympathy" for enforcement of gambling laws, but that, as a result of this committee's exposure of the Lookout House as a syndicate operation, "people became exercised and the laws are easy to enforce now." He was reminded that the people were exercised as far back as 1939, as evidenced by the injunction that nobody bothered to enforce. His reply was that this was an action brought by the attorney general of Kentucky and the primary responsibility for its enforcement rested with the attorney general.

Mr. Quill asserted that gambling at the Lookout House ceased after the committee's Cleveland hearings and that he would have pressed contempt proceedings under the injunction had operations there continued. He professed to have no personal knowledge of gambling at the Lookout House since he became commonwealth attorney but acknowledged that several years ago, while he was a member of the legislature, he had lost $40 in a dice game there.

Sheriff Henry A. Berndt of Kenton County, when asked whether he was the chief law enforcement officer of the county, retorted: "I am the chief law enforcement officer. I am the chief fire marshal. I am the chief dog catcher. I am the chief tax collector. I guess I have probably 150 duties according to the statute." Berndt said he had nine deputies, six of whom collect taxes. The other three serve processes. Berndt obeys the statute requiring inspections insofar as it is possible. The chief deputy, he said, does the work when he can be spared from his other duties, otherwise there are no inspections. No gambling was ever found during the inspections.

"We do not really try to make any attempt at law enforceing," Berndt said bluntly. He claimed that he repeatedly had told the grand jury that his office could not do so and at the same time per-form its other duties, too. Berndt never heard of the Cleveland syndicate until the committee exposed their interests in northern Kentucky. He has not been on the lookout for any of the members, would not know them if he saw them, and would not know where to start looking for them.

Chief of Police Alfred Schild of Covington testified that his chief of detectives and other members of his staff had been looking for the source of the race wire service for 4 or 5 months without success. He has never been inside the Kentucky Club in Covington so he does not know what is going on there, although he did know of a $75,000 robbery there at one time. This was the biggest haul by gunmen in the history of the city but he did not consider that it required any personal investigation by him.

It was Schild who told the committee that gambling clubs in Kenton County advertised in the Kentucky Peace Officers Association magazine. Asked if he thought it was all right for the magazine to accept advertisements from gamblers, Schild asserted that "they didn't advertise as gamblers," and besides they advertised in other magazines, as well.

Schild could not tell the committee how the gamblers receive "tip-offs" about impending raids. He conceded that his department had a rule requiring that all warrants be registered at headquarters before being served. "I don't know why. It's been a rule for years and years," he added. Schild testified that he was a friend of John Rigney but professed not to know that Rigney was a leader of the slot machine syndicate, a matter of common knowledge in Covington.

Turning to Campbell County, the committee heard testimony describing the commendable efforts being made to restore order in the field of law enforcement in the city of Newport, while conditions in the county surrounding Newport are allowed to run wild.

A reform administration came into control of the city government of Newport in January 1950. Three officials of that administration testified before the committee, namely, City Solicitor Fred Warren, City Manager Malcolm Rhoads, and City Commissioner Charles J. Eha.

Mr. Warren testified regarding the injunction proceedings brought by the attorney general of Kentucky against the gambling interests in Campbell County in 1943 resulting in a permanent injunction. He said that during the period of the litigation all gambling was eradicated. After the injunction was obtained, however, gambling gradually was resumed and continued unchecked until 1950. He testified that no explanation was ever given as to why no move was made to enforce the mandate of the court and he expressed the opinion that gambling casinos could not have operated too openly and regularly and for such protracted periods without protection.

Commissioner Eha, who was one of the candidates supported by the Newport Civic Association, related some of the difficulties experienced by the reform group in its war against the gambling interests. He declared that the citizens are now aware that the city is better off without gambling. He, too, has received threats because of his activities against gambling.

City Manager Rhoads, who had been a witness at the committee's Cleveland hearings, testified again in June and July. At an executive session of the committee held on June 20, he indicated some surprise when informed that a committee investigator had found gambling in the Alexandria Club just a couple of weeks before. When he returned for the July 23 hearing, Mr. Rhoads told the committee that he was certain that gambling had ceased there because two detectives had been stationed in the place between 10 p. m. and 2 a. m. every night to make sure no gambling went on. He said the city has had some difficulty because of "tip-offs" of projected raids but an effort is being made to determine their source.

The Bobben Realty Co. clearing house bookmaking operation has been broken up and a similar outfit has been routed from the Finance Building in recent weeks. Mr. Rhoads said he has been trying to break up the wire service to bookmakers but the Ace Research Service has moved from its former location and he has been unable to learn the source from which the wire service now emanates.

Mr. Rhoads reiterated a statement he gave to the committee in Cleveland that he did not feel he could place any confidence in Chief George Gugel of the Newport Police Department. He has tried to cure the situation, he explained, by bypassing Gugel and using men in the department he knows to be reliable. The gamblers, he said, had also made efforts to buy him off. He told of a telephone call he received in which he was informed that if he would let things alone the gambling interests would be willing to pay $1,000 a week. The same figure, he declared, was repeated to him soon after the incident by a visitor to his office who he knew was not connected with the rackets. Telephone calls and letters containing threats of harm to him and members of his family also have been received by Mr. Rhoads.

The gambling interests, according to Mr. Rhoads, first try "to buy what they want." If unsuccessful they move into the second stage, which is to harass officials moving against their operations. The third is a smear campaign impugning the integrity of those who oppose gambling activities.

Gambling in Newport in 1949 enjoyed somewhat of a blessing from the administration then in power which adopted legislation levying certain taxes on the gambling interests. The tax bill for the Yorkshire was $8,090.40 under this measure, clearing houses paid $500, and bookmakers were assessed $250. The city treasury was enriched to the extent of $50,109.99 in 1949 but, on the eve of its departure from office, the former administration repealed the taxing ordinance. Mr. Rhoads said that the new administration would never have tolerated the special taxing system because "I cannot see any difference between a city and an individual taking graft."

Suppression of gambling has helped business in Newport, according to Mr. Rhoads. Bank deposits are higher and there has been a substantial increase in inquiries from industrial enterprises interested in the possibility of erecting plants there.

Chief of Police Gugel when called as a witness, also expressed surprise that a committee investigator had found gambling in the Alexandria Club in June because his men had told him there was none. Since the Cleveland hearings, Gugel said, he has been endeavoring to get rid of all gambling. When pressed to define specifically what course of action he was pursuing, Gugel replied, "Still issuing orders to my subordinates." Gugel was asked what he had done about the Ace Research Service, which supplied wire service to more than 100 bookmakers in Covington and more than 60 in Newport. He said he sent his detectives to the outfit's headquarters but they could not find anything.

Lack of cooperation on the part of Chief Gugel serves as an obstacle to law enforcement in Newport. However, the city administration is to be congratulated on the progress it is making.

It is a pity that the law enforcement officers of the rest of Campbell County cannot be persuaded to follow the excellent example of the city of Newport.

William J. Wise, Commonwealth attorney of Campbell County, for almost 9 years, was called upon to explain the widespread commercialized gambling in his section. He said, "I suppose it was just like Topsy, it just grew up. It has been in existence long before I appeared on the political scene, and I suppose it has existed by sufferance, at least that is my opinion." He confessed that he was "generally aware" of the operations of the casinos, but insisted that he has told every grand jury it was their prerogative to investigate them, although none ever did. He did succeed in getting an indictment against one member of the Cleveland syndicate, Samuel Tucker, 5 or 6 years ago, but Tucker was acquitted.

The committee's investigation showed that the Beverly Hills Country Club had gross receipts of $975,000 for 1948 and 1949, a net of $426,199 for that period, distributed to the following: Samuel Tucker, Moe Dalitz, Rothkopf, and Kleinman, $44,019 each; Charles Polizzi, $32,014; T. J. McGinty, $34,301; John Croft, $26,583; Harry Potter, $20,008; Mitchell Meyer, $17,150; Samuel Schroeder, $54,024; and Marion Brink, $40,017.   In addition, Tucker was paid a salary of $10,000 annually from 1945 to 1948, Meyer and Potter were paid $3,900 each for 1948 and $4,110 each for 1949.   The money wheels took in $70,000, chuck-a-luck, $17,000; blackjack, $51,000; craps, etc., $244,000, and slots, $69,000.

It is of interest to note that the partners of Beverly Hills are practically the same as in the case of the Lookout House in Covington, and that both operations include members of the Cleveland mob.

When confronted with these figures, Mr. Wise conceded that they were "fabulous" and admitted that he had never heard of some of the individuals named.

The committee found that the operations at the Yorkshire Club were even more extensive for the same 2 years, with gross receipts amounting to $1,526,000, the gross profit was $614,000 and the net income, $427,597.   The following shared in the profits: Maurice Ryan, Fort Thomas, Ky., $30,018; Fred Hallam, Bellevue, Ky., $47,662; Morris Nemmo, Fort Thomas, Ky., $30,493; Robert Bergen, Fort Thomas, Ky., $24,121; Sam Gutterman, Cincinnati, $10,496; A. R. Masterson, Fort Thomas, Ky.; E. R. Lowe, Tucson, Ariz.; James H. Brink, Fort Mitchell, Ky.; Claude Hines, Fort Mitchell, Ky.; George and Frieda Bregal, Melbourne, Ky., $17,493 each; Alfred Goltsman, George Gordon, Samuel Tucker, and Ruby Kolad, all of Cleveland, $20,992 each; Abe Schneider and John Croft, Cincinnati, $34,987 and $33,092, respectively; and George Bear, Detroit, $24,296.

Mr. Wise conceded that this operation was "much more sizable than any of us thought or could have imagined."

Sheriff Ray Diebold of Campbell County, whose principal qualification for his job seems to have been that he once served as a "good will" man for a brewery, made two appearances before the committee. The first time he testified that he had never been in the Beverly Hills Club, the Latin Quarter or the Yorkshire Club, and that he had never raided them because he had been informed by the county police that there was no gambling in any of them.   He had only "heard" that the Cleveland syndicate was involved in operations of the casinos and he had learned from his lawyer only a short time before the June hearing about the law requiring him, as sheriff, to inspect dance halls and roadhouses at least once a month.   When he testified in July, he was emphatic in declaring he had been diligent in his inspections and promised to furnish the committee with copies of his monthly reports from then on.   He still has a clear record of no arrests for gambling since he had been sheriff.   The committee asked why he had never visited any of the casinos, at least as "good will" man for the brewery.   He replied that the casinos use premium beers only, whereas he was stimulating business for a local product.

James Winters, chief of the Campbell County police, told the committee that he had reason to believe that gambling was going on in places like the Beverly Hills Club and the Latin Quarter but his men never found any when they made inspections. Pleading that he had only six men to patrol 508 miles of highway in the county, Winters said they had little time to look for gambling violations.

Jack Kuresman, Cincinnati public accountant who represents the Latin Quarter, Yorkshire, Beverly Hills, and the Merchants Club, testified that his office received daily sheets which showed wins, losses, expenses and the bankroll at the beginning and end of each day. He admitted that he had no means of verifying the wins and losses. Asked why he was unable to produce the records of the Latin Quarter, Kuresman said that as soon as his clients learned that the committee was interested in northern Kentucky again they came to his office and retrieved the records, together with his work sheets.

(c) SCRANTON, PA.

The committee's survey of conditions in the area of Scranton, Pa., included some investigation in nearby Wilkes-Barre and Hazleton. The committee concentrated on the ramifications of a multi-million-dollar Treasury-balance lottery of which Louis Cohen is believed to be the ruler. Cohen has a long history of lottery operations. For years, he and his several brothers have ruled a lottery empire that covers several States. Louis Cohen divides his time between a home in Florida and a residence in the Pocono Mountains outside of Scranton. His name has been linked to night-club and gambling enterprises in Florida.

The Treasury-balance lottery, according to testimony obtained by the committee, operates in most of the Eastern States and in sections of the Midwest. Tickets are sold for 25 cents and 50 cents, with occasional "specials" during the year selling for $1. The last five figures of the daily balance issued by the United States Treasury determine the winners. The ticket plays for 5 days, and top prize in most instances is $3,000. The odds against the betters are extremely heavy, and the profit of the racketeers who run the lottery is enormous.

A special service of the Western Union Telegraph Co. speeds the number daily from Washington to 51 subscribers who have been identified either as the principals or chief agents in the operation of the racket throughout the East. An additional 16 subscribers located in Chicago, Ill.; Alliance, Barnesville, Berea, Canton, Cleveland Heights, Cleveland, Toledo, and Youngstown, Ohio, and Indianapolis, Ind., are serviced out of the Chicago office of the telegraph company.

Law-enforcement officials in Scranton seemingly are afflicted with the same peculiar blindness toward organized gambling that has been apparent to the committee in its inquiries in other cities. Four horserooms running wide open and heavily patronized were found by committee investigators. A numbers banker testified that he did business for 20 years without ever having been arrested himself, although there were three or four occasions when his runners were picked up. Punchboards littered store counters, and Treasury-balance tickets were openly sold.

It is clearly evident that there is a strange reluctance on the part of the police in Scranton to arrest anybody for violations of the gambling laws. Horserooms are never raided. Periodically, when "the heat is on," the order goes out to "close and stay closed," but such an edict lacks any prolonged or lasting effectiveness. The same can also be said for the cities of Pittston and Wilkes-Barre in adjoining Luzerne County.

To units of the Pennsylvania State Police must go credit for the only successful forays against the gambling interests, even though they usually follow a policy of not going into the cities unless requested to do so by the district attorney or city officials themselves.

In March of this year, without notice to the Scranton police, several details of State police staged a series of raids in the city designed to cripple the operations of Louis Cohen. Vast quantities of Treasury-balance tickets, printing equipment, engraving plates, stapling machines, and supplies were seized. Seven persons were arrested. The value of the seized material was in excess of $50,000 and the tickets being processed were intended for distribution in the months between October 1951 and February 1952.

A similar seizure in Wilkes-Barre, also by the State police, yielded an even greater volume of tickets, materials, and equipment, and struck hard at the source of supply for so-called independent operators not linked with Cohen.

The committee endeavored unsuccessfully to serve a subpena on Cohen prior to its hearing in Washington on August 7 in connection with the Scranton investigation. Accompanied by counsel, Cohen subsequently appeared in Washington and presented himself to the committee, but insufficient time remained for proper interrogation of the witness.

While Cohen was evading process, the committee subpenaed his chief lieutenant in Pennsylvania, Patrick Joseph Size, of Scranton. Claiming that his answers would tend to incriminate him, Size refused to give any testimony about his activities or his dealings with Cohen. He also refused to explain suspicious long-distance telephone calls made every Friday from his home to Allentown, Reading, Schuylkill Haven, Wilkes-Barre, and Williamsport.

Jimmy Mack, of Wilkes-Barre, also known as Vincenzo Maccarone, testified before the committee. He admitted owning pinball machines and a few slot machines and said that he grossed $50 to $60 a day as a numbers banker in Wilkes-Barre. Pretending that he did not know whether the numbers business was against the law, he pointed to the fact that the police never interfered with him or gave him trouble in connection with his slot machines. He added that he operated the slot machines in private clubs outside the city and none of them ever was seized.

Capt. Harry E. McElroy, director of the bureau of criminal identification and information of the Pennsylvania State Police with headquarters at Harrisburg, told the committee that Sgt. Charles Hartman of the State police had reported a bribe offer from Jimmy Mack, acting on behalf of Cohen, and that the State police commissioner had given instructions to Hartman "to string Mack along," because all signs indicated that the time was approaching to close in on the Cohen operations. The advisability of trying to bait Cohen into passing the bribe was considered but this was eventually abandoned in favor of the direct thrust that would cripple his operations. Mack denied the bribe offer but the committee sees no reason for doubting the word of Captain McElroy.

The treasury-balance racket, Captain McElroy said, has two divisions. In one division are a number of independent operators. The other division consists of the syndicate headed by Cohen. The State is divided into districts with separate organizations in each district. The racket runs into many millions, in fact, Captain McElroy estimated that it grosses more than $30,000,000 a year, with the syndicate operation accounting for more than $20,000,000 of this figure. He identified Size as Cohen's principal representative in Pennsylvania and declared that information in the hands of the State police indicates that Cohen operates on an interstate basis.

Captain McElroy told the committee that raids made during the past 1½ years have resulted in confiscation of millions of tickets and printing equipment, material and supplies worth tremendous amounts of money, but he complained that it is difficult to get evidence against the leaders. "They sit behind somewheres and the money comes in to them and they don't have direct operations, and that's that," Captain McElroy declared. He estimated that the operators realize net profit of about 20 percent of the gross intake. He said he had heard of many instances where the racket interests refused to pay the big "hits."

Captain McElroy was asked whether use of the Treasury balance has the psychological effect of giving the lottery the benefit of the prestige of the Federal Government. He testified that he was certain that this was so.

George T. Harris, superintendent of the Washington office of Western Union, testified that a Western Union employee is sent every morning to obtain the Treasury balance and he transmits it directly from the Treasury Department to Western Union's commercial news department in New York. The number is wired from there to Chicago from which it is wired to 16 subscribers to this special service. Fifty-one subscribers in the East are serviced from New York. Three Scranton subscribers are included in the list. They are Size, Jack Richards, and R. E. Booth. The other cities to which the number is sent are Rochester, N. Y.; Plattsburg, N. Y.; Syracuse, N. Y.; Boston, Mass.; Allentown, Pa.; Niagara Falls, N. Y.; Pittsburgh, Pa.; Manchester, N. H.; Olean, N. Y.; Johnstown Pa.; Rome, N. Y.; Utica, N. Y.; Elizabeth, N. J.; Worcester, Mass.; Trenton, N. J.; Williamsport, Pa.; Jeannette, Pa.; Salamanca, N. Y.; Lewistown, Pa.; Burlington, Vt.; Monessen, Pa.; Buffalo, N. Y.; Baltimore, Md.; Concord, N. H.; Cortland, N. Y.; Geneva, N. Y.; Elmira, N. Y.; Johnson City, N. Y.; Beacon, N. Y.; Endicott. N. Y.; Ilion, N. Y.; Edgewood, R. I.; Fall River, Mass.; Altoona, Pa.; Easton, Pa.; and Newburgh, N. Y.

The committee also questioned Joseph Baldassari, a partner in the Baldassari Amusement Co., but he proved to be extremely uncooperative. The committee had information to the effect that Baldassari and his brother Al are engaged in an extensive gambling enterprise operating under official sanction. However, he refused to answer most of the questions put to him on the ground that his answer might tend to incriminate him. He produced voluminous records but refused to disclose their contents. He refused to say whether he knew Louis Cohen and other underworld characters or whether he took Scranton police on trips in his airplane. He did admit, however, that his father was Ulisses Baldassari, who furnished the bail for the seven defendants arrested by the State police in the raids on Cohen's printing operations.

He declined to say whether he owned any slot machines and whether his brother ran a horse room at 108 Adams Avenue. He also refused to say whether he had paid protection money to any official or whether it was true that he had given a $2,500 ring to the director of public safety.

At first he refused to name the partners in Baldassari Amusement Co. but he was finally compelled to admit that they consisted of himself, his brother Al, and their two wives. He was unwilling to try to reconcile this with the fact that the firm's income tax returns listed only the two wives as the partners.

The District Attorney of Lackawanna County, Carlon M. O'Malley, gave what seemed to the committee to be a rather unsatisfactory explanation of the small number of gambling prosecutions in his county. He said his office by tradition is a prosecuting office, not a policing agency, although he does have four county detectives. He said he would be naive if he attempted to tell the committee that the Scranton horse rooms did not exist or had not existed for a number of years, but he claimed that the responsibility for any laxity rested with the city police department, which has 175 uniformed men and 12 detectives. He referred to the State police raids on the Cohen lottery ticket printing establishment last March in connection with which Patrick Joseph Size, Gregory Size, and others received fines ranging from $200 to $300 but no jail sentences were imposed.

Mr. O'Malley stated that on June 29, while on vacation, he issued orders to his staff to conduct a survey of gambling in the areas of Lackawanna County outside of Scranton. This was prompted, he said, by the reappearance of Cohen-controlled Treasury-balance lottery tickets in the county. It is significant to note that this committee's investigators entered Scranton on June 20 and their presence was publicly announced several days before Mr. O'Malley ordered his survey.

He said his staff reported back that they and the State police had communicated with all police chiefs in the communities outside of Scranton and had been informed that they had no knowledge of any gambling, with the exception of punchboards, which they promised to suppress forthwith.

Mr. O'Malley submitted to the committee a report of the survey which showed that warnings to cease operations had been given to all suspected gamblers, including Louis Cohen, although Cohen's chief lieutenant, Patrick Joseph Size, was not in Scranton when the warning was issued. In spite of Mr. O'Malley's disclaimer of responsibility for gambling in the city of Scranton, the "close and stay closed" order described in his report was issued to a number of Scranton gamblers. Those warned included: Richard Booth, distributor for the Square Deal and Penn Limited Treasury-balance lotteries; Joe and Al Baldassari, partners in the horse room at 108 Adams Avenue; Charles Pascucci and Nick Rosse, operators of the horse room in the Greyhound Terminal Building, 218 Adams Avenue; Peter Genello, a bookie associated with the Baldassari brothers; James "Bus" Caffrey, operator of a horse room at 217 Penn Avenue; Michael Nemetz, operator of a horse room at 226 Lackawanna Avenue; Eugene Allegrucci, distributor of the Domino Treasury-balance lottery; James

Martin, distributor of the Black Diamond Treasury-balance lottery; Adolph "Dolly" Rosar, distributor for the New Deal Treasury-balance lottery; Michael Size, distributor for the Emperial Treasury-balance lottery; Dickey Rose, a telephone bookmaker; and Thomas Sesso, head of the numbers racket.

Committee counsel posed this question to Mr. O'Malley: "I wonder if you can explain why it is the place stays wide open until our investigators arrive and our investigators can find it (gambling) like any other citizen, yet the police are not doing anything about it. Are the police receiving protection for that?" His answer was, "I have no knowledge of that and cannot answer it." Mr. O'Malley's attention was also called to the fact that the horse room in the Greyhound Terminal Building was across the street from the district attorney's office and the Baldassari horse room was in the next block. He acknowledged that a gambling place in Carbondale was located in a building owned by the mother of the prothonotary of Lackawanna County.

Mr. O'Malley argued that crime conditions in Lackawanna County are far better than they were prior to World War II. He attributed this improvement largely to the action of the Army and the FBI.

Joseph Scalleat, Hazleton racketeer, was recommended for contempt by the committee after a brief but highly irritating appearance. He refused to bring records as directed by the subpena because he "didn't think it was necessary" and he defiantly told the committee at the outset that he was going to refuse to answer all questions. He refused to tell the committee what business he was pursuing, whether he had any brothers named Sam and Albert, or if he knew Jack Parisi, a former New York convict, or had any contacts with him. He refused to say if he remembered Parisi's arrest by State police in a hide-out located in a building occupied by his sister and her husband.

David F. Haggerty, a constable in Scranton for 12 years and an owner of harness-racing horses, refused to tell the committee whether or not he had any interest in the horse room on Penn Avenue operated by James "Buz" Caffrey. He admitted that he gave no attention to his duties as constable because it was strictly a commission or fee office and "I just never went in for it." He testified that he derives no income from being a constable and that he "just about breaks even" in the operation of his stable, but he declined to answer when questioned about the source of $19,500 in "commissions" listed in his income-tax returns for 1949 and 1950.

The committee asked Mr. Haggerty, "Do you know of any political contributions made from the gambling interests in connection with the political life of Scranton?" His answer was, "I will have to decline to answer that on the grounds it may tend to incriminate me."

Thomas Sesso, who has lived in Scranton 33 years, has been a numbers banker for 20 years and has never been arrested himself, although his runners were apprehended three or four times. He told the committee he grossed $15,000 to $20,000 a year and operated only in a couple of blocks in the central city because "when a man don't stretch too far the police never get you."

There were times during his years as a numbers banker that he was compelled to suspend operations. How did he know "when the heat was on?". His answer, "The city gives the order out to the cops, something comes out, then I just stop." As a numbers banker he has done well financially. When he gave up his shoemaking establishment 20 years ago, he had nothing. Now he has $15,000 in cash, three properties, invested money in a mortgage, and a Lincoln automobile. He was asked, "You are retiring now on your earnings?" He replied, "That's right. Right now I don't know nothing. When the future coming, I don't know what I do."

Two Scranton police captains appearing before the committee blandly insisted that their manifold duties in other fields of police work left them with little time to enforce gambling laws. Richard Beynon, the day captain, maintained that he was responsible only for traffic control. He knew the horse rooms were operating but didn't know if they had wire service. He knew Treasury tickets were sold in the city but he claimed he never personally witnessed any sales. He didn't know the Cohens or anything about them but he knew the Baldassari brothers as "businessmen" and he also knew that the numbers lottery was operating. He did not know of any numbers bankers other than Sesso, but he did not think there were any.

The only slot machines Beynon knew anything about were located in veterans' posts and private clubs but he had no knowledge about whether they were operating. Asked about a raid on a gambling house in West Scranton in which the raiding detail seized eight or nine men but "lost" all but two of them before the arrival of the lieutenant, Beynon said he didn't know whether any disciplinary action had been taken on account of the "loss" of prisoners because that was not under his jurisdiction.

James G. Conaboy, captain on the 4 p. m. to midnight shift, testified he knew very little about the numbers business because operations were virtually over before his shift began. Office details and handling of complaints about disorderly conduct, mischievous boys, etc., keep him so busy "that I do not have the time to personally go out and observe every activity in the city or under my jurisdiction. From the fact that no patrolman, sergeant, or lieutenant has ever submitted verbally or written any complaint to me, I had presumed that the conditions in Scranton were at least favorable, and I had no occasion to suspect anything else."

If any gambling violation had been brought to his attention, Conaboy said, he would have made out a report to the superintendent of police, but "I never had a complaint from a subordinate, citizen, or anybody else as to the activities of a horse room or numbers, and therefore I would have no occasion or necessity to submit a report to my superior."

The Scranton, Pittston, and Wilkes-Barre horse rooms were all "drops" for wire service being supplied by Metro-Globe News Service of Hoboken, N. J. In Scranton, only one operator applied for the service under his own name. The other three adopted the obviously fictitious names of the "Greek Social Club," the "Modern Amusement Co." and the "B. & B. Club." The Pittston subscribers were the "Pittston Social Club" and the "Wyoming Valley Social Club." In Wilkes-Barre the service was furnished to J. Sheerin.

The committee sought the testimony of Jack Parisi, long-time associate of Albert Anastasia, reputed head of Murder, Inc., in New York, about his activities in Hazleton, Pa., but Parisi entered a Philadelphia hospital the day before the committee's hearing on

August 7. Doctors confirmed that he was suffering from a chronic leg injury directly attributed to a bullet wound in the hip sustained many years ago.

Parisi vanished from New York in 1939 when police began hunting him for two murders. For 10 years he enjoyed sanctuary in Pennsylvania coal field communities until State police flushed him out of a specially designed hide-out in Hazleton and turned him over to the New York authorities. Parisi "beat the rap" in the two murder cases and returned to Hazleton where he blossomed out as production manager in the Nuremberg Dress Co. factory at Nuremberg, a few miles from Hazleton. The owner of the company is Harry Strasser, alias Cohen, alias Lefty, with a New York criminal record. Strasser and Anastasia are partners in the Madison Dress Co. in Hazleton, and Strasser is also listed as the owner of the Mount Carmel Garment Co., in Mount Carmel, Pa.; the Bobby Dress Co. in Dickson City, Pa.; and the Interstate Dress Transportation Co. The committee also has evidence of additional infiltration of the garment industry in Pennsylvania by racket interests but lack of time and funds compelled the committee to forego a more intensive investigation of this phase of racketeering activity in legitimate business.

Except for the aggressive investigative accomplishments of the Pennsylvania State Police and their noteworthy efforts to cripple lottery operations centered in the cities of northeastern Pennsylvania, the committee finds that official lethargy toward organized gambling is so appalling as to be shocking to the public conscience.

The "slap on the wrist" attitude evidenced by the "close and stay closed" orders of nebulous tenure can hardly be regarded as an adequate substitute for rigid enforcement that is marked by arrest and conviction and, where the circumstances warrant it, imprisonment.

(d) READING, PA.

Testimony dealing with Reading, Pa., was heard by the committee at a hearing held in Washington on June 28, 1951.

It was immediately apparent that Reading was what law-enforcement officers describe as an "open town." (i) Two horse rooms operated without molestation within a short distance of the center of the city, one within the shadow of city hall itself; (ii) slot machines were openly exposed except for periodic pronouncements by the district attorney that they must stop, warnings that received scant attention; (iii) punchboards littered store counters, with change from purchases being deliberately placed on them to induce play by minors as well as adults; (iv) numbers were written openly in many places, including newsstands and barber shops.

Numerous complaints were made in vain to enforcement officers. District Attorney John E. Ruth answered that he viewed gambling as part of the life of the community that had to be accepted and, anyhow, he was a prosecutor and not an investigator. This was on May 2, 1949, and the following month church groups who approached Mayor John Davis were told that gambling was part of the nature of the people of Reading and that the city was not any worse than other cities of its size. He said it was not his responsibility as mayor to rid the city of gambling. He said it was the responsibility of the clergy to induce the people to stop gambling.

Western Union records introduced at the hearing showed that a horse room at 601 Franklin Street had been receiving wire service from March 22, 1950, until May 28, 1951, when it became known that the committee was making its investigation. However, service to a horse room at 31 Poplar Street, which began on March 4, 1950, was still being continued as of June 7, 1951, the date upon which Western Union supplied the data. The subscriber for the Franklin Street place was listed as "Ben Moyer" and in the case of the Poplar Street operation the subscriber was "Moyer A. C." The service came from Metro-Globe News Service, Hoboken, N. J., a distributor for Continental News Service.

Actually the operator of the Franklin Avenue horse room was Alex Fudeman, nephew of Abraham and Isadore Minker, long-standing racket powers in Reading and in control of practically all gambling. The building in which it operated was owned by Thomas A. Williams, who admitted that the horse room had been located in the basement of the building for years. Williams displayed some remorse over the committee's entry into Reading and the danger of losing his tenant. As he put it, "Who else would pay $150 a month for it?"

The committee secured from Ralph S. Kreitz, a lifelong resident of Reading and an operator of slot machines for more than 20 years, some idea of the "take" realized by the owners of these machines and their locations. He said he owned about 100 machines and had been operating until the committee's investigators came to town. He insisted that the machines were all in chartered clubs and that there were no machines located where youngsters could play them. These "clubs" were found to have practically no restrictions on membership, payment of nominal annual dues being practically the only requirement for membership.

According to Kreitz, profits from the machines were split on a 50–50 basis between the owner of the establishment and himself. He estimated the share received by his locations during the preceding 14 months at $180,000. His share, he maintained, was only about $60,000 because of heavy expenditures for beer, lunches, and so forth, to insure "good will." Kreitz figures his net income "in a good year" at $25,000 to $30,000 after the payment of all salaries and expenses, but asserted that there were times when he was forced to close down and "live off his fat." He also admitted that he operated punchboards and console slot machines, but declared that he realized very little revenue from these.

Kreitz was never arrested for gambling or slot-machine operations except once 15 years ago by the State police, but if too many complaints were made, the local police sometimes chased him out of his locations. One such period lasted 9 months. He admitted that there were others in the same racket but he would not name them. The State police had "knocked off" his machines on two occasions, once putting him completely out of business. It was some time before he was able to accumulate enough funds to obtain more machines. He admitted also that the Federal Government caught up to him in 1948 for income-tax evasion for which he went to jail.

Kreitz defended gambling and even tried to picture Reading gamblers as benevolent characters. According to him, if a man were to lose $500 betting on a horse and the "bookie" learned that he couldn't afford it, the money would be returned to the man's family. He said there had been occasions when a player lost $60 or $70 in his slot machines and he saw to it that the money was refunded "rather than have any trouble."

Kreitz' personal relationships with public officials were not without significance. He holds "open house" for men in all walks of life, including important city officials. The district attorney visited him once when he was sick and a State policeman once took him for a plane ride to Florida. He could not remember whose plane it was. Also, he admitted having given $800 to Lieutenant Hoffman of the Reading police "to save his life when he was sick" and that he didn't expect to get the money back. Kreitz is only one of several racketeers in Reading and his operations are probably dwarfed by those of the Minker brothers.

Abraham and Isadore Minker, on the surface, are in the wholesale fruit and produce business and operate two realty companies. Behind the scenes they engage in activities about which they refused to testify on the ground that their testimony might tend to incriminate them. Their nephew, Alex Fudeman, a former bootlegger who operates the two horse rooms, also refused to testify on the same ground.

Abraham Minker, a Russian immigrant who was penniless in 1939 when he was released from Lewisburg Federal penitentiary, is far from penniless now. He and his brother Isadore refused to say whether they knew Frank Costello, Owney Madden, Nig Rosen, Willie Weisberg, or Muggsy Taylor, and they refused to identify the source of large amounts of miscellaneous income reported in at least one case in an income-tax return as being derived from "gambling."

The conduct of all three of these witnesses before the committee was such that they were subsequently cited for contempt of Congress and their cases are now in the hands of the United States attorney for the District of Columbia for prosecution.

Perhaps some light is thrown on the Minkers' affairs by the testimony of their bookkeeper, Miss Ann Brenner, a reluctant witness whose unexplained accumulation of wealth still remains a mystery. Over the 4-year period of 1946 to 1949 the combined income of herself and her sister was approximately $37,000. Yet, during that time they had invested $17,000 in Government bonds, made loans totaling $21,000, purchased stocks worth more than $22,000, put $7,500 in Federal savings and loan bonds, and loaned $24,000 to the Minkers' Brighton Realty Co. In addition, they had $15,910 in cash in a safe-deposit box and had three bank accounts. Miss Brenner could not even hazard a guess as to the balances remaining in these accounts. The bank records showed deposits over the 4-year period aggregating $61,037.18. She admitted that the deposits looked high but she guessed, "It may be the same money rotating."

Miss Brenner's investments included loans of $4,000 to Lt. Albert M. Hoffman of the Reading police and $2,400 to Richard Birney, son of the chief of police, but she denied that these were to incur police sympathy toward the Minkers' operations.

Her explanation consisted of vague statements about family savings and frugal living, along with a few claims that were not entirely consistent with her income-tax returns. She recalled vaguely that the tax returns of Isadore Minker showed "miscellaneous income or gambling or something to that effect," and that she might have seen that on the returns of Isadore or Abraham, or both, but she brushed this aside by saying, "I am a bookkeeper. I am not to judge other people's lives."

The most dismal and distressing aspect of the story of the failure of the law enforcement in Reading was extracted from Chief Birney, the final witness. The committee can classify his testimony only as "pitiful." Chief Birney has held his job for more than 7 years and is the head of a department with a personnel of 155, including policemen and civilian employees. But he solemnly told the committee that the top law enforcement officer in Reading was the sheriff and that the mayor, and not he, was the man who had complete supervision over the police department under the Third Class City Act of the State of Pennsylvania.

Chief Birney said he had "assumed" that the Minkers and Alex Fudeman had been "partly at the head" of the rackets in Reading for a period of years but it had never been proved. He had "heard" there had been two wide-open horse rooms in the city for 20 years but no investigation was ever made because he did not receive any complaints. He admitted that the horse rooms were never raided and no arrests for bookmaking had ever been made since he became chief.

"The policy of the department is to act on complaints only on orders from the mayor. No complaints were received, nor no orders given," was a stock answer made repeatedly to questions addressed to Chief Birney by the committee. He asserted that a report of a violation submitted by an officer on the beat was not considered a complaint.

Chief Birney said he never consulted with the mayor about rumors that the horse rooms were operating. He said his orders were that if complaints were received the police were to warn the parties responsible, but that no arrests were to be made "unless absolutely necessary."

"In a small department you don't initiate action. You wait for orders. You don't set a policy, you merely carry out a policy. That is what I did," said Birney in defense of his position. He admitted that he had seen a newspaper article in 1949 which stressed that gambling was wide open in Reading and that "the syndicate" was getting $5,000,000 annually, but he had done nothing about it. He denied knowing anything about the special "pagoda" stamp which was attached to punchboards, suspected as being a sign that those particular boards were protected, and he admitted that he had never investigated to find out what he could about any such stamp.

Chief Birney did recall one occasion when a ban on punchboards was ordered, but he insisted that tobacco and candy companies in Reading stormed the mayor's office complaining that the ban was interfering with trade and compelled the mayor to lift the ban.

The committee has no difficulty, after reviewing the Reading testimony and particularly that of Chief Birney, in arriving at the conclusion that Reading is a classic example of political strangulation of a police department at the behest of gambling interests seeking to thwart any interference with their activities.

D. CRIME IN LARGE CITIES

(a). NEW YORK CITY

When the committee concluded its public hearings in New York City in March 1951, there was one witness whose name had appeared time and again in the testimony of other witnesses but whose presence could not be obtained. He is Irving Sherman, one-time intimate friend of William O'Dwyer at the time O'Dwyer was mayor of New York.

The committee's desire to question Sherman in the March hearings had been widely publicized and it was later learned that Sherman was aware of the fact that he was being sought, but he failed to appear. Shortly after the New York hearings closed, Sherman's lawyer accepted service of a committee subpena for him, but there has never been a satisfactory explanation of his reason for desiring to avoid the committee's process.

Sherman had been described as a man of great mystery who might furnish information regarding the relationship between some of the officials of New York City and the gangster syndicates who control bookmaking and the wire service monopoly.

The intimate friendship between O'Dwyer and Sherman had already been established, as had the friendship between Sherman and Costello.

From the testimony at previous hearings of the committee and from the indictments obtained through the fine work of District Attorney Frank Hogan of New York County and District Attorney Miles F. McDonald of Kings County, it had become apparent that substantial sums had been paid in graft in recent years. Bookmakers operating on an enormous scale paid regular protection to the police department but no one was able to ascertain how much of the "take" filtered through to the top.

In the fire department, it was known that James Moran, O'Dwyer's loyal friend, who has been convicted of perjury for his false testimony before this committee, had established a regular system for collecting graft required to be paid for oil-burner installation permits.

James Moran, the man who probably knows more than any other about New York graft, lied before this committee and has since refused to talk at all. After his conviction for perjury, he was offered the opportunity to tell the truth but he declined the invitation, perhaps because the 5-year sentence he has received for perjury is less that what the truth would bring.

With Moran silent, it was hoped that Irving Sherman might be able to throw some light on the subject. Sherman had friends on all sides of the fence. Besides being an intimate of O'Dwyer, he knew Congressmen and other public officials. He was widely known in the garment industry. And he had known such men as "Bugsy" Siegel, Frank Costello, "Niggy" Rutkin, and other underworld characters. He would be a natural for the role of go-between.

The committee found that Sherman would not be the fertile source of information that many had expected. However, it felt that he should be called as a witness and the testimony he gave was not without interest.

He appeared before the committee in a public hearing in Washington, D. C., accompanied by counsel. He refused to testify unless all radio, newsreel cameras, and television cameras were turned off. With great reluctance the committee complied with this demand because it was faced with the choice of holding him for contempt or obtaining his testimony. It came to the conclusion that the public interest would best be served by doing what was necessary to have him talk. His testimony confirmed previous testimony of other witnesses to the effect that he was formerly a good friend of O'Dwyer, working strenuously for him in the 1945 New York mayoralty election. He admitted his acquaintanceship with Costello and "Bugsy" Siegel.

Perhaps the most sensational part of his testimony was to the effect that in late October 1945, just before the election, he left town at the urgent request of O'Dwyer, who sent a messenger urging him to leave immediately in order to be unavailable to the press. The reason given was that the former expected a newspaper blast linking Sherman to himself on the one hand and to Frank Costello and "Bugsy" Siegel on the other. Sherman acceded promptly to this request, leaving the next day with his family on a trip that had no destination but which eventually took him to Florida, where he waited until the campaign was over. When asked why he would make such a sacrifice, he said, "because the man asked me to, and I thought enough of him to do it."

When Sherman returned, he found himself to be an outcast. O'Dwyer would not see him and when he went to see Moran his identity was mysteriously shrouded in the fictitious name "Dr. Cooper." Sherman said he thought use of this name was intended as a joke, but he admitted it might have been for purposes of concealment.

Sherman was closely questioned concerning his avoidance of the New York hearings. He admitted discussing his absence with several friends during the time the committee was actively seeking him, but he denied that he was waiting for the committee to go out of existence before appearing.

Sherman testified that during the twenties he had been an adjuster for the American Cloak and Suit Association, that in 1937 he had gone to California for about 3 years and then returned to New York in 1940. He described himself as a legitimate businessman throughout and stated that presently he is in the clothing manufacturing business. He admitted to an arrest for gambling but denied any other illegitimate activities.

The following associations of Sherman were developed in the hearing: While working for the Cloak and Suit Association, he met and knew Louis "Lepke" Buchalter and Jacob "Gurrah" Shapiro because "you had to know them * * * they would make you do that." Sherman denied having had any dealings with them, but admitted their power over the industry. While in California from 1937 to 1940, he became friendly with Benjamin "Bugsy" Siegel, and went to the track with him. He said that Frank Orsatti, of the Orsatti Bros. Theatrical Agency, introduced them. Sherman gave no satisfactory answer as to his purpose of his occupation in California, although he denied having left New York, as did many others, because of the "heat" put on by Gov. Thomas E. Dewey, then district attorney of New York. He also denied participation in the then incipient labor shake-down in the movie industry.

According to his testimony, Sherman returned to New York in 1940, as general manager of Phono-Vision Co., a New York subsidiary of a

California company of the same name of which Frank Orsatti was president; Frank Orsatti brought Sherman into contact with Frank Costello, who was represented as being interested in investing in the enterprise; Sherman negotiated with Costello with a view to giving him the Louisiana distributorship for Phono-Vision's slot machine type of projector by which the customer may select and view a movie for 10 cents; Costello wanted the distributorship for "Dandy Phil" Kastel. Sherman claimed that no significance should be attached to the fact that Phil Kastel was also Costello's slot machine distributor for Louisiana. Sherman's idea was that slot machines and Phono-Vision projectors might well be used by the same customers, including bars, night clubs, and casinos.

Sherman said that he and Costello negotiated at some length with Costello coming "to the office, oh, once or twice a week for quite some time," although Sherman does not know whether Costello actually put up any money for stock. In this connection it is of note that Costello, when before the committee in New York last March, answering a question as to whether he and Sherman engaged in business together said, "Absolutely not."

In addition, Sherman admitted knowing Meyer Lansky, James "Niggy" Rutkin, Joe Adonis, and Joe Stacher, alias Doc Rosen alias Doc Harris, all of whom are known gamblers and racketeers.

Turning next to Sherman's association with Ambassador O'Dwyer, Sherman said he met O'Dwyer in the winter of 1941–42 with James J. Moran in a Broadway restaurant, the introduction being made by a now deceased New York detective named Jack Gorman; the friendship quickly grew and they saw each other frequently in Washington; in fact, they stayed at the Mayflower Hotel simultaneously on 15 occasions during the war years. Sherman thought O'Dwyer "was a real nice man." Sherman attempted to explain his continual presence in Washington by saying that he was there to sell Phono-Vision's 300 completed projectors to the Army Signal Corps, and to obtain business for other corporations.

Sherman's testimony concerning the 1942 meeting at Frank Costello's apartment on the subject of Joe Baker's Air Corps contracts differed somewhat from that of O'Dwyer. The latter had testified in March that he thought he had asked Sherman to arrange the meeting because "I knew he knew Costello." Sherman, on the other hand, said Moran came to him and asked him to attend, and O'Dwyer was incorrect when he said that Sherman arranged it. Sherman said he did not learn what the meeting concerned until afterward because he was detained at the bar by Mrs. Costello and another man and gained the impression that he was not wanted in the "huddle" which included Costello and O'Dwyer.

Sherman denied that there was any standing arrangement under which he would be brought into New York City from La Guardia Airport by Abraham Goldman, deputy chief inspector, New York Police Department, but he said that Goldman had brought him and Frank V. Connolly, Chief, Special Rating Division, WPB, and friend of O'Dwyer, in from La Guardia several times. He said that Goldman was a close friend of O'Dwyer's.

Sherman was in Washington at the Mayflower at the same time as O'Dwyer at least once a week between February 14 and March 29, 1945. On the latter date, O'Dwyer announced his candidacy for the New York mayoralty. However, Sherman said he had "nothing whatsoever" to do with the decision. Sherman, nevertheless, asked people in the garment industry "to do everything they can, to vote for him, to help him," and collected and turned over to Moran or Moe Sherman (a deceased raincoat manufacturer) "between four, five, maybe six thousand dollars at different intervals." This money, Sherman guessed, was turned over to O'Dwyer.

As a result of the treatment of Sherman after the election, he and O'Dwyer are no longer friendly.

Sherman was closely questioned concerning his selective service registration and classification of 4-A, essential occupation. In his selective service occupational questionnaire, filed July 17, 1942, on which his classification was granted, he listed himself as working exclusively for Federal Aircraft Products, Inc. But the pay roll records of Federal Aircraft indicate that Sherman was not carried until the week of October 29, 1942. Sherman continued on the pay roll until the week of October 8, 1943, approximately 3 weeks after he was deferred and never notified selective service of his change in occupation. His only explanation was that the books must be wrong.

(b). NORTHERN NEW JERSEY

The committee renewed its investigation of Abner Zwillman because it felt that his previous testimony before the committee had not been complete.

The committee was greatly handicapped in its investigation of Zwillman by the fact that honest citizens who were glad to tell the committee's investigators in confidence what they knew about his great influence in important governmental circles were too terrified to testify in the open for fear of personal or political reprisal or financial ruin. The committee's staff knows that his influence extends to Newark and other political bailiwicks but time did not permit full development of these aspects of the investigation.

Like Frank Costello in New York, Zwillman exercises his influence in New Jersey in a manner that makes detection almost impossible. He makes it a practice never to attend any public function and he avoids wherever possible having his name appear openly in any financial transaction. Twice he sought to avoid testifying before the committee. In March, after a long search and extensive conferences with his counsel, he at last testified briefly before the committee at a time when its time was too limited for a thorough examination. Many questions asked of him at that time he refused to answer on the ground that his answers might tend to incriminate him.

When counsel for the committee advised his counsel in July that he was wanted again for questioning, he vanished entirely. His counsel claimed they did not know of his whereabouts, his home was empty with no one to receive telegrams or mail and a Nation-wide search by the United States marshals, the Coast Guard, and the committee's staff failed to reveal his whereabouts. The inference is inescapable that Zwillman, in spite of his wealth and political power, has a great deal to hide.

Zwillman's beginnings were as a vegetable cart peddler in the third ward of Newark. His great opportunity came when he and his childhood friend, Joseph Stacher, found a chance to go into bootlegging.

They eventually became partners in what became the largest bootlegging syndicate of the prohibition era.

The fabulous bootlegger incarnate

The committee was most fortunate in having testimony from Mr. Edwin A. Baldwin, a recently retired member of the Intelligence Unit, United States Treasury, who, with other revenue agents, conducted an intensive investigation of Zwillman and his associates covering the period between approximately 1926 and the beginning of World War II. Mr. Baldwin's testimony and that of Joseph H. Reinfeld given in the 1950 tax fraud case of *United States* v. *Rutkin* (in which Rutkin was convicted and received a 4-year sentence and a $10,000 fine) together paint an amazing picture of Zwillman the bootlegger. The picture had been known only dimly before the public hearings in Washington on August 16 and 17, 1951.

From a background of poverty and privation, he rose in a decade to become the holder of a 40 or 50 percent interest in the Reinfeld Syndicate, an organization which imported nearly 40 percent of all the illicit alcohol consumed in the United States during prohibition. The sums of money involved were staggering, as the following excerpt from the record attests:

Q. Now, Mr. Baldwin, as a result of your investigation, can you give us an approximation in money of how much this syndicate collected from 1926 to 1933?
A. All I can tell you is what we found * * *. We uncovered bank deposits of around $25,000,000, then we found out that was only part of the syndicate's operations. We found that the cash they took in they never deposited. * * * Mr. Stacher at one time told me that they collected at least as much cash as they collected (checks). * * *
Q. So that roughly the Reinfeld Syndicate collected approximately $60,000,000 from their illegal liquor distributorships?
A. Based on my investigation, I would say yes.

In the early days Zwillman was big and tough. He was arrested several times for assault and battery, and once in 1930 he was convicted of atrocious assault and battery when he beat a numbers runner almost to death. He came out of the notorious third ward in Newark, where he helped organize the Third Ward Political Club which had its headquarters in or near a saloon run by one "Pop" Handler, whose son, Charles, is presently statutory representative for several of Zwillman's legitimate companies as well as corporation counsel of the city of Newark. Among his associates were Joseph "Doc" Stacher, alias "Doc" Rosen, alias "Doc" Harris, a big-time gambler with a record; Jerry Catena, whose participation in gambling operations is well known; Willy Tiplitz recently convicted with Zwillman's cousin, Daniel, for running a fixed numbers game; Charles Haber, alias Charles Haberman, recently convicted and sentenced to 10 years on a narcotics charge; James "Niggy" Rutkin, known in prohibition days as Zwillman's "enforcer."

These men, or most of them, joined the group led by Joseph Reinfeld, known as the Reinfeld Syndicate. This syndicate, dealing largely with the Bronfman interests which owned the Bronfman Distillery of Canada, carried on what they described as the "high seas operation." The system under which they operated consisted of bringing liquor from Canada, France, England, Scotland, and Germany to the little St. Lawrence River island of St. Pierre et Miquelon and there transshipping it to "rum runway" 12 miles off Sandy Hook.

At that point the syndicate's customers took over and ran the liquor into the United States. Much of the money received would be sent in $100,000 and $500,000 lots, frequently in gold, to Canada "so that in case this country got too hot for them, they would have something if they had to flee."

When the customs authorities investigated the settlement and obtained a payment of $3,000,000, Zwillman immediately filed several delinquent income-tax returns. When Mr. Baldwin asked Zwillman why he had done this, Zwillman said, "I saw what happened to Al Capone, and I said to myself, 'Who am I? If they can put Al Capone in jail, these fellows, they can also put me in.' "

Zwillman after repeal, legitimate businessman

When Zwillman appeared before the public hearing of the committee in Washington on March 26, 1951, the following question and answer occurred:

Q. Did I understand from your testimony that since prohibition days you claim you have gone legitimate in your business?

A. From that period of 1935 or 1936 up, I have been trying, Mr. Senator * * * I am trying—trying hard.

This endeavor has been signally successful financially, more so even than the endeavor made by a great, good friend of Zwillman's, Frank Costello. A short summary of Zwillman's legitimate activities will demonstrate this.

After repeal, several members of the Reinfeld Syndicate, including Zwillman and Joseph H. Reinfeld, put the final liquidation dividend of $250,000 into the new liquor-importing corporation of Browne-Vintners. To avoid public disclosure of the participants, all the stock of this corporation was held by a nominee. The original cost was $1,000 a share. In 1940 Browne-Vintners was sold to Seagrams for $7,500,000, the sale price per share being approximately $3,000. Zwillman was alleged to have had a 50 percent stock interest in the company from its inception, but received only 16 percent of the proceeds of dissolution. His complaint on this score plus complaints concerning the allocation of the tax burden and the diversion of corporate business led to a settlement in late 1942 under which Reinfeld paid $308,000 to Zwillman, $50,000 to Stacher and $250,000 to Rutkin. Rutkin failed to report this income in his income-tax returns with the result that he was prosecuted and convicted in 1950 for tax evasion. Reinfeld testified in that case that he had been questioned in late 1949 concerning Zwillman's failure to report the $308,000 he received in this settlement but no action against Zwillman on this score has been taken.

While Zwillman's income-tax returns were being investigated the confidential agents' reports mysteriously disappeared from the files of the Bureau of Internal Revenue in Washington. Later direct quotations from these reports appeared in legal papers used by Rutkin.

Browne-Vintners was not by any means Zwillman's only legitimate venture after prohibition. In 1935, the United States Yeast Co. was incorporated and Zwillman at its inception held 40 percent of the stock for which he paid $10,000. The company operated at a loss despite the fact that Zwillman poured money into it. As of August 31, 1936, it owed him $55,947.08 and it was sold in early 1947. There was also the Harr Kegtap System, Inc., incorporated in 1936, and which at the time of its liquidation in 1938 owed Zwillman $24,252.41.

There are at least six other more successful ventures in which Zwillman has participated in a managerial capacity. There is Public Service Tobacco, distributor of cigarettes through vending machines, owned one-half by Zwillman's immediate family and one-half by the family of "Big Mike" Lascari, a close friend of "Lucky" Luciano, who took $2,500 to Luciano in Italy in 1949. This company for the fiscal year ending November 30, 1949, had gross sales of $1,421,881.38.

Another enterprise is Federal Automatic Co., Inc., which rents washing machines and which reported gross receipts for the year 1949 of $114,872.34. Zwillman also owns 97 percent of the shares of E & S Trading Co., dealers in iron and steel for which he paid $97,000. Finally there are his General Motors distributorship, parts and service agency, and used-car business. In the year 1948 alone, the city of Newark, for which Zwillman's lawyer, Charles Handler, is corporation counsel, purchased $379,983.36 worth of trucks from Zwillman's business, despite the fact that the other bids were lower and the same trucks could probably have been bought elsewhere by the city for $16,000 less.

Zwillman has also invested money in enterprises in which he takes no part in the management, sometimes using a "front" to conceal his participation. The committee received testimony regarding several of these but it is certain that these are by no means all. In 1944–45, he invested approximately $60,000 in two independent movie-producing companies; he put about $400,000 into the purchase of the former United States post office site in Louisville, Ky., which was later sold at a profit, although he reported a loss in his income tax returns; and he bought $41,000 worth of bonds in a New York hotel and $21,000 worth of bonds of the Hudson & Manhattan Railroad.

Zwillman and his wife own 42,714 shares (slightly under 2 percent) of the stock of Barium Steel Corp. which is controlled by J. A. Sisto. Out of fairness, it should be said that although Zwillman and Sisto have been close friends for a number of years, the committee found no evidence that Zwillman exercises any influence over the company's affairs. This stock has a present value of about $600,000.

The rough total of these known investments is $1,100,000, a sum which is substantially greater than the legitimate investments admittedly owned by Zwillman's intimate, Frank Costello. Committee testimony indicates that Costello made a $119,000 capital gain from his Wall Street property, has an interest in an infra-red-ray broiler company, and a $41,000 investment in oil wells.

One of the nominees commonly used by Zwillman is Arthur Garfield Hays of the New York bar. Another man who has acted as a nominee for Zwillman is Jules Endler, Newark restaurateur, who was very cooperative in his testimony before the committee. He asked Zwillman why he needed a "front" and Zwillman replied that his known presence "might injure" other participants. Mr. Endler went on to say that in none of the deals in which he had been associated with Zwillman, had there been a full disclosure of his participation even to the other investors.

Zwillman the politician

Although Zwillman has been "trying hard" to be a legitimate businessman since the repeal of prohibition, business has not been the sole outlet for his funds and energies. He seems to have turned to politics on a rather impressive scale, always behind the scenes, of course. His reasons for wanting to exercise political inference are quite obscure.

(i) *State-wide.*—In the 1949 New Jersey gubernatorial campaign, Zwillman, through an intermediary, offered Democratic candidate Elmer Wene $300,000 in return for the right to approve the man appointed attorney general of the State of New Jersey. It is to Mr. Wene's great credit that he turned this offer down flatly, without even permitting the proposal to be fully explained to him. Mr. James A. Bishop who was Mr. Wene's adviser at the time and who testified on this subject before the committee, stated that he was approached by one George Kesselhant, assistant to the Democratic leader of Essex County, N. J., who came to him to say that he had a very important offer to make to Mr. Wene. The offer was that "Zwillman would go for $300,000 to Senator Wene because Zwillman does not want the Wene administration to hurt him * * * that is all he asks." When pressed for more specifications, Kesselhant told Mr. Bishop that Zwillman "would want a friend in the State attorney general's office." Mr. Bishop went on to say that he understood this to mean that Zwillman desired to name the State attorney general.

Wene was not elected governor and his Republican opponent received a heavy vote in Hudson County, a county which has always been overwhelmingly Democratic. As will be seen from the discussion below, there is a strong chance that Zwillman had something to do with having that vote swing away from Wene.

On June 26, 1949, a testimonial dinner was tendered Harold Krieger, assistant corporation counsel of Jersey City and a close friend of Zwillman's. This dinner was held at the Essex House, Newark, and was attended by about 1,100 people, mainly labor leaders and politicians. Krieger as guest of honor received, among other gifts, a gold-plated typewriter and money toward a new car. The toastmaster was Harold G. Hoffman, former Governor of New Jersey, who appeared admittedly on the invitation of Zwillman.

Previously, in the 1946 Republican primary for the governorship, ex-Governor Hoffman had solicited Zwillman's help in the Newark-Essex County area, both by telephoning him personally and by sending an emissary, Joseph Bozzo. Although Bozzo insisted that Zwillman contributed no money, he did say that Zwillman was asked to give all the help he could. The telephone company and hotel records indicate that on March 26 and April 9, 1946, Zwillman called the hotel room in Trenton of State Senator Charles K. Barton, at the time majority leader of the New Jersey Senate. On the first call he asked for Bozzo and on the second, he asked for and apparently spoke to Senator Barton. Bozzo believes that these calls were in reference to Governor Hoffman's candidacy in the Republican primary.

These incidents contrast sharply with the following testimony given by Zwillman when he testified last March:

Q. Will you tell the committee whether in the last 3 years you made any political contributions? * * *
A. I have not made anything of substance anyhow. * * *
Q. Did you ever contribute to a gubernatorial campaign in the State of New Jersey?
A. I am quite sure I did not.

(ii) *The local level.*—In May 1949, the Hague-Eggers administration of Jersey City terminated after approximately 30 years of uninterrupted rule. John V. Kenny and four other city commissioners were elected on the so-called Freedom Ticket. Of these five men, only three remain in power today. The other two have been stripped of their powers because they would not "work in harmony" with the new administration. One is Charles Witkowski, formerly director of public safety, in charge of the police department, who has been stripped of his powers and today is in charge of the city's lighting system, while the other is James M. Murray, formerly commissioner of parks and public property, who presently has under his control only a public bathhouse.

Commissioners Witkowski and Murray together with the former head of the city police racket squad, and one of the patrolmen on the racket squad described for this committee the present picture in Jersey City. Upon entering office in May 1949, the Kenny administration continued for about 6 weeks the racket squad it had inherited from the old Hague-Eggers regime. As this squad proved to be inefficient in the eyes of Commissioner Witkowski, he recommended a change of personnel to Mayor Kenny, who suggested replacements. The new squad, composed of men suggested by Mayor Kenny, made only one arrest in 7 months. Thereupon, Commissioner Witkowski replaced it with men of his own choosing under Detective Joseph Brooks. This squad went immediately to work and made approximately 180 arrests in a comparable 7-month period, with a 95-percent conviction rate. In the 16-month period of the squad's operation, over 325 arrests for gambling, numbers, etc., were made, the highest per capita percentage in the United States. It was estimated by Mr. Brooks that the operation of his squad had, since January 1, 1951, "cost the bookmakers in Jersey City in bail alone approximately $800,000." At the same time, Commissioner Witkowski organized a water-front squad which made a vigorous effort to eradicate usury and gambling, and generally to maintain peace along the notorious Jersey City water front.

The efforts of these squads, and the success of those efforts, caused Mayor Kenny to say to Commissioner Witkowski, "Between the gambling squad and the water-front squad, you are hurting our friends." Kenny attempted to get the same message across to Witkowski through Commissioner Murray.

Among these friends may have been Zwillman associates, even though Zwillman, at the public hearing last March, responding to a question concerning a $50,000 contribution to Mayor Kenny's 1949 campaign, said:

Not 50,000 cents * * * Mr. Senator, that is another fantasy, and whoever gave it to you ought to—I never gave him 50 cents.

Mr. Bishop, when testifying about the $300,000 contribution offered to Senator Wene in return for the right to select the State's attorney general in the 1949 gubernatorial campaign, stated that the intermediary who made the offer for Zwillman said, "You can tell the Senator that Zwillman will do more for Wene than he did for Johnny Kenny." Mayor Kenny, in his testimony, denied he had received help from Zwillman but Bishop seemed quite certain of the accuracy of his own recollections.

Testimony was taken both first from Harold Krieger, labor lawyer and assistant corporation counsel of Jersey City, and then from his former wife, Mrs. Muriel Krieger, resulting in many discrepancies and contradictions. However, Commissioner Murray, to a degree, confirmed part of Mrs. Krieger's statements, and Mrs. Krieger herself testified in a manner that gained the credence of the committee.

Krieger claimed not to remember very clearly about his dealings with Zwillman. He said he met Zwillman at a restaurant just before World War II and learned he was in the tobacco business. He said he might have talked to Zwillman occasionally about legislation affecting the tobacco business but he could not recall clearly. He was sure he had never discussed politics with Zwillman. He said he has seen Zwillman only occasionally but has never represented him legally or otherwise. He said that the acquaintance was casual and social, and that he had never sought Zwillman out, although he might have dropped in at Zwillman's house on occasions when he happened to be near there on other business. He said that in Florida, he had seen Zwillman once or twice on a casual basis just because Zwillman happened to be staying at the same hotel as some of Krieger's friends. Krieger was asked particularly about visiting Zwillman at his hotel in Florida in the winter of 1948 and 1949. Krieger was quite vague about the number of times they had met: "It may have been 10. It may have been two or three. It may have been 12 or 4."

Krieger admits that he occasionally talked to Zwillman on the telephone, but he could not recall why he should have placed two calls costing approximately $6 each to Zwillman in Waukesha, Wis., on January 20 and 22, 1951.

Mr. Krieger's testimony impressed the committee as being vague and general, perhaps even to the point of being evasive. His recollection regarding a number of events seemed to be dubiously dim.

Mrs. Krieger, on the other hand, was much more definite and positive in her testimony. Although she had refused to testify except under subpena, when she actually reached the stand she testified freely, openly, and in a straightforward manner. As she was not in the hearing room at the time Mr. Krieger testified and did not hear his testimony, it cannot be claimed that she was deliberately contradicting her former husband.

Mrs. Krieger said that Zwillman and Krieger consulted each other often on labor and political matters; that during some periods Krieger would call Zwillman "quite frequently," and that "there were times when [Krieger] would see [Zwillman] once a week * * * on Saturdays generally * * * sometimes for 2 months at a time." She said these visits were always prearranged by telephone and that Krieger went to Zwillman's house for the specific purpose of seeing him. She said Krieger's statement that he dropped in at Zwillman's house only when in his neighborhood was not correct.

Regarding visits by Krieger to Zwillman in Florida in the winter of 1948 and 1949, Mrs. Krieger testified that "they used to confer almost every afternoon" by prearrangement. She had been present on several occasions when they conferred beside the pool at the Hotel Martinique, and at other times, Krieger would tell her that he was going over to talk to Zwillman and on his return he would report that he had done so. Mrs. Krieger also said that in Florida, Krieger would see Jerry Catena, Zwillman's former associate, the person from whom Zwillman and Lascari bought the Public Service Tobacco Co. Catena is a big-time gambling operator who was suspected by Mr. Baldwin, former Treasury intelligence agent, of being a front for Zwillman.

Mr. Krieger denied ever using the term "Big Fellow" when referring to Zwillman and "Little Fellow" when referring to Mayor Kenny. Mrs. Krieger, on the other hand, was quite definite in saying that Krieger used those terms almost exclusively in referring to Zwillman and Kenny and called Zwillman the "Big Fellow" even when talking to him. She added that these nicknames were used partly to conceal the identity of the individuals when talking on the telephone. Under persistent questioning, she also said Zwillman clearly dominated Krieger. She said, "Well, he would consult with him and ask his opinion, and if Zwillman said anything, I believe it was done."

Krieger admitted doing for Mayor Kenny everything "an individual can do to elect a candidate" in the 1949 campaign in Jersey City but he denied having directed the campaign, swinging the labor vote, or discussing the campaign with Zwillman. Mrs. Krieger, on the other hand, stated that Krieger had discussed the campaign with Zwillman on several occasions, and she recalled a dinner with Kenny's son-in-law and his wife at which Krieger virtually promised to swing the labor vote to Kenny. This testimony was supported by that of Commissioner Murray, who testified that Kenny told him, in an effort to make Murray more agreeable to the use of Krieger's law office for press releases, photographs, etc., that "Mr. Krieger was most instrumental, in fact almost solely instrumental, in getting a labor parade, which was a very big parade there, during our campaign and that he did that job almost alone."

The committee believes that Krieger knows more about Zwillman's participation in politics than he is willing to admit.

Associations

Zwillman apparently has found it somewhat difficult to shake off his past associations with criminals. Indeed, he maintains contacts with so many of them that it would probably be closer to the truth to say that his effort to "go straight" in this respect is more half-hearted than difficult. A list of his associates since repeal and his conversion to legitimate activities reads like a "Who's Who" in big-time, interstate crime.

Frank Costello, whom he met in the prohibition era, and whom he admits knowing "very well," is still close enough to him to be in fairly regular telephone contact. He knew and called "Bugsy" Siegel, west coast mobster, before the latter's still unsolved murder in 1947. He admits knowing "fairly well" Meyer Lansky, E. J. Catena, a convicted murderer, Willie Moretti, Solly Moretti, Charles "Lucky" Luciano, Frank Erickson, "one, maybe two" of the Fischettis (Capone's legatees in Chicago), Joe "Doc" Stacher, and Joe Adonis. The following testimony indicates what Zwillman thinks about these associations:

Q. Costello is a big racketeer, isn't he?
A. If I got to believe what they say about him in the papers, then people will believe what they say about me, so I am not believing it.

The original purpose of these associations is illustrated by the following excerpt from Zwillman's testimony:

Q. Did you have any business with Joe Adonis during prohibition?

A. Nothing of importance. The only reason, you sometimes can't tell. If you sold an office and you didn't know who the partner was in the office, so he might have been a partner.

It is to be remembered that the above-named racketeers, gangsters, and gamblers continue as associates of Zwillman as of the last few years. In addition, he maintains close present contacts with Jerry Catena. Catena is a hoodlum whose convictions include one for bribing a juror when Nicky Delmore was tried for the murder of a prohibition agent. In the year 1946 Catena and Joe Adonis as partners received $120,000 from one gambling establishment alone. Catena is vice president and majority stockholder of People's Express Co., an organization which attempted to rent for $96,000 per year the $8,300,000 Newark Union Truck Terminal, the carrying charges of which are close to $500,000 per year. The local teamsters' union had virtually closed the terminal down by one of its loading rules but Catena's representative was able to assure the Port of New York Authority which built and owns the terminal that People's Express would have no labor trouble.

Zwillman's partner in Public Service Tobacco Co. is Michael "Big Mike" Lascari who was brought up in the same household as "Lucky" Luciano. So close is Lascari to Luciano that he visited Luciano in 1949 in Italy for a week and admits that he took Luciano at least $2,500. Lascari also gave "Lucky's" brother a Manhattan juke-box distributorship after "Lucky's" deportation because, as he put it, "our relationship, so far as the Luciano family was concerned, was very close. He was not doing anything; as a matter of providing a means of making a living I gave it to him."

When asked how he reconciled these unsavory associations with his endeavor to become and remain legitimate, Zwillman said:

Truthfully, I am traveling by myself. I am not looking to run away from anybody if they are not breaking the law. If they are breaking the law, they could go their own way, it is none of my business. I am trying to—I spend my time in the office all day and home all night.

This is the language of the man who craftily evaded the committee's Nation-wide hunt in July and August 1951, when it was seeking his presence again for a public hearing in Washington.

(c) FLORIDA

The return visit

The committee returned to the Miami area in June to view developments since its last investigation. Information as to events occurring since that last visit was furnished by the testimony of Dan P. Sullivan, operating director of the Crime Commission of Greater Miami. Mr. Sullivan expressed concern that little had been done regarding an investigation of contributors to the 1948 gubernatorial campaign with its interstate racket implications, nor had the Florida State Racing Commission effectively removed the cloud over the dog racing in the state because of disclosures of the holdings and activities of Capone associates.

With regard to the 1948 campaign, three of the major contributors were Louis E. Wolfson, C. V. Griffin, and William H. Johnston, principal operator of four Florida dog tracks and an Illinois race track and an old-time associate of Al Capone's legatees. The total contribution of these three alone was in excess of $400,000. Yet the incumbent, Gov. Fuller Warren, submitted an affidavit purporting to reflect the total of contributions to his campaign as required by Florida law that accounted for $8,825, and he omitted from his schedule of contributors the foregoing named persons. Further, there seemed to have been no State interest manifested in the apparent violation of section 550.07 of the Florida statutes concerning campaign contributions by an officer or stockholder of a racing licensee corporation. At previous hearings Johnston had sworn to substantial campaign contributions to Governor Warren's gubernatorial campaign. Notwithstanding, Johnston and his tracks seem to enjoy immunity from State level inquiry.

Racket attempt to control public opinion through the press and radio

Information was obtained in this return visit to Miami concerning the infiltration of out-of-State racketeers into the Miami newspaper area in order to protect and insure the tremendous illicit profit to be made from gambling in that area. Testimony was received concerning the sponsorship and purpose of a newspaper founded in 1949 and known as the Daily Mail. An exconvict named Harry I. Voiler testified that he had started the newspaper but denied that any money had been invested by Martin Accardo, formerly of the Capone gang. However, Mrs. Oretta Y. Carroll, who had been married to Accardo, testified and produced documentary proof that Accardo had invested $125,000 in this journal. Mrs. Carroll also said that Voiler had attempted to enlist her aid in persuading Tony "The Enforcer" Accardo (Martin's brother), sometimes described as the "new Capone," to "solicit" advertisements from night-club owners and movie operators. She stated that the purposes of this paper were (1) to provide prompt dissemination of racing results and (2) to create a favorable atmosphere toward out-of-State racketeer elements to be found in Miami. In support of this latter purpose an editorial from the Daily Mail welcoming the notorious Frank Costello to Miami was received in the record.

The revelation that Lee Mason, alias Chicago Phil Friedlander, a man with a lengthy criminal record of many types of offenses, had been recently serving Miami area radio stations as a disc jockey and commentator with obvious potentialities as a molder of public opinion from a point of view most advantageous to the racket interests, was topped only by Mason's modest admission that "I am considered more or less of an authority on law-enforcement matters" and "for 5 years I did a program known as Criminal Court Notes." The committee did not doubt that Mason could speak with the authority of one who had viewed law enforcement from many angles, but could scarcely approve the use of the air waves to the unsuspecting public as a medium for the expression of his beliefs.

The committee experienced considerable difficulty in obtaining testimony from the former sheriff of Dade County (which embraces the Greater Miami area), James A. Sullivan. This man, who had been removed and shortly thereafter reinstated by Governor Warren, resigned almost immediately after the committee subpenaed him on its return visit to Florida. Sullivan presented the dismal picture of a former standard bearer of public trust asserting his constitutional privilege against self-incrimination and refusing to answer questions concerning property acquisition and campaign contributions.

Mrs. Ethel Sullivan, wife of the ex-sheriff, who had personally participated in collecting money for her husband's 1944 and 1948 campaigns, said that the money just flowed and much of it was diverted by her into funds which she used to pay off a mortgage on the home of her parents in Perryman, Md., and to build a home for her sister in Aberdeen, Md. At least $30,000 was misapplied in this way and apparently unreported as income, as both Sullivans have since been indicted for income tax violations. Mrs. Sullivan was not above affixing her husband's name to property conveyances and talking an unsuspecting notary public into the acknowledgment. To believe that ex-Sheriff Sullivan was not aware of these doings is incredible.

Just outside of Miami, there is a town of Hollywood, Fla., with a population of about 18,000 people. Hollywood has been known as a wide-open town. The former city tax assessor, Lee A. Wentworth, told a lurid tale of vast gambling operations which opened after the 1948 election. Wentworth and several citizens formed a committee with the express purpose of combatting the vast gambling operations in Florida. They had no success whatever in obtaining aid from the local authorities, so they informed Governor Warren by telegram and telephone of the situation. They received no reply to either message. Their efforts evidently harassed the gambling interests somewhat, as Wentworth stated that on two different occasions he had been offered $25,000 to stop his campaign against gambling in Hollywood.

Three witnesses testified that the mayor of Hollywood, Lester C. Boggs, was actively aiding gambling interest in the city. The testimony revealed that Boggs was on friendly terms with Jake Lansky, Meyer Lansky, and other big-time gamblers in Hollywood.

When Boggs took the witness stand, he emphatically denied most of the above testimony, claiming that these witnesses were political soreheads and disgruntled defeated candidates. Boggs denied receiving any money from gamblers for protection and glossed over the "exaggerated" claims that Hollywood was a wide-open town. Boggs admitted, however, knowing the gamblers named heretofore but really didn't know what business they were in—especially if it was gambling.

The committee reviewed the powerful position of affluence and influence in Florida State affairs wielded by Johnston, who in some investments and operations has fronted for Johnny Patton, former "Boy Mayor of Burnham, Ill." and currently described as probably the most important surviving member of the Capone hierarchy. Attorney Albert D. Hubbard of Miami hesitatingly explained the reason for a trip made by Raymond Craig, a top Miami gambling figure, and himself to Chicago in April of 1949. Hubbard had been retained by Craig to prepare and attempt to push through the Florida Legislature a bill designed to legalize the handling of off-track bets by bookies. When shown copies of hotel bills reflecting a visit to the Blackstone Hotel in Chicago on April 21, 1949, where Johnston maintained an apartment, Hubbard conceded that he and Craig had gone to Chicago to see Johnston about the proposed legislation. When asked why Johnston, who had no official standing, had been sought out, Hubbard acknowledged, "I knew that Mr. Johnston was a long-time friend of Governor Warren's. I knew that he was in the racing business and I knew that he would be the logical man to whom Governor Warren would turn for advice concerning racing legislation."

Throughout the Florida testimony the name of Governor Warren cropped up frequently in questionable connections. The committee felt that it was only fair on its part to offer the Governor an opportunity to answer the allegations and charges made against him. Opportunity to appear voluntarily before the committee was extended to the Governor on three separate occasions prior to the June 1951 hearings in Florida. These three invitations were rejected. As the investigation and then the hearings proceeded, it became increasingly apparent to the committee that the taking of testimony from Governor Warren would be desirable. Finally, in light of the Governor's refusals to appear voluntarily, the committee issued a subpena requiring his appearance before the committee in Washington, D. C., on July 9, 1951. Governor Warren refused to respond to the subpena, resting his refusal on the ground of State sovereignty.

The committee again offered to obtain testimony from the Governor and notified him that it would receive his sworn testimony in Tallahassee. Governor Warren replied that he would be happy to have a "conference" in Tallahassee with the committee, but left no doubt that he would refuse to take oath in testifying as had been required by rules of the committee of every other witness who had appeared before it. In other words, the Governor took the unusual position that while he would talk to the Senate committee, he would not swear that his statements were the truth. Such unsworn statements could not be the basis of perjury charges if they were found untrue. Faced with the persistent refusal of the Governor to appear and testify under the usual form of oath the committee terminated its efforts to obtain his testimony.

The conclusion reached by the committee after its return visit in the summer of 1951 is that despite the most commendable efforts of certain groups and organizations in Florida, such as the Crime Commissions of Greater Miami and Tampa, illegitimate activities, such as gambling continue to exist on an extensive scale. This gambling is controlled by interstate syndicates and unsavory associates of some men in high office.

(d) MARYLAND

Since the population of Baltimore city represents approximately half of that of the entire State of Maryland, the committee's inquiries were directed at first to Baltimore where the Nation-wide wire service was found to have an important subsidiary. Anne Arundel County, immediately adjacent to Baltimore city, came in for scrutiny, and a $6,000,000 gambling operation in Prince Georges and Calvert Counties was uncovered.

This operation disclosed a welter of law enforcement complications and jurisdictional problems because of its interstate character. The District of Columbia and Virginia were encompassed by the venture, and although the pick-up men and runners traveled daily across State lines, law enforcement authorities had not uncovered the operations which had carried on over a considerable period and involved sizable amounts.

Baltimore City.—Maryland is a racing State. The Baltimore gambling pattern seemed to have sprung from the bookies' penchant to exploit off-track betting in the territory contiguous to race tracks. The bookie wire service, scratch sheet business, and their running mate, the lucrative numbers business, thrived. That the situation could not have existed without police knowledge and permission goes without saying.

There is substantial evidence that more than a decade ago, after the end of the prohibition era, national racketeers began to muscle in on Baltimore gambling. A bombing episode in the thirties involving Julius "Blinky" Fink, associate of Nig Rosen's Philadelphia mob, and numbers operator "Willie" Adams, marked the beginning of the effort of out-of-State hoodlums to declare themselves "in" on Baltimore's lucrative numbers business and other gambling. Investigation developed the fact that the head of one of Baltimore's several large numbers syndicates was directly approached by an out-of-town mobster who stated that his outfit was taking over 75 percent of the Baltimore operation. This muscle man pointed out that even after such a cut there would still be more profit because of enlarged operations. Evidently this "muscle" succeeded, as the local operator withdrew to less dangerous endeavors.

Much of Baltimore's gambling has been funneled through night club and tavern operations. The club or bar operation is run in the name of a front in whose name the license is held. In one case the front, Myer Rosen, frankly admitted under oath that he had no financial interest whatever and was merely the bartender for gambler and narcotic violator Louis Oppelman at Phil's Bar. In another instance the front man, Samuel Aaronson, admitted that he had borrowed the entire sum to start the business from Ike Saperstein, a racketeer with a criminal record who was using the Blue Mirror in conjunction with his gambling operations.

The size of such operations by gamblers requires, for their own protection, the laying off of parts of their bets with gamblers in other States. They have done business by telephone with well-known betting commissioners in various cities, such as Edward Dobkin of Chicago, "Sleep-Out Louie" Levinson of Cincinnati, and Louis Dove of Washington, D. C. Settlement was sometimes made by check and, of course, the amount of these checks gives no real idea of the full extent of the gambling operation. One Baltimore night club front operation showed nearly $200,000 in 1 year moving through its accounts to gamblers in other States.

Baltimore has not been without its other gambling activities—crap games (with loaded dice), numbers racket, etc. Willie Adams, one of Baltimore's principal numbers syndicate operators, admitted his "take" was $1,000 a week.

George Goldberg, long a figure in the sporting fraternity of Baltimore, came before the committee with an imposing array of lawyers. He refused to answer all questions except as to his name. At the public hearing he failed to answer the subpena of the committee.

Narcotics.—The narcotics situation in Baltimore has presented a serious problem. The increased use of drugs by teen-agers has been particularly alarming. The pattern, generally speaking, followed that of a youth being induced by a friend to try a "reefer" of marijuana. Later he was induced to try something stronger. After sniffing heroin a few times, he learned about "mainlining" or injecting the drug directly into his veins. In short order, he became a slave to drugs. The cost of satisfying his habit almost inevitably led to crime. It also led to the enslavement of others because the young addict soon found that selling the drug was one means of supporting his own habit.

An extremely interesting revelation occurred when a committee staff member testified that, following a tip that a major portion of the marijuana supply for the Baltimore–Washington area was growing wild in western Maryland and West Virginia, he explored the countryside along the Potomac near Kitzmiller, Md., and found marijuana growing in large quantities as a weed on the land of several unsuspecting farmers. The ease with which the weed can be grown presents a serious problem in the path of the Bureau of Narcotics in its efforts to wipe out the use of this stepping stone to misery.

As to the vice and prostitution situation, undercover investigators of the American Social Hygiene Association made a survey in late June of 1951 in Baltimore. They found the city not infested with open or flagrant houses of prostitution. Numerous bellboys, cab drivers, and others were contacted but refused to act as go-betweens. However, they found that in 21 bars and night clubs in Baltimore's notorious "Block," prostitutes were encountered plying their trade somewhat cautiously. The report then described in detail the methods of operation in each of the 21 places in the "Block."

The wire service

Howard Sports Daily, the racing wire service satellite in Baltimore, for years has occupied a key position in the scheme to furnish bookmakers with the vital instantaneous racing news, odds, conditions, results, and prices which are the sine qua non of their multi-million-dollar empire. Testimony of Harry Bilson, boss of Howard Sports, and Leonard Matusky, of the World Wide News & Music Co., an associated organization, served further to debunk and explode the feeble claims that the vast wire service network is not in fact controlled and guided by Continental Press and its Capone gang counterparts in Chicago.

From Bilson the committee learned that his company, which has been described as a dummy, performs the function of gathering the racing news from the tracks in Maryland, New Jersey, and Florida which is sold to Continental. In turn, Howard Sports buys the news from Continental and sells it to east coast subscribers invariably found to be engaged in the bookmaking business. While it is true that some of the news is sent to newspapers, this excuse for existence was found to be but a sham when it was learned that the papers receive the news free or pay a comparative pittance. In previous hearings the committee had learned how Howard Sports employees acted as wigwag men in the vicinity of the race tracks to purloin the race results by telescope and binoculars, then relay it by telephone or telegraph to Baltimore whence it was introduced into the Nation-wide circuit. These wigwag men, hired by Continental Press, were thereafter shunted about like pawns on a chess board on the payroll of Continental's subsidiaries, such as Illinois Press and Howard Sports. When information was sought as to the nature of expenditures aggregating some $50,000 per year for "rent" ostensibly paid by Bilson's track crew, Bilson was vague and referred the committee to his track-crew boss Roscoe Odle, who could not be found either by the committee or Bilson. The question of whether or not this substantial sum of money which Howard Sports carries on its books as an operating expense and consequently a deductible item in its income tax is actually spent for legitimate purposes remains unanswered. Similar tax deductions which reduce the amount paid to the Government were claimed for such items as auto expense for Bilson who admitted that his health would not permit him to drive a car.

Bilson recited a tale incredulous in the extreme when he told the committee that the news at the tracks is now being gathered by a mysterious individual whom he has never seen and could not help the committee to locate, despite the fact that over the past several months he has paid this man over $800 a week. Following the passage of a law in Florida calling for a 20-minute delay in the transmission of racing results this ghost figure telephoned to Bilson and offered to furnish him with the news. Bilson claimed that he contracted with the man over the telephone and supplied his track crew to work with the man whose name was variously furnished to the committee as R. Gorman, Al Gorman, George Gorman, and George Baker, doing business as the Tropical News.

The news was supplied with Howard Sports paying for the crew and the telephone calls from "the voice." Checks were mailed to him at General Delivery, Hialeah, Fla., and promptly cashed, but never deposited. Thereafter, "the voice" moved his activities to the Maryland and New Jersey tracks. Although when at Pimlico race track in Baltimore, he was practically at Bilson's elbow, the latter still claimed he had no idea of his true identity. An interesting sidelight was the fact that when "the voice" reached New Jersey he found it possible to cash his checks at the office of another wire service distributor in Camden, N. J., called Malbro Communications Engineers. Malbro officials cashed checks for "the voice," but also disclaimed knowing his identity. When the committee pressed for leads to find "the voice," Bilson professed an inability to find his own track crew who were in daily telephone touch with him.

Obviously in an effort to thwart law enforcement, the wire service distributors in Baltimore, as elsewhere, have resorted to a unique method of dealing with their bookmaker customers. Bilson and Matusky told the committee that they were servicing customers who paid them in the neighborhood of $50 per week for the privilege of calling in on the telephone to get the racing news. The identities of these people were unknown to them and no names were used, but each customer was assigned a code number. Payment for the service was received from these "numbers" when some nameless individual would pay cash at the companies' offices weekly. The committee noted that the wire service account books reflected discontinuance of these coded accounts simultaneously with raids by Baltimore police on bookmaking establishments.

The interlocking nature of the wire service outlets came out in the testimony of Matusky of World Wide News and Music. It was found that the owner of all of the stock of World Wide was Sanford Niles of Chicago whom Matusky described as a "roadman" for Continental

Press. Matusky was to receive $400 per week for 20 years under the arrangement. The company was set up by John D. McInerney of Chicago who is also an officer of Howard Sports Daily. At one time a 50-percent stockholder was Roscoe Odle who was boss of the track crew of Howard Sports. He was drawing $200 per week from World Wide for duties which Matusky was unable to outline although they seemed to be his same wigwag work performed for Howard Sports at the tracks. The three "companies" worked together without written contracts, paying hundreds of dollars per week for the news, with the price fluctuating apparently according to the whims of Continental's bosses. No dividends were ever paid on stockholdings of Howard or World Wide, the practice being for Continental to drain off any surplus at year's end as payment for the news.

Although the master plan evidently called for an avoidance of direct relationship or privity of contract between Continental and World Wide and an insulated set-up whereby Continental sold to Howard Sports and Howard Sports to World Wide, Matusky of World Wide testified that he received calls from representatives of Continental who reviewed his business and upped the price he had to pay Howard for the news. Further, and most indicative of all, was the fact that when World Wide was suffering financial distress in 1951, Matusky admittedly bypassed the chain of command and directly called Tom Kelly, general manager of Continental and acknowledged wire service kingpin and sought his assistance.

Kelly, although having no interest on the surface in the welfare of World Wide, went into action and caused Sanford Niles to pour more money from undisclosed sources into World Wide. The facade of separate corporate entities was completely torn from Continental's house of cards when Senator Kefauver asked Matusky this question: "The truth about the matter, Mr. Matusky, is that while you have these different companies, some of Kelly's employees own the stock in several corporations and all of you look to Continental and to Mr. Kelly as being the daddy of the whole thing, don't you?" Matusky slowly answered, "Well—I did."

Anne Arundel County

Law enforcement in Anne Arundel County where several wire service customers remained undisturbed for years seems to have left something to be desired. It was developed that the county chief of police, since retired, "investigated" allegations that a gambling casino was being operated on St. Helenas Island in the Severn River by viewing the place from the mainland and that police officers checking into a report of a late shooting involving known gambling figures reported it was a "backfire" although applicable hospital records reflected the admission and treatment of the victim for a gunshot wound.

A gentleman farmer

For nearly a decade Charles E. Nelson seemingly enjoyed the pleasures and travels generally associated with the life of a prosperous gentleman farmer. Owner of a beautiful and completely equipped stock farm, even to air conditioning, in Prince Georges County adjacent to Washington, D. C., Nelson, as owner of a string of race horses, became a well-known figure at auction sales of expensive thoroughbreds. He rose to prominence as the buyer of blooded stock who could bid and buy for cash without hesitation over the price.

In his appearance before the committee at its closing hearings, Nelson attempted to masquerade as the country bumpkin even to the point of feigning deafness until committee members, not satisfied with his pretended naïveté about the source of his income, finally elicited his answer that "he thought" that his income was from gambling. Pursuing this opening the committee investigated further and proved that it was indeed gambling, estimated to gross at least $6,000,000 per year from the numbers business in Washington, D. C., and the nearby counties in Maryland and Virginia.

Nelson conceded that he was the principal owner of "Uncle Billy's" a collection of concessions at North Beach, Md. The foremost attraction there unquestionably was the imposing array of "one-arm bandits" whose profit-making possibilities have been well established. Claiming inability to discuss his business affairs without access to what he termed his "little red book," at the committee's suggestion Nelson was accompanied to his elaborate farm by a staff member where the "little red book" proved to be a file cabinet of ledgers and records.

Examination reflected receipts for bondsmen's fees, lawyer fees, fines of associated individuals for gambling arrests, receipts for vast purchases of numbers books, adding machines, coin wrappers, and other accoutrements peculiar to the numbers business. From the records Nelson was found to have realized a net of more than $250,000 over a 4-year period from the business he "thought" might have been gambling. He had acquired in recent years properties estimated to be worth over $1,000,000.

Notwithstanding the fact that Nelson's books reflected a net income from his gambling accounts of more than $50,000 during 1950, not 1 cent of tax did he pay to the Government. How did he explain this? As a gentleman farmer his losses from the operation of the farm, which included such questionable deductions as mileage charges for as many as seven automobiles, exceeded his admitted gains and thus his method of computation left the Government without any tax payment.

But the figure which was charged off as an operating expense that interested the committee the most was the $10,000 which he annually entered as "good will—advertising." Why did he seek good will? It was shown that one of his practices was to distribute turkeys at Christmastime to various individuals, some of whom were members of the police department charged with investigating numbers operators.

Sheriff Carlton G. Beall of Prince Georges County told how he had been approached by Nelson recently with an offer of graft of $15,000 per month to be paid by Nelson and Sam Beard, a notorious Washington area gambler, to the sheriff, chief of police, and State's attorney for the privilege of running their gambling enterprises unmolested. According to the sheriff, Nelson had even embellished his proposal with an offer to help the sheriff find and makes cases against Nelson's competitors and thus obtain the necessary publicity and statistics to convince the voters that the laws were being enforced.

These proclivities on Nelson's part to ingratiate himself with police officials caused the committee to question several county policemen after a witness told of complaining of Nelson's operations and assisting the police to obtain the evidence only to find that a planned raid

executed simultaneously with the committee hearings apparently was
aborted by an alleged tip-off.

Since the hearings,.State, county, and Federal law enforcement and
prosecutive officials have manifested interest in Nelson's activities.

The pattern

Judge Joseph Sherbow of the Supreme Bench of Baltimore City, a
fearless jurist, summarized the Maryland picture when he said—

Lottery operations have slowed down.   Bookmaking has taken a definite turn.
It has slowed down somewhat.

He then went on to point out that bookmakers were very resourceful
and had changed their method of operation.

To some extent—

Judge Sherbow said—

they moved out of Baltimore City and into adjacent counties and now the operation is a little different.

He pointed out that they had not gone out of business but were
following the pattern this committee has found in other parts of the
country where they have withdrawn into an "insulated" operation,
where they move into an apartment or some similar place and take
bets over the telephone without the bettor ever making physical
contact with the bookmaker.

It was further stated by Judge Sherbow that—

if any gambling or other illegal venture is in existence for any length of time and
is not discovered by the police, then one of the following several things is true:
(1) The policeman on the beat is blind; (2) or he is incompetent; or (3) he is
corrupt.

Judge Sherbow went on to say that from his intimate contact with
the Baltimore Police Department, he has found that the vast majority
are competent, upstanding, decent policemen.   It was obvious, however, from his testimony that he did not want to imply that there were
not some lax policemen—for the committee's findings indicate that
there has not been 100 percent faithful performance of duty.   There
was, on the other hand, definite evidence that the Baltimore Police
Department was under the direction of an absolutely honest and
forthright police commissioner who would vigorously clamp down on
any departure from accepted principles.   This was evidenced by his
prompt dismissal of a ranking officer proven to have "borrowed" a
substantial sum from Willis M. "Buzz" King, widely-known gambler
who had been called before the committee.

Immediate reaction to the committee's activities in the Maryland
area has been noteworthy.   State's attorneys in several instances have
initiated grand jury action, and have already brought to trial some
of the principals in a large "come-back money" conspiracy found in
existence at the Bowie race track.   The committee from the inception
of its investigation in the Baltimore area was assisted materially by
prosecuting and court officers.   The State's attorney, Anselm Sodaro,
manifested a keen interest in every particular and not only was his
cooperation most valuable but his prompt action on the local level
was in keeping with his policy of effective law enforcement.   Mr.
Sodaro, a well-qualified prosecutor, is vigorously probing the situation
in the city in the wake of committee disclosures.   The State's attorney
in Prince Georges County is committed to further exploring the

$6,000,000 interstate numbers business of Charles E. Nelson and its attendant implications of police and public official connections. The Maryland General Assembly has authorized a legislative committee to explore the possibilities of organized crime within the State. This Senate committee expresses its approval and commendation of these positive steps for remedial action at the State and local level which have resulted directly from revelations and investigation of the Senate group.

(e) STRAGGLER WITNESSES

During the past 4 months the committee at various times has conducted hearings to secure the testimony of several witnesses for whom arrest warrants had been issued by the Senate. In February after unsuccessful attempts had been made to serve subpenas, warrants were voted for 17 persons. Those named in the warrants were Rocco Fischetti; Charles Fischetti; Murray L. "The Camel" Humphreys; Jacob "Greasy Thumb" Guzik; William G. O'Brien; John Angersola, alias King; Moe Dalitz, alias Davis; Samuel T. Haas; Morris Kleinman; Louis Rothkopf, alias Rhody; Samuel "Gameboy" Miller; Morris "Mushy" Wexler; Samuel Tucker; George Angersola, alias King; John Croft; James Brink; and Louis Levinson.

The warrants were placed in the hands of Mr. Joseph Duke, the Sergeant at Arms of the Senate. The committee greatly appreciates the vigilant efforts of Mr. Duke and of the various agencies of Government which brought about the eventual apprehension of all the persons named.

Dalitz and Tucker made arrangements to present their testimony before the committee at the hearing in Los Angeles on February 28. Guzik, O'Brien, Kleinman, Rothkopf, Croft, and Brink testified before the committee in Washington prior to the filing of the committee's Third Interim Report on May 1. Charles Fischetti and Louis Levinson both succumbed to heart attacks after their apprehension and before the committee had an opportunity to interrogate them.

The questioning of Rocco Fischetti and Murray "The Camel" Humphreys, both of whom have been connected with the Capone syndicate in Chicago, took place at an executive session of the committee on May 28. Fischetti at the outset read a prepared statement in which he advised the committee that he would refuse to answer any questions on the ground of possible self-incrimination. Fischetti refused to tell the committee who prepared the statement, and he also refused to say if he was married or if he had any children or what means of transportation he used to come to the hearing. He has been cited for contempt and his case is presently in the hands of the United States attorney for the District of Columbia.

Humphreys, a member of the old Capone mob, was also a recalcitrant witness and, like Fischetti, he insisted on reading into the record a statement claiming his privilege against self-incrimination in terms almost identical with the statement used by Fischetti. Like Fischetti, he also refused to say who prepared it. He admitted that he had used the alias of J. Harris during the past but refused to say why. He also admitted having served 18 months for tax evasion. Humphreys also refused to say that he knew Ralph O'Hara, Jake Guzik, Al Capone, "Machine Gun" Jack McGurn, Frank "The Enforcer" Nitti, or the late James Ragen, who was slain in warfare arising out of efforts by the Capone syndicate to muscle into the wire service. Humphreys also refused to say whether or not he knew Hymie Levin, Phil Katz, Roy Jones, Willie Nemoth, Frank Costello, Joe Adonis, or Jack Dragna. He would not tell the committee whether he had ever been to California, Florida, or New York and declined to say whether he knew Ralph Pierce, Rocco Fischetti, Paul "The Waiter" Ricca, or Louis "Little New York" Campagna. Committee counsel asked Humphreys, "Do you know who killed James Ragen?" He replied, "I am going to have to claim my privilege on that also, sir." He was asked, "Do you know who killed William Drury?" Again he replied, "I am going to have to claim my privilege on that also, sir."

Despite his earlier refusal to say whether he knew Rocco Fischetti, Humphreys finally was forced to admit in the concluding stages of his testimony that he and Fischetti had flown to Washington in the same plane and had eaten breakfast together in a Washington hotel just before the hearing.

Humphreys has also been cited for contempt.

At an executive session of the hearing held on June 19, the committee heard the testimony of Samuel T. Haas, a Cleveland lawyer; Morris "Mushy" Wexler, of Cleveland Heights, operator of the Empire News Service, a distributor for Continental Press Service; and Samuel "Gameboy" Miller, a partner of Wexler in the Empire News and identified with gambling establishments in Ohio, Kentucky, and Florida.

At the outset of his testimony, Haas admitted that he had been indicted for arson in 1919, that he had been convicted in police court and sentenced to 1 to 20 years, but the conviction was reversed by the Supreme Court, and the case remanded for new trial. Indictment was subsequently nol-prossed, and disbarment proceedings arising out of the indictment were also dismissed. He also acknowledged that in 1932 he filed a petition of bankruptcy in which he said that his assets consisted only of $100 and his lawbooks. He testified that he knew "Big Al" Polizzi, Thomas J. McGinty, and Arthur "Mickey" McBride and that he was attorney for Wexler in the Empire News Service. He said that he had known Kleinman since 1925, and that he had known Rothkopf for about 15 years and Dalitz for about 18 or 19 years.

Haas was questioned extensively about his connection with the financial maneuvers which brought about the merger of the Reliance Steel Corp. and the Detroit Steel Corp. leading to the vesting of control of the merged companies in Dalitz, Tucker, Rothkopf, and Kleinman. Haas testified that some time after 1940, Dalitz brought to his office M. J. Zivian who outlined to him a plan whereby the stock of Reliance Steel Corp. was to be acquired as a preliminary to the merger with Detroit Steel. As $200,000 was needed, a transaction was worked out whereby $100,000 of Detroit Steel stock was to be purchased and deposited along with Zivian's Reliance Steel stock as collateral for a $200,000 loan. Haas put up one-third and Dalitz supplied two-thirds of the $100,000. Haas said that his one-third share of the financing represented his own funds and that he received 333 shares of Detroit Steel which he retained until 1950, when he sold them. He admitted that it was a very profitable investment and that he subsequently learned that the two-thirds share put up by Dalitz was on behalf of Dalitz, Tucker, Kleinman, and Rothkopf.

Haas explained his relationship with Wexler by saying that back in 1924 he represented William Swartz, Wexler's predecessor as owner of the wire service, in a proceeding brought to restrain a police officer stationed in front of the wire-service establishment from interfering with its activity. He insisted that this was the only time he represented Swartz, who subsequently was indicted for murder and who was also the owner of the Chesapeake Operating Co. which ran a club located on the border between Ohio and West Virginia. When reminded that he had made telephone calls to Swartz in 1950, Haas insisted that the calls were on behalf of James "Shimmy" Patton, another client of his. Haas admitted that his brother, Morgan C. Haas, had been an employee of the Buckeye Catering Co., a concern engaged in the operation of slot machines. He had obtained the job for his brother through Nate Weisenberg, known as the slots king of Ohio, who was found murdered in a ditch in 1945. Haas said that he knew that Al Polizzi was a partner in this concern but professed not to know Jerry Milano, the present owner.

Haas acknowledged also that he at one time had an interest in the Modern Music Co. of Colorado Springs, Colo., that went bankrupt but he claimed to be surprised to learn that 35 percent of the final inventory consisted of slot machines. He admitted that he had received a $5,000 bequest from Fred Koehler, former Cleveland chief of police, county commissioner, mayor, and sheriff, in whose safety-deposit box $500,000 worth of securities was found after his death. Haas referred to Koehler as "a very dear friend of mine" but declared that he had no idea of how Koehler accumulated this wealth because Koehler was "very incommunicative."

Haas was examined as to his extensive real estate holdings in Cleveland but insisted that it was just coincidence that the holders of adjoining properties in some instances were Kleinman and Rothkopf. He admitted that in 1944 he had a 37½ percent interest in the Burroughs Book Store which he purchased for $450,000. He acknowledged that he had received $75,000 for the sale of land on which the Palm Beach Ambassador Hotel in Florida was built in 1946. His former law partner was Harry Cohen, who is now practicing law in Florida. Cohen represented Jack Friedlander, member of the S & G Syndicate, when Friedlander testified before the committee.

In view of his bankruptcy in 1932, Haas' accumulation of wealth has been phenomenal.

Wexler told the committee that he was the owner of the Theatrical Grill and a partner of Samuel "Gameboy" Miller and Robert Kaye in the Empire News Service. He said that he was in Florida when he learned that he was wanted but refused to tell the committee with whom he stayed. From Florida he went to a hotel just outside Pittsburgh and remained there until he learned of the issuance of the warrant, at which time he came to Washington and surrendered. Wexler admitted that he was a subscriber to Continental Press Service but he refused to answer practically every other question which dealt with his 26 years in the wire service business. He would not discuss the amount of the annual payments from Empire to Continental except to say that they varied from year to year. He admitted knowing Arthur "Mickey" McBride very well but he refused to say how well he knew Pete Licavoli. He denied that he knew Allan Smiley, west coast racket figure, or that he knew anything about telephone calls placed to Smiley from the Theatrical Grill. He refused to answer any questions about telephone calls placed from the Theatrical Grill to Mike Farah, owner of the Jungle Inn in Mahoning County, Ohio, or to the Merchants Club in Newport, Ky. He admitted that McBride had served as an accommodation endorser in connection with loans he had obtained from a Cleveland bank.

Samuel "Gameboy" Miller listed his address as Miami, Fla., when questioned by the committee, but he said that he had lived in Cleveland for 50 years. He admitted that he had been a partner in the Island Club in Miami with some members of the S. & G. Syndicate and that he had also been a partner in the Lookout House in northern Kentucky with James Brink, but he refused to say whether he had brought Kleinman, Rothkopf, Tucker, or Dalitz into that operation. He also admitted that he was a partner of Wexler's in the Empire News Service and that he had been a partner in the Thomas Club in Cleveland which ceased operating in 1945. He said he acquired his interests in the Island Club in Miami through Sam Cohen, one of the members of the S. & G. Syndicate. He estimated his income from the Island Club at about $15,000. He said he was receiving $30,000 or $40,000 annually from the Empire News Service for which he performed no services whatever. He was not sure just why he had a share in that enterprise.

John Angersola, alias John King, claimed Miami Beach as his residence when he appeared before the committee at an executive session on August 6 and said he had not been in Cleveland in 15 years. He admitted that he served time in the Ohio State Penitentiary 30 years ago for robbery and that he might have used the name of John DiMarco on an occasion about 20 years ago in Detroit when he was picked up for suspicion. He refused to say whether or not he had ever been connected with the Buckeye Catering Co. in Cleveland and admitted that he had purchased a fishing boat named the *Wood Duck* from Arthur "Mickey" McBride for $6,000 or $7,000 about 10 years ago. He claimed the longest trip he ever made in the boat was to Bimini and he denied that he had ever taken the boat to either Cuba or Mexico. He said he sold the boat to "Big Al" Polizzi in 1946 or 1947 for $5,000.

He acknowledged that he had paid $40,000 in cash for his present home 4 or 5 years ago but he refused to say how he had acquired this money. The home that he had occupied before that time he had sold to "Trigger Mike" Coppola for $30,000. He admits that he had kept cash in a safety deposit box but claimed there was no cash in it now. When asked what he had done with this cash, he replied that he might have purchased real estate with it. He admitted that he is now the owner of the Grand Hotel in Miami Beach and that he had had an interest in the Woffard Hotel since 1939 or 1940. He has also admitted having an interest in the Yorkshire Club in Newport, Ky., but he claimed he did not know where the Yorkshire Club was located as he had never been there. He refused to say how he acquired his interest in it. He also admitted knowing Dalitz, Kleinman, and Rothkopf but he refused to say whether he had had any dealings with them.

The committee developed some interesting testimony in the questioning of George Angersola, alias George King, who still resides in

Cleveland. Angersola listed his occupation as an organizer for the Cleaners and Dyers International Union at $100 a week but he was somewhat vague about his duties. He admitted that he also served as floor manager for the 23 Room, a Miami Beach establishment, during the winter months for which he also received $100 a week. He testified that he was able to do this because he received a 10-week paid vacation from his union duties. Under questioning he finally admitted that he has not worked actually for the union for a couple of years, although he was still being paid at the rate of $100 a week. When the committee sought an explanation for this, George Angersola replied, "They may need me."

George Angersola admitted that he had been in jail twice, once for a period of 3 months on a bootlegging charge and again for 3 months following his conviction for extortion in 1939. He admitted that he knew all of the members of the Cleveland Syndicate but he denied ever having had any dealings with any of them.

A witness who gave the committee considerable trouble before he finally accepted a subpena was George S. May, prominent Chicago business figure and head of the George S. May Co., which specializes in business engineering. Although May claimed to have been in Chicago for 53 days during which time efforts were being made to serve him with a subpena, he admitted that he had never communicated with the United States marshal or the committee to express his willingness to accept service and to appear before the committee.

He testified before the committee in Washington on May 28. He refused to answer any questions about his connections with the Tam O'Shanter Country Club. He refused to say who the directors were, who kept the records, who the manager was, who owned the real estate, or whether there were any slot machines in the club. He refused to tell the committee whether he knew Ed Vogel, the slot machine king of Cook County, or whether he had ever had any agreement with Vogel for a 60–40 split of the proceeds from the slot machines located in the club.

The committee had information to the effect that May owned 93 percent of the stock of Tam O'Shanter, Inc., which is believed to own the land and buildings occupied by the Tam O'Shanter Country Club and that the club receives $120,000 a year in dues, $400,000 from the dining room, $325,000 from the bar, $650,000 for outside parties, and $45,000 a year from slot machines. May refused to confirm or deny these figures. He also refused to say whether the club had been tipped off about impending raids. In the final stages of the hearing, he admitted that he had told counsel for the committee on one occasion that if he gave any information "he would not last 48 hours."

May also admitted to the committee that he had pleaded guilty to a charge of forgery 35 years ago and had been sentenced to 11 months, but he declared that he had gone straight ever since.

Because of his refusal to answer pertinent questions put to him by the committee, May has been cited for contempt.

E. INTRODUCTION OF CORRECTIVE LEGISLATION

Exposing the facts about organized criminal activities has been only a portion of the task. Disclosures in the committee's records make an overwhelming case for effective remedial legislation. Its investigations and hearings have awakened Nation-wide interest which may be counted on to support Congress in enacting effective laws where they are needed. Accordingly, the development of a legislative program has been given major emphasis in concluding the committee's work. A number of proposals for new laws were put forth in the Third Interim Report; these have been developed and enlarged, and other avenues of approach have been carefully explored. The committee has introduced 23 bills.

It must be borne in mind that the challenge of organized crime in interstate commerce is not new. In the last half century the Federal power has had to be invoked many times to deal with the interstate expansion of criminal activities which could no longer be curbed by local laws and local enforcement agencies, e. g., lotteries (1895); poaching (1900); train robberies (1902); white slavery (1910); liquor traffic (1913); theft of vehicles (1919); kidnaping (1923); bank robbery (1934); general larceny (1934); extortion (1934); theft of cattle (1941). What the committee has brought to light is the same old problem, but in startling new proportions: the train robbers, kidnapers, and bootleggers of another era have shifted to new fields, principally illegal gambling, where they have taken on an aura of pseudo-respectability and reaped enormous wealth. Their power is so great that local officials are often bought and sold, sometimes by mobs located in other States many miles away. Clearly this is a responsibility of the Federal Government, calling for action by Congress to impose better national controls and to insure that the national enforcement machinery will take hold effectively.

I. GAMBLING: S. 1563, 1564, 1624, 2061

Illegal gambling activities are the principal source of revenue for today's hoodlums and racketeers, and the heart of illegal gambling is bookmaking. The "bookie" empire has two vulnerable points within reach of Congress' power over interstate commerce: The essential flow of specialized gambling information to the bookmaker, and his dependence on interstate facilities in placing lay-off and come-back bets. The committee has introduced three bills designed to strike at these points.

S. 1563 would substantially eliminate the so-called wire services, exemplified by Continental Press Service, Inc., from interstate commerce. To avoid risks of evasion which are obvious in applying an inflexible criminal prohibition to so nebulous and far-flung an activity, the bill makes use of a licensing procedure, to be administered by the Federal Communications Commission. Any person (excepting newspapers, broadcasters, and legitimate press services) who wishes to disseminate gambling information, as defined in the bill, must apply for a license which can only be issued on a showing (1) that the applicant is of good moral character; (2) that the proposed operation is in the public interest; and (3) that the information is not "primarily for use in facilitating gambling activities which constitute violations of" State laws.

S. 1564 reflects the committee's recognition that the ultimate effects of S. 1563 may be delayed by hearings, appeals and court tests, the initial weakness of any administrative device, and it therefore strikes straight at the source of the bookmakers' information with a narrow criminal prohibition. The proprietors of almost all legitimate race tracks and sports events have long been fighting the wire-service operators, by denying them the right to send out their bulletins on betting odds, scratches, times, results, etc. Consequently the operators have been driven to elaborate subterfuge, sometimes stealing the information from blinds outside the track or enclosure, sometimes using wig-wag signals, semaphores, special codes, and even walkie-talkie radio equipment from inside. S. 1564 would make it a Federal crime for any person to transmit in interstate commerce gambling information "obtained surreptitiously or through stealth and without the permission of" the proprietor of the event, when such information is intended to be used for illegal gambling purposes. It is believed that this measure would be effective at once to stop the flow of such information, and thus to cripple the wire services before they are brought completely in hand by regulation under the FCC.

S. 1624 is a combination bill which consolidates two of the committee's original proposals with certain new matters. It contains a flat criminal prohibition against using interstate facilities in connection with any bet or wager, thus putting an end to lay-off and come-back transactions between gamblers in different States. The committee has stressed in the record, and will continue to emphasize, that this law is not intended to punish casual, private users of the telephone; no drafting technique seemed adequate to separate the casual user and the professional bettor; the matter is therefore left to sound discretion at the enforcement level. Telephone companies would not be affected, since they do not "send or transmit" messages (see *Southern Tel. Co.* v. *King*, 103 Ark. 160 (1912)), and other carriers would be liable only if shown to have violated the prohibition "knowingly." The bill also extends chapter 61 of the Criminal Code, the old lottery law, to include any other "gambling enterprise" or "scheme of any kind offering money or other prizes dependent in whole or in part upon lot or chance," and brings pushcards and punchboards specifically within its prohibitions. The Slot Machine Act (Public Law 906, 81st Cong.) is amended by substituting for the present controlling definition, which has proved inadequate, a general description of mechanical gambling devices, which would bring roulette wheels and so-called one-ball machines, as well as all variations of the orthodox slot machine, within the scope of the law. Ordinary pinball amusement devices would not be reached, under the judicial construction that "free games," when confined to a mere right to operate the machine, do not constitute a thing of value (see *Washington Coin Machine Ass'n* v. *Callahan*, 142 F. 2d 97 (C. A. D. C., 1944)).

A further improvement in the enforcement machinery relating to slot machines is proposed in S. 2059, discussed under part VI, Tax Measures, post.

The committee lately exposed another interstate gambling empire of impressive proportions, which has grown up in defiance of the old lottery law by decentralizing its operations and attenuating its interstate ties: The Treasury balance lottery racket. A large part of the success of this operation depends on the confidence inspired in its patrons by the integrity of the United States Treasury.   Thus the prestige of the Federal Government itself is being traded upon, and the committee feels that this is an abuse which can and should be stopped.

S. 2061 would make it a misdemeanor for any person to base a "gambling enterprise, lottery, gift enterprise, or scheme of any kind * * * which offers prizes dependent in whole or in part upon lot or chance" on any official publication or data issued by the United States.

Additional measures relating to gambling are proposed as revisions of the tax laws.   See S. 1529 and 1532, discussed under part VI, Tax Measures, post.

II. NARCOTICS: S. 1695, 1900

Despite existing Federal and State laws on the subject, the traffic in narcotics still flourishes.   The committee found no deficiencies in the pattern of statutory control, however, and attributes the present acute problem to a shortage—quantative, not qualitative—of enforcement personnel, and to the comparatively gentle treatment narcotics offenders have been receiving at the hands of the courts.   The first part of the problem is an appropriations matter; providing adequate personnel and facilities to check this "slow form of murder" is a responsibility which the committee urges Congress never to shrug off or take lightly.

The second relates to the administration of criminal penalties.   It is indisputable that more severe sentences, meted out to narcotics offenders when they are detected and apprehended, would facilitate enforcement and tend to discourage the traffic.   The committee unqualifiedly approves efforts to impress the seriousness of narcotics offenses upon the judges who ultimately bring this vicious type of criminal to account, and has accordingly sponsored two bills on the subject.

S. 1695 (companion to H. R. 3490, passed by the House of Representatives July 16, 1951) would impose the following penalties for any violation of the narcotics laws: First offense, up to $2,000 fine and 2 to 5 years' imprisonment; second offense, up to $2,000 and 5 to 10 years' imprisonment; subsequent offense, up to $2,000 and 10 to 20 years' imprisonment.   No sentence may be suspended, or probation granted, in any case of a second or subsequent offender.

S. 1900 would impose a special penalty of up to $2,000 and 20 years to life imprisonment, without suspended sentence or probation, for any violation involving the sale of narcotics (by a person over 21) to a person under 17 years of age.

Questions have been raised from a number of sources, however, as to the propriety of imposing arbitrary minimum sentences in all cases. The committee recognizes the possible merit of these objections and suggests that they be given due weight in further consideration of the bills.

The committee discovered a slight conflict in jurisdiction and practice, relating to narcotics, between the Narcotics Bureau of the Treasury Department, and the Passport Division of the Department of State.   Since the illegal narcotics traffic is exclusively international in origin, the Narcotics Bureau has a keen interest in restricting the movements of American citizens known or strongly suspected to be engaged in the traffic, a matter which is within the absolute discretion of the Passport Division. After full exploration the committee believes that this conflict does not warrant legislative intervention; closer cooperation between the agencies themselves, and full recognition that the suppression of this traffic is intimately related to the public welfare of the country, coupled with the manifest intelligence and good faith found on both sides, promise an adequate solution.

Although the committee explored the matter thoroughly and is convinced that controls should be imposed upon barbiturates, no legislation has been proposed to deal with them, because of the pendency of a joint plan now being worked out by the Treasury Department, the Department of Justice, and the Federal Security Agency as a result of the efforts of the Committee on Ways and Means of the House of Representatives. This plan is expected to result in an adequate pattern of control.

III. LIQUOR TRAFFIC: S. 1530, 1663, 2062

The traffic in bootleg liquor into dry States and dry local-option areas is of sizable proportions and seems clearly to call for congressional intervention. The committee disapproves the present tendency among Federal enforcement officials to make a sharp distinction between tax collection and general law enforcement, and to concentrate on the former. The laws themselves account for part of this emphasis, and changes have been proposed accordingly.

S. 1530 would amend the basic permit section of the Federal Alcohol Administration Act so as to fix the life of such permits at 2 years. They are presently issued for an indefinite period, subject to revocation only by affirmative administrative action and on certain specified grounds. The proposed change would make all such permits reviewable biennially, and thus facilitate periodic clean-ups of the industry. The basic permit is the primary control imposed on all manufacturers, importers, and wholesalers of alcoholic beverages.

S. 1663 (companion to H. R. 1278) would extend the Federal prohibition against importing liquor into States which have outlawed the *importation* thereof (18 U. S. C. 1262) to include dry areas in local-option States.

S. 2062 is proposed to cure a fundamental defect in the present law which remains even with the change worked by.S. 1663. Only two States, Kansas and Oklahoma, are affected by 18 United States Code 1262, for the reason indicated by emphasizing the word "importation" above. The courts have held that States in which the *sale* or *use* of liquor is prohibited do not qualify for Federal protection, *Dunn* v. *U. S.*, 98 F. 2d 119 (C. C. A. 10, 1938). The committee therefore proposes that the Webb-Kenyon Act (27 U. S. C. 122) which prohibits importation into any dry State or area, and which has been a Federal statute since 1913, should be called into play again (the act has been a dead letter since 1936 for want of a penalty section, which was repealed by Congress in that year). S. 2062 imposes a fine of $1,000 and 1 year imprisonment for any violation of section 122. The committee recognizes that in making this proposal it is reopening an old debate in the Congress; but experience since the matter was last considered, as brought out in the committee's hearings and investigations, suggests a thorough reappraisal. Amendment 21 of the Constitution was manifestly not intended to be a shield for bootlegging activities which fatten organized crime. The committee believes that this, like gambling, narcotics, and other illegal activities which pollute the flow of interstate commerce, calls again for a direct assertion of the Federal power.

The committee also proposes a change in the penalties affecting the occupational tax imposed on liquor retailers, in S. 2059, discussed under part VI, Tax Measures, post.

IV. UNLAWFUL ENTRY BY ALIENS: S. 1661, 1662

A number of important criminals were discovered by the committee to have entered the United States illegally, and this type of offense frequently appears in the backgrounds of career gangsters and hoodlums. Besides endorsing S. 716, which would liberalize the entire process of deportation, the committee has sponsored two bills relating to this subject.

S. 1661 (companion to H. R. 2793) would revise section 8 of the Immigration Act of 1917, punishing the smuggling and concealing of aliens, to eliminate a technical flaw which has caused the section to be nullified by the courts. See *U. S.* v. *Evans,* 333 U. S. 483 (1948).

S. 1662 (companion to H. R. 2258) would provide for the reopening of certain cases in which illegal immigrants may now secure an unassailable congressional suspension of deportation proceedings against them, when after-acquired evidence shows new grounds for deportation.

V. CRIMINAL TACTICS IN TRANSPORTATION: S. 1899

In several parts of the country evidence of gangster activities and "muscle" tactics was found in connection with over-the-road trucking. Moreover, the committee is impressed with the fact that the trucking and forwarding industries have been peculiarly vulnerable to such activities and tactics in the past. When interstate hoodlums are flushed out of gambling they may be expected to turn up, as they did when repeal disrupted bootlegging, in other sensitive areas, and the transportation industries are a likely field for invasion. After a careful analysis of the Interstate Commerce Act it was concluded that the act itself needed no revisions, since the powers of the Interstate Commerce Commission, under the present pattern of the law, are ample and effective. The matter has therefore been dealt with in a proposed addition to the statement of national transportation policy, first enacted in the Transportation Act of 1940.

S. 1899 adds a paragraph at the end of the statement of national transportation policy enjoining the Interstate Commerce Commission to keep all forms of transportation subject to its control "free of terrorism, extortion, racketeering and similar unlawful or unethical business tactics"—with the practical effect of removing all doubt that the Commission may take such tactics into account whenever it applies the standards of fitness, ability, and public convenience and necessity to applicants for and holders of certificates, licenses, and permits under the Act.

VI. TAX MEASURES: S. 1529, 1531, 1532, 1660, 2059

The Internal Revenue Code has been analyzed with a view to tightening controls over organized crime through the Federal taxing powers. The committee is not persuaded that the direct imposition of taxes, as exemplified by the Harrison Narcotics Act, is a suitable general device for curbing illegal activities, and for this reason it has rejected numerous proposals to impose direct, confiscatory taxes on various types of organized criminal enterprises. There is force in the argument that recognizing gangsters and hoodlums directly for tax purposes tends to compromise the dignity of the Federal Government and to complicate local enforcement problems. Moreover, the direct, confiscatory tax might be subject to grave questions on constitutional grounds. See *U. S.* v. *Constantine,* 296 U. S. 287 (1935).

On the other hand, it is felt that the power to require disclosures and information incidental to the imposition and collection of Federal taxes should be fully used, when it appears justified as an appropriate adjunct of general tax measures, both to protect the Federal revenues and to expose illegal operations.

S. 1529 is a bill to facilitate the collection of taxes from gambling casinos, whose large cash transactions and inadequate records very frequently mask revenue frauds. Casinos which operate lawfully would be required to maintain daily totals of winnings and losses; those which operate clandestinely would be further required to record each separate wagering transaction.

S. 1531 would impose a definite statutory requirement on all taxpayers to preserve the records supporting their income-tax returns for a period of 7 years. The present regulation governing this practice is vague and unsatisfactory, requiring records to be kept, "so long as the contents thereof may become material in the administration of any internal revenue law." Periods of limitation under the Internal Revenue Code vary, the limit for prosecutions for income tax evasion being 6 years. Actions for recovery of taxes under certain circumstances are never barred. The proposed bill would therefore not only place an unequivocal statutory duty on persons who now frustrate the collection of taxes by destroying their records, but would at the same time clarify the position of honest taxpayers who are uncertain as to their obligations under the present regulation.

S. 1532 relates to the deduction of expenses and losses by gamblers in reporting their net income. The first section of the bill would prohibit the deduction of any expense "incurred in or as a result of illegal wagering." The committee is mindful of the logic of imposing a similar prohibition with regard to expenses incurred in other illegal activities as well, and further consideration might be given to this possibility. The second section changes the present right of taxpayers to deduct wagering losses up to the amount of wagering gains, by prohibiting the deduction of all losses incurred in illegal wagering transactions. This would make total winnings, of the amateur and professional gambler alike, taxable as net income without any offset for losses, where the transactions involved are violations of applicable laws.

S. 1660 would require any taxpayer who reports more than $2,500 as income from unlawful sources, for the current year or any of the 5 years prior thereto, to append a statement of his net worth to his return.   Both in collecting taxes and in enforcing other laws, enforcement officials have been much handicapped by a lack of information as to the net worth of gangsters and racketeers.   Such information, over a spread of several years, would provide a multiple-point check on the rise of underworld characters.   There is precedent for this requirement: the Treasury Department has required net-worth statements, from certain persons reporting large incomes, since 1937.   And it is not believed that the measure could be effectively resisted on the grounds of self-incrimination.   See *U. S.* v. *Sullivan*, 274 U. S. 259 (1927).

S. 2059 is a bill to write effective penalties, fashioned after section 145 of chapter 1 of the Internal Revenue Code, into parts VII and IX of chapter 27, Internal Revenue Code.   These are the parts which impose occupational taxes on the retail liquor traffic and on slot-machine vendors.   In both cases, adequate returns by the taxpayers affected, and strict compliance with the registration and information requirements of the chapter, would produce records of great value to local enforcement officials in detecting and apprehending violators of their laws.   At present these requirements are indifferently enforced with respect to the liquor traffic, in part, at least, because the supporting penalty provisions are vague and unsatisfactory.   The problem has not become acute in policing the slot-machine industry, but the same deficiency exists and should be corrected.

VII. ENFORCEMENT OF CRIMINAL LAWS—S. 1625, 1747, 2060

In the course of its work the committee had many occasions to confer with Federal prosecutors and other officials who are concerned with enforcing Federal laws.   Considerable attention has been given to analyzing the problems raised by these officers and their suggestions for improving the enforcement machinery with which they work.   As a result, the committee is sponsoring three bills.

S. 1625 (companion to H. R. 2260) would relieve the Government of the wholly unrealistic burden, in perjury cases based on contradictory statements made under oath, of proving which of such statements is false.

S. 1747 would remedy a glaring deficiency.   Although many Federal agencies and quasi-judicial bodies have statutes which allow them to compel witnesses to testify over a plea of privilege based on self-incrimination, the Department of Justice itself, with its general responsibility for Federal law enforcement, has no such power at its disposal.   This bill would authorize the compulsion of such testimony, with an adequate grant of immunity from prosecution for matters revealed in the course thereof, in all Federal court and grand jury proceedings, with the added safeguard that the Attorney General must determine that granting immunity in each individual case is "necessary to the public interest."   S. 1747 is intended to be complementary with S. 1570, discussed in "Part VIII, Congressional investigations," post, which confers the same power, amply safeguarded, on congressional committees.

S. 2060 proposes an important addition to the Government's rights of appeal in criminal cases. Under present law, there is no recourse when, at the outset of a criminal case, the defense successfully moves to suppress evidence upon which the prosecution is relying. Good cases have been effectively destroyed by this tactic. The Government should be empowered to seek review of such orders when it believes they are erroneous, so long as the defendant has not been put in jeopardy at the time of the appeal. S. 2060 would accomplish this.

The committee heard numerous complaints of the wholly unsatisfactory situation which prevails with respect to wire-tapping and the use of wire-tapping evidence in the courts. Study of this matter has suggested that the strong divergence of views which has heretofore defeated wire-tapping legislation may now be resolved; communication and enforcement interests alike agree that the present situation is intolerable. The committee believes that some interested agency should take the initiative in working out a generally acceptable plan of control, and as a starting point, commends the pattern which appears to have worked satisfactorily in the State of New York (N. Y. Const., art. I, sec. 12; Code Cr. Proc., sec. 813–a; Penal Code, sec. 552–a).

VIII. CONGRESSIONAL INVESTIGATIONS, S. 2058, 2057

The problems encountered by the committee in compelling the appearance of witnesses and eliciting their testimony, although concededly arising in part from the antisocial characteristics of the type of witness involved, have shown the need for a thorough study of the investigative machinery which is available to the two Houses of Congress. This machinery has been found wanting in some particulars.

The most glaring weakness, which proved highly embarrassing to the committee and continuously frustrated its investigations, was the defect in the immunity statute governing congressional investigations (18 U. S. C. 3486). This section has been lifeless since the Supreme Court decision in *Counselman* v. *Hitchcock* (284 U. S. 141 (1891)). That case held invalid a law similar to the present congressional immunity statute. The basis of the decision was that the immunity granted in the statute was not completely coextensive with the scope of the fifth amendment, and that it was thus ineffective as a substitute for the privilege against self-incrimination. S. 1570, introduced by Senator McCarran, as amended by Senator Ferguson, meets this objection, and is strongly endorsed by the committee.

The evasive tactics of witnesses sought by the committee suggest permanent legislation patterned after Senate Resolution 65, Eighty-second Congress, which brought witnesses in under warrants of arrest.

S. 2058 would create permanent machinery for the apprehension under warrants of arrest of persons found to be evading a congressional subpena, in order to serve process on them or to exact security for their appearance. This machinery could only be set in motion after diligent efforts to obtain service in the usual manner, and only upon a proper finding, by the committee issuing the subpena, that the witness was willfully evading service. The mere existence of such a law would put an end to the undignified spectacle of witnesses playing at hide and seek with committee personnel and Congressional Sergeants at Arms.

S. 2057 gives definite statutory sanction to present practices in issuing and serving subpenas. The authority of deputies and committee personnel in this respect is sometimes nebulous at present, and the committee feels that, since the courts are scrupulously exacting in all matters relating to the perfection of service, a statute, to remove all doubts in all cases, is highly desirable.

Attention is also called to a drafting deficiency which, while not within the committee's compass, should be corrected. Four of the sections in title 2 U. S. C. (191-4) which control the power of congressional bodies to take testimony under oath, to punish for contempt, etc., apply to joint committees only when the same are created "by a joint or concurrent resolution"—with the result that joint committees created by act of Congress are left without such powers.

IX. FEDERAL CRIME COMMISSION

Senate Joint Resolution 65 is intended to accomplish the proposal contained in the committee's Third Interim Report calling for establishment of a Federal Crime Commission. It would authorize creation of a permanent commission in the executive branch of the Government, organized and staffed independently of other Government agencies but coordinating its efforts with, and reporting to, Congress.

This proposal has encountered opposition on the part of the Treasury Department and the Department of Justice. Furthermore, Senator Wiley dissented from it at the time it was made.

The committee does not recede from this proposal but acknowledges that its enactment may encounter difficulty and that in any event enactment would take some time. It is therefore proposing, in addition to this, the establishment of a privately constituted National Crime Coordinating Council organized in the manner described elsewhere in this report.

F. STATUS OF CONTEMPT PROCEEDINGS

In the course of the committee's hearings, it encountered many examples of witnesses who refused to answer material questions or to disclose the contents of subpenaed records, on the ground that to do so would tend to incriminate them. Forty of these recalcitrant witnesses were cited for contempt by the Senate and their cases were placed in the hands of the appropriate United States attorneys for prosecution.

The committee has reported to the Senate the contempts committed by four other witnesses, but the Senate had not certified the committee reports to the United States attorney as of the time that this report was filed.

Two recalcitrant witnesses, namely, Morris Kleinman and Louis Rothkopf, who have also been cited for contempt, did not rely upon the privilege against self-incrimination but based their refusal upon the novel ground that the procedure adopted by the committee in requiring them to testify at a hearing which was being televised, broadcast, and photographed by newsreel cameras was generally a violation of their constitutional rights. The issues raised by Mr. Kleinman and Mr. Rothkopf by their refusal to testify will ultimately be resolved by the courts.

The persons who have been cited by the Senate for contempt, together with the status of their cases, and the persons whose contempts have been reported to the Senate by the committee, but not certified to the United States attorney as of the time this report was filed, are as follows:

DISTRICT OF COLUMBIA

Cases in which the committee report has been certified to United States attorney, but the cases have not as yet been presented to grand jury:

Anthony J. Accardo, Chicago, Ill.
George L. Bowers, Miami, Fla.
John Croft, Cincinnati, Ohio
Joseph Doto, alias Joe Adonis, Palisades, N. J.
John Doyle, Gary, Ind.
Julius Fink, Baltimore, Md.
Rocco Fischetti, Chicago, Ill.
Alex Fudeman, Reading. Pa.
Jacob Guzik, Chicago, Ill.

Murray L. Humphreys, Chicago, Ill.
Morris Kleinman, Cleveland, Ohio
Arthur Longano, Englewood, N. J.
James Lynch, Palisades, N. J.
George S. May, Chicago, Ill.
Abraham Minker, Reading, Pa.
Isadore Minker, Reading, Pa.
Salvatore Moretti, Demarest, N. J.
William G. O'Brien, Miami, Fla.

Case disposed of:

Harry Russell, Miami Beach, Fla. (acquitted on February 5, 1951, on motion for a directed verdict).

Cases in which committee report has been filed with Senate, but not certified to United States attorney as of the time that this report was filed:

Joseph Baldassari, Scranton, Pa.
Joseph Scalleat, Hazleton, Pa.
Patrick Joseph Size, Scranton, Pa.

DISTRICT OF NEW JERSEY

Case in which the committee report has been filed with Senate, but not certified to United States attorney as of the time that this report was filed:

Herman Orman, Atlantic City, N. J.

SOUTHERN DISTRICT OF NEW YORK

Indictments for contempt were filed in the following cases (trial dates not set):

Frank Costello, New York City.
Joseph Doto, alias Joe Adonis, Palisades, New Jersey.
Frank Erickson, New York City.

EASTERN DISTRICT OF MICHIGAN

Indictments for contempt filed and defendants' motion to dismiss to be heard some time in September 1951. Trial dates not set:

Peter Licavoli, Grosse Pointe, Mich.
Mike Rubino, Grosse Pointe, Mich.

Case disposed of. Acquitted on grounds that notice was defective. The subpena served upon Trilck required his appearance in Washington and the court held that notice given to his attorney, directing him to appear in Detroit instead, was not sufficient:

Russell Trilck, Detroit, Mich.

NORTHERN DISTRICT OF OHIO

Indictments for contempt were filed in the following cases which will be tried some time in September 1951:

Joseph Aiuppa, Cicero, Ill.   (Decision on defendant's motion to dismiss deferred until trial.)
Joseph Di Carlo, Youngstown, Ohio.   (Decision on defendant's motion to dismiss deferred until trial.)
James Licavoli, Cleveland, Ohio.   (Motion for bill of particulars denied.)

NORTHERN DISTRICT OF CALIFORNIA

Indictments for contempt were filed in the following cases:

Stanley Cohen, San Francisco, Calif.   (Trial date not set.)
David N. Kessel, Piedmont, Calif.   (Trial January 7, 1952.)
Walter M. Pechart, El Cerrito, Calif.   (Trial January 7, 1952.)

SOUTHERN DISTRICT OF FLORIDA

Information for contempt filed in one case:

Martin Accardo, Coral Gables, Fla.   (Arraignment October 5, 1951, on which date defendant's motion requiring filing of new information will be argued. If the court should grant defendant's motion, new information will be filed immediately; if the court denies motion, case to be set for trial on October 22, 1951.)

NORTHERN DISTRICT OF ILLINOIS

Indictment for contempt filed:

Ralph O'Hara, Tiedtville, Ill.   (Trial date not set.)

Cases in which the committee report has been certified to United States attorney, but cases have not as yet been presented to grand jury:

Jack Dragna, Los Angeles, Calif.
Pat Manno, Chicago, Ill.
Peter Tremont, Chicago, Ill.

EASTERN DISTRICT OF LOUISIANA

Cases disposed of:

John J. Fogarty, New Orleans, La.   (Plea of nolo contendere and sentenced to 30 days in jail and to pay $300 fine, with jail sentence suspended and defendant placed on probation for 90 days.)
Phil Kastel, New Orleans, La.   (Defendant's motion to dismiss was granted on June 27, 1951.)
Carlos Marcello, Marrero, La.   (Tried and found guilty. Sentenced to 6 months in jail and to pay $500 fine and required to post $3,000 bond pending appeal.)

Indictments for contempt filed and defendants' motions to dismiss denied.   Trial dates not set:

Anthony Marcello, Gretna, La.
Joseph A. Poretto, New Orleans, La.

The contempt cases recently decided by the Supreme Court of the United States have greatly expanded the scope of the constitutional privilege against self-incrimination. It would seem, under the present state of the law, that a witness may invoke the privilege even where the possibility of incrimination is quite remote. The most recent Supreme Court decision on the matter is *United States* v. *Hoffman*, 341 U. S. 479 (1951), upholding the right of a defendant appearing before a Federal grand jury to refuse to state even the nature of his business. There would seem to be a distinction between appearance before a body like a grand jury which has power to indict the witness and appearance before a congressional committee which is empowered to obtain information for legislative purposes only. As a matter of law, there is considerable uncertainty as to the extent to which the court will apply the Hoffman case to the cases of witnesses appearing before this and other congressional committees.

The contempt cases which have been certified to the United States attorneys, but which have not as yet been presented to grand juries, are being reexamined, in the light of the opinion in the Hoffman case, with a view to determining whether or not indictments should be sought in those cases.

G. USE OF TELEVISION, NEWSREELS AND RADIO IN CONGRESSIONAL HEARINGS

As the first congressional committee to encounter television on an extensive scale at its hearings, this committee feels that a report regarding its experience and attitude in that connection would be desirable.

There has been a great deal of public discussion regarding the advisability of permitting congressional hearings to be televised. It should be understood at the outset, however, that the issue does not relate to television as such. Television is essentially another improved method of public communication.

If hearings are to be conducted in public, obviously public access to the proceedings cannot be limited to those who are able to attend in person. No one can object to having reporters present who report everything they believe to be of public interest irrespective of whether the witness likes it or not. No serious objection has been raised to the use of flash-bulb photographs for newspaper publication and the use of radio to broadcast public hearings has been a common practice. Newsreel cameras present the most difficult problem because of their bulk and the brilliance of the lights required for their use.

All of these media of news collection and dissemination have been in use for many years. Adding television merely has the effect of increasing the number of people who can actually see the proceedings. Television cameras are quiet and unobtrusive and they require considerably less light than newsreel cameras.

If the subject matter being investigated by a congressional committee is of limited public interest the demand made upon it for access to the hearing by the various media of public news collection and dissemination will be similarly limited. If its subject matter is of great public interest, it will be besieged with requests from the press, the radio, the newsreel producers, and the television firms for the right to publish and broadcast the hearings. It is incumbent upon a committee faced with these requests not to discriminate unjustly among the various media.

The committee found, for example, that when its hearings involved large cities or notorious characters whose names were of great public interest, all of these media of communication sought access to the hearings, whereas hearings covering medium-size cities, where the subject matter was less spectacular, attracted the press only. Presumably, because of the expense of handling their equipment, newsreel and television firms attend only if the material has unusual publicity value.

Accordingly, it is the degree of public interest, not the desires of the committee, which governs the number of news representatives and the amount of equipment that the committee will be asked to allow in the hearing room.

The public has a right to be informed of the activities of its Government and it is entitled to have access to public hearings of congressional committees. The witnesses appearing before the committee also have rights that must be respected, but a witness does not have any inherent right to interfere with the rights of the public in this regard. There falls upon the shoulders of the committee conducting the hearing the responsibility of maintaining a fair and equitable balance between the rights of both the public and the witness.

The degree to which a witness is distracted by news devices depends on many factors, including the health and temperament of the witness. Giving testimony of any kind under any conditions may be nerve-wracking to some witnesses. Some can bear the strain more easily than others. Much depends upon the willingness of the witness to cooperate. A friendly and cooperative witness seldom objects to being photographed or televised and does not find these factors to be distracting. The reluctant witness, on the other hand, is necessarily under greater strain and is more easily distracted by outside forces. This gives rise to the question of whether the friendly witness should be given less favorable treatment that the recalcitrant one.

The committee must always be conscious of its responsibility to obtain from its witnesses the information required to fulfill its mission. If a witness refuses to testify unless all media of news dissemination are diverted from him, the committee either may recommend that he be cited for contempt of Congress or it may accede to his request for the purpose of obtaining the information the witness is able to supply. This requires a careful exercise of judgment as to which course will be in the best interests of the public.

Crime is nearly always a matter that attracts wide public attention and it is for this reason that at some of the more newsworthy hearings of the committee, the various media of news dissemination requested the right to bring in all of their facilities and equipment. Drawing the line was not easy.

In order to reduce the amount of equipment in the hearing room, the committee ordinarily required the television networks to form a pool so that only one set of cameras would be in the room. It also attempted to limit the number of newsreel cameras and in some instances it forbade the taking of still photographs with flash bulbs during the time when a witness was actually testifying. In other cases where the witness requested it, cameras, both newsreel and television, were required to be turned away from the witness during his testimony. In one case, where the testimony of the witness was deemed to be of considerable importance, all cameras, radio, and recording devices were silenced.

The policy adopted generally by the committee throughout was to attempt to recognize the public's right of access to the hearings, to avoid unfair discrimination between the various news media and at the same time to avoid subjecting the witness to an ordeal that would unduly interfere with the giving of his testimony. The committee exercised its judgment according to the individual circumstances of each case.

One of the important factors that affects the decision of a congressional committee in regard to the amount of facilities and equipment to be allowed in a hearing room is the size and character of the room itself. Congress does not have a hearing room adequately suited for a hearing that is of such widespread interest that newsreels and television networks will be attracted to it. Such rooms as it has are not equipped to accommodate modern photographing and televising equipment in an inconspicuous manner.

An example of the modern method of handling such equipment is found in the United Nations assembly room at Lake Success where the room itself is well lighted and newsreel and television cameras are installed behind a glass partition which blocks all operational noise. In such an arrangement the equipment is hardly noticed. If similar facilities were available for the hearings of congressional committees there would be few occasions when a witness could justifiably claim that his ability to testify was unduly hampered by the presence of news disseminating equipment.

Considerable confusion of thought has resulted from the error of placing congressional hearings in the same category as trials in court. While it is true that gangsters and hoodlums when called before this committee and asked to give information regarding organized crime, were in an uncomfortable position while being interrogated by counsel and Senators, they were not on trial.

A court trial is entirely different. It is a judicial proceeding involving the specific facts of an individual case. A jury is present and must be able to hear and weigh the evidence without distraction. The fate of an individual defendant is at stake and great weight must be given to his right to be tried in an atmosphere that is strictly calm and judicial. It is for these reasons that the Federal Rules of Criminal Procedure specifically forbid radio broadcasting of court proceedings.

The function of a congressional committee, on the other hand, is to obtain information for the purpose of enacting legislation. The legislative process includes the important step of enlightening the public regarding the matters under inquiry in order that intelligent public opinion will be developed. The more access the public has to the hearings the more thoughtful will its opinion be. This is a necessary part of the democratic process.

A final point that deserves comment is the question of commercial sponsorship of the broadcasting of committee hearings. Unlike most public-interest programs, a congressional hearing if fully broadcast, occupies long periods of time, often extending over several days. During this period, a radio or television station or network, in order to carry the hearings, is required to cancel all of its regular commercial programs. This involves not only loss of revenue but also, in some cases, the payment of cancellation penalties. Seldom can a station or network afford to bear this enormous financial burden.

Unless sponsorship is permitted, the public will be deprived of the privilege of witnessing many important events. At the same time, it is important to avoid a type of sponsorship which permits the broadcasting to be done in a manner that detracts from the dignity of the proceedings.

After extensive study by the committee and its staff, and discussion with representatives of the radio and television industry, the committee in an effort to reach an understanding with the industry adopted a proposed code of conditions covering the use of sponsored radio and television at its hearings. The plan adopted is as follows:

1. No television network or station shall use for the hearings a commercial sponsor not specifically approved in writing by the committee or its designated representative, and no sponsor shall be charged by a network or station more than such reasonable amount as may be consistent with the usual charges for other programs emanating from a public source.

2. No commercial announcement shall be broadcast from the hearing room.

3. Breaks for station identification during the hearings shall be limited to 10 seconds.

4. No network or station shall make any comment or commercial announcement during the testimony of a witness, or interrupt the broadcasting of the testimony of a witness for the purpose of making any such comment or announcement.

5. During each pause or intermission in the hearings, the network may make a commercial announcement lasting not more than 1 minute and, except in the case of a newspaper, magazine, or other publication of general circulation referring to reports of the hearings to appear in its columns, such commercial shall be institutional in character and shall make no reference to the hearings.

6. No local station shall interrupt any portion of the broadcasting of the hearings as received from a network for the purpose of making any spot or other commercial announcement.

7. A network or situation may, at any time, make a complete break from the broadcasting of the hearings for the purpose of broadcasting other programs.

8. At the beginning and end of the broadcasting of the hearings for any day, the network carrying the hearings shall make the following announcement or its equivalent:

These hearings are brought to you as a public service by the X Company in cooperation with the Y Television Network.

It is hoped that the committee's experience in this matter will be of some guide to other congressional committees faced with similar problems.

The committee, immediately after its creation in May 1950, adopted a code of procedure for its hearings. This code provided among other things that a witness before the committee should have the benefit of counsel when requested. Also the counsel could ask his client questions designed to bring out full information on a particular matter; questions or interrogatories could be submitted to the committee to be asked other witnesses who gave testimony concerning a particular witness. The code also provided that any persons or organizations whose names were mentioned in a hearing should be afforded an opportunity to give their side of the story by testifying or filing a statement or data in the record designed to clarify any point in controversy.

Later, when requests were made to permit televising of the hearings, the committee gave a great deal of consideration to this problem and ultimately adopted the set of conditions for sponsored broadcasts set forth heretofore. The committee had to act on all matters in its hearings without the benefit of precedent of other committees.

The committee feels that much time in the development of individual codes for congressional committees would be saved and hearings would be expedited if the Senate or the Congress would adopt an over-all code of procedure for all such committees. Witnesses appearing before the committees and their counsel would then know the rules of the game and much bickering, questioning and delay would be avoided.

The committee gives its wholehearted approval to the proposals which are now pending before the Senate Committee on Rules and Administration and other congressional committees for the adoption of such an over-all code of procedure.

ADDENDUM

After this report was filed, the committee received notice from the Western Union Telegraph Co. to the effect that its service regarding the United States Treasury Balance Reports, originating at Washington, D. C., is being discontinued, pursuant to the company's policy of cooperating with law-enforcement agencies.

Hearings held by the committee under the chairmanship of Senator Kefauver, were printed in volumes as follows:

Part 1. Florida.
Part 1A. Florida.
Part 2. Federal and State Officials; California Crime Commission and Chicago Crime Commission.
Part 3. Black Market Operations.
Part 4. Missouri.
Part 4A. Missouri.
Part 5. Illinois.
Part 6. Ohio–Kentucky.
Part 7. New York–New Jersey.
Part 8. Louisiana.
Part 9. Michigan.
Part 10. Nevada–California.
Part 11. Pennsylvania.
Part 12. Federal and State Officials, and Miscellaneous Witnesses.

Prior to May 1, 1951, the committee issued three Interim Reports, Nos. 2370, 141, and 307.

The Library of Congress, Legislative Reference Service, has prepared an index of all the names found in the printed hearings listed above, which is being put into print at the Government Printing Office, and will make the hearings double valuable to crime commissions, libraries, law-enforcement officials, the press, etc., to whom the index will be made available.

The hearings held by the committee since May 1, 1951, under the chairmanship of Senator O'Conor, will be printed in volumes as follows:

Part 13. Miscellaneous Witnesses.
Part 14. Narcotics.
Part 15. Kentucky.
Part 16. Florida.
Part 17. Maryland–District of Columbia.
Part 18. New York–New Jersey.
Part 19. Pennsylvania.

The latter hearings are presently being printed, and will soon be available to interested parties.

104

○